Hands-On Reinforcement Learning for Games

Implementing self-learning agents in games using artificial intelligence techniques

Micheal Lanham

BIRMINGHAM - MUMBAI

Hands-On Reinforcement Learning for Games

Commissioning Editor: Sunith Shetty
Acquisition Editor: Reshma Raman
Content Development Editor: Nathanya Dias
Senior Editor: Ayaan Hoda
Technical Editor: Joseph Sunil
Copy Editor: Safis Editing
Project Coordinator: Aishwarya Mohan
Proofreader: Safis Editing
Indexer: Pratik Shirodkar
Production Designer: Alishon Mendonsa

First published: January 2020

Production reference: 2240120

Published by Packt Publishing Ltd.
Livery Place
35 Livery Street
Birmingham
B3 2PB, UK.

ISBN 978-1-83921-493-6

www.packt.com

To Larry Hamilton and his late wife Leona. They helped get me started...

Packt.com

Subscribe to our online digital library for full access to over 7,000 books and videos, as well as industry leading tools to help you plan your personal development and advance your career. For more information, please visit our website.

Why subscribe?

- Spend less time learning and more time coding with practical eBooks and Videos from over 4,000 industry professionals

- Improve your learning with Skill Plans built especially for you

- Get a free eBook or video every month

- Fully searchable for easy access to vital information

- Copy and paste, print, and bookmark content

Did you know that Packt offers eBook versions of every book published, with PDF and ePub files available? You can upgrade to the eBook version at www.packt.com and as a print book customer, you are entitled to a discount on the eBook copy. Get in touch with us at customercare@packtpub.com for more details.

At www.packt.com, you can also read a collection of free technical articles, sign up for a range of free newsletters, and receive exclusive discounts and offers on Packt books and eBooks.

Contributors

About the author

Micheal Lanham is a proven software and tech innovator with 20 years of experience. During that time, he has developed a broad range of software applications in areas such as games, graphics, web, desktop, engineering, artificial intelligence, GIS, and machine learning applications for a variety of industries as an R&D developer. At the turn of the millennium, Micheal began working with neural networks and evolutionary algorithms in game development. He was later introduced to Unity and has been an avid developer, consultant, manager, and author of multiple Unity games, graphic projects, and books ever since.

About the reviewers

Tony V. Le works in **experience design** (**XD**) and specializes in game and web design/development. Tony graduated from DePaul University with a master of arts in experience design and from Columbia College, Chicago, with a bachelor of arts in game design. Tony currently runs and operates a small development studio known as tvledesign LLC, whose core focus is to create unique interactive experiences and help clients create better experiences for their customers.

Micael DaGraça is a professional game designer and interactive creator who works with independent video game studios and creates interactive apps focused on the health and pharmaceutical industries. He studied digital arts at the University of IESA Multimedia, Paris, and ESAD Matosinhos. He started his career as a project manager in a small studio and then gradually started working as a game developer by helping other studios to develop their games. More recently, he has been creating interactive content for the pharmaceutical industry.

Packt is searching for authors like you

If you're interested in becoming an author for Packt, please visit `authors.packtpub.com` and apply today. We have worked with thousands of developers and tech professionals, just like you, to help them share their insight with the global tech community. You can make a general application, apply for a specific hot topic that we are recruiting an author for, or submit your own idea.

Table of Contents

Preface

This book is your one-stop shop for learning how various **reinforcement learning** (**RL**) techniques and algorithms play an important role in game development using Python.

The book will start with the basics to provide you with the necessary foundation to understand how RL is playing a major role in game development. Each chapter will help you implement various RL techniques, such as Markov decision processes, Q-learning, the actor-critic method, **state-action-reward-state-action** (**SARSA**), and the deterministic policy gradients algorithm, to build logical self-learning agents. You will use these techniques to enhance your game development skills and add various features to improve your overall productivity. Later in the book, you will learn how deep RL techniques can be used to devise strategies that enable agents to learn from their own actions so that you can build fun and engaging games.

By the end of the book, you will be able to use RL techniques to build various projects and contribute to open source applications.

Who this book is for

This book is for game developers who are looking to add to their knowledge by implementing RL techniques to build games from scratch. This book will also appeal to machine learning and deep learning practitioners, and RL researchers who want to understand how self-learning agents can be used in the game domain. Prior knowledge of game development and a working knowledge of Python programming are expected.

What this book covers

Chapter 1, *Understanding Rewards-Based Learning*, explores the basics of learning, what it is to learn, and how RL differs from other, more classic learning methods. From there, we explore how the Markov decision process works in code and how it relates to learning. This leads us to the classic multi-armed and contextual bandit problems. Finally, we will learn about Q-learning and quality-based model learning.

Chapter 2, *Dynamic Programming and the Bellman Equation*, digs deeper into dynamic programming and explores how the Bellman equation can be intertwined into RL. Here, you will learn how the Bellman equation is used to update a policy. We then go further into detail about policy iteration or value iteration methods using our understanding of Q-learning, by training an agent on a new grid-style environment.

Chapter 3, *Monte Carlo Methods*, explores model-based methods and how they can be used to train agents on more classic board games.

Chapter 4, *Temporal Difference Learning*, explores the heart of RL and how it solves the temporal credit assignment problem often discussed in academia. We apply **temporal difference learning** (**TDL**) to Q-learning and use it to solve a grid world environment (such as FrozenLake).

Chapter 5, *Exploring SARSA*, goes deeper into the fundamentals of on-policy methods such as SARSA. We will explore policy-based learning through understanding the partially observable Markov decision process. Then, we'll look at how we can implement SARSA with Q-learning. This will set the stage for the more advanced policy methods that we will explore in later chapters, called PPO and TRPO.

Chapter 6, *Going Deep with DQN*, takes the Q-learning model and integrates it with deep learning to create advanced agents known as **deep Q-learning networks** (**DQNs**). From this, we explain how basic deep learning models work for regression or, in this case, to solve the Q equation. We will use DQNs in the CartPole environment.

Chapter 7, *Going Deeper with DDQNs*, looks at how extensions to **deep learning** (**DL**) called **convolutional neural networks** (**CNNs**) can be used to observe a visual state. We will then use that knowledge to play Atari games and look at further enhancements.

Chapter 8, *Policy Gradient Methods*, delves into more advanced policy methods and how they integrate into deep RL agents. This is an advanced chapter as it covers higher-level calculus and probability concepts. You will get to experience the MuJoCo animation RL environment in this chapter as a reward for your hard work.

Chapter 9, *Optimizing for Continuous Control*, looks at improving the policy methods we looked at previously for continuously controlling advanced environments. We start off by setting up and installing the MuJoCo environment. After that, we look at a novel improvement called recurrent networks for capturing context and see how recurrent networks are applied on top of PPO. Then we get back into the actor-critic method and this time look at asynchronous actor-critic in a couple of different configurations, before finally progressing to actor-critic with experience replay.

Chapter 10, *All Together Rainbow DQN*, tells us all about Rainbow. Google DeepMind recently explored the combination of a number of RL enhancements all together in an algorithm called Rainbow. Rainbow is another advanced toolkit that you can explore and either borrow from or use to work with more advanced RL environments.

Chapter 11, *Exploiting ML-Agents*, looks at how we can either use elements from the ML-Agents toolkit in our own agents or use the toolkit to get a fully developed agent.

Chapter 12, *DRL Frameworks*, opens up the possibilities of playing with solo agents in various environments. We will explore various multi-agent environments as well.

Chapter 13, *3D Worlds*, trains us to use RL agents effectively to tackle a variety of 3D environmental challenges.

Chapter 14, *From DRL to AGI*, looks beyond DRL and into the realm of AGI, or at least where we hope we are going with AGI. We will also looks at various DRL algorithms that can be applied in the real world.

To get the most out of this book

A working knowledge of Python and game development is essential. A good PC with a GPU would be beneficial.

Download the example code files

You can download the example code files for this book from your account at www.packt.com. If you purchased this book elsewhere, you can visit www.packtpub.com/support and register to have the files emailed directly to you.

You can download the code files by following these steps:

1. Log in or register at www.packt.com.
2. Select the **Support** tab.
3. Click on **Code Downloads**.
4. Enter the name of the book in the **Search** box and follow the onscreen instructions.

Once the file is downloaded, please make sure that you unzip or extract the folder using the latest version of:

- WinRAR/7-Zip for Windows
- Zipeg/iZip/UnRarX for Mac
- 7-Zip/PeaZip for Linux

The code bundle for the book is also hosted on GitHub at `https://github.com/PacktPublishing/Hands-On-Reinforcement-Learning-for-Games`. In case there's an update to the code, it will be updated on the existing GitHub repository.

We also have other code bundles from our rich catalog of books and videos available at `https://github.com/PacktPublishing/`. Check them out!

Download the color images

We also provide a PDF file that has color images of the screenshots/diagrams used in this book. You can download it here: `http://www.packtpub.com/sites/default/files/downloads/9781839214936_ColorImages.pdf`.

Conventions used

There are a number of text conventions used throughout this book.

`CodeInText`: Indicates code words in text, database table names, folder names, filenames, file extensions, pathnames, dummy URLs, user input, and Twitter handles. Here is an example: "The three functions `make_atari`, `wrap_deepmind`, and `wrap_pytorch` are all located in the new `wrappers.py` file we imported earlier."

A block of code is set as follows:

```
env_id = 'PongNoFrameskip-v4'
env = make_atari(env_id)
env = wrap_deepmind(env)
env = wrap_pytorch(env)
```

When we wish to draw your attention to a particular part of a code block, the relevant lines or items are set in bold:

```
epsilon_start = 1.0
epsilon_final = 0.01
epsilon_decay = 30000

epsilon_by_episode = lambda episode: epsilon_final + (epsilon_start -
epsilon_final) * math.exp(-1. * episode / epsilon_decay)

plt.plot([epsilon_by_episode(i) for i in range(1000000)])
plt.show()
```

Any command-line input or output is written as follows:

```
pip install mujoco
```

Bold: Indicates a new term, an important word, or words that you see onscreen. For example, words in menus or dialog boxes appear in the text like this. Here is an example: "Building on that, we'll look at a variant of the DQN called the **DDQN**, or **double (dueling) DQN**."

Warnings or important notes appear like this.

Tips and tricks appear like this.

Get in touch

Feedback from our readers is always welcome.

General feedback: If you have questions about any aspect of this book, mention the book title in the subject of your message and email us at customercare@packtpub.com.

Errata: Although we have taken every care to ensure the accuracy of our content, mistakes do happen. If you have found a mistake in this book, we would be grateful if you would report this to us. Please visit www.packtpub.com/support/errata, selecting your book, clicking on the Errata Submission Form link, and entering the details.

Piracy: If you come across any illegal copies of our works in any form on the Internet, we would be grateful if you would provide us with the location address or website name. Please contact us at copyright@packt.com with a link to the material.

If you are interested in becoming an author: If there is a topic that you have expertise in and you are interested in either writing or contributing to a book, please visit authors.packtpub.com.

Reviews

Please leave a review. Once you have read and used this book, why not leave a review on the site that you purchased it from? Potential readers can then see and use your unbiased opinion to make purchase decisions, we at Packt can understand what you think about our products, and our authors can see your feedback on their book. Thank you!

For more information about Packt, please visit packt.com.

Section 1: Exploring the Environment

Reinforcement Learning (**RL**) is a complex topic comprising of terminology and concepts that all seem to blend together. In this section, we uncover the terminology and basics of RL for the novice or more advanced user.

This section contains the following chapters:

- Chapter 1, *Understanding Rewards-Based Learning*
- Chapter 2, *Monte Carlo Methods*
- Chapter 3, *Dynamic Programming and the Bellman Equation*
- Chapter 4, *Temporal Difference Learning*
- Chapter 5, *Exploring SARSA*

Understanding Rewards-Based Learning

1

The world is consumed with the machine learning revolution and, in particular, the search for a functional **artificial general intelligence** or **AGI**. Not to be confused with a conscious AI, AGI is a broader definition of machine intelligence that seeks to apply generalized methods of learning and knowledge to a broad range of tasks, much like the ability we have with our brains—or even small rodents have, for that matter. Rewards-based learning and, in particular, **reinforcement learning** (**RL**) are seen as the next steps to a more generalized intelligence.

> "Short-term AGI is a serious possibility."
> – OpenAI Co-founder and Chief Scientist, **Ilya Sutskever**

In this book, we start from the beginning of rewards-based learning and RL with its history to modern inception and its use in gaming and simulation. RL and, specifically, deep RL are gaining popularity in both research and use. In just a few years, the advances in RL have been dramatic, which have made it both impressive but, at the same time, difficult to keep up with and make sense of. With this book, we will unravel the abstract terminology that plagues this multi-branch and complicated topic in detail. By the end of this book, you should be able to consider yourself a confident practitioner of RL and deep RL.

For this first chapter, we will start with an overview of RL and look at the terminology, history, and basic concepts. In this chapter, the high-level topics we will cover are as follows:

- Understanding rewards-based learning
- Introducing the Markov decision process
- Using value learning with multi-armed bandits
- Exploring Q-learning with contextual bandits

We want to mention some important technical requirements before continuing in the next section.

Technical requirements

This book is a hands-on one, which means there are plenty of code examples to work through and discover on your own. The code for this book can be found in the following GitHub repository: `https://github.com/PacktPublishing/Hands-On-Reinforcement-Learning-for-Games`.

As such, be sure to have a working Python coding environment set up. Anaconda, which is a cross-platform wrapper framework for both Python and R, is the recommended platform to use for this book. We also recommend Visual Studio Code or Visual Studio Professional with the Python tools as good **Integrated development editors**, or **IDEs**.

 Anaconda, recommended for this book, can be downloaded from `https://www.anaconda.com/distribution/`.

With that out of the way, we can move on to learning the basics of RL and, in the next section, look at why rewards-based learning works.

Understanding rewards-based learning

Machine learning is quickly becoming a broad and growing category, with many forms of learning systems addressed. We categorize learning based on the form of a problem and how we need to prepare it for a machine to process. In the case of supervised machine learning, data is first labeled before it is fed into the machine. Examples of this type of learning are simple image classification systems that are trained to recognize a cat or dog from a prelabeled set of cat and dog images. Supervised learning is the most popular and intuitive type of learning system. Other forms of learning that are becoming increasingly powerful are unsupervised and semi-supervised learning. Both of these methods eliminate the need for labels or, in the case of semi-supervised learning, require the labels to be defined more abstractly. The following diagram shows these learning methods and how they process data:

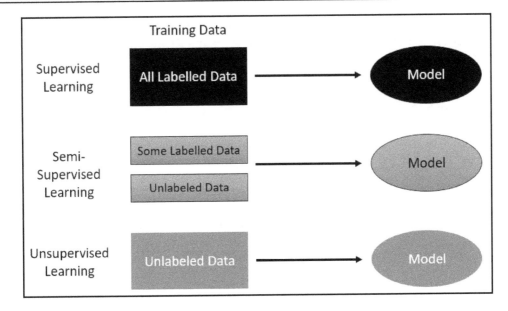

Training Data

Supervised Learning — All Labelled Data — Model

Semi-Supervised Learning — Some Labelled Data / Unlabeled Data — Model

Unsupervised Learning — Unlabeled Data — Model

Variations of supervised learning

A couple of recent papers on `arXiv.org` (pronounced archive.org) suggest the use of semi-supervised learning to solve RL tasks. While the papers suggest no use of external rewards, they do talk about internal updates or feedback signals. This suggests a method of using internal reward RL, which, as we mentioned before, is a thing.

While this family of supervised learning methods has made impressive progress in just the last few years, they still lack the necessary planning and intelligence we expect from a truly intelligent machine. This is where RL picks up and differentiates itself. RL systems learn from interacting and making selections in the environment the agent resides in. The classic diagram of an RL system is shown here:

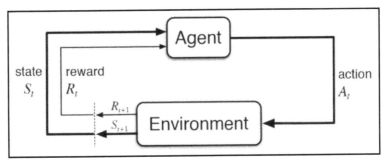

An RL system

In the preceding diagram, you can identify the main components of an RL system: the **Agent** and **Environment**, where the **Agent** represents the RL system, and the **Environment** could be representative of a game board, game screen, and/or possibly streaming data. Connecting these components are three primary signals, the **State**, **Reward**, and **Action**. The **State** signal is essentially a snapshot of the current state of **Environment**. The **Reward** signal may be externally provided by the **Environment** and provides feedback to the agent, either bad or good. Finally, the **Action** signal is the action the **Agent** selects at each time step in the environment. An action could be as simple as *jump* or a more complex set of controls operating servos. Either way, another key difference in RL is the ability for the agent to interact with, and change, the **Environment**.

Now, don't worry if this all seems a little muddled still—early researchers often encountered trouble differentiating between supervised learning and RL.

In the next section, we look at more RL terminology and explore the basic elements of an RL agent.

The elements of RL

Every RL agent is comprised of four main elements. These are **policy**, **reward function**, **value function**, and, optionally, **model**. Let's now explore what each of these terms means in more detail:

- **The policy**: A policy represents the decision and planning process of the agent. The policy is what decides the actions the agent will take during a step.
- **The reward function**: The reward function determines what amount of reward an agent receives after completing a series of actions or an action. Generally, a reward is given to an agent externally but, as we will see, there are internal reward systems as well.
- **The value function**: A value function determines the value of a state over the long term. Determining the value of a state is fundamental to RL and our first exercise will be determining state values.
- **The model**: A model represents the environment in full. In the case of a game of tic-tac-toe, this may represent all possible game states. For more advanced RL algorithms, we use the concept of a partially observable state that allows us to do away with a full model of the environment. Some environments that we will tackle in this book have more states than the number of atoms in the universe. Yes, you read that right. In massive environments like that, we could never hope to model the entire environment state.

We will spend the next several chapters covering each of these terms in excruciating detail, so don't worry if things feel a bit abstract still. In the next section, we will take a look at the history of RL.

The history of RL

An Introduction to RL, by Sutton and Barto (1998), discusses the origins of modern RL being derived from two main threads with a later joining thread. The two main threads are trial and error-based learning and dynamic programming, with the third thread arriving later in the form of temporal difference learning. The primary thread founded by Sutton, trial and error, is based on animal psychology. As for the other methods, we will look at each in far more detail in their respective chapters. A diagram showing how these three threads converged to form modern RL is shown here:

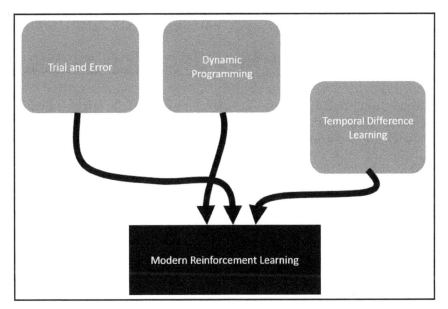

The history of modern RL

 Dr. Richard S. Sutton, a distinguished research scientist for DeepMind and renowned professor from the University of Alberta, is considered the father of modern RL.

Lastly, before we jump in and start unraveling RL, let's look at why it makes sense to use this form of learning with games in the next section.

Why RL in games?

Various forms of machine learning systems have been used in gaming, with supervised learning being the primary choice. While these methods can be made to look intelligent, they are still limited by working on labeled or categorized data. While **generative adversarial networks** (**GANs**) show a particular promise in level and other asset generation, these families of algorithms cannot plan and make sense of long-term decision making. AI systems that replicate planning and interactive behavior in games are now typically done with hardcoded state machine systems such as finite state machines or behavior trees. Being able to develop agents that can learn for themselves the best moves or actions for an environment is literally game-changing, not only for the games industry, of course, but this should surely cause repercussions in every industry globally.

In the next section, we take a look at the foundation of the RL system, the Markov decision process.

Introducing the Markov decision process

In RL, the agent learns from the environment by interpreting the state signal. The state signal from the environment needs to define a discrete slice of the environment at that time. For example, if our agent was controlling a rocket, each state signal would define an exact position of the rocket in time. State, in that case, may be defined by the rocket's position and velocity. We define this state signal from the environment as a Markov state. The Markov state is not enough to make decisions from, and the agent needs to understand previous states, possible actions, and any future rewards. All of these additional properties may converge to form a Markov property, which we will discuss further in the next section.

The Markov property and MDP

An RL problem fulfills the Markov property if all Markov signals/states predict a future state. Subsequently, a Markov signal or state is considered a Markov property if it enables the agent to predict values from that state. Likewise, a learning task that is a Markov property and is finite is called a finite **Markov decision process**, or **MDP**. A very classic example of an MDP used to often explain RL is shown here:

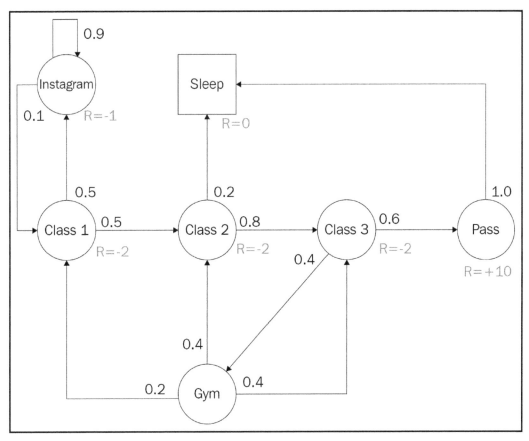

The Markov decision process (Dr. David Silver)

 The preceding diagram was taken from the excellent online lecture by Dr. David Silver on YouTube (https://www.youtube.com/watch?v= 2pWv7GOvuf0). Dr. Silver, a former student of Dr. Sutton, has since gone on to great fame by being the brains that power most of DeepMind's early achievements in RL.

The diagram is an example of a finite discrete MDP for a post-secondary student trying to optimize their actions for maximum reward. The student has the option of attending class, going to the gym, hanging out on Instagram or whatever, passing and/or sleeping. States are denoted by circles and the text defines the activity. In addition to this, the numbers next to each path from a circle denote the probability of using that path. Note how all of the values around a single circle sum to 1.0 or 100% probability. The **R=** denotes the reward or output of the reward function when the student is in that state. To solidify this abstract concept further, let's build our own MDP in the next section.

Building an MDP

In this hands-on exercise, we will build an MDP using a task from your own daily life or experience. This should allow you to better apply this abstract concept to something more tangible. Let's begin as follows:

1. Think of a daily task you do that may encompass six or so states. Examples of this may be going to school, getting dressed, eating, showering, browsing Facebook, and traveling.
2. Write each state within a circle on a full sheet of paper or perhaps some digital drawing app.
3. Connect the states with the actions you feel most appropriate. For example, don't get dressed before you shower.
4. Assign the probability you would use to take each action. For example, if you have two actions leaving a state, you could make them both 50/50 or 0.5/0.5, or some other combination that adds up to 1.0.
5. Assign the reward. Decide what rewards you would receive for being within each state and mark those on your diagram.
6. Compare your completed diagram with the preceding example. How did you do?

Before we get to solving your MDP or others, we first need to understand some background on calculating values. We will uncover this in the next section.

Using value learning with multi-armed bandits

Solving a full MDP and, hence, the full RL problem first requires us to understand values and how we calculate the value of a state with a value function. Recall that the value function was a primary element of the RL system. Instead of using a full MDP to explain this, we instead rely on a simpler single-state problem known as the multi-armed bandit problem. This is named after the one-armed slot machines often referred to as bandits by their patrons but, in this case, the machine has multiple arms. That is, we now consider a single-state or stationary problem with multiple actions that lead to terminal states providing constant rewards. More simply, our agent is going to play a multi-arm slot machine that will give either a win or loss based on the arm pulled, with each arm always returning the same reward. An example of our agent playing this machine is shown here:

Illustration of an agent playing multi-armed bandits

We can consider the value for a single state to be dependent on the next action, provided we also understand the reward provided by that action. Mathematically, we can define a simple value equation for learning like so:

$$V(a) = V(a) + \alpha(r - V(a))$$

In this equation, we have the following:

- *V(a)*: the value for a given action
- *a*: action
- *α*: alpha or the learning rate
- *r*: reward

Notice the addition of a new variable called α (alpha) or the learning rate. This learning rate denotes how fast the agent needs to learn the value from pull to pull. The smaller the learning rate (0.1), the slower the agent learns. This method of action-value learning is fundamental to RL. Let's code up this simple example to solidify further in the next section.

Coding a value learner

Since this is our first example, make sure your Python environment is set to go. Again for simplicity, we prefer Anaconda. Make sure you are comfortable coding with your chosen IDE and open up the code example, Chapter_1_1.py, and follow along:

1. Let's examine the first section of the code, as shown here:

```
import random

reward = [1.0, 0.5, 0.2, 0.5, 0.6, 0.1, -.5]
arms = len(reward)
episodes = 100
```

```
learning_rate = .1
Value = [0.0] * arms
print(Value)
```

2. We first start by doing `import` of `random`. We will use `random` to randomly select an arm during each training episode.

3. Next, we define a list of rewards, `reward`. This list defines the reward for each arm (action) and hence defines the number of arms/actions on the bandit.

4. Then, we determine the number of arms using the `len()` function.

5. After that, we set the number of training episodes our agent will use to evaluate the value of each arm.

6. Set the `learning_rate` value to `.1`. This means the agent will learn slowly the value of each pull.

7. Next, we initialize the value for each action in a list called `Value`, using the following code:

```
Value = [0.0] * arms
```

8. Then, we print the `Value` list to the console, making sure all of the values are 0.0.

The first section of code initialized our rewards, number of arms, learning rate, and value list. Now, we need to implement the training cycle where our agent/algorithm will learn the value of each pull. Let's jump back into the code for `Chapter_1_1.py` and look to the next section:

1. The next section of code in the listing we want to focus on is entitled `agent learns` and is shown here for reference:

```
# agent learns
for i in range(0, episodes):
    action = random.randint(0, arms-1)
    Value[action] = Value[action] + learning_rate * (
        reward[action] - Value[action])

print(Value)
```

2. We start by first defining a `for` loop that loops through `0` to our number of episodes. For each episode, we let the agent pull an arm and use the reward from that pull to update its determination of value for that action or arm.

3. Next, we want to determine the action or arm the agent pulls randomly using the following code:

```
action = random.randint(0, arms-1)
```

4. The code just selects a random arm/action number based on the total number of arms on the bandit (minus one to allow for proper indexing).

5. This then allows us to determine the value of the pull by using the next line of code, which mirrors very well our previous value equation:

```
Value[action] = Value[action] + learning_rate * (
reward[action] - Value[action])
```

6. That line of code clearly resembles the math for our previous `Value` equation. Now, think about how `learning_rate` is getting applied during each iteration of an episode. Notice that, with a rate of `.1`, our agent is learning or applying $1/10^{th}$ of what `reward` the agent receives minus the `Value` function the agent previously equated. This little trick has the effect of averaging out the values across the episodes.

7. Finally, after the looping completes and all of the episodes are run, we print the updated `Value` function for each action.

8. Run the code from the command line or your favorite Python editor. In Visual Studio, this is as simple as hitting the play button. After the code has completed running, you should see something similar to the following, but not the exact output:

```
C:\Users\Micheal\Anaconda3\python.exe                          —   □   ×
[0.0, 0.0, 0.0, 0.0, 0.0, 0.0, 0.0]
[0.7941088679053511, 0.37290670858355, 0.17298296564654017, 0.30628975550000004,
0.4888187886688896, 0.0814697981114816, -0.3587852317595]
Press any key to continue . . .
```

Output from Chapter_1_1.py

You will most certainly see different output values since the random action selections on your computer will be different. Python has many ways to set static values for random seeds but that isn't something we want to worry about quite yet.

Now, think back and compare those output values to the rewards set for each arm. Are they the same or different and if so, by how much? Generally, the learned values after only 100 episodes should indicate a clear value but likely not the finite value. This means the values will be smaller than the final rewards but they should still indicate a preference.

The solution we show here is an example of **trial and error** learning; it's that first thread we talked about back in the history of RL section. As you can see, the agent learns by randomly pulling an arm and determining the value. However, at no time does our agent learn to make better decisions based on those updated values. The agent always just pulls randomly. Our agent currently has no decision mechanism or what we call a **policy** in RL. We will look at how to implement a basic greedy policy in the next section.

Implementing a greedy policy

Our current value learner is not really learning aside from finding the optimum calculated value or the reward for each action over several episodes. Since our agent is not learning, it also makes it a less efficient learner as well. After all, the agent is just randomly picking any arm each episode when it could be using its acquired knowledge, which is the `Value` function, to determine it's next best choice. We can code this up in a very simple policy called a greedy policy in the next exercise:

1. Open up the `Chapter_1_2.py` example. The code is basically the same as our last example except for the episode iteration and, in particular, the selection of action or arm. The full listing can be seen here—note the new highlighted sections:

```
import random

reward = [1.0, 0.5, 0.2, 0.5, 0.6, 0.1, -.5]
arms = len(reward)
learning_rate = .1
episodes = 100
Value = [0.0] * arms
print(Value)

def greedy(values):
    return values.index(max(values))

# agent learns
for i in range(0, episodes):
    action = greedy(Value)
    Value[action] = Value[action] + learning_rate * (
        reward[action] - Value[action])

print(Value)
```

2. Notice the inclusion of a new greedy() function. This function will always select the action with the highest value and return the corresponding index/action index. This function is essentially our agent's policy.

3. Scrolling down in the code, notice inside the training loop how we are now using the greedy() function to select our action, as shown here:

```
action = greedy(Value)
```

4. Again, run the code and look at the output. Is it what you expected? What went wrong?

Looking at your output likely shows that the agent calculated the maximum reward arm correctly, but likely didn't determine the correct values for the other arms. The reason for this is that, as soon as the agent found the most valuable arm, it kept pulling that arm. Essentially the agent finds the best path and sticks with it, which is okay in this single step or stationary environment but certainly won't work over a many step problem requiring multiple decisions. Instead, we need to balance the agents need to explore and find new paths, versus maximizing the immediate optimum reward. This problem is called the **exploration versus exploitation** dilemma in RL and something we will explore in the next section.

Exploration versus exploitation

As we have seen, having our agent always make the best choice limits their ability to learn the full values of a single state never mind multiple connected states. This also severely limits an agent's ability to learn, especially in environments where multiple states converge and diverge. What we need, therefore, is a way for our agent to choose an action based on a policy that favors more equal action/value distribution. Essentially, we need a policy that allows our agent to explore as well as exploit its knowledge to maximize learning. There are multiple variations and ways of balancing the trade-off between exploration and exploitation. Much of this will depend on the particular environment as well as the specific RL implementation you are using. We would never use an absolute greedy policy but, instead, some variation of greedy or another method entirely. In our next exercise, we show how to implement an initial optimistic value method, which can be effective:

1. Open Chapter_1_3.py and look at the highlighted lines shown here:

```
episodes = 10000
Value = [5.0] * arms
```

2. First, we have increased the number of episodes to 10000. This will allow us to confirm that our new policy is converging to some appropriate solution.

3. Next, we set the initial value of the `Value` list to `5.0`. Note that this value is well above the reward value maximum of `1.0`. Using a higher value than our reward forces our agent to always explore the most valuable path, which now becomes any path it hasn't explored, hence ensuring our agent will always explore each action or arm at least once.

4. There are no more code changes and you can run the example as you normally would. The output of the example is shown here:

Output from Chapter_1_3.py

Your output may vary slightly but it likely will show very similar values. Notice how the calculated values are now more relative. That is, the value of `1.0` clearly indicates the best course of action, the arm with a reward of `1.0`, but the other values are less indicative of the actual reward. Initial option value methods are effective but will force an agent to explore all paths, which are not so efficient in larger environments. There are of course a multitude of other methods you can use to balance exploration versus exploitation and we will cover a new method in the next section, where we introduce solving the full RL problem with Q-learning.

Exploring Q-learning with contextual bandits

Now that we understand how to calculate values and the delicate balance of exploration and exploitation, we can move on to solving an entire MDP. As we will see, various solutions work better or worse depending on the RL problem and environment. That is actually the basis for the next several chapters. For now, though, we just want to introduce a method that is basic enough to solve the full RL problem. We describe the full RL problem as the non-stationary or contextual multi-armed bandit problem, that is, an agent that moves across a different bandit each episode and chooses a single arm from multiple arms. Each bandit now represents a different state and we no longer want to determine just the value of an action but the quality. We can calculate the quality of an action given a state using the Q-learning equation shown here:

$$Q_{t+1} = Q(s_t, a_t) + \alpha(r_{t+1} + \Upsilon_{a'}^{max} Q(s_{t+1}, a) - Q(s'_{t+1}, a_t))$$

In the preceding equation, we have the following:

- s_t: state
- s'_{t+1}: current state
- a': next action
- a_t: current action
- Υ: gamma—reward discount
- α: alpha—learning rate
- r: reward
- r_{t+1}: next reward
- Q_{t+1}: quality

Now, don't get overly concerned if all of these terms are a little foreign and this equation appears overwhelming. This is the Q-learning equation developed by Chris Watkins in 1989 and is a method that simplifies the solving of a **Finite Markov Decision Process** or **FMDP**. The important thing to observe about the equation at this point is to understand the similarities it shares with the earlier action-value equation. In Chapter 2, *Dynamic Programming and the Bellman Equation*, we will learn in more detail how this equation is derived and functions. For now, the important concept to grasp is that we are now calculating a quality-based value on previous states and rewards based on actions rather than just a single action-value. This, in turn, allows our agent to make better planning for multiple states. We will implement a Q-learning agent that can play several multi-armed bandits and be able to maximize rewards in the next section.

Implementing a Q-learning agent

While that Q-learning equation may seem a lot more complex, actually implementing the equation is not unlike building our agent that just learned values earlier. To keep things simpler, we will use the same base of code but turn it into a Q-learning example. Open up the code example, Chapter_1_4.py, and follow the exercise here:

1. Here is the full code listing for reference:

```
import random

arms = 7
bandits = 7
learning_rate = .1
gamma = .9
episodes = 10000
```

```
reward = []
for i in range(bandits):
    reward.append([])
    for j in range(arms):
        reward[i].append(random.uniform(-1,1))
print(reward)

Q = []
for i in range(bandits):
    Q.append([])
    for j in range(arms):
        Q[i].append(10.0)
print(Q)

def greedy(values):
    return values.index(max(values))

def learn(state, action, reward, next_state):
    q = gamma * max(Q[next_state])
    q += reward
    q -= Q[state][action]
    q *= learning_rate
    q += Q[state][action]
    Q[state][action] = q

# agent learns
bandit = random.randint(0,bandits-1)
for i in range(0, episodes):
    last_bandit = bandit
    bandit = random.randint(0,bandits-1)
    action = greedy(Q[bandit])
    r = reward[last_bandit][action]
    learn(last_bandit, action, r, bandit)
print(Q)
```

2. All of the highlighted sections of code are new and worth paying closer attention to. Let's take a look at each section in more detail here:

```
arms = 7
bandits = 7
gamma = .9
```

3. We start by initializing the `arms` variable to 7 then a new `bandits` variable to 7 as well. Recall that `arms` is analogous to `actions` and `bandits` likewise is to `state`. The last new variable, `gamma`, is a new learning parameter used to discount rewards. We will explore this discount factor concept in future chapters:

```
reward = []
for i in range(bandits):
    reward.append([])
    for j in range(arms):
        reward[i].append(random.uniform(-1,1))
print(reward)
```

4. The next section of code builds up the reward table matrix as a set of random values from -1 to 1. We use a list of lists in this example to better represent the separate concepts:

```
Q = []
for i in range(bandits):
    Q.append([])
    for j in range(arms):
        Q[i].append(10.0)
print(Q)
```

5. The following section is very similar and this time sets up a Q table matrix to hold our calculated quality values. Notice how we initialize our starting Q value to 10.0. We do this to account for subtle changes in the math, again something we will discuss later.

6. Since our states and actions can be all mapped onto a matrix/table, we refer to our RL system as using a model. A model represents all actions and states of an environment:

```
def learn(state, action, reward, next_state):
    q = gamma * max(Q[next_state])
    q += reward
    q -= Q[state][action]
    q *= learning_rate
    q += Q[state][action]
    Q[state][action] = q
```

7. We next define a new function called `learn`. This new function is just a straight implementation of the Q equation we observed earlier:

```
bandit = random.randint(0,bandits-1)
for i in range(0, episodes):
    last_bandit = bandit
    bandit = random.randint(0,bandits-1)
```

```
        action = greedy(Q[bandit])
        r = reward[last_bandit][action]
        learn(last_bandit, action, r, bandit)
    print(Q)
```

8. Finally, the agent learning section is updated significantly with new code. This new code sets up the parameters we need for the new learn function we looked at earlier. Notice how the bandit or state is getting randomly selected each time. Essentially, this means our agent is just randomly walking from bandit to bandit.

9. Run the code as you normally would and notice the new calculated Q values printed out at the end. Do they match the rewards for each of the arm pulls?

Likely, a few of your arms don't match up with their respective reward values. This is because the new Q-learning equation solves the entire MDP but our agent is NOT moving in an MDP. Instead, our agent is just randomly moving from state to state with no care on which state it saw before. Think back to our example and you will realize since our current state does not affect our future state, it fails to be a Markov property and hence is not an MDP. However, that doesn't mean we can't successfully solve this problem and we will look to do that in the next section.

Removing discounted rewards

The problem with our current solution and using the full Q-learning equation is that the equation assumes any state our agent is in affects future states. Except, remember in our example, the agent just walked randomly from bandit to bandit. This means using any previous state information would be useless, as we saw. Fortunately, we can easily fix this by removing the concept of discounted rewards. Recall that new variable, gamma, that appeared in this complicated term: $\gamma_{a'}^{max} Q(s_{t+1}, a)$. Gamma and this term are a way of discounting future rewards and something we will discuss at length starting in Chapter 2, *Dynamic Programming and the Bellman Equation*. For now, though, we can fix this sample up by just removing that term from our learn function. Let's open up code example, Chapter_1_5.py, and follow the exercise here:

1. The only section of code we really need to focus on is the updated learn function, here:

```
def learn(state, action, reward, next_state):
    #q = gamma * max(Q[next_state])
    q = 0
    q += reward
    q -= Q[state][action]
    q *= learning_rate
```

```
q += Q[state][action]
Q[state][action] = q
```

2. The first line of code in the function is responsible for discounting the future reward of the next state. Since none of the states in our example are connected, we can just comment out that line. We create a new initializer for `q = 0` in the next line.

3. Run the code as you normally would. Now you should see very close values closely matching their respective rewards.

By omitting the discounted rewards part of the calculation, hopefully, you can appreciate that this would just revert to a value calculation problem. Alternatively, you may also realize that if our bandits were connected. That is, pulling an arm led to another one arm machine with more actions and so on. We could then use the Q-learning equation to solve the problem as well.

That concludes a very basic introduction to the primary components and elements of RL. Throughout the rest of this book, we will dig into the nuances of policies, values, actions, and rewards.

Summary

In this chapter, we first introduced ourselves to the world of RL. We looked at what makes RL so unique and why it makes sense for games. After that, we explored the basic terminology and history of modern RL. From there, we looked to the foundations of RL and the Markov decision process, where we discovered what makes an RL problem. Then we looked to building our first learner a value learner that calculated the values of states on an action. This led us to uncover the need for exploration and exploitation and the dilemma that constantly challenges RL implementers. Next, we jumped in and discovered the full Q-learning equation and how to build a Q-learner, where we later realized that the full Q equation was beyond what we needed for our unconnected state environment. We then reverted our Q learned back into a value learner and watched it solve the contextual bandit problem.

In the next chapter, we will continue from where we left off and look into how rewards are discounted with the Bellman equation, as well as look at the many other improvements dynamic programming has introduced to RL.

Questions

Use these questions and exercises to reinforce the material you just learned. The exercises may be fun to attempt, so be sure to try atleast two to four questions/exercises:

Questions:

1. What are the names of the main components of an RL system? Hint, the first one is **Environment**.
2. Name the four elements of an RL system. Remember that one element is optional.
3. Name the three main threads that compose modern RL.
4. What makes a Markov state a Markov property?
5. What is a policy?

Exercises:

1. Using `Chapter_1_2.py`, alter the code so the agent pulls from a bandit with 1,000 arms. What code changes do you need to make?
2. Using `Chapter_1_3.py`, alter the code so that the agent pulls from the average value, not greedy/max. How did this affect the agent's exploration?
3. Using `Chapter_1_3.py`, alter the `learning_rate` variable to determine how fast or slow you can make the agent learn. How few episodes are you required to run for the agent to solve the problem?
4. Using `Chapter_1_5.py`, alter the code so that the agent uses a different policy (either the greedy policy or something else). Take points off yourself if you look ahead in this book or online for solutions.
5. Using `Chapter_1_4.py`, alter the code so that the bandits are connected. Hence, when an agent pulls an arm, they receive a reward and are transported to another specific bandit, no longer at random. **Hint:** This likely will require a new destination table to be built and you will now need to include the discounted reward term we removed.

Even completing a few of these questions and/or exercises will make a huge difference to your learning this material. This is a hands-on book after all.

2
Dynamic Programming and the Bellman Equation

Dynamic programming (**DP**) was the second major thread to influence modern **reinforcement learning** (**RL**) after trial-and-error learning. In this chapter, we will look at the foundations of DP and explore how they influenced the field of RL. We will also look at how the Bellman equation and the concept of optimality have interwoven with RL. From there, we will look at policy and value iteration methods to solve a class of problems well suited for DP. Finally, we will look at how to use the concepts we have learned in this chapter to teach an agent to play the FrozenLake environment from OpenAI Gym.

Here are the main topics we will cover in this chapter:

- Introducing DP
- Understanding the Bellman equation
- Building policy iteration
- Building value iteration
- Playing with policy versus value iteration

For this chapter, we look at how to solve a finite **Markov decision process** (**MDP**) with DP using the Bellman equation of optimality. This chapter is meant as a history lesson and background to DP and Bellman. If you are already quite familiar with DP, then you may want to bypass this chapter since we will just explore entry-level DP, covering just enough background to see how it has influenced and bettered RL.

Introducing DP

DP was developed by Richard E. Bellman in the 1950s as a way to optimize and solve complex decision problems. The method was first applied to engineering control problems but has since found uses in all disciplines requiring the analytical modeling of problems and subproblems. In effect, all DP is about is solving subproblems and then finding relationships to connect those to solve bigger problems. It does all of this by first applying the Bellman optimality equation and then solving it.

Before we get to solving a finite MDP with DP, we will want to understand, in a little more detail, what it is we are talking about. Let's look at a simple example of the difference between normal recursion and DP in the next section.

Regular programming versus DP

We will do a comparison by first solving a problem using regular methods and then with DP. Along the way, we will identify key elements that make our solution a DP one. What most experienced programmers find is that they likely have done DP in some capacity, so don't be surprised if this all sounds really familiar. Let's open up the Chapter_2_1.py example and follow the exercise:

1. The code is an example of finding the nth number in the Fibonacci sequence using recursion and is shown as follows:

```
def Fibonacci(n):
    if n<0:
        print("Outside bounds")
    elif n==1:
        return 0 # n==1, returns 0
    elif n==2:
        return 1 # n==2, returns 1
    else:
        return Fibonacci(n-1)+Fibonacci(n-2)
print(Fibonacci(9))
```

2. Recall that we can resolve the nth element in the Fibonacci sequence by summing the two previous digits in the sequence. We consider that when n == 1, the value is 0, and when n == 2, the returned value is 1. Hence, the third element in the sequence would be the sum of Fibonacci(1) and Fibonacci(2) and would return a value of 1. This reflects in the code shown in the following line:

```
return Fibonacci(n-1)+Fibonacci(n-2)
```

3. Hence, the solution for finding the fourth element using the linear programming version of recursion is shown in the following diagram:

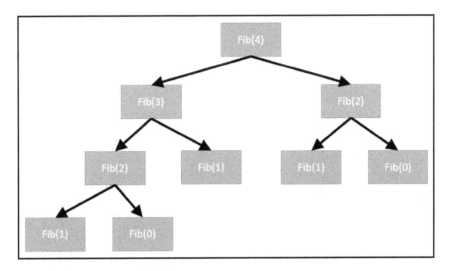

Solving the fourth element of the Fibonacci sequence

We can note the following:

- The preceding diagram shows each recursive call to the Fibonacci function required to calculate previous elements. Notice how this method requires the solution to solve or call the Fibonacci(2) function twice. Of course, that additional call in this example is trivial but these additional calls can quickly add up.
- Run the code as you normally would and see the printed result for the ninth element.

To appreciate how inefficient recursion can be, we have modified our previous example and saved it as Chapter_2_2.py. Open up that example now and follow the next exercise:

1. The modified code, with the extra line highlighted, is shown for reference:

```
def Fibonacci(n):
    if n<0:
        print("Outside bounds")
    elif n==1:
        return 0 # n==1, returns 0
    elif n==2:
        return 1 # n==2, returns 1
    else:
```

```
        print("Solving for {}".format(n))
        return Fibonacci(n-1)+Fibonacci(n-2)
print(Fibonacci(9))
```

2. All we are doing is printing out when we need to calculate two more sequences to return the sum. Run the code and notice the output, as shown in the following screenshot:

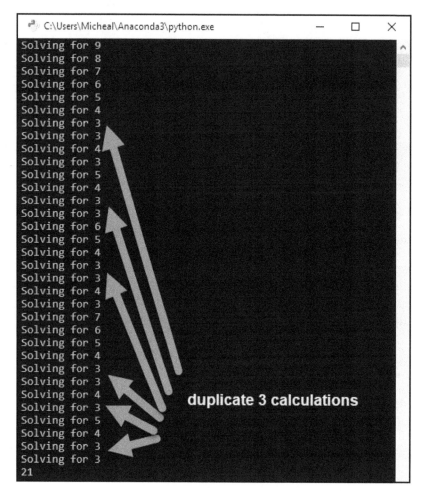

Output from example Chapter_2_1.py

3. Notice, for just calculating the ninth element of the Fibonacci sequence using recursion, the number of times just `Fibonacci(3)` is called.

Now, the solution works and, as they say, it is pretty and clean. In fact, as a programmer, you may have been taught to worship this style of coding at one time. However, we can clearly see how inefficient this method is to scale and that is where DP comes in, which we will discuss in the next section.

Enter DP and memoization

A key concept in DP is to break down larger problems into smaller subproblems, then solve said smaller problems and store the result. The fancy name for this activity is called **memoization** and the best way to showcase how this works is with an example. Open up `Chapter_2_3.py` and follow the exercise:

1. For reference, the entire block of code from our previous example has been modified as follows:

```python
fibSequence = [0,1]

def Fibonacci(n):
    if n<0:
        print("Outside bounds")
    elif n<= len(fibSequence):
        return fibSequence[n-1]
    else:
        print("Solving for {}".format(n))
        fibN = Fibonacci(n-1) + Fibonacci(n-2)
        fibSequence.append(fibN)
        return fibN
print(Fibonacci(9))
```

2. Again, the highlighted lines denote code changes, but, in this case, we will go over each code change in more detail starting with the first change, as follows:

```python
fibSequence = [0,1]
```

3. This new line creates a new starting Fibonacci list with our two base numbers, 0 and 1. We will still use a recursive function, but now we also store the results of every unique calculation for later:

```python
elif n<= len(fibSequence):
        return fibSequence[n-1]
```

4. The next code change is where the algorithm returns a previously stored value, as in 0 or 1, or as calculated and then stored in the `fibSequence` list:

```
fibN = Fibonacci(n-1) + Fibonacci(n-2)
fibSequence.append(fibN)
return fibN
```

5. The last group of code changes now saves the recursive calculation, adding the new value to the entire sequence. This now requires the algorithm to only calculate each nth value of the sequence once.

6. Run the code as you normally would and look at the results shown in the following screenshot:

```
C:\Users\Micheal\Anaconda3\python.exe          —    □    ×
Solving for 9
Solving for 8
Solving for 7
Solving for 6
Solving for 5
Solving for 4
Solving for 3
21
Press any key to continue . . .
```

Example output from example Chapter_2_3.py

Notice how we are now only calculating the numbers in the sequence and not repeating any calculations. Clearly, this method is far superior to the linear programming example that we looked at earlier, and the code actually doesn't look bad either. Now, as we said, if this type of solution seems obvious, then you probably already understand more about DP than you realize.

 We will only cover a very simple introduction to DP as it relates to RL in this book. As you can see, DP is a powerful technique that can benefit any developer who is serious about optimizing code.

In the next section, we look further at the work of Bellman and the equation that was named after him.

Understanding the Bellman equation

Bellman worked on solving finite MDP with DP, and it was during these efforts he derived his famed equation. The beauty behind this equation—and more abstractly, the concept, in general—is that it describes a method of optimizing the value or quality of a state. In other words, it describes how we can determine the optimal value/quality for being in a given state given the action and choices of successive states. Before breaking down the equation itself, let's first reconsider the finite MDP in the next section.

Unraveling the finite MDP

Consider the finite MDP we developed in Chapter 1, *Understanding Rewards Learning*, that described your morning routine. Don't to worry if you didn't complete that exercise previously as we will consider a more specific example, as follows:

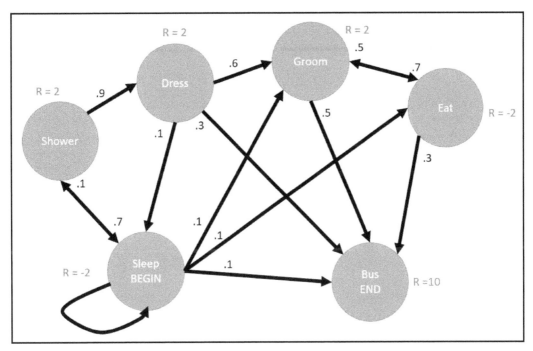

MDP for waking up and getting on the bus

The preceding finite MDP describes a possible routine for someone waking up and getting ready to get on a bus to go to school or work. In this MDP, we define a beginning state (**BEGIN**) and an ending state, that is, getting on the bus (**END**). The **R =** denotes the reward allotted when moving to that state and the number closest to the end of the action line denotes the probability of taking that action. We can denote the optimum path through this finite MDP, as shown in the following diagram:

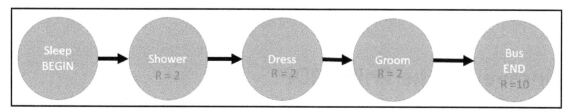

The optimum solution to the MDP

Mathematically, we can describe the optimum result, therefore, as the sum of all rewards traversed through the environment to obtain the total reward. More formally, we can also write this mathematically like so:

$$R_{total} = R_{t+1} + R_{t+2} + R_{t+2} + \ldots$$

However, and this is where Bellman comes in, we can't consider all rewards as equal. Without exploring the math in more exhaustive detail, the Bellman equation introduced the concept that future rewards should be discounted. This is also quite intuitive when you think about it. The experience or effect we feel from future actions is weakened depending on how far in the future we need to decide. This is the same concept we apply with the Bellman equation. Hence, we can now apply a discounting factor (gamma) to the previous equation and show the following:

$$R_{total} = R_{t+1} + \gamma R_{t+2} + \gamma^2 R_{t+3} + \ldots = \sum_{k=0}^{\infty} \gamma^k R_{t+k+1}$$

Gamma (γ), shown in the equation, represents a future rewards discount factor. The value can be from 0.0 to 1.0. If the value is 1.0, then we consider no discount of future rewards, whereas a value of 0.1 would heavily discount future rewards. In most RL problems, we keep this number fairly high and well above 0.9. This leads us to the next section where we discuss how the Bellman equation can optimize a problem.

The Bellman optimality equation

The Bellman equation shows us that you can solve any MDP by first finding the optimal policy that allows an agent to traverse that MDP. Recall that a policy defines the decisions for each action that will guide an agent through an MDP. Ideally, what we want to find is the optimal policy: a policy that can maximize the value for each state and determine which states to traverse for maximum reward. When we combine this with other concepts and apply more math wizardry and then combine it with the Bellman optimality equation, we get the following optimal policy equation:

$$\pi(s) = \underset{a}{argmax} \mathbb{E}[R_{t+1} + \gamma v_\pi(S_{t+1})|S_t = s, A_t = a]$$

That strange term at the very beginning ($\underset{a}{argmax\mathbb{E}}$) is a way of describing a function that maximizes the rewards given a set of states and actions considering that we discount future rewards by a factor called gamma. Notice how we also use π to denote the policy equation but we often think of this as a quality and may refer to this as q or Q. If you think back to our previous peek at the Q-learning equation, then now you can clearly see how the rewards' discount factor, gamma, comes into play.

In the next section, we will look at methods to solve an MDP using DP and a method of policy iteration given our understanding of the Bellman optimality principle and resulting policy equation.

Building policy iteration

For us to determine the best policy, we first need a method to evaluate the given policy for a state. We can use a method of evaluating the policy by searching through all of the states of an MDP and further evaluating all actions. This will provide us with a value function for the given state that we can then use to perform successive updates of a new value function iteratively. Mathematically, we can then use the previous Bellman optimality equation and derive a new update to a state value function, as shown here:

$$v_{k+1} = \mathbb{E}[R_{t+1} + \gamma v_k(S_{t+1}|S_t = s]$$

In the preceding equation, the $\mathbb{E}$ symbol represents an expectation and denotes the expected state value update to a new value function. Inside this expectation, we can see this dependent on the returned reward plus the previous discounted value for the next state given an already chosen action. That means that our algorithm will iterate over every state and action evaluating a new state value using the preceding update equation. This process is called backing up or planning, and it is helpful for us to visualize how this algorithm works using backup diagrams. The following is an example of the backup diagrams for action value and state value backups:

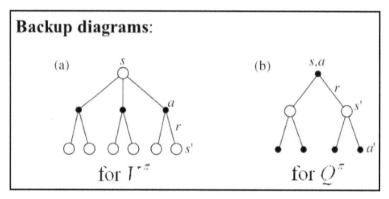

Backup diagrams for action value and state value backups

Diagram **(a)** or V^{π} is the part of the backup or evaluation that tries each action and hence provides us with action values. The second part of the evaluation comes from the update and is shown in diagram **(b)** for Q^{π}. Recall, the update evaluates the forward states by evaluating each of the state actions. The diagrams represent the point of evaluation with a filled-in solid circle. Notice how the action value only focuses on the forward actions while the state value focuses on the action value for each forward state. Of course, it will be helpful to look at how this comes together in code. However, before we get to that, we want to do some housekeeping in the next section.

Installing OpenAI Gym

To help to encourage research and development in RL, the OpenAI group provides an open source platform for RL training called Gym. Gym, provided by OpenAI, comes with plenty of sample test environments that we can venture through while we work through this book. Also, other RL developers have developed other environments using the same standard interface Gym uses. Hence, by learning to use Gym, we will also be able to explore other cutting-edge RL environments later in this book.

The installation for Gym is quite simple, but, at the same time, we want to avoid any small mistakes that may cause you frustration later. Therefore, it is best to use the following instructions to set up and install an RL environment for development.

 It is highly recommended that you use Anaconda for Python development with this book. Anaconda is a free open source cross-platform tool that can significantly increase your ease of development. Please stick with Anaconda unless you consider yourself an experienced Python developer. Google `python anaconda` to download and install it.

Follow the exercise to set up and install a Python environment with Gym:

1. Open a new Anaconda Prompt or Python shell. Do this as an admin or be sure to execute the commands as an admin if required.
2. From the command line, run the following:

```
conda create -n chapter2 python=3.6
```

3. This will create a new virtual environment for your development. A virtual environment allows you to isolate dependencies and control your versioning. If you are not using Anaconda, you can use the Python virtual environment to create a new environment. You should also notice that we are forcing the environment to use Python 3.6. Again, this makes sure we know what version of Python we are using.
4. After the installation, we activate the environment with the following:

```
activate chapter2
```

5. Next, we install Gym with the following command:

```
pip install gym
```

6. Gym will install several dependencies along with the various sample environments we will train on later.

Before we get too far ahead though, let's now test our Gym installation with code in the next section.

Testing Gym

In the next exercise, we will write code to test Gym and an environment called FrozenLake, which also happens to be our test environment for this chapter. Open the Chapter_2_4.py code example and follow the exercise:

1. For reference, the code is shown as follows:

```python
from os import system, name
import time
import gym
import numpy as np

env = gym.make('FrozenLake-v0')
env.reset()

def clear():
    if name == 'nt':
        _ = system('cls')
    else:
        _ = system('clear')

for _ in range(1000):
    clear()
    env.render()
    time.sleep(.5)
    env.step(env.action_space.sample()) # take a random action
env.close()
```

2. At the top, we have the imports to load the system modules as well as gym, time, and numpy. numpy is a helper library we use to construct tensors. Tensors are a math/programming concept that can describe single values or multidimensional arrays of numbers.

3. Next, we build and reset the environment with the following code:

```python
env = gym.make('FrozenLake-v0')
env.reset()
```

4. After that, we have a clear function, which we use to clear rendering that is not critical to this example. The code should be self-explanatory as well.

5. This brings us to the `for` loop and where all of the actions, so to speak, happen. The line of most importance is shown as follows:

```
env.step(env.action_space.sample())
```

6. The `env` variable represents the environment, and, in the line, we are letting the algorithm take a random action every step or iteration. In this example, the agent learns nothing and just moves at random, for now.

7. Run the code as you normally would and pay attention to the output. An example of the output screen is shown in the following:

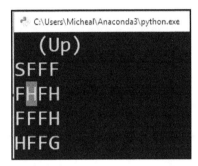

Example render from the FrozenLake environment

Since the algorithm/agent moves randomly, it is quite likely to hit a hole, denoted by `H` and just stay there. For reference, the legend for FrozenLake is given here:

- **S** = start: This is where the agent starts when reset is called.
- **F** = frozen: This allows the agent to move across this area.
- **H** = hole: This is a hole in the ice; if the agent moves here, it falls in.
- **G** = goal: This is the goal the agent wants to reach, and, when it does, it receives a reward of 1.0.

Now that we have Gym set up, we can move to evaluate the policy in the next section.

Policy evaluation

Unlike the trial-and-error learning, you have already been introduced to DP methods that work as a form of static learning or what we may call planning. Planning is an appropriate definition here since the algorithm evaluates the entire MDP and hence all states and actions beforehand. Hence, these methods require full knowledge of the environment including all finite states and actions. While this works for known finite environments such as the one we are playing within this chapter, these methods are not substantial enough for real-world physical problems. We will, of course, solve real-world problems later in this book. For now, though, let's look at how to evaluate a policy from the previous update equations in code. Open `Chapter_2_5.py` and follow the exercise:

1. For reference, the entire block of code, `Chapter_2_5.py`, is shown as follows:

```
from os import system, name
import time
import gym
import numpy as np
env = gym.make('FrozenLake-v0')
env.reset()

def clear():
    if name == 'nt':
        _ = system('cls')
    else:
        _ = system('clear')

def act(V, env, gamma, policy, state, v):
    for action, action_prob in enumerate(policy[state]):
        for state_prob, next_state, reward, end in
env.P[state][action]:
            v += action_prob * state_prob * (reward + gamma *
V[next_state])
            V[state] = v
def eval_policy(policy, env, gamma=1.0, theta=1e-9, terms=1e9):
    V = np.zeros(env.nS)
    delta = 0
    for i in range(int(terms)):
        for state in range(env.nS):
            act(V, env, gamma, policy, state, v=0.0)
        clear()
        print(V)
        time.sleep(1)
        v = np.sum(V)
        if v - delta < theta:
            return V
```

```
            else:
                    delta = v
          return V

    policy = np.ones([env.env.nS, env.env.nA]) / env.env.nA
    V = eval_policy(policy, env.env)

    print(policy, V)
```

2. At the beginning of the code, we perform the same initial steps as our test example. We load `import` statements and initialize and load the environment, then define the `clear` function.

3. Next, move to the very end of the code and notice how we are initializing the policy using `numpy as np` to fill a tensor of the size of the environment, `state x action`. We then divide the tensor by the number of actions in a state—4, in this case. This gives us a distributed probability of `0.25` per action. Remember that the combined action probability in a Markov property needs to sum up to `1.0` or 100%.

4. Now, move up the `eval_policy` function and focus on the double loop, as shown in the following code block:

```
    for i in range(int(terms)):
      for state in range(env.nS):
        act(V, env, gamma, policy, state, v=0.0)
      clear()
      print(V)
      time.sleep(1)
      v = np.sum(V)
      if v - delta < theta:
        return V
      else:
        delta = v
    return V
```

5. The first `for` loop loops on the number of terms or iterations before termination. We set a limit here to prevent endless looping. In the inner loop, all of the states in the environment are iterated through and acted on using the `act` function. After that, we use our previous render code to show the updated values. At the end of the first `for` loop, we check whether the calculated total change in the `v` value is less than a particular threshold, `theta`. If the change in value is less than the threshold, the function returns the calculate value function, `V`.

6. At the core of the algorithm is the `act` function and where the update equation operates; the inside of this function is shown as follows:

```
for action, action_prob in enumerate(policy[state]):
  for state_prob, next_state, reward, end
 in env.P[state][action]:
    v += action_prob * state_prob * (reward + gamma *
 V[next_state]) #update
      V[state] = v
```

7. The first `for` loop iterates through all of the actions in the policy for the given state. Recall that we start by initializing the policy to 0.25 for every `action` function, `action_prob = 0.25`. Then, we loop through every transition from the state and action and apply the update. The update is shown in the highlighted equation. Finally, the `value` function, `V`, for the current state is updated to `v`.

8. Run the code and observe the output. Notice how the `value` function is continually updated. At the end of the run, you should see something similar to the following screenshot:

Running example Chapter_2_5.py

If it seems off that the policy is not updated, that is actually okay, for now. The important part here is to see how we update the `value` function. In the next section, we will look at how we can improve the policy.

Policy improvement

With policy evaluation under our belt, it is time to move on to improving the policy by looking ahead. Recall we do this by looking at one state ahead of the current state and then evaluating all possible actions. Let's look at how this works in code. Open up the Chapter_2_6.py example and follow the exercise:

1. For brevity, the following code excerpt from Chapter_2_6.py shows just the new sections of code that were added to that last example:

```
def evaluate(V, action_values, env, gamma, state):
    for action in range(env.nA):
        for prob, next_state, reward, terminated in
env.P[state][action]:
            action_values[action] += prob * (reward + gamma *
V[next_state])
    return action_values

def lookahead(env, state, V, gamma):
    action_values = np.zeros(env.nA)
    return evaluate(V, action_values, env, gamma, state)

def improve_policy(env, gamma=1.0, terms=1e9):
    policy = np.ones([env.nS, env.nA]) / env.nA
    evals = 1
    for i in range(int(terms)):
        stable = True
        V = eval_policy(policy, env, gamma=gamma)
        for state in range(env.nS):
            current_action = np.argmax(policy[state])
            action_value = lookahead(env, state, V, gamma)
            best_action = np.argmax(action_value)
            if current_action != best_action:
                stable = False
                policy[state] = np.eye(env.nA)[best_action]
            evals += 1
        if stable:
            return policy, V

#replaced bottom code from previous sample with
policy, V = improve_policy(env.env)
print(policy, V)
```

2. Added to the last example are three new functions: improve_policy, lookahead, and evaluate. improve_policy uses a limited loop to loop through the states in the current environment; before looping through each state, it calls eval_policy to update the value function by passing in the current policy, environment, and gamma parameters (discount factor). Then, it calls the lookahead function, which internally calls an evaluate function that updates the action values for the state. evaluate is a modified version of the act function.

3. While both functions, eval_policy and improve_policy, use limited terms for loops to prevent endless looping, they still use very large limits; in the example, the default is 1e09. Therefore, we still want to determine a condition to hopefully stop the loop much earlier than the term's limit. In policy evaluation, we controlled this by observing the change or delta in the value function. In policy improvement, we now look to improve the actual policy and, to do this, we assume a greedy policy. In other words, we want to improve our policy to always pick the highest value action, as shown in the following code:

```
action_value = lookahead(env, state, V, gamma)best_action =
np.argmax(action_value)
if current_action != best_action:
  stable = False
  policy[state] = np.eye(env.nA)[best_action]
evals += 1

if stable:
  return policy, V
```

4. The preceding block of code first uses the numpy function—np.argmax on the list of action_value returns from the lookahead function. This returns the max or best_action, or in other words, the greedy action. We then consider whether current_action is not equal to best_action; if it is not, then we consider the policy is not stable by setting stable to false. Since the action is not the best, we also update policy with the identity tensor using np.eye for the shape defined. This step simply assigns the policy a value of 1.0 for the best/greedy actions and 0.0 for all others.

5. At the end of the code, you can see that we now just call improve_policy and print the results of the policy and value functions.

6. Run the code as you normally would and observe the output, as shown in the following screenshot:

```
C:\Users\Micheal\Anaconda3\python.exe                                          —    □   ×
[0.01070127 0.01147851 0.0178007  0.00593357 0.02062529 0.
 0.03804234 0.         0.06308208 0.12130938 0.13436865 0.
 0.         0.16647742 0.37812288 0.         ]
[[0.   1.   0.   0.  ]
 [0.   0.   0.   1.  
 [0.25 0.25 0.25 0.25]
 [0.   0.   0.   1.  ]
 [0.25 0.25 0.25 0.25]
 [0.25 0.25 0.25 0.25]
 [0.25 0.25 0.25 0.25]
 [0.25 0.25 0.25 0.25]
 [0.   0.   0.   1.  ]
 [0.   1.   0.   0.  ]
 [0.25 0.25 0.25 0.25]
 [0.25 0.25 0.25 0.25]
 [0.25 0.25 0.25 0.25]
 [0.   0.   1.   0.  ]
 [0.   0.   1.   0.  ]
 [0.25 0.25 0.25 0.25]] [0.01070127 0.01147851 0.0178007  0.00593357 0.02062529 0.
 0.03804234 0.         0.06308208 0.12130938 0.13436865 0.
 0.         0.16647742 0.37812288 0.         ]
Press any key to continue . . .
```

1.0 best action

Example output for Chapter_2_6.py

This sample will take a while longer to run and you should see the value function improve as the sample runs. When the sample completes, it will print the value function and policy. You can now see how the policy clearly indicates the best action for each state with a 1.0 value. The reason some states still have the 0.25 value for all actions is that the algorithm sees no need to evaluate or improve the policy in those states. They were likely states that were holes or were outside the optimal path.

Policy evaluation and improvement is one method we can use for planning with DP, but, in the next section, we will look at a second method called value iteration.

Building value iteration

Iterating over values may seem a step back to what we referred to as policy iteration in the last section, but it is actually more of a side step or companion method. In value iteration, we loop through all states in the entire MDP looking for the best value for each state, and when we find that, we stop or break. However, we don't stop there and we continue by looking ahead of all states and then assuming a deterministic probability of 100% for the best action. This yields a new policy that may perform better than the previous policy iteration demonstration. The differences between both methods are subtle and best understood with a code example. Open up `Chapter_2_7.py` and follow the next exercise:

1. This code example builds on the previous example. New code changes in example `Chapter_2_7.py` are shown in the following code:

```
def value_iteration(env, gamma=1.0, theta=1e-9, terms=1e9):
    V = np.zeros(env.nS)
    for i in range(int(terms)):
        delta = 0
        for state in range(env.nS):
            action_value = lookahead(env, state, V, gamma)
            best_action_value = np.max(action_value)
            delta = max(delta, np.abs(V[state] -
best_action_value))
            V[state] = best_action_value
        if delta < theta: break
    policy = np.zeros([env.nS, env.nA])
    for state in range(env.nS):
        action_value = lookahead(env, state, V, gamma)
        best_action = np.argmax(action_value)
        policy[state, best_action] = 1.0
    return policy, V

#policy, V = improve_policy(env.env)
#print(policy, V)

policy, V = value_iteration(env.env)
print(policy, V)
```

2. The bulk of this code is quite similar to code we already reviewed in the previous examples, but there are some subtle differences worth noting.

3. First, this time, inside the limited terms loop, we iterated through the states and performed a straight lookahead with the `lookahead` function. The details of this code are as follows:

```
for state in range(env.nS):
  action_value = lookahead(env, state, V, gamma)
  best_action_value = np.max(action_value)
  delta = max(delta, np.abs(V[state] - best_action_value))
  V[state] = best_action_value
```

4. The slight difference in the preceding code versus policy evaluation and improvement is that, this time, we do an immediate lookahead and iterate over action values and then update the `value` function based on the best value. In this block of code, we also calculate a new `delta` value or amount of change from the previous best action value:

```
if delta < theta: break
```

5. After the loop, there is an `if` statement that checks whether the calculated `delta` value or the amount of action value change is below a particular threshold, `theta`. If `delta` is sufficiently small, we break the limited terms loop:

```
policy = np.zeros([env.nS, env.nA])
  for state in range(env.nS):
    action_value = lookahead(env, state, V, gamma)
    best_action = np.argmax(action_value)
    policy[state, best_action] = 1.0
return policy, V
```

6. From there, we initialize `policy` this time to all zeros with the `numpy np.zeros` function. Then, we loop through all of the states again and perform another one-step lookahead using the `lookahead` function. This returns a list of action values, which we determine the max index of, `best_action`. We then set `policy` to `1.0`; we assume the best action is always the one chosen for the state. Finally, we return the new policy and the `value` function, `V`.

7. Run the code as you have and examine the output as shown in the following screenshot:

Example output from Chapter_2_8.py

This time, we don't do any policy iteration or improvement so the sample runs faster. You should also note how the policy has been updated for all states. Recall, in policy iteration, only the relevant states the algorithm/agent could move through were evaluated.

In the next section, we turn an actual agent loose on the environment using the policy calculated with policy iteration and improvement versus value iteration in the next section.

Playing with policy versus value iteration

Policy and value iteration methods are quite similar and looked at as companion methods. As such, to evaluate which method to use, we often need to apply both methods to the problem in question. In the next exercise, we will evaluate both policy and value iteration methods side by side in the FrozenLake environment:

1. Open the `Chapter_2_8.py` example. This example builds on the previous code examples, so we will only show the new additional code:

```
def play(env, episodes, policy):
    wins = 0
    total_reward = 0
    for episode in range(episodes):
        term = False
        state = env.reset()
        while not term:
            action = np.argmax(policy[state])
            next_state, reward, term, info = env.step(action)
            total_reward += reward
            state = next_state
            if term and reward == 1.0:
                wins += 1
    average_reward = total_reward / episodes
    return wins, total_reward, average_reward

policy, V = improve_policy(env.env)
print(policy, V)

wins, total, avg = play(env.env, 1000, policy)
print(wins)

policy, V = value_iteration(env.env)
print(policy, V)

wins, total, avg = play(env.env, 1000, policy)
print(wins)
```

2. The additional code consists of a new function, `play`, and different test code at the end. At the code at the end, we first calculate a policy using the `improve_policy` function, which performs policy iteration:

```
wins, total, avg = play(env.env, 1000, policy)print(wins)
```

3. Next, we evaluate the number of wins for `policy` by using the `play` function. After this, we print the number of wins.

4. Then, we evaluate a new policy using value iteration, again using the `play` function to evaluate the number of wins and printing the result:

```
for episode in range(episodes):
  term = False
  state = env.reset()
  while not term:
    action = np.argmax(policy[state])
    next_state, reward, term, info = env.step(action)
    total_reward += reward
    state = next_state
    if term and reward == 1.0:
      wins += 1
average_reward = total_reward / episodes     return wins,
total_reward, average_reward
```

5. Inside the `play` function, we loop through the number of episodes. Each episode is considered to be one attempt by the agent to move from the start to the goal. In this example, the termination of an episode happens when the agent encounters a hole or the goal. If it reaches the goal, it receives a reward of 1.0. Most of the code is self-explanatory, aside from the moment an agent conducts an action and is shown again as follows:

```
next_state, reward, term, info = env.step(action)
```

6. Recall, in our Gym environment test, we just randomly stepped the agent around. Now, in the preceding code, we execute a specific action set by the policy. The return from taking the action is `next_state`, `reward` (if any), `term` or termination, and an `info` variable. This line of code entirely controls the agent and allows it to move and interact with the environment:

```
total_reward += reward
state = next_state
if term and reward == 1.0:
  wins += 1
```

7. After the agent takes a step, we then update `total_reward` and `state`. Then, we test to see whether the agent won, the environment was terminated, and the returned reward was 1.0. Otherwise, the agent continues. The agent may also terminate an episode from falling into a hole.

8. Run the code as you normally would and examine the output, as shown in the
following screenshot:

```
C:\Users\Micheal\Anaconda3\python.exe                                    —    □    ×
[0.01402847 0.01350705 0.01987033 0.00662344 0.02338524 0.
 0.04180654 0.         0.06957365 0.13315616 0.14735612 0.
 0.         0.18253931 0.41446192 0.        ]
[[1.   0.   0.   0.  ]
 [0.   0.   0.   1.  ]
 [0.25 0.25 0.25 0.25]
 [0.   0.   0.   1.  ]
 [0.25 0.25 0.25 0.25]
 [0.25 0.25 0.25 0.25]
 [0.25 0.25 0.25 0.25]
 [0.25 0.25 0.25 0.25]
 [0.   0.   0.   1.  ]
 [0.   1.   0.   0.  ]
 [0.25 0.25 0.25 0.25]
 [0.25 0.25 0.25 0.25]
 [0.25 0.25 0.25 0.25]
 [0.   0.   1.   0.  ]
 [0.   1.   0.   0.  ]
 [0.25 0.25 0.25 0.25]] [0.01402847 0.01350705 0.01987033 0.00662344 0.02338524 0.
 0.04180654 0.         0.06957365 0.13315616 0.14735612 0.
 0.         0.18253931 0.41446192 0.        ]
767  ←————————————————————  policy iteration
[[1. 0. 0. 0.]
 [0. 0. 0. 1.]
 [0. 0. 0. 1.]
 [0. 0. 0. 1.]
 [1. 0. 0. 0.]
 [1. 0. 0. 0.]
 [1. 0. 0. 0.]
 [1. 0. 0. 0.]
 [0. 0. 0. 1.]
 [0. 1. 0. 0.]
 [1. 0. 0. 0.]
 [1. 0. 0. 0.]
 [1. 0. 0. 0.]
 [0. 0. 1. 0.]
 [0. 1. 0. 0.]
 [1. 0. 0. 0.]] [0.82352939 0.82352939 0.82352939 0.82352938 0.8235294  0.
 0.52941175 0.         0.8235294  0.8235294  0.76470587 0.
 0.         0.88235293 0.94117647 0.        ]
851  ←————————————————————  value iteration
Press any key to continue . . . _
```

Example output from example Chapter_2_8.py

Notice the difference in results. This is the difference in policy iteration with value iteration over the FrozenLake problem. You can play with and adjust the parameters of theta and gamma to see whether you get better results for either method. Again, much like RL itself, you will need to perform a little trial and error on your own to determine the best DP method to use.

In the next section, we look at some additional exercises that can help you further your understanding of the material.

Exercises

Completing the exercises in this section is entirely optional, but, hopefully, you can start to appreciate that we, as reinforcement learners ourselves, learn best by doing. Do your best and attempt to complete at least 2-3 exercises from the following:

1. Consider other problems you could use DP with? How would you break the problem up into subproblems and calculate each subproblem?
2. Code up another example that compares a problem programmed linearly versus dynamically. Use the example from *Exercise 1*. The code examples, Chapter_2_2.py and Chapter_2_3.py, are good examples of side-by-side comparisons.
3. Look through the OpenAI documentation and explore other RL environments.
4. Create, render, and explore other RL environments from Gym using the sample test code from Chapter_2_4.py.
5. Explain the process/algorithm of evaluating and improving a policy using DP.
6. Explain the difference between policy iteration and value iteration.
7. Open the Chapter_2_5.py policy iteration example and adjust the theta and gamma parameters. What effect do these have on learning rates and values?
8. Open the Chapter_2_6.py policy improvement example and adjust the theta and gamma parameters. What effect do these have on learning rates and values?
9. Open the Chapter_2_7.py value iteration example and adjust the theta and gamma parameters. What effect do these have on learning rates and values?
10. Complete all of the policy and value iteration examples using the FrozenLake 8x8 environment. This a much larger version of the lake problem. Now, which method performs better?

Use these exercises to strengthen your knowledge of the material we just covered in this chapter. In this next section, we will summarize what we covered in this chapter.

Summary

In this chapter, we took an in-depth look at DP and the Bellman equation. The Bellman equation with DP has influenced RL significantly by introducing the concept of future rewards and optimization. We covered the contribution of Bellman in this chapter by first taking a deep look at DP and how to solve a problem dynamically. Then, we advanced to understanding the Bellman optimality equation and how it can be used to account for future rewards as well as determine expected state and action values using iterative methods. In particular, we focused on the implementation in Python of policy iteration and improvement. Then, from there, we looked at value iteration. Finally, we concluded this chapter by setting up an agent test against the FrozenLake environment using a policy generated by both policy and value iteration. For this chapter, we looked at a specific class of problems well suited to DP that also helped us to derive other concepts in RL such as discounted rewards.

In the next chapter, we continue with this theme by looking at Monte Carlo methods.

3
Monte Carlo Methods

For this chapter, we will jump back to the trial-and-error thread of **reinforcement learning (RL)** and look at Monte Carlo methods. This is a class of methods that works by episodically playing through an environment instead of planning. We will see how this improves our RL search for the best policy and we now start to think of our algorithm as an actual agent—one that explores the game environment rather than preplans a policy, which, in turn, allows us to understand the benefits of using a model for planning or not. From there, we will look at the Monte Carlo method and how to implement it in code. Then, we will revisit a larger version of the FrozenLake environment with our new Monte Carlo agent algorithm.

In this chapter, we will continue looking at how RL has evolved and, in particular, focus on the trial and error thread with the Monte Carlo method. Here is a summary of the main topics we will cover in this chapter:

- Understanding model-based and model-free learning
- Introducing the Monte Carlo method
- Adding RL
- Playing the FrozenLake game
- Using prediction and control

We again explore more foundations of RL, variational inference, and the trial and error method. This knowledge will be essential for anyone who is serious about finishing this book, so please don't skip this chapter.

Understanding model-based and model-free learning

If you recall from our very first chapter, Chapter 1, *Understanding Rewards-Based Learning*, we explored the primary elements of RL. We learned that RL comprises of a policy, a value function, a reward function, and, optionally, a model. We use the word *model* in this context to refer to a detailed plan of the environment. Going back to the last chapter again, where we used the FrozenLake environment, we had a perfect model of that environment:

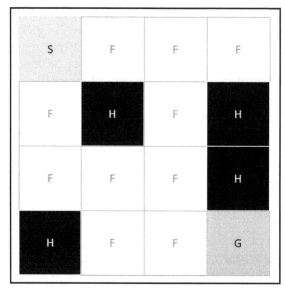

Model of the FrozenLake environment

Of course, looking at problems with a fully described model in a finite MDP is all well and good for learning. However, when it comes to the real world, having a full and completely understood model of any environment would likely be highly improbable, if not impossible. This is because there are far too many states to account for or model in any real-world problem. As it turns out, this can also be the case for many other models as well. Later in this book, we will look at environments with more states than the number of atoms in the known universe. We could never possibly model such environments. Hence, the planning methods we learned in Chapter 2, *Dynamic Programming and the Bellman Equation*, won't work. Instead, we need a method that can explore an environment and learn from it. This is where Monte Carlo comes in and is something we will cover in the next section.

Introducing the Monte Carlo method

The Monte Carlo method was so named because of its similarity to gambling or chance. Hence, the method was named after the famous gambling destination at the time. While the method is extremely powerful, it has been used to describe the atom, quantum mechanics, and the quantity of π itself. It is only until fairly recently, within the last 20 years, that it has seen widespread acceptance in everything from engineering to financial analysis. The method itself has now become foundational to many aspects of machine learning and is worth further study for anyone in the AI field.

In the next section, we will see how the Monte Carlo method can be used to solve for π.

Solving for π

The standard introduction to Monte Carlo methods is to show how it can be used to solve for π. Recall from geometry, π represents half the circumference of a circle and 2π represents a full circle. To find this relationship and value, let's consider a unit circle with a radius of 1 unit. That unit could be feet, meters, parsecs, or whatever—it's not important. Then, if we place that circle within a square box with dimensions of 1 unit, we can see the following:

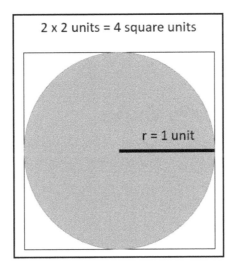

A unit circle inside a unit square

Given the preceding, we know that we have a square that encompasses dimensions of 2 units by 2 units or 100% of the area with an area of 4 square units. Going back to geometry again, we know that the area of a circle is given by πr^2. Knowing that the circle is within the square and knowing the full area, we can then apply the Monte Carlo method to solve for the following:

$$A = 4 = \pi r^2$$

The Monte Carlo method works by randomly sampling an area and then determining what percentage of that sample is correct or incorrect. Going back to our example, we can think of this as randomly dropping darts onto the square and then counting how many land within the circle. By counting the number of darts that land within the circle, we can then backcalculate a number for π using the following equation:

$$\pi = 4 * ins/total$$

In the preceding equation, we have the following:

- *ins*: The total number of darts or samples that fell within the circle
- *total*: The total number of darts dropped

The important part about the preceding equation is to realize that all we are doing here is taking a percentage (*ins/total*) of how many darts fell within the circle to determine a value for π. This may still be a little unclear, so let's look at a couple of examples in the next sections.

Implementing Monte Carlo

In many cases, even understanding simple concepts that are abstract can be difficult without real-world examples. Therefore, open up the Chapter_3_1.py code sample.

 We should mention before starting that π, in this case, refers to the actual value we estimate at 3.14.

Follow the exercise:

1. The following is the entire code listing for reference:

```
from random import *
from math import sqrt

ins = 0
n = 100000

for i in range(0, n):
    x = (random()-.5) * 2
    y = (random()-.5) * 2
    if sqrt(x*x+y*y)<=1:
        ins+=1

pi = 4 * ins / n
print(pi)
```

This code solves for π using the Monte Carlo method, which is quite impressive when you consider how simple the code is. Let's go over each section of the code.

2. We start with the `import` statements, and here we just import `random` and the `math` function, `sqrt`.

3. From there, we define a couple of variables, `ins` and `n`. The `ins` variable holds the number of times a dart or sample is inside the circle. The n variable represents how many iterations or darts to drop.

4. Next, we randomly drop darts with the following code:

```
for i in range(0, n):
    x = (random()-.5) * 2
    y = (random()-.5) * 2
    if sqrt(x*x+y*y)<=1:
      ins+=1
```

5. All this code does is randomly sample values in the range of −1 to 1 for x and y and then determine whether they are within a circle radius of 1, which is given by the calculation within the square root function.

6. Finally, the last couple of lines do the calculation and output the result.

7. Run the example as you normally would and observe the output.

What you will likely find is the guess may be a bit off. That all depends on the number of samples. You see, the confidence of the Monte Carlo method and therefore the quality of the answer goes up with the more samples you do. Hence, to improve the last example, you will have to increase the value of the variable, n.

In the next section, we look at this example again but this time look at what those dart samples may actually look like in the next section.

Plotting the guesses

If you are still having problems grasping this concept, visualizing this example may be more helpful. Run the exercise in the next section if you want to visualize what this sampling looks like:

1. Before starting this exercise, we will install the `matplotlib` library. Install the library with `pip` using the following command:

   ```
   pip install matplotlib
   ```

2. After the install, open up the `Chapter_3_2.py` code example shown here:

   ```python
   import matplotlib.pyplot as plt
   from random import random

   ins = 0
   n = 1000

   x_ins = []
   y_ins = []
   x_outs = []
   y_outs = []

   for _ in range(n):
       x = (random()-.5) * 2
       y = (random()-.5) * 2
       if (x**2+y**2) <= 1:
           ins += 1
           x_ins.append(x)
           y_ins.append(y)
       else:
           x_outs.append(x)
           y_outs.append(y)

   pi = 4 * ins/n
   print(pi)

   fig, ax = plt.subplots()
   ax.set_aspect('equal')
   ax.scatter(x_ins, y_ins, color='g', marker='s')
   ax.scatter(x_outs, y_outs, color='r', marker='s')
   plt.show()
   ```

3. The code is quite similar to the last exercise and should be fairly self-explanatory. We will just focus on the important sections of code highlighted in the preceding.

4. The big difference in this example is we remember where the darts are dropped and identify whether they fell inside or outside of the circle. After that, we plot the results. We plot a point for each and color them green for inside the circle and red for outside.

5. Run the sample and observe the output, as shown here:

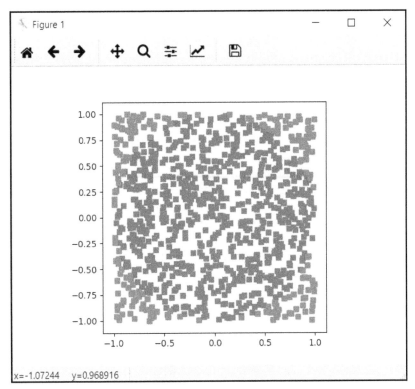

Example output from Chapter_3_2.py

The output looks like a circle, as much as we would expect it to. However, there is a problem with the output value of π. Notice how the estimated value of π is now quite low. This is because the value of n—the number of darts or samples—is only 1,000. That means, for the Monte Carlo method to be a good estimator, we also need to realize it needs a sufficiently large number of guesses.

In the next section, we look to see how we can apply this method to an expanded version of the FrozenLake problem with RL.

Adding RL

Now that we understand the Monte Carlo method, we need to understand how to apply it to RL. Recall that our expectation now is that our environment is relatively unknown, that is, we do not have a model. Instead, we now need to develop an algorithm by which to explore the environment by trial and error. Then, we can take all of those various trials and, by using Monte Carlo, average them out and determine a best or better policy. We can then use that improved policy to continue exploring the environment for further improvements. Essentially, our algorithm becomes an explorer rather than a planner and this is why we now refer to it as an agent.

Using the term **agent** reminds us that our algorithm is now an explorer and learner. Hence, our agents not only explore but also learn from that exploration and improve on it. Now, this is real artificial intelligence.

Aside from the exploration part, which we already visited earlier in Chapter 1, *Understanding Rewards-Based Learning*, the agent still needs to evaluate a value function and improve on a policy. Hence, much of what we covered in Chapter 2, *Dynamic Programming and the Bellman Equation*, will be applicable. However, this time, instead of planning, our agent will explore the environment and then, after each episode, re-evaluate the value function and update the policy. An episode is defined as one complete set of moves from the start to termination. We call this type of learning episodic since it refers to the agent only learning and improving after an episode. This, of course, has its limitations and we will see how continuous control is done in Chapter 4, *Temporal Difference Learning*. In the next section, we jump in and look at the code and how this all works.

Monte Carlo control

There are two ways to implement what is called **Monte Carlo control** on an agent. The difference between the two is how they calculate the average return or sampled mean. In what is called **First-Visit Monte Carlo**, the agent only samples the mean the first time a state is visited. The other method, **Every-Visit Monte Carlo**, samples the average return every time a state is visited. The latter method is what we will explore in the code example for this chapter.

The original source code for this example was from Ankit Choudhary's blog (https://www.analyticsvidhya.com/blog/2018/11/reinforcement-learning-introduction-monte-carlo-learning-openai-gym/).

The code has been heavily modified from the original. Ankit goes far more heavily into the mathematics of this method and the original is recommended for those readers interested in exploring more math.

Open up `Chapter_3_3.py` and follow the exercise:

1. Open the code and review the imports. The code for this example is too large to place inline. Instead, the code has been broken into sections.

2. Scroll to the bottom of the sample and review the following lines:

```
env = gym.make('FrozenLake8x8-v0')
policy =
monte_carlo_e_soft(env,episodes=50000)print(test_policy(policy,
env))
```

3. In the first line, we construct the environment. Then, we create `policy` using a function called `monte_carlo_e_soft`. We complete this step by printing out the results from the `test_policy` function.

4. Scroll up to the `monte_carlo_e_soft` function. We will get to the name later but, for now, the top lines are shown:

```
if not policy:
  policy = create_random_policy(env)
Q = create_state_action_dictionary(env, policy)
returns = {}
```

5. These lines create a policy if there is none. This shows how the random policy is created:

```
def create_random_policy(env):
  policy = {}
  for key in range(0, env.observation_space.n):
    p = {}
    for action in range(0, env.action_space.n):
      p[action] = 1 / env.action_space.n
      policy[key] = p
  return policy
```

6. After that, we create a dictionary to store state and action values, as shown here:

```
def create_state_action_dictionary(env, policy):
  Q = {}
  for key in policy.keys():
    Q[key] = {a: 0.0 for a in range(0, env.action_space.n)}
  return Q
```

7. Then, we start with a `for` loop that iterates through the number of episodes, like so:

```
for e in range(episodes):
    G = 0
    episode = play_game(env=env, policy=policy, display=False)
    evaluate_policy_check(env, e, policy, test_policy_freq)
```

8. Change `display=False` as highlighted in the preceding to `display=True`, as shown here:

```
episode = play_game(env=env, policy=policy, display=True)
```

9. Now, before we get too far ahead, it may be helpful to see how the agent is playing a game. Run the code example and watch the output. Don't run the code until completion—just for a few seconds or up to a minute is fine. Make sure to undo your code changes before saving:

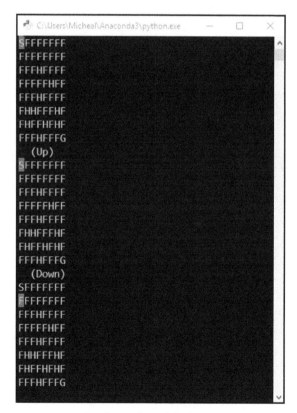

Example output of agent playing the game

This screenshot shows an example of the agent exploring the expanded 8 x 8 FrozenLake environment. In the next section, we look at how the agent plays the game.

> Again, make sure you undo your code and change display=True to display=False before proceeding.

Playing the FrozenLake game

The agent code now plays or explores the environment and it is helpful if we understand how this code runs. Open up Chapter_3_3.py again and follow the exercise:

1. All we need to focus on for this section is how the agent plays the game. Scroll down to the play_game function, as shown in the following:

```python
def play_game(env, policy, display=True):
    env.reset()
    episode = []
    finished = False
    while not finished:
        s = env.env.s
        if display:
            clear_output(True)
            env.render()
            sleep(1)
        timestep = []
        timestep.append(s)
        n = random.uniform(0, sum(policy[s].values()))
        top_range = 0
        action = 0
        for prob in policy[s].items():
            top_range += prob[1]
            if n < top_range:
                action = prob[0]
                break
        state, reward, finished, info = env.step(action)
        timestep.append(action)
        timestep.append(reward)
        episode.append(timestep)
    if display:
        clear_output(True)
        env.render()
        sleep(1)
    return episode
```

2. We can see the function takes the `env` and `policy` environment as inputs. Then, inside, it resets the environments with `reset` and then initializes the variables. The start of the `while` loop is where the agent begins playing the game:

```
while not finished:
```

3. For this environment, we are letting the agent play infinitely. That is, we are not limiting the number of steps the agent may take. However, for this environment, that is not a problem since it is quite likely the agent will fall into a hole. But, that is not always the case and we often need to limit the number of steps and agent takes in an environment. In many cases, that limit is set at `100`, for example.

4. Inside the `while` loop, we update the agent's state, `s`, then display the environment is `display=True`. After that, we set up a `timestep` list to hold that `state`, `action`, and `value`. Then, we append the state, `s`:

```
s = env.env.s
if display:
  clear_output(True)
  env.render()
  sleep(1)
timestep = []
timestep.append(s)
```

5. Next, we look at the code that does the random sampling of the action based on the `policy` values, as shown:

```
n = random.uniform(0, sum(policy[s].values())) top_range = 0
action = 0
for prob in policy[s].items():
  top_range += prob[1]
  if n < top_range:
    action = prob[0]
    break
```

6. This is essentially where the agent performs a uniform sampling of the policy with `random.uniform`, which is the Monte Carlo method. Uniform means that sampling is uniform across values and not skewed if it were from a normal or Gaussian method. After that, an action is selected in the `for` loop based on a randomly selected item in the policy. Keep in mind that, at the start, all actions may have an equal likelihood of `0.25` but later, as the agent learns policy items, it will learn to distribute accordingly as well.

Monte Carlo methods use a variety of sampling distributions to determine randomness. So far, we have extensively used uniform distributions, but in most real-world environments, a normal or Gaussian sampling method is used.

7. Then, after a random action is chosen, the agent takes a step and records it. It already recorded `state` and it now appends `action` and `reward`. Then, it appends the `timestep` list to the `episode` list, as shown:

```
state, reward, finished, info = env.step(action)
timestep.append(action)
timestep.append(reward)
episode.append(timestep)
```

8. Finally, when the agent has `finished`, by finding the goal or dropping in a hole, it returns the list of steps in `episode`.

Now, with our understanding of how the agent plays the game, we can move on evaluating the game and optimizing it for prediction and control.

Using prediction and control

When we previously had a model, our algorithm could learn to plan and improve a policy offline. Now, with no model, our algorithm needs to become an agent and learn to explore and, while doing that, also learn and improve. This allows our agent to now learn effectively by trial and error. Let's jump back into the `Chapter_3_3.py` code example and follow the exercise:

1. We will start right from where we left off and review the last couple of lines including the `play_game` function:

```
episode = play_game(env=env, policy=policy, display=False)
evaluate_policy_check(env, e, policy, test_policy_freq)
```

2. Inside `evaluate_policy_check`, we test to see whether the `test_policy_freq` number has been reached. If it has, we output the current progress of the agent. In reality, what we are evaluating is how well the current policy will run an agent. The `evaluate_policy_check` function calls `test_policy` to evaluate the current policy. The `test_policy` function is shown here:

```
def test_policy(policy, env):
    wins = 0
```

```
r = 100
for i in range(r):
    w = play_game(env, policy, display=False)[-1][-1]
    if w == 1:
        wins += 1
return wins / r
```

3. `test_policy` evaluates the current policy by running the `play_game` function and setting a new agent loose for several games set by `r = 100`. This provides a `wins` percentage, which is output to show the agent's progress.

4. Back to the main function, we step into a `for` loop that loops through the last episode of gameplay in reverse order, as shown here:

```
for i in reversed(range(0, len(episode))):
    s_t, a_t, r_t = episode[i]
    state_action = (s_t, a_t)
    G += r_t
```

5. Looping through the episode in reverse order allows us to use the last reward and apply it backward. Hence, if the agent received a negative reward, all actions would be affected negatively. The same is also true for a positive reward. We keep track of the total reward with the `G` variable.

6. Inside the last loop, we then check whether the state was already evaluated for this episode; if not, we find the list of returns and average them. From the averages, we can then determine the best action, `A_star`. This is shown in the code block:

```
if not state_action in [(x[0], x[1]) for x in episode[0:i]]:
    if returns.get(state_action):
        returns[state_action].append(G)
    else:
        returns[state_action] = [G]
    Q[s_t][a_t] = sum(returns[state_action]) /
len(returns[state_action])
    Q_list = list(map(lambda x: x[1], Q[s_t].items()))
    indices = [i for i, x in enumerate(Q_list) if x == max(Q_list)]
    max_Q = random.choice(indices)
A_star = max_Q
```

7. A lot is going on in this block of code, so work through it slowly if you need to. The key takeaway is that all we are doing here is averaging returns or a state and then determining the most likely best action, according to Monte Carlo, within that state.

8. Before we jump to the last section of code, run the example as you normally would. This should yield a similar output to the following:

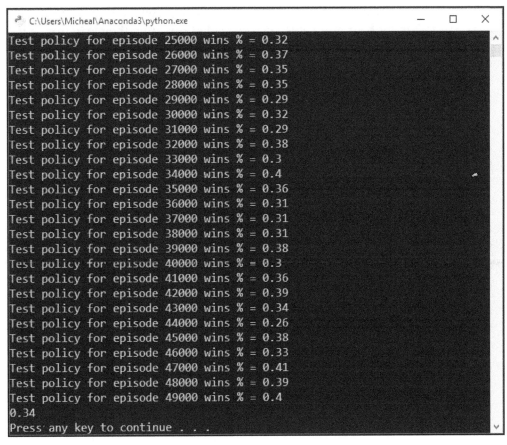

Test policy for episode 25000 wins % = 0.32
Test policy for episode 26000 wins % = 0.37
Test policy for episode 27000 wins % = 0.35
Test policy for episode 28000 wins % = 0.35
Test policy for episode 29000 wins % = 0.29
Test policy for episode 30000 wins % = 0.32
Test policy for episode 31000 wins % = 0.29
Test policy for episode 32000 wins % = 0.38
Test policy for episode 33000 wins % = 0.3
Test policy for episode 34000 wins % = 0.4
Test policy for episode 35000 wins % = 0.36
Test policy for episode 36000 wins % = 0.31
Test policy for episode 37000 wins % = 0.31
Test policy for episode 38000 wins % = 0.31
Test policy for episode 39000 wins % = 0.38
Test policy for episode 40000 wins % = 0.3
Test policy for episode 41000 wins % = 0.36
Test policy for episode 42000 wins % = 0.39
Test policy for episode 43000 wins % = 0.34
Test policy for episode 44000 wins % = 0.26
Test policy for episode 45000 wins % = 0.38
Test policy for episode 46000 wins % = 0.33
Test policy for episode 47000 wins % = 0.41
Test policy for episode 48000 wins % = 0.39
Test policy for episode 49000 wins % = 0.4
0.34
Press any key to continue . . .

Example output from Chapter_3_3.py

Notice how we can now visualize the agent's progress as it randomly explores. The percentage of wins you may see could be entirely different and in some cases, they may be much higher or lower. This is because the agent is randomly exploring. To evaluate an agent entirely, you would likely need to run the agent for more than 50,000 episodes. However, continually averaging a mean after a new sample is added over 50,000 iterations would be far too computationally expensive. Instead, we use another method called an incremental mean, which we will explore in the next section.

Incremental means

An incremental or running mean allows us to keep an average for a list of numbers without having to remember the list. This, of course, has huge benefits when we need to keep a mean over 50,000, 1 million, or more episodes. Instead of updating the mean from a full list, for every episode, we hold one value that we incrementally update using the following equation:

$$V(S_t) = V(S_t) + \alpha(G_t + V(S_t))$$

In the preceding equation, we have the following:

- $V(S_t)$ = The current state value for the policy
- α = Represents a discount rate
- G_t = The current total return

By applying this equation, we now have a method to update the policy and, coincidentally, we use a similar method in the full Q equation. However, we are not there yet and, instead, we update the value using the following algorithm:

Initialize, for all $s \in \mathcal{S}$, $a \in \mathcal{A}(s)$:
    $Q(s, a) \leftarrow$ arbitrary
    $Returns(s, a) \leftarrow$ empty list
    $\pi \leftarrow$ an arbitrary ε-soft policy

Repeat forever:
    (a) Generate an episode using π
    (b) For each pair s, a appearing in the episode:
        $R \leftarrow$ return following the first occurrence of s, a
        Append R to $Returns(s, a)$
        $Q(s, a) \leftarrow$ average($Returns(s, a)$)
    (c) For each s in the episode:
        $a^* \leftarrow \arg\max_a Q(s, a)$
        For all $a \in \mathcal{A}(s)$:
        $\pi(s, a) \leftarrow \begin{cases} 1 - \varepsilon + \varepsilon/|\mathcal{A}(s)| & \text{if } a = a^* \\ \varepsilon/|\mathcal{A}(s)| & \text{if } a \neq a^* \end{cases}$

The Monte Carlo ε-soft policy algorithm

The algorithm shows how the e-soft or epsilon soft version of the Monte Carlo algorithm works. Recall this is the second method we can use to define an agent with Monte Carlo. While the preceding algorithm may be especially scary, the part we are interested in is the last one, shown in this equation:

$$\pi(s, a) = \begin{cases} 1 - \epsilon + \epsilon/|A(s)| & a = a^* \\ \epsilon/|A(s)| & a \neq a^* \end{cases}$$

This becomes a more effective method for policy updates and is what is shown in the example. Open up `Chapter_3_3.py` and follow the exercise:

1. Scroll down to the following section of code:

```
for a in policy[s_t].items():
  if a[0] == A_star:
    policy[s_t][a[0]] = 1 - epsilon + (epsilon /
abs(sum(policy[s_t].values())))
  else:
    policy[s_t][a[0]] = (epsilong / abs(sum(policy[s_t].values())))
```

2. It is in this last block of code that we incrementally update the policy to the best value, as shown here:

```
policy[s_t][a[0]] = 1 - alpha + (alpha /
abs(sum(policy[s_t].values())))
```

3. Or we assign it some base value, as shown in the following:

```
policy[s_t][a[0]] = (alpha / abs(sum(policy[s_t].values())))
```

4. From here, we can run the example again and enjoy the output.

Now that you understand the basics of the Monte Carlo method, you can move on to more sample exercises in the next section.

Exercises

As always, the exercises in this section are here to improve your knowledge and understanding of the material. Please attempt to complete 1-3 of these exercises on your own:

1. What other constants like π could we use Monte Carlo methods to calculate? Think of an experiment to calculate another constant we use.

2. Open the `Chapter_3_1.py` sample code and change the value of n, that is, the number of darts dropped. How does that affect the calculated value for π? Use higher or lower values for n.

3. When we calculated π, we assumed a uniform distribution of darts. However, in the real world, the darts would likely be distributed in a normal or Gaussian manner. How would this affect the Monte Carlo experiment?

4. Refer to sample `Chapter_3_2.py` and change the value of n. How does that affect plot generation? Are you able to fix it?

5. Open `Chapter_3_3.py` and change the number of test episodes to run in the `test_policy` function to a higher or lower value.

6. Open `Chapter_3_3.py` and increase the number of episodes that are used to train the agent. How does the agent's performance increase, if at all?

7. Open `Chapter_3_3.py` and change the value of alpha that is used to update the incremental mean of averages. How does that affect the agent's ability to learn?

8. Add the ability to visualize each policy test in a graph. See whether you can transfer the way we created the plots in example `Chapter_3_2.py`.

9. Since the code is fairly generic, test this code on another Gym environment. Start with the standard 4 x 4 FrozenLake environment and see how well it performs.

10. Think of ways in which the Monte Carlo method given in this example could be improved upon.

These exercises do not take much additional time and they can make the world of difference to your understanding of the materials in this book. Please use them.

Summary

In this chapter, we extended our exploration of RL and looked again at trial-and-error methods. In particular, we focused on how the Monte Carlo method could be used as a way of learning from experimenting. We first looked at an example experiment of the Monte Carlo method for calculating π. From there, we looked at how to visualize the output of this experiment with matplotlib. Then, we looked at a code example that showed how to use the Monte Carlo method to solve a version of the FrozenLake problem. Exploring the code example in detail, we uncovered how the agent played the game and, through that exploration, learned to improve a policy. Finally, we finished this chapter by understanding how the agent improves this policy using an incremental sample mean.

The Monte Carlo method is powerful but, as we learned, it requires episodic gameplay while, in the real world, a working agent needs to continuously learn as it controls. This form of learning is called temporal difference learning and is something we will explore in the next chapter.

Temporal Difference Learning

4

In our previous discussion on the history of reinforcement learning, we covered the two main threads, trial and error and **Dynamic Programming** (**DP**), which came together to derive current modern **Reinforcement Learning** (**RL**). As we mentioned in earlier chapters, there is also a third thread that arrived late called **Temporal Difference Learning** (**TDL**). In this chapter, we will explore TDL and how it solves the **Temporal Credit Assignment** (**TCA**) problem. From there, we will explore how TD differs from **Monte Carlo** (**MC**) and how it evolves to full Q-learning. After that, we will explore the differences between on-policy and off-policy learning and then, finally, work on a new example RL environment.

For this chapter, we will introduce TDL and how it improves on the previous techniques we looked at in previous chapters. Here are the main topics we will cover in this chapter:

- Understanding the TCA problem
- Introducing TDL
- Applying TDL to Q-learning
- Exploring TD(0) in Q-learning
- Running off-policy versus on-policy

This chapter introduces TDL and Q-learning in detail. Therefore, it is worth reviewing and understanding the material well. Knowing the foundational material well will only ease your learning later.

Understanding the TCA problem

The credit assignment problem is described as the task of understanding what actions you need to take to receive the most credit or, in the case of RL, rewards. RL solves the credit assignment problem by allowing an algorithm or agent to find the optimum set of actions to maximize the rewards. In all of our previous chapters, we have seen how variations of this can be done with DP and MC methods. However, both of these previous methods are offline, so they cannot learn while performing a task.

The TCA problem is differentiated from the credit assignment CA problem in that it needs to be solved across time; that is, an algorithm needs to find the best policy across time steps instead of learning after an episode, in the case of MC, or needing to plan before, as DP does. This also means that an algorithm that solves the CA problem across time can also or should be able to learn in real time, that is, be able to make updates to a policy during the progression of the task, rather than before or after as we have seen in earlier chapters.

By introducing the concept of time or a progression of events, we also allow our agent to learn the importance of event timing. Previously, our agents would have no awareness of time-critical events such as hitting a moving target or timing a running jump just right. TDL, on the other hand, allows an agent to understand event timing and take appropriate action. We will introduce the concept and intuition of TDL in the next section.

Introducing TDL

TDL was introduced by the father of RL himself, Dr. Richard Sutton, in 1988. Sutton had developed the method as an improvement to MC/DP but, as we will see, the method itself led to the development of Q-learning by Chris Watkins in 1989. The method itself is model-free and does not require episode completion before an agent learns. This makes this method very powerful for exploring unknown environments in real time, as we will see.

Before we get into discovering the updated mathematics to this approach, it may be helpful to look at the backup diagrams of all of the methods covered so far in the next section.

Bootstrapping and backup diagrams

TDL can learn during an episode by approximating the updated value function given previous experience. This allows the algorithm to learn while it is in an episode and hence make corrections as needed. To understand the differences further, let's review a composite of the backup diagrams for DP, MC, and TD in the following diagram:

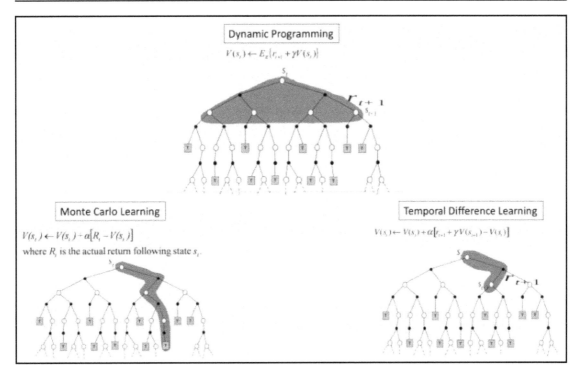

Backup diagrams for DP, MC, and TDL

The diagram was taken from *An Introduction to Reinforcement Learning* by Barto and Sutton (2018). In the diagram, you can see our previous two methods, DP and MC, as well as TDL. The shaded area (red or black) denotes the algorithm's learning space. That is the area the agent will need to explore before being able to update its value function and, hence, policy. Notice how, as the diagrams progress from DP to TDL, the shaded area becomes smaller—that is, for each advancing algorithm, that agent needs to explore less and less area initially or during an episode before learning. As we will see, this allows an agent to learn before even finishing an episode.

Before we look at the code, we should take a look at how this new approach revises the math of our value function in the next section.

Applying TD prediction

Throughout this book, we will explore methods for allowing an algorithm to predict and control an agent to complete a task. Prediction and control are at the heart of RL, and previously we had both methods separate. That is, they either ran before (DP) or after (MC). Now, for an agent to learn in real time, we need an online update rule that will update the value function after a designated time step. In TDL, this is called the TD update rule.

The rule is shown here in equation form:

$$V(S_t) = V(S_t) + \alpha[R_{t+1} + \gamma V(S_{t+1}) - V(S_t)]$$

In the previous equation, we have the following:

- $V(S_t)$: The value function for the current state
- α: Alpha, the learning rate
- R_{t+1}: The reward of the next state
- γ: A discount factor
- $V(S_{t+1})$: The value of the next state

Hence, we can say that the value of the current state is equal to the value of the current state plus alpha, times the summation of the next reward, plus a discount factor, gamma, times the difference between the next state value and the current state value.

To understand this better, let's look at a code example in the next section.

TD(0) or one-step TD

One thing we should identify before getting too far ahead is that the method we look at here is for one-step TD or what we refer to as TD(0). Remember, as programmers, we start counting at 0, so TD(0) essentially means TD one-step. We will look at multiple-step TD in Chapter 5, *Exploring SARSA*.

For now, though, we will look at an example of using one-step TD in the next exercise:

1. Open the Chapter_4_1.py source code example, as seen in the following code:

```
import numpy as np
from tqdm import tqdm
import random
```

```
gamma = 0.5
rewardSize = -1
gridSize = 4
alpha = 0.5
terminations = [[0,0], [gridSize-1, gridSize-1]]
actions = [[-1, 0], [1, 0], [0, 1], [0, -1]]
episodes = 10000

V = np.zeros((gridSize, gridSize))
returns = {(i, j):list() for i in range(gridSize) for j in
range(gridSize)}
deltas = {(i, j):list() for i in range(gridSize) for j in
range(gridSize)}
states = [[i, j] for i in range(gridSize) for j in range(gridSize)]

def generateInitialState():
    initState = random.choice(states[1:-1])
    return initState

def generateNextAction():
    return random.choice(actions)

def takeAction(state, action):
  if list(state) in terminations:
    return 0, None
  finalState = np.array(state)+np.array(action)
  if -1 in list(finalState) or gridSize in list(finalState):
    finalState = state
  return rewardSize, list(finalState)

for it in tqdm(range(episodes)):
  state = generateInitialState()
  while True:
    action = generateNextAction()
    reward, finalState = takeAction(state, action)
    if finalState is None:
      break
  before =  V[state[0], state[1]]
  V[state[0], state[1]] += alpha*(reward + gamma*V[finalState[0],
finalState[1]] - V[state[0], state[1]])
  deltas[state[0], state[1]].append(float(np.abs(before-V[state[0],
state[1]])))
  state = finalState

print(V)
```

2. This is a straight code example demonstrating how value updates work and that uses no RL environment. The first section we will focus on is where we initialize our parameters just after the imports. Here, we initialize the learning rate, `alpha` (`0.5`); discount factor, `gamma` (`0.5`); the size of the environment, `gridSize` (4); a list of state `terminations`; list of `actions`; and finally, `episodes`. Actions represent the movement vector and terminations represent the grid square where an episode will terminate.

3. Next, we initialize the value function, `V`, with all zeros using the `numpy` function, `zeros`. We then create three lists, `returns`, `deltas`, and `states` using Python list comprehensions. These lists hold values for later retrieval and notice how this relates to a DP technique.

4. Then, we define some utility functions, `generateInitialState`, `generateNextAction`, and `takeAction`. The first two functions are self-explanatory but let's focus on the `takeAction` function:

```
def takeAction(state, action):
  if list(state) in terminations:
    return 0, None
  finalState = np.array(state)+np.array(action)
  if -1 in list(finalState) or gridSize in list(finalState):
    finalState = state
  return rewardSize, list(finalState)
```

5. The preceding function takes the current `state` and `action` as inputs. It then determines whether the current state is terminal; if it is, it returns. Otherwise, it calculates the next state using simple vector math to get `finalState`.

6. Then, we enter the `for` loop that starts episodic training. Note that, although the agent explores the environment episodically, since the environment has a beginning and an end, it still learns temporally. That is, it learns after every time step. The `tqdm` library is a helper enumerator, which prints a status bar when we run a `for` loop.

7. The first thing that happens at the start of the `for` loop is the agent's state is initialized randomly. After that, it enters a `while` loop that runs one entire episode. Most of this code is self-explanatory, aside from the implementation of the value update equation, as shown here:

```
V[state[0], state[1]] += alpha*(reward + gamma*V[finalState[0],
finalState[1]] - V[state[0], state[1]])
```

8. The block of code is an implementation of the previous value update function. Notice the use of the learning rate, `alpha`, and discount factor, `gamma`.

9. Run the code as you normally would and notice the output of the `Value` function:

```
C:\Users\Micheal\Anaconda3\python.exe                                    —    □    ×
100%|################################################| 10000/10000 [00:21<00:00, 458.54it/s]
[[ 0.         -1.49423831 -1.9958849  -1.99776133]
 [-1.2447176  -1.98811069 -1.98747494 -1.98064978]
 [-1.86806477 -1.98964328 -1.88924666 -1.49072661]
 [-1.98202495 -1.90378281 -1.55590434  0.        ]]
Press any key to continue . . .
```

Running example in Chapter_4_1.py

Now, the function is less than optimal and that has more to do with the training or hyperparameters we used. We will look at the importance of tuning hyperparameters in the next section.

Tuning hyperparameters

The collection of training parameters that we investigated at the top of the last code example are called hyperparameters, so named to differentiate them from normal parameters or weights we use in deep learning. We have yet to look at deep learning in detail, but it is important to understand why they are called **hyperparameters**. Previously, we played around with the concept of a learning rate and discount factor but now we need to formalize them and understand their effect across methods and environments.

In our last example, both the learning rate (alpha) and discount factor (gamma) were set to .5. What we need to understand is what effect these parameters have on training. Let's open up sample code `Chapter_4_2.py` and follow the next exercise:

1. `Chapter_4_2.py` is almost identical to the previous example, aside from a few minor differences. The first of these is we `import matplotlib` here to be able to view some results later.
2. Recall, you can install `matplotlib` from a Python console with the following command:

```
pip install matplotlib
```

3. We use `matplotlib` to render the results of our training efforts. As we progress through this book, we will look at more advanced methods later.

4. Next, we see that the hyperparameters, alpha and gamma, have been modified to values of `0.1`:

```
gamma = 0.1
rewardSize = -1
gridSize = 4
alpha = 0.1
```

5. Now, as you often refine training, you likely will only want to modify a single parameter at a time. This will give you more control and understanding of the effect a parameter may have.

6. Finally, at the end of the file, we see the code to output the training values or change in training values. Recall the list we created earlier called `deltas`. Captured in this list are all of the deltas or changes made during training. This can be extremely useful to visualize, as we'll see:

```
plt.figure(figsize=(20,10))
all_series = [list(x)[:50] for x in deltas.values()]
for series in all_series:
    plt.plot(series)

plt.show()

print(V)
```

7. This code just loops through the list of changes made during training for each episode. What we expect is that over training, the amount of change will reduce. Reducing the amount of change allows the agent to converge to some optimal value function and hence policy later.

8. Run the code as you normally would and notice how the output of the value function has changed substantially but we can also see how the agent's training progressed:

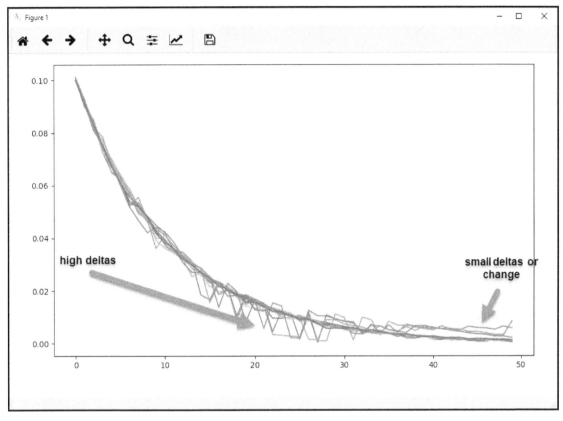

Example output from Chapter_4_2.py

On the plot, you can now see how the training converges over time. The plot is represented over the number of steps in an episode. Notice how the amount of change or delta is greater to the left of the plot, with fewer steps in an episode, and then it decreases over time with more steps. This convergence assures us that the agent is indeed learning using the provided hyperparameters.

 Tuning hyperparameters is foundational to deep learning and deep reinforcement learning. Many consider the tuning practice to be where all of the work is done and, for the most part, that is true. You may often spend days, weeks, or months tuning hyperparameters of a single network model.

Feel free to explore playing with the hyperparameters on your own and see what effect each has on training convergence. In the next section, we look at how TD is combined with Q-learning.

Applying TDL to Q-learning

Q-learning is considered one of the most popular and often used foundational RL methods . The method itself was developed by Chris Watkins in 1989 as part of his thesis, *Learning from Delayed Rewards*. Q-learning or rather Deep Q-learning, which we will cover in `Chapter 6`, *Going Deep with DQN*, became so popular because of its use by DeepMind (Google) to play classic Atari games better than a human. What Watkins did was show how an update could be applied across state-action pairs using a learning rate and discount factor gamma.

This improved the update equation into a Q or quality of state-action update equation, as shown in the following formula:

$$Q(S_t, A_t) = Q(S_t, A_t) + \alpha[R_{t+1} + \gamma \max_a Q(S_{t+1}, a) - Q(S_t, A_t)]$$

In the previous equation, we have the following:

- $Q(S_t, A_t)$ =The current state-action quality being updated
- $\alpha = alpha$ =The learning rate
- R_{t+1} =The reward for the next state
- $\gamma = gamma$ =Gamma, the discount factor
- $\max_a Q(S_{t+1}, a) =$ Take the max best or greedy action

This equation allows us to update state-action pairs based on learned future state-action pairs. It also does not require a model as the algorithm explores by trial and error and can learn during an episode since updates are run during the episode.

This method can now solve the temporal credit assignment problem and we will look at a code example in the next section.

Exploring TD(0) in Q-learning

TDL for first step or TD(0) then essentially simplifies to Q-learning. To do a full comparison of this method against DP and MC, we will first revisit the FrozenLake environment from Gym. Open up example code `Chapter_4_4.py` and follow the exercise:

1. The full listing of code is too large to show. Instead, we will review the code in sections starting with the imports:

   ```
   from os import system, name
   from time import sleep
   ```

```
import numpy as np
import gym
import random
from tqdm import tqdm
```

2. We have seen all of these imports before, so there is nothing new here. Next, we cover the initialization of the environment and outputting some initial environment variables:

```
env = gym.make("FrozenLake-v0")
env.render()
action_size = env.action_space.n
print("Action size ", action_size)
state_size = env.observation_space.n
print("State size ", state_size)
```

3. There's nothing new here either. Next, we introduce the concept of a Q table or quality table that now defines our policy in terms of state-action pairs. We set this to an equal quality for each state-action pair by dividing one by the total number of actions in a state (action-size):

```
qtable = np.ones((state_size, action_size))/action_size
print(qtable)
```

4. Next, we can see a section of hyperparameters:

```
total_episodes = 50000
total_test_episodes = 100
play_game_test_episode = 1000
max_steps = 99
learning_rate = 0.7
gamma = 0.618
```

5. There are two new parameters here called play_game_test_episode and max_steps. max_steps determine the number of maximum steps our algorithm may run in an episode. We do this to limit the agent from getting into possible endless loops. play_game_test_episode sets the episode number to show a preview of the agent playing based on the current best Q table.

6. Next, we introduce an entirely new set of parameters that have to deal with exploration and exploitation:

```
epsilon = 1.0
max_epsilon = 1.0
min_epsilon = 0.01
decay_rate = 0.01
```

7. Recall that we discussed the exploration versus exploitation dilemma in RL in `Chapter 1`, *Understanding Rewards-Based Learning*. In this section, we introduce `epsilon`, `max_epsilon`, `min_epsilon`, and `decay_rate`. These hyperparameters control the exploration rate of the agent while it explores, where `epsilon` is the current probability of an agent exploring during a time step. Maximum and minimum epsilon represent the limits of how much or little the agent explores, with `decay_rate` controlling how much the `epsilon` value decays from time step to step.

8. Understanding the exploration versus exploitation dilemma is essential to RL so we will pause here and let you run the example. The following is an example of the agent playing on the FrozenLake environment:

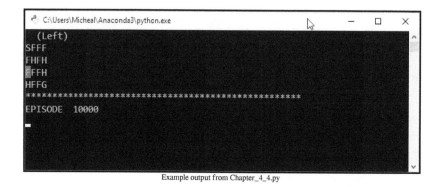

Example output from Chapter_4_4.py

Watch how the agent plays the game in the later episodes, after 40,000, and you will see that the agent can move around the holes and find the goal in short order, usually. The reason it may not do this has to do with exploration/exploitation and something we will review again in the next section.

Exploration versus exploitation revisited

For several chapters now, we have always assumed our agent to be greedy. That is, it always chooses the best action given a choice in policy. However, as we have seen, this does not always provide the best path to optimum reward. Instead, what we find is that by allowing an agent to randomly explore early and then over time reduce the chance of exploration, there is a substantial improvement in learning. Except, if the environment is too large or complex, an agent may need more exploration time compared to a much smaller environment. If we maintained high exploration in a small environment, our agent would just waste time exploring. This is the trade-off you need to balance and it is often tied to the task required to perform.

The method of exploration we are using in this example is called e-greedy or epsilon-greedy. It's so named because we start out greedy with high epsilon and then decrease it over time. There are several exploration methods we may use and a list of the more common versions and a description of each is shown here:

- **Random**: This is the always random method, which can be an effective baseline test to perform on a new environment.
- **Greedy**: This is always taking the greedy or best action in a state. As we have seen, this can have bad consequences.
- **E-greedy**: Epsilon greedy allows for a method to balance exploration rate over time by decreasing epsilon (exploration rate) by a factor during each time step or episode.
- **Bayesian or Thompson sampling**: This uses statistics and probability to best choose an action over a random distribution of sampled actions. Essentially, the action is chosen from across action distributions. For example, if a state has a bag of actions to choose from, each bag then also stores previous rewards for each action. A new action is chosen by taking a random choice from each action bag and comparing it to all of the other choices. The best action, the one giving the highest value, is selected. We don't actually store all of the rewards for all previous actions but, rather, we determine the sample distribution that describes these returned rewards.

 If the concepts of statistics and probability we just discussed are foreign to you, then you should engage in some free online learning of these topics. These concepts will be covered over and over again in-depth in later chapters.

There are other methods that provide additional options for strategies on how to pick the best action for a Q-learner. For now, though, we will stick to e-greedy as it is relatively simple to implement and is quite effective.

Now, if you go back to example `Chapter_4_4.py` and watch closely, you will see the agent may reach the goal, or it may not. In fact, the FrozenLake environment is more treacherous than we give it credit for. What that means is that rewards in that environment are more sparse and it often takes considerably longer to train with trial and error techniques. Instead, this type of learning method performs better in environments with continuous rewards. That is, when an agent receives a reward during an episode and not just at termination.

Fortunately, Gym has plenty of environments we can play with that will allow us more continuous rewards and we will explore a fun example in the next section.

Teaching an agent to drive a taxi

OpenAI Gym has plenty of fun environments that allow us to switch out and test new environments very easily. This, as we have seen, allows us to compare results of algorithms far easier. However, as we have also seen, there are limitations to various algorithms, and the new environment we explore in this section introduces the limitation of time. That is, it places a time limit on the agent as part of the goal. In doing this, our previous algorithms, DP and MC, become unable to solve such a problem, which makes this a good example to also introduce time-based or time-critical rewards.

What better way to introduce time-dependent learning than to think of a time-dependent task? There are plenty of tasks, but one that works well is an example of a taxi. That is, the agent is a taxi driver and must pick up passengers and drop them off at their correct destinations but promptly. In the Gym Taxi-v2 environment, it is the goal of the agent to pick up a passenger at a location and then drop them off at a goal. The agent gets a reward of +20 points for a successful drop off and -1 point for every time step it takes. Hence, the agent needs to pick up and drop off passengers as quickly as possible.

An example of an agent playing this environment is shown here:

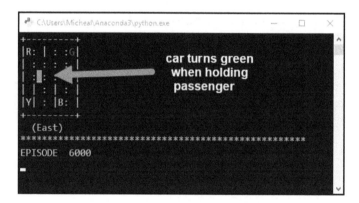

Example output from the Taxi-v2 Gym environment

In the screenshot, the car is green, meaning it has picked up a passenger from one of the symbols. The current goal is for the agent to drop off the passenger at their designated goal (symbol) highlighted. Let's now go back to the code, this time, to `Chapter_4_5.py`, which is an updated version of our last example now using the Taxi-v2 environment.

After you have the code opened, follow the exercise:

1. This code example is virtually identical to Chapter_4_4.py, aside from the initialization of the environment shown:

   ```
   env = gym.make("Taxi-v2")
   ```

2. We will use all of the same hyperparameters as before, so there's no need to look at those again. Instead, skip down to the play_game function, as shown in the following code block:

   ```
   def play_game(render_game):
     state = env.reset()
     step = 0
     done = False
     total_rewards = 0
     for step in range(max_steps):
       if render_game:
         env.render()
         print("**...****************")
         print("EPISODE ", episode)
         sleep(.5)
         clear()
       action = np.argmax(qtable[state, :])
       new_state, reward, done, info = env.step(action)
       total_rewards += reward
       if done:
         rewards.append(total_rewards)
         if render_game:
           print ("Score", total_rewards)
         break
       state = new_state
     return done, state, step, total_rewards
   ```

3. The play_game function essentially uses the qtable list, which is essentially the generated policy of qualities for state-action pairs. The code should be comfortable now and one detail to notice is how the agent selects an action from the qtable list using the following code:

   ```
   action = np.argmax(qtable[state, :])
   ```

4. The play_game function here takes the role of our agent test function previously. This function will allow you to see the agent play the game as it progresses through training. This is accomplished by setting render_game to play_game to True. Doing this allows you to visualize the agent playing an episode of the game.

You will often want to watch how your agent is training, at least initially. This can provide you with clues as to possible errors in your implementation or the agent finding possible cheats in new environments. We have found agents to be very good cheaters or at least be able to find cheats quite readily.

5. Next, we jump down to the next for loop that iterates through the training episodes and trains the `qtable`. When a threshold set by `play_game_test_episode` of episodes has elapsed, we allow the agent to play a visible game. Doing this allows us to visualize the overall training progress. However, it is important to remember that this is only a single episode and the agent could be doing extensive exploration. So, it is important to remember that, when watching the agent, they may just occasionally randomly explore. The code shows how we loop through the episodes:

```
for episode in tqdm(range(total_episodes)):
  state = env.reset()
  step = 0
  done = False
  if episode % play_game_test_episode == 0:
    play_game(True)
  for step in range(max_steps):
    exp_exp_tradeoff = random.uniform(0,1)
    if exp_exp_tradeoff > epsilon:
      action = np.argmax(qtable[state,:])
    else:
      action = env.action_space.sample()
    new_state, reward, done, info = env.step(action)
    qtable[state, action] = qtable[state, action] + learning_rate *
(reward + gamma * np.max(qtable[new_state, :]) - qtable[state,
action])
    state = new_state
    if done == True:
      break
  epsilon = min_epsilon + (max_epsilon - min_epsilon)*np.exp(-
decay_rate*episode)
```

6. First, inside the episode loop, we handle the exploration-exploitation dilemma by sampling a random value and then comparing it to epsilon. If it is greater than the greedy action, it is selected; otherwise, a random exploratory action is selected, as shown in the code:

```
exp_exp_tradeoff = random.uniform(0,1)
if exp_exp_tradeoff > epsilon:
  action = np.argmax(qtable[state,:])
else:
  action = env.action_space.sample()
```

7. Then, the next line is where the step is taken with the selected action. After that, `qtable` is updated based on the previous Q-learning equation. There is a lot going on in this single line of code, so make sure you understand it:

```
qtable[state, action] = qtable[state, action] + learning_rate *
(reward + gamma * np.max(qtable[new_state, :]) - qtable[state,
action])
```

8. After that, we check whether the episode is done with the `done` flag. If it is, we terminate and continue with another episode. Otherwise, we update the value of `epsilon` with the following code:

```
epsilon = min_epsilon + (max_epsilon - min_epsilon)*np.exp(-
decay_rate*episode)
```

9. Finally, the remainder of the code is shown:

```
env.reset()
print(qtable)

for episode in range(total_test_episodes):
  done, state, step, total_rewards = play_game(False)

env.close()
print ("Score over time: " + str(sum(rewards)/total_test_episodes))
```

10. The last piece of code resets and then tests the environment with the trained `qtable` for `total_test_episodes` and then outputs the average score or reward for an episode.

11. Finally, run the code as you normally would and observe the output carefully. Pay particular attention to how the taxi picks up and drops off passengers in later episodes. Sample output from the training is shown here:

```
C:\Users\Micheal\Anaconda3\python.exe                                           —   □   ×
Score 4
100%|################################################################| 50000/50000 [10:15<00:00, 81.21it/s]
[[  0.16666667    0.16666667    0.16666667    0.16666667    0.16666667
    0.16666667]
 [ -1.8953181   -1.44880345   -1.8953178    -1.44819268   -0.72512948
  -10.44789578]
 [ -0.72617581    0.4446       -0.84835659    0.44421064    2.33782249
   -8.55527336]
 ...
 [ -2.14796729    5.15374787   -2.18733027   -2.13442453   -9.94738054
   -9.31336954]
 [ -2.30243816   -1.46591343   -2.30243816   -2.35177552  -10.65814823
  -10.18335066]
 [ 12.69124466   -0.89999954   -0.5779       31.35602094    0.16666667
    0.16666667]]
Score over time: 12.64
Press any key to continue . . .
```

Best score averaged over 100 episodes

The final output from sample Chapter_4_5.py

In this example, you will clearly see how the agent progresses in training from doing nothing to picking up and dropping off passengers in short order. The agent will actually perform remarkably better in this environment than in other apparently simpler environments such as the FrozenLake. This has more to do with the method of learning and the related task and suggests that we need to be careful as to what methods we use for which problems. You may find, in some cases, that certain advanced algorithms perform poorly on simple problems and that the converse may happen. That is, simpler algorithms such as Q-learning when paired with other technologies can become far more powerful as we will see in Chapter 6, *Going Deeper with DQN*.

In the last section of this chapter, we look at how the previous Q-learning method could be improved.

Running off- versus on-policy

We covered the terms on- and off-policy previously when we looked at MC training in Chapter 2, *Monte Carlo Methods*. Recall that the agent didn't update its policy until after an episode. Hence, this defines the TD(0) method of learning in the last example as an off-policy learner. In our last example, it may seem that the agent is learning online but it still, in fact, trains a policy or Q table externally. That is, the agent needs to build up a policy before it can learn to make decisions and play the game. Ideally, we want our agent to learn or improve its policy as it plays through an episode. After all, we don't learn offline nor does any other biological animal. Instead, our goal will be to understand how an agent can learn using on-policy learning. On-policy learning will be covered in Chapter 5, *Exploring SARSA*.

Exercises

As we progress through this book, the exercises at the end of each chapter will be more directed toward providing you with agent training experience. Training RL agents not only requires a fair amount of patience but also intuition on how to spot whether something is wrong or right. That only comes with training experience, so use the following exercises to learn that:

1. Open example `Chapter_4_2.py` and change the `gridSize` variable to see what effect this has on convergence.
2. Open example `Chapter_4_2.py` and tune the hyperparameters for alpha and gamma. Try to find the optimum values for both. This will require you to run the example multiple times.
3. Open example `Chapter_4_2.py` and change the number of episodes, up or down. See what effect a large number of episodes, such as 100,000 or 1,000,000, has on training.
4. Tune the `learning_rate` and `gamma` hyperparameters in example `Chapter_4_4.py`. Can they be improved upon?
5. Adjust the exploration (`epsilon`, `max_epsilon`, `min_epsilon`, and `decay_rate`) hyperparameters from example `Chapter_4_4.py`. How does changing these values affect training performance or lack thereof?
6. Tune the `learning_rate` and `gamma` hyperparameters in example `Chapter_4_5.py`. Can they be improved upon?

7. Adjust the exploration (`epsilon`, `max_epsilon`, `min_epsilon`, and `decay_rate`) hyperparameters from example `Chapter_4_5.py`. How does changing these values affect training performance or lack thereof?

8. Add the ability to track the deltas or change in Q values during training to examples `Chapter_4_4.py` or `Chapter_4_5.py`. Recall how we tracked and output the deltas to a plot in example `Chapter_4_2.py`.

9. Add the ability to render plots of the training performance to example `Chapter_4_4.py` or `Chapter_4_5.py`. This will require you to complete the previous exercise as well.

10. Use the code in example `Chapter_4_5.py` and try the Q-learner on other environments. The Mountain Car or Cart Pole environments from Gym are interesting and ones we will be exploring soon.

At this stage in your RL training career, it is important to get how hyperparameters work. The right or wrong hyperparameters can make or truly break an experiment. This leaves you with two options: read a lot of boring math-induced papers or just do it. Since this is a hands-on book, we are expecting you prefer the latter.

Summary

In this chapter, we discussed how temporal difference learning, the third thread of RL, combined to develop TD(0) and Q-learning. We did that by first exploring the temporal credit assignment problem and how it differed from the credit assignment problem. From that, we learned how TD learning works and how TD(0) or first step TD can be reduced to Q-learning.

After that, we again played on the FrozenLake environment to understand how the new algorithm compared to our past efforts. Using model-free off-policy Q-learning allowed us to tackle the more difficult Taxi environment problem. This is where we learned how to tune hyperparameters and finally looked at the difference between off- and on-policy learning. In the next chapter, we continue where we left off with on- versus off-policy as we explore SARSA.

Exploring SARSA 5

In this chapter, we continue with our focus on **Temporal Difference Learning** (TDL) and expand on it from TD (0) to multi-step TD and beyond. We will look at a new method of **Reinforcement Learning** (**RL**) called SARSA, explore what it is, and how it differs from Q-learning. From there, we will look at a few examples with new continual control learning environments from Gym. Then, we will move to a deeper understanding of TDL and introduce concepts called **TD lambda** (λ) and **eligibility traces**. Finally, we will finish off this chapter by looking at an example of SARSA.

For this chapter, we will extend our discussion of TDL and uncover **State Action Reward State Action** (**SARSA**), continuous action spaces, TD (λ), eligibility traces, and on-policy learning. Here is an overview of what we will cover in this chapter:

- Exploring SARSA on-policy learning
- Using continuous spaces with SARSA
- Extending continuous spaces
- Working with TD (λ) and eligibility traces
- Understanding SARSA (λ)

This chapter is very much a continuation of `Chapter 4`, *Temporal Difference Learning*. Please read that chapter before this one. In the next section, we continue right where we left off in the last chapter.

Exploring SARSA on-policy learning

SARSA, which is the process this method emulates. That is, the algorithm works by moving to a state, then choosing an action, receiving a reward, and then moving to the next state action. This makes SARSA an on-policy method, that is, the algorithm works by learning and deciding with the same policy. This differs from Q-learning, as we saw in `Chapter 4`, *Temporal Difference Learning*, where Q is a form of off-policy learner.

The following diagram shows the difference in backup diagrams for Q-learning and SARSA:

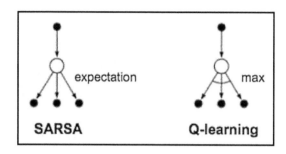

Backup diagrams for Q and SARSA

Recall that our Q-learner is an off-policy learner. That is, it requires the algorithm to update the policy or Q table offline and then later make decisions from that. However, if we want to tackle the TDL problem beyond one step or TD (0), then we need to have an on-policy learner. Our learning agent or algorithm must be able to update its policy in between whatever number of TD steps we may be looking at. This also requires us to update our Q update equation with a new SARSA update equation, as shown here:

$$Q(S_t, A_t) = Q(S_t, A_t) + \alpha[R_{t+1} + \gamma Q(S_{t+1}, A_{t+1}) - Q(S_t, A_t)]$$

Recall that our Q-learning equation was like so:

$$Q(S_t, A_t) = Q(S_t, A_t) + \alpha[R_{t+1} + \gamma \max_a Q(S_{t+1}, a) - Q(S_t, A_t)]$$

In the previous equation, we have the following:

- $Q(S_t, A_t)$ = The current state-action quality being updated
- $\alpha = alpha$ = The learning rate
- R_{t+1} = The reward for the next state
- $\gamma = gamma$ = Gamma, the discount factor
- $\max_a Q(S_{t+1}, a) =$ The maximum best or greedy action

We can further visualize this as shown in the following diagram:

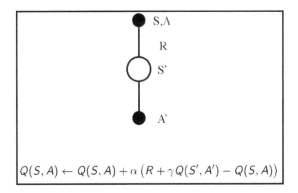

SARSA diagram and equation

Notice how that funny *max* term is gone now in SARSA and we use the expectation now and not just the best. This has to do with the action selection strategy. If you recall in Q-learning, we always used the max or best action according to averaging rewards. Recall that Q-learning assumes that you average the maximum reward. Instead, we want to select the action the agent perceives to be the one that will return the best possible returns. Hopefully, you have also noticed how we have progressed from speaking about rewards to value, state actions, state values, and now returns, where a return represents the perceived value for an action. We will discuss maximizing returns in more detail later in this chapter.

In the next section, we will learn how to solve a new type of problem called **continuous action spaces**. Then, we will look at how to use SARSA to solve a new Gym environment.

Using continuous spaces with SARSA

Up until now, we have been exploring the **finite Markov Decision Process** or **finite MDP**. These types of problems are all well and good for simulation and toy problems, but they don't show us how to tackle real-world problems. Real-world problems can be broken down or discretized into finite MDPs, but real problems are not finite. Real problems are infinite, that is, they define no discrete simple states such as showering or having breakfast. Infinite MDPs model problems in what we call continuous space or continuous action space, that is, in problems where we think of a state as a single point in time and state defined as a slice of that time. Hence, the discrete task of **eat breakfast** could be broken down to each time step including individual chewing actions.

Solving an infinite MDP or continuous space problem is not trivial with our current toolset, but it will require us to apply discretization tricks. Applying discretization or breaking the continuous space into discrete spaces will make this problem solvable with our current toolset. In Chapter 6, *Going Deep with DQN*, we will look to apply deep learning to a continuous action space, which allows us to solve these environments without using these discretization tricks.

Many continuous RL environments have more environmental states than atoms in the observable universe, and yes, that is a very big number. We have managed to solve these problems by applying deep learning and hence deep RL starting in Chapter 6, *Going Deep with DQN*.

The code for this chapter was originally sourced from this GitHub repository: https://github.com/srnand/Reinforcement-Learning-using-OpenAI-Gym. It looks like the author, Shrinand Thakkar, has since moved on to other pursuits and did not complete this excellent work as he intended.

Open Chapter_5_1.py and follow the exercise shown here:

1. The full source code for the listing is as follows:

```python
import gym
import math
from copy import deepcopy
import numpy as np
import matplotlib.pyplot as plt

env = gym.make('MountainCar-v0')
Q_table = np.zeros((20,20,3))
alpha=0.3
buckets=[20, 20]
gamma=0.99
rewards=[]
episodes = 3000

def to_discrete_states(observation):
 interval=[0 for i in range(len(observation))]
 max_range=[1.2,0.07]

 for i in range(len(observation)):
  data = observation[i]
  inter = int(math.floor((data +
max_range[i])/(2*max_range[i]/buckets[i])))
  if inter>=buckets[i]:
    interval[i]=buckets[i]-1
```

```
    elif inter<0:
      interval[i]=0
    else:
      interval[i]=inter
  return interval

def expect_epsilon(t):
  return min(0.015, 1.0 - math.log10((t+1)/220.))

def expect_alpha(t):
  return min(0.1, 1.0 - math.log10((t+1)/125.))

def get_action(observation,t):
 if np.random.random()<max(0.001, expect_epsilon(t)):
  return env.action_space.sample()
 interval = to_discrete_states(observation)
 return np.argmax(np.array(Q_table[tuple(interval)]))

def update_SARSA(observation,reward,action,ini_obs,next_action,t):
 interval = to_discrete_states(observation)
 Q_next = Q_table[tuple(interval)][next_action]
 ini_interval = to_discrete_states(ini_obs)
 Q_table[tuple(ini_interval)][action]+=max(0.4,
expect_alpha(t))*(reward + gamma*(Q_next) -
Q_table[tuple(ini_interval)][action])

for episode in range(episodes):
  observation = env.reset()
  t=0
  done=False
  while (done==False):
    env.render()
    print(observation)
    action = get_action(observation,episode)
    obs_next, reward, done, info = env.step(action)
    next_action = get_action(obs_next,episode)
update_SARSA(obs_next,reward,action,observation,next_action,episode
)
    observation=obs_next
    action = next_action
    t+=1
  rewards.append(t+1)
plt.plot(rewards)
plt.show()
```

2. Moving past the imports, we will look at the hyperparameter initialization code:

```
env = gym.make('MountainCar-v0')
Q_table = np.zeros((20,20,3))
alpha=0.3
buckets=[20, 20]
gamma=0.99
rewards=[]
episodes = 3000
```

3. We start the code block with the instantiation of a new environment, `MountainCar-v0`, which is in a continuous space environment. We then see the `Q_table` table is initialized with all zeros. Then, we set values for the learning rate, `alpha`; the discount factor, `gamma`; and the number of `episodes`. Also, we see a new list called `buckets` constructed. We will cover what buckets do shortly.

4. From there, jump to the end of the code. We want a high-level overview of what the code does first. Take a look at the episode `for` loop, shown here:

```
observation = env.reset()
t=0
done=False
while (done==False):
 env.render()
 print(observation)
 action = get_action(observation,episode)
 obs_next, reward, done, info = env.step(action)
 next_action = get_action(obs_next,episode)
update_SARSA(obs_next,reward,action,observation,next_action,episode
)
   observation=obs_next
   action = next_action
   t+=1
rewards.append(t+1)
```

5. The preceding code is the episode loop code and very much follows the pattern that we have seen in several previous chapters. The one major point of difference here is the way the algorithm/agent seemingly picks an action twice, as can be seen in the following block of code:

```
action = get_action(observation,episode)
obs_next, reward, done, info = env.step(action)
next_action = get_action(obs_next,episode)
```

6. The difference from Q-learning here is that the agent in SARSA is on-policy, that is, the action it picks needs to also decide its next action. Recall, in Q-learning, the agent works off-policy, that is, it takes an action from a previously learned policy. Again, this also goes back to TD (0) or one step, where the algorithm is still only looking one step ahead.

7. At this point, let's run the algorithm to see how this works. A few examples of the car climbing the hill can be seen here:

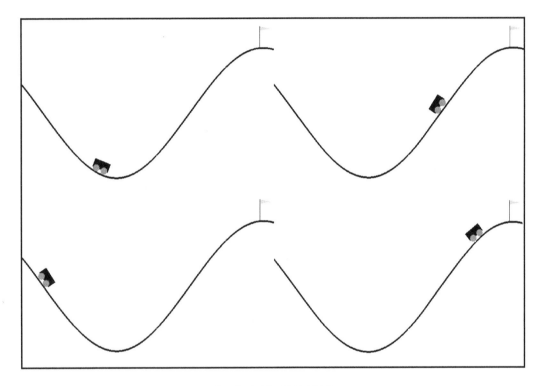

Example output from Chapter_5_1.py

From the preceding screenshot, we can see that the agent is climbing the hill. Let the agent continue climbing until it reaches the flag; it should almost get there. Now, this is cool and fairly powerful stuff, but even more so considering we can do this by assuming our infinite MDP (continuous space) is controllable in discrete steps and hence a finite MDP. To do that, we have to learn how to discretize a continuous action space and we will see how to do that in the next section.

Discretizing continuous state spaces

RL is limited to discrete spaces or what we learned previously as a finite MDP. A finite MDP describes a discrete set of steps or states with an action to move between states decided by a probability. The infinite version of this may define an infinite number of state-actions between any set of states. Hence, a basketball player moving from one end of the court to score a basket describes an infinite MDP or continuous space. That is, for each point in time, the ball player could be in an infinite number of positions, dribbling or not dribbling, or shooting the ball and so on. Likewise, in the `MountainCar` environment, the car can be moving up or down the hill in either direction at any point in time. This makes the `MountainCar` environment a continuous state space, but just barely. Fortunately, we can use a clever trick to discretize the state space as follows:

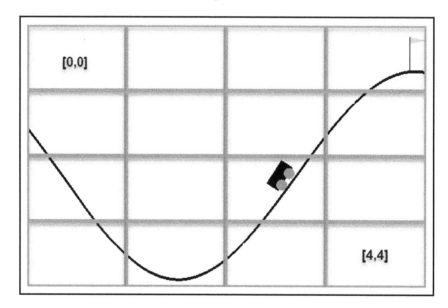

Example discretization of MountainCar

In the preceding diagram, we have overlaid a grid on top of the environment to represent state spaces the cart may be in. For the sample, a 4 x 4 grid is used, but in our code, we will use a much larger grid. Doing this allows us to capture the position of the cart as if it was on a grid. Since the goal of this task is to move the cart up the hill, then discretizing the space by applying a gridding technique works quite well. In more complex continuous spaces, your grid may represent multiple dimensions in space or across other features. Fortunately, we won't have to worry about those complex mathematics when we learn how to apply deep learning to continuous spaces.

Now that we understand how the space is discretized, let's jump back to the sample code in `Chapter_5_1.py` and review how this works in the following exercise:

1. We will start by picking up where we last left off. At the last point, we were just updating the `Q_table` table with the following line inside the episode `for` loop:

```
update_SARSA(obs_next,reward,action,observation,next_action,episode
)
```

2. This calls the `update_SARSA` function, shown here:

```
def update_SARSA(observation,reward,action,ini_obs,next_action,t):
  interval = to_discrete_states(observation)
  Q_next = Q_table[tuple(interval)][next_action]
  ini_interval = to_discrete_states(ini_obs)
  Q_table[tuple(ini_interval)][action]+=max(0.4,
expect_alpha(t))*(reward + gamma*(Q_next) –
Q_table[tuple(ini_interval)][action])
```

3. For now, ignore the `Q_table` update code and instead focus on the highlighted calls to `to_discrete_states`. These calls take an observation as input. An observation denotes the cart's absolute position in the x,y coordinates. This is where we discretize the state using the following function:

```
def to_discrete_states(observation):
 interval=[0 for i in range(len(observation))]
 max_range=[1.2,0.07]
 for i in range(len(observation)):
   data = observation[i]
   inter = int(math.floor((data +
max_range[i])/(2*max_range[i]/buckets[i])))
   if inter>=buckets[i]:
     interval[i]=buckets[i]-1
   elif inter<0:
     interval[i]=0
   else:
     interval[i]=inter
 return interval
```

4. The `to_discrete_states` function returns the grid interval the cart is currently in. Back in the `update_SARSA` function, we change the interval list back to a tuple with the following:

```
tuple(interval)
```

5. Run the sample as you normally would again, just to confirm it works as expected.

This simple method of discretization works well for this task but can quickly fall down or become overtly complex depending on the complexity of the environment. Before we move on to other matters, we want to return and look at how we update `Q_table` with SARSA in the next section.

Expected SARSA

Vanilla SARSA is quite similar to Q-learning in terms of how we choose values. It will generally just use an epsilon-greedy max action strategy, not unlike what we used previously; however, what we find, especially when working on-policy, is that the algorithm needs to be more selective. Now, this is very much the goal of all RL, but, in this particular case, we manage these trade-offs a bit better by introducing an expectation. When we combine this with SARSA, we call it **expected SARSA**.

In expected SARSA, we assume an unknown learning rate alpha, and hence an unknown exploration rate epsilon as well. Instead, we equate the learning rate alpha and exploration rate epsilon using functions based on assigned rewards. We assign a reward of one timepoint for each time step and then calculate the new alpha and epsilon based on those. Open `Chapter_5_2.py` back up and let's see how this works by following the exercise here:

1. The two functions of code we are interested in are shown here:

```
def expect_epsilon(t):
  return min(0.015, 1.0 - math.log10((t+1)/220.))

def expect_alpha(t):
  return min(0.1, 1.0 - math.log10((t+1)/125.))
```

2. The two functions, `expect_epsilon` and `expect_alpha`, calculate an expectation or ratio based on the rewards returned so far, `t`, where `t` equals the total time the cart has been moving in the environment.

3. We can focus on how `expect_epsilon` is used by looking at the `get_action` function shown here:

```
def get_action(observation,t):
  if np.random.random()<max(0.001, expect_epsilon(t)):
    return env.action_space.sample()
  interval = to_discrete_states(observation)
  return np.argmax(np.array(Q_table[tuple(interval)]))
```

4. `get_action` returns the action based on the observation (*x* and *y* positions of the cart). It does this by first checking whether a random action is to be sampled or, instead, the best action. We determine the probability of this by using the `expect_epsilon` equation, which calculates epsilon based on the total episode time playing the environment. This effectively means the epsilon in this example will range between 0.001 and 0.0015; see whether you can figure that out in the code.

5. Next, we do something similar to calculate `alpha` shown in the `update_SARSA` function. The single line where this is used is shown again:

```
Q_table[tuple(ini_interval)][action]+=max(0.4,
expect_alpha(t))*(reward + gamma*(Q_next) -
Q_table[tuple(ini_interval)][action])
```

6. The preceding code should be familiar by now as it looks like our regular policy update equation, except, in this instance, we are tuning the value for `alpha` using an expectation based on the current time on the task. You can also think of this in some ways as a secondary reward.

7. Run the code again and let it finish to completion. Notice the output as we will use that as a comparison soon:

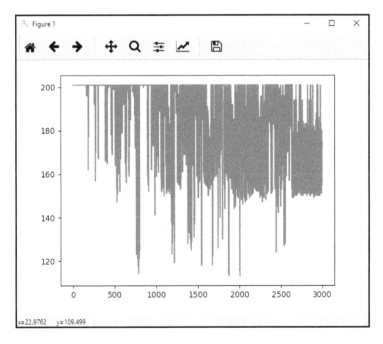

The output of returns/rewards over training time

The plot shows the accumulated rewards/time the cart spends in the environment. The cost is awarded a time reward for each time slice it remains in the environment, where if the cart remains stationary or relatively still for more than a few time slices, the episode is over. Therefore, the more time the cart stays in the environment also equates to more movement.

Continuous states or continuous observations are not the only things we need to concern ourselves when considering real-time problems. In the real world, we also deal with continuous action spaces as well. Currently, we have been looking at problems with discrete action spaces, that is, environments that use arbitrary discrete actions to control the agent. These actions are typically up, down, left, and right. However, for the real world, we need finer control and often categorize actions as turn left by amount x or right by amount y. By adding continuous action spaces, our RL algorithms become less robotic and provide finer control. Discretizing discrete action spaces into continuous action spaces is more difficult and not something we will concern ourselves with. Instead, we will look at how to convert another more popular continuous action space we use for deep RL in the following section.

Extending continuous spaces

Typically, we leave problems with large observation spaces to be tackled with deep learning. Deep learning, as we will learn, is very well-suited to such problems. However, deep learning is not without its own issues and it is sometimes prudent to try and solve an environment without deep learning. Now, not all environments will discretize well, as we mentioned previously, but we do want to look at another example. The next example we will look at is the infamous Cart Pole environment, which is almost always tackled with deep RL, primarily because it uses a continuous action space with four dimensions. Keep in mind that our previous observation spaces only had one dimension, and, in our last example, we only had two.

 Being able to convert an agent's observation space can be a useful trick especially in more abstract game environments. Remember, good game mechanics are often more about being fun rather than accurate. This certainly applies to some AI elements in games.

You can find the specifics of the observation and state spaces by going to the environment's GitHub page if it has one. Most of the more popular environments have their own page. The **Cart Pole** and **Mountain Car** observation and action spaces are shown in the following excerpts:

| **Mountain Car** | | | | **Cart Pole** | | | |

Mountain Car

Observation

Type: Box(2)

Num	Observation	Min	Max
0	position	-1.2	0.6
1	velocity	-0.07	0.07

Actions

Type: Discrete(3)

Num	Action
0	push left
1	no push
2	push right

Cart Pole

Observation

Type: Box(4)

Num	Observation	Min	Max
0	Cart Position	-2.4	2.4
1	Cart Velocity	-Inf	Inf
2	Pole Angle	~ -41.8°	~ 41.8°
3	Pole Velocity At Tip	-Inf	Inf

Actions

Type: Discrete(2)

Num	Action
0	Push cart to the left
1	Push cart to the right

Spaces of Mountain Car and Cart Pole environments

The preceding excerpts show a comparison of the **Mountain Car** versus the **Cart Pole** environments. Both environments use discrete action spaces, which is good. However, the **Cart Pole** environment uses a 4-dimensional observation space with values shown in the ranges in the table in the screenshot. This can be a little tricky and it will be helpful to understand how multidimensional observation spaces work in more detail.

Open `Chapter_5_3.py` and follow this exercise to see how our last example can be converted into **Cart Pole**:

1. For the most part, the code is identical to the last two examples, so we only need to look at the differences. We will start with the environment construction section at the top, as follows:

   ```
   env = gym.make('CartPole-v0')
   ```

2. This constructs the infamous **Cart Pole** environment. Again, switching environments is easy but your code has to adapt to the observation and action spaces. **Cart Pole** and **Mountain Car** share the same observation/action space types. That is, its observation space is continuous but with a discrete action space.

3. Next, we will look and see how this affects our Q_table table initialization with the code here:

```
Q_table = np.zeros((20,20,20,20,3))
```

4. Notice how the table is now configured with four dimensions at size 20. Previously, this was just two dimensions of size 20. Go back and check the last code examples for comparison if you need to.

5. With more dimensions added to the Q_table table, that means we also need to add more dimensions to our discretization buckets, as shown here:

```
buckets=[20, 20, 20, 20]
```

6. Again, we increase the buckets array from two dimensions to four, all of size 20. We are arbitrarily using a size of 20 but we could use a larger or smaller value.

7. The last thing we need to do is redefine the boundaries of the environment's observations. Recall we were able to extract this information from the GitHub page. This is the table that shows the min/max values in the ranges. The line of code we are interested in is just inside the to_discrete_states function, as shown here:

```
def to_discrete_states(observation):
 interval=[0 for i in range(len(observation))]
 max_range=[2.4,999999, 41.8,999999]
```

8. The line is highlighted and declares the max_range variable. max_range sets the max value along each dimension in the observation space. We populate this with the values from the table and, in the case of infinity, we use six 9s (999999), which often works for the upper limits of values with infinity.

9. Next we, need to update the axis dimensions we use for indexing into the Q_table table, as shown in the code here:

```
Q_table[:,:,:,:,action]+=lr*td_error*(eligibility[:,:,:,:,action])
```

10. In the preceding code, notice how we are now indexing to the four dimensions and the action.

11. Run the code as you normally would and observe the output; an example is shown here:

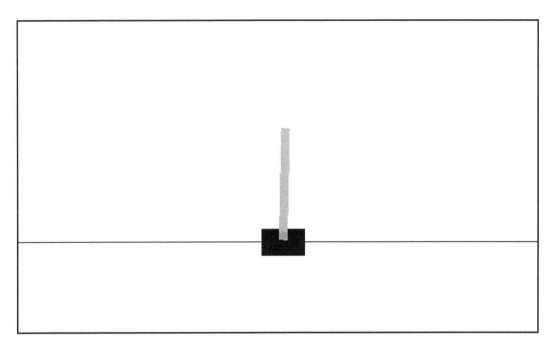

Example Chapter_5_3.py

Eventually, SARSA using a discretized observation space can solve the `CartPole` environment. This one may take a while to learn so be patient, but the agent will learn to balance the pole on the cart. You should have a fairly good understanding of how discretization works and SARSA at TD (0). In the next section, we will look at looking ahead/behind more than one step.

Working with TD (λ) and eligibility traces

Up until now, we have looked at the forward view or what the agent perceives to be as the next best reward or state. In **MC**, we looked at the entire episode and then used those values to reverse calculate returns. For TDL methods such as Q-learning and SARSA, we looked a single step ahead or what we referred to as TD (0). However, we want our agents to be able to take into account several steps, *n*, in advance. If we can do this, then surely our agent will be able to make better decisions.

As we have seen previously, we can average returns across steps using a discount factor, gamma. However, at this point, we need to more careful about how we average or collect returns. Instead, we can define the averaging of all returns over an infinite number of steps forward as follows:

$$G_t^\lambda = (1 - \lambda) \sum_{n=1}^{\infty} \lambda^{n-1} G_{t:t+n}$$

In the preceding equation, we have the following:

- G_t^λ = This is the weighted average of all returns.
- $G_{t:t+n}$ = This is the return of individual episodes from t to $t+n$.
- λ = Lambda, a weight value between [0,1].

Since lambda is less than one, as values of n increase, the amount of contribution to the final average return becomes smaller. This is due to raising lambda (λ) to the power of n as in the preceding equation. Again, this is the same principle as using the discount factor, gamma. Now that we are thinking in terms of n steps or what we will refer to as lambda, we can revisit how this looks in the following diagram:

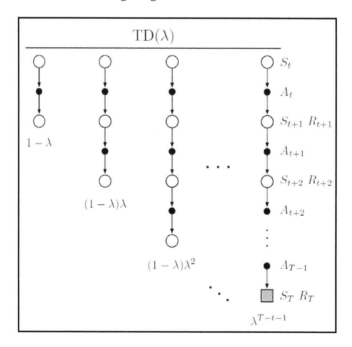

Progression of TD (λ)

To find the general solution for n time steps, where n is an unknown we call lambda (λ), we need to determine a general solution for finding lambda, that is, the value of lambda that generalizes the problem. We can do that by first assuming that any episode will end at time step, t, and then rewriting our previous equation as follows:

$$G_t^\lambda = (1 - \lambda) \sum_{n=1}^{T-t-1} \lambda^{n-1} G_{t:t+n} + \lambda^{T-t-1} G_t$$

When a value of 0 for lambda is used, this represents TD (0). A value of 1 for lambda represents MC or a need for a complete episode lookahead. However, it is complicated to implement this form of lookahead models and, intuitively, looking ahead is a very small part of what biological animals learn. In fact, our primary source of learning is experience, and that is exactly what we start to consider in the next section.

Backward views and eligibility traces

Do you recall the last time you found a coin on the floor or street? After you picked up the coin, did you think to yourself: a) "I knew looking down all that time would pay off," or b) "Wow, I found a coin, how did I do that?" In fact, in most cases, it would be option b, that is, we learned something was good and then thought back to how we discovered it. The moment of brilliance in option a is akin to believing in quantum particles, atoms, and bacteria. This is no different in RL, and what we find is that it is often more useful to look back at what happened in the past; however, not so far back as to be a past event as in MC.

We can use TDL to take a backward look at the returns for several steps. However, we can't just use an absolute value for the state transitions. Instead, we need to determine the predicted error for each step back using the following equation:

$$\delta_t = R_{t+1} + \gamma V(S_{t+1}) - V(s_t)$$

In the preceding equation, we have the following:

- δ_t = This is the TD error or delta.
- $V()$ = The value function, which can be further defined by the following:

$$V(s) = V(s) + \alpha \delta_t E_t(s)$$

We can further define the following:

$$E_0(s) = 0$$

$$E_t(s) = \gamma\alpha E_{t-1}(s) + 1(S_t = s)$$

In the preceding equation, $1(S_t = s) =$ assigns the full value of 1 when the state is at s.

E denotes the eligibility factor or the amount the value should be considered in the TD error. What is happening here is that the value function is being updated by the number of TD errors over n steps, but, instead of looking forward, we look backward. Much like all things in RL, it seems this has to be applied across several variations of algorithms. For n step TDL or TD (λ), we have three variations we concern ourselves with. They are Tabular TD (λ), SARSA (λ), and Q (λ). Each algorithm variation in pseudocode is shown in the following diagram:

Tabular TD(λ)	SARSA(λ)	Q(λ)

Initialize $V(s)$ arbitrarily and $e(s) = 0$, for all $s \in S$
Repeat (for each episode):
  Initialize s
  Repeat (for each step of episode) :
    $a \leftarrow$ action given by π for s
    Take action a, observe reward, r, and next state s'
    $\delta \leftarrow r + \gamma V(s') - V(s)$
    $e(s) \leftarrow e(s) + 1$
    For all s:
      $V(s) \leftarrow V(s) + \alpha\delta e(s)$
      $e(s) \leftarrow \gamma\lambda e(s)$
    $s \leftarrow s'$
  Until s is terminal
	Initialize $Q(s,a)$ arbitrarily and $e(s,a) = 0$, for all s,a
	Repeat (for each episode):
	  Initialize s,a
	  Repeat (for each step of episode):
	    Take action a, observe r, s'
	    Choose a' from s' using policy derived from Q (e.g. ? - greedy)
	    $\delta \leftarrow r + \gamma Q(s',a') - Q(s,a)$
	    $e(s,a) \leftarrow e(s,a) + 1$
	    For all s,a:
	      $Q(s,a) \leftarrow Q(s,a) + \alpha\delta e(s,a)$
	      $e(s,a) \leftarrow \gamma\lambda e(s,a)$
	    $s \leftarrow s'; a \leftarrow a'$
	  Until s is terminal
		Initialize $Q(s,a)$ arbitrarily and $e(s,a) = 0$, for all s,a
		Repeat (for each episode):
		  Initialize s,a
		  Repeat (for each step of episode):
		    Take action a, observe r, s'
		    Choose a' from s' using policy derived from Q (e.g. ? - greedy)
		    $a^* \leftarrow \arg\max_b Q(s',b)$ (if a ties for the max, then $a^* \leftarrow a'$)
		    $\delta \leftarrow r + \gamma Q(s',a^*) - Q(s,a^*)$
		    $e(s,a) \leftarrow e(s,a) + 1$
		    For all s,a:
		      $Q(s,a) \leftarrow Q(s,a) + \alpha\delta e(s,a)$
		      If $a' = a^*$, then $e(s,a) \leftarrow \gamma\lambda e(s,a)$
		        else $e(s,a) \leftarrow 0$
		    $s \leftarrow s'; a \leftarrow a'$
		  Until s is terminal

TD (λ), SARSA (λ), and Q (λ)

Each algorithm has a slight variation in the way it calculates values and TD errors. In the next section, we will look at a full implementation of SARSA (λ) in code.

Understanding SARSA (λ)

We could, of course, implement TD (λ) using the tabular online method, which we haven't covered yet, or with Q-learning. However, since this is a chapter on SARSA, it only makes sense that we continue with that theme throughout. Open `Chapter_5_4.py` and follow the exercise:

1. The code is quite similar to our previous examples, but let's review the full source code, as follows:

```python
import gym
import math
from copy import deepcopy
import numpy as np
import matplotlib.pyplot as plt
import seaborn as sns

env = gym.make('MountainCar-v0')
Q_table = np.zeros((65,65,3))
alpha=0.3
buckets=[65, 65]
gamma=0.99
rewards=[]
episodes=2000
lambdaa=0.8

def to_discrete_states(observation):
 interval=[0 for i in range(len(observation))]
 max_range=[1.2,0.07]
 for i in range(len(observation)):
  data = observation[i]
  inter = int(math.floor((data +
max_range[i])/(2*max_range[i]/buckets[i])))
  if inter>=buckets[i]:
   interval[i]=buckets[i]-1
  elif inter<0:
   interval[i]=0
  else:
   interval[i]=inter
 return interval

def expect_epsilon(t):
   return min(0.015, 1.0 - math.log10((t+1)/220.))

def get_action(observation,t):
 if np.random.random()<max(0.001, expect_epsilon(t)):
  return env.action_space.sample()
```

```
    interval = to_discrete_states(observation)
    return np.argmax(np.array(Q_table[tuple(interval)]))

def expect_alpha(t):
    return min(0.1, 1.0 - math.log10((t+1)/125.))

def
updateQ_SARSA(observation,reward,action,ini_obs,next_action,t,eligi
bility):
    interval = to_discrete_states(observation)
    Q_next = Q_table[tuple(interval)][next_action]
    ini_interval = to_discrete_states(ini_obs)
    lr=max(0.4, expect_alpha(t))
    td_error=(reward + gamma*(Q_next) -
Q_table[tuple(ini_interval)][action])
    Q_table[:,:,action]+=lr*td_error*(eligibility[:,:,action])
for episode in range(episodes):
    observation = env.reset()
    t=0
    eligibility = np.zeros((65,65,3))
    done=False
    while (done==False):
        env.render()
        action = get_action(observation,episode)
        next_obs, reward, done, info = env.step(action)
        interval = to_discrete_states(observation)
        eligibility *= lambdaa * gamma
        eligibility[tuple(interval)][action]+=1
        next_action = get_action(next_obs,episode)
updateQ_SARSA(next_obs,reward,action,observation,next_action,episod
e,eligibility)
        observation=next_obs
        action = next_action
        t+=1
    rewards.append(t+1)
plt.plot(rewards)
plt.show()
```

2. The top section of code is quite similar with some notable differences. Notice the initialization of the MountainCar environment and the Q_table table setup using the following code:

```
env = gym.make('MountainCar-v0')
Q_table = np.zeros((65,65,3))
```

3. Notice how we increase the number of discretized states from 20 x 20 to 65 x 65 as we initialize the `Q_table` table.

4. The next major difference now is the calculation of eligibility using lambda. We can find this code in the bottom episode `for` loop, as shown in the following code:

```
env.render()
action = get_action(observation,episode)          next_obs, reward,
done, info = env.step(action)
interval = to_discrete_states(observation)
eligibility *= lambdaa * gamma
eligibility[tuple(interval)][action]+=1
next_action = get_action(next_obs,episode)
updateQ_SARSA(next_obs,reward,action,observation,next_action,episod
e,eligibility)
observation=next_obs
action = next_action
t+=1
```

5. The calculation for eligibility is done in the highlighted lines. Notice how we multiply `eligibility` by `lambda` and `gamma`, then add one for the current state. This value is then passed into the `update_SARSA` function, as follows:

```
def
updateQ_SARSA(observation,reward,action,ini_obs,next_action,t,eligi
bility):
  interval = to_discrete_states(observation)
  Q_next = Q_table[tuple(interval)][next_action]
  ini_interval = to_discrete_states(ini_obs)
  lr=max(0.4, expect_alpha(t))
  td_error=(reward + gamma*(Q_next) -
Q_table[tuple(ini_interval)][action])
  Q_table[:,:,action]+=lr*td_error*(eligibility[:,:,action])
```

6. Notice how we now update the `Q_table` table based on a determination of `td_error` and `eligibility`. In other words, we take into consideration now how current the information is and how much it was valued in the past.

7. Run the code example again as you normally would and watch the agent play the task. The training output for this task is shown in the following diagram:

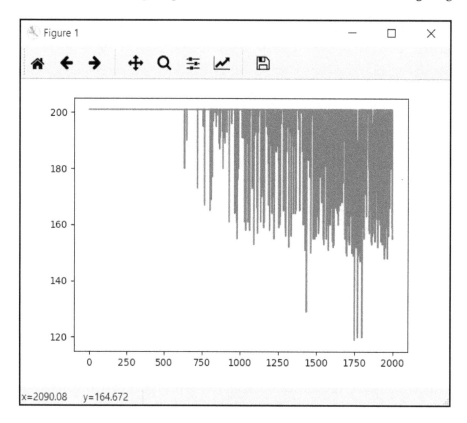

Output plot of rewards for SARSA (λ)

It may take a few minutes to generate the plot shown in the preceding diagram, so please be patient. Be sure to note how this compares with the previous examples we already ran in this chapter. You did run all of the sample exercises to completion, right? Notice how the output of returns/rewards of the time on each episode increases quicker and converges quicker.

We want to look at one more complex example that puts our use of discretization to the extreme in the next example.

SARSA lambda and the Lunar Lander

As the algorithms we develop get more complicated, their capabilities also get more powerful. However, there are limits and it is important to understand the limits of any technology. To test those limits, we want to look at an example that pushes them. For this particular case, we will look at the Lunar Lander environment from Gym. This environment is modeled after the old classic arcade game of the same name, where the object is to land a lunar module on the surface of the moon. In this environment, the observation space is described in eight dimensions and the action space in four. As we will see, this can quickly go beyond our current computational limits.

The `LunarLander` environment requires the installation of a special module called `Box2D`. This is essentially a graphics package.

Follow the exercise in the next section to set up and run the advanced `Box2D` modules for Gym:

- Follow these steps for Windows (Anaconda):

1. Open an Anaconda Prompt as an administrator. Run the following command:

   ```
   conda install swig
   ```

   SWIG is a requirement of `Box2D`.

2. Next, run the following command to install Box2D:

   ```
   pip install box2d-py
   ```

- Follow these steps for Mac/Linux (or Windows without Anaconda):

1. Open a Python shell and run the following command:

   ```
   pip install gym[all]
   ```

2. If you encounter issues, consult the instructions for the Windows installation.

This installation now allows you to run all of the more advanced Box2D environments. These are far more game-like and interesting to train on as well. Open up Chapter_5_5.py and follow the exercise to set up and train SARSA on Lunar Lander:

1. The source code for Chapter_5_5.py is almost identical to Chapter_5_4.py aside from minor differences in setting up the discrete states. We will first look at how we set up the Q_table table with the following code:

    ```
    env = gym.make('LunarLander-v2')
    Q_table = np.zeros((5,5,5,5,5,5,5,5,4))
    ```

2. Notice how we went from values of 65 steps down to 5. The last value denotes the action space size and this has gone from three in MountainCar to four for LunarLander. However, with eight dimensions, we have to be careful about the size of the array. Hence, we need to limit each step size to five, in this example.

3. Next, we initialize the buckets state:

    ```
    buckets=[5,5,5,5,5,5,5,5]
    ```

4. Again, initialized to a size of three for the eight dimensions.

5. Then, we set the max_range values for the maximum values we want our step to span, like so:

    ```
    max_range=[100,100,100,100,100,100,100,100]
    ```

6. We use a value of 100 here to denote some arbitrary max value. Altering or tweaking these values could improve training efficiency.

7. Next, we need to expand the Q_table indexing to include 8 dimensions, like so:

    ```
    Q_table[:,:,:,:,:,:,:,:,action]+=lr*td_error*(eligibility[:,:,:,:,:
    ,:,:,:,action])
    ```

8. Be aware of the limits we are applying to the agent in this example. We are effectively making the agent see in big sections, where each section or axis feature is only divided into three slices. It is surprising how effective this method can be.

9. Run the sample and let it go to completion. Yes, this one will take a while but it is worth it. An example output from the Lunar Lander environment can be seen in the following diagram:

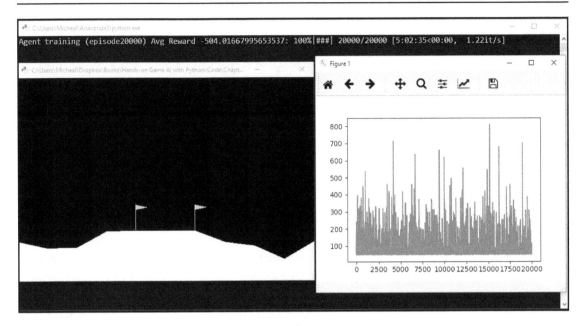

Example output from Chapter_5_5.py

In the last example, we briefly looked at using SARSA on another continuous observation space environment, the Lunar Lander. While it can be fun to play with these environments and see how our discretization can manage an infinite MDP adequately, it is time we moved on to using the big guns of deep learning to manage continuous observation spaces. From the output of rewards, we can see that the example does not converge at all. This is likely because the discretization is not fine enough; perhaps you can improve on that?

The discretization process in this example is not optimal and could certainly be improved upon with some DP methods.

Deep learning networks applied to RL allow us to tackle enormous continuous observation and action spaces. As such, discretization of spaces won't be needed regularly going forward but it can be a useful trick or advantage for simpler problems.

This completes this chapter and I encourage you to move on and explore the exercises to improve your own learning.

Exercises

These exercises are here for you to use and learn from. Attempt at least 2-3, and the more you do, the easier later chapters will also be:

1. What is the difference between an online and offline policy agent?
2. Tune the hyperparameters for any or all of the examples in this chapter, including the new hyperparameter, `lambda`.
3. Change the discretization steps in any example that uses discretization and see what effect it has on training.
4. Use example `Chapter_5_3.py`, **SARSA(0)**, and adapt it to another Gym environment that uses a continuous observation space and discrete action space.
5. Use example `Chapter_5_4.py`, **SARSA(λ)**, and adapt it to another Gym environment that uses a continuous observation space and discrete action space.
6. There is a hyperparameter shown in the code that is not used. Which parameter is it?
7. Use example `Chapter_5_5.py`, **SARSA(λ)**, Lunar Lander and optimize the discretization so that it performs better. For example, you are still limited by array dimensions but you can increase or decrease some more important dimensions.
8. Use example `Chapter_5_5.py`, **SARSA(λ)**, Lunar Lander and optimize the `max_range` values so that it performs better. For example, instead of setting all values to 999, check whether certain values can be narrowed or need expanding.
9. Update an example to work with a continuous action environment. This will require you to discrete the action space.
10. Convert one of the samples into Q-learning, that is, it uses an offline policy.

Feel free to also explore more on your own. We barely scratched the surface of the intricacies of these methods. Finally, we come to our summary in the next section.

Summary

For this chapter, we continued exploring TD learning. We looked at an example of an online TD (0) method called **SARSA**. Then, we looked at how we can discretize an observation space to tackle harder problems but still use the same toolset. From there, we looked at how we could tackle harder continuous space problems such as `CartPole`. After that, we revisited TDL and then looked to n step forward views, decided that was less than optimal, and then moved to backward views and eligibility traces, which led to us uncovering TD (λ), SARSA(λ), and Q (λ). Using SARSA(λ), we were able to solve the `MountainCar` environment in far less time. Finally, we wanted to tackle a far more difficult environment, `LunarLander` using SARSA(λ) without deep learning.

In the next chapter, we look at introducing deep learning and escalate ourselves to deep reinforcement learners.

Section 2: Exploiting the Knowledge

After exploring the basics of RL and using it in toy environments, it is time to take our agents to the next level with the addition of deep learning and several other advanced methods.

This section contains the following chapters:

Going Deep with DQN

6

In this chapter, you will be introduced to **deep learning** (**DL**) in order to handle newer, more challenging infinite **Markov decision process** (**MDP**) problems. We will cover some basics about DL that are relevant to **reinforcement learning** (**RL**), and then look at how we can solve a Q-learning. After that, we will look at how to build a Deep Q-learning or DQN agent in order to solve some Gym environments.

Here is a summary of the topics we will cover in this chapter:

- DL for RL
- Using PyTorch for DL
- Building neural networks with PyTorch
- Understanding DQN in PyTorch
- Exercising DQN

In this chapter, we introduce DL with respect to RL. Applying DL to **deep reinforcement learning** (**DRL**) is quite specific and is not covered in detail here.

DL for RL

Over the course of the previous five chapters, we learned how to evaluate the value of state and actions for a given finite MDP. We learned how to solve various finite MDP problems using methods from MC, DP, Q-learning, and SARSA. Then we explored infinite MDP or continuous observation/action space problems, and we discovered this class of problems introduced computational limits that can only be overcome by introducing other methods, and this is where DL comes in.

 DL is so popular and accessible now that we have decided to cover only a very broad overview of the topic in this book. Anyone serious about building DRL agents should look at studying DL further on their own.

For many, DL is about image classification, speech recognition, or that new cool thing called a **generative adversarial network** (**GAN**). Now, these are all great applications of DL, but, fundamentally, DL is about learning to minimize loss or errors. So when an image is shown to a network in order to learn the image, it is first split up and then fed into the network. Then the network spits out an answer. The correctness of the answer is determined, and any error is pushed back into the network as a way of learning. This method of pushing errors back through the network is called **backpropagation**.

The basics of this whole system are shown here:

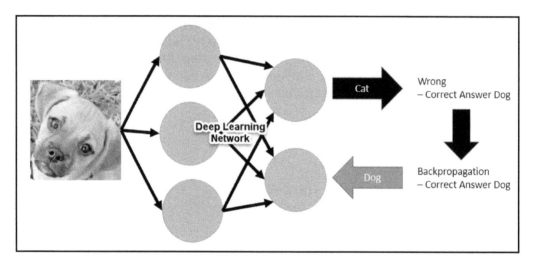

DL oversimplified

The DL network learns by backpropagating the errors back through the network as corrections to each cell, called a neuron, and internal to the neuron are parameters called weights. Each weight controls the strength of a connection to that neuron. The strength of each connection or weight in the network is modified using an optimization method based on the gradient descent. **Gradient descent** (**GD**) is a method derived from calculus that allows us to calculate the effect each connection/weight has on the answer. Working back, we can, therefore, use GD to determine the amount of correction each weight needs.

The major downside to using backpropagation with GD is that the training or learning needs to happen very slowly. Thus, many, perhaps thousands or millions of, images need to be shown to the network in order for it to learn. This actually works well when we apply DL to RL since our trial-and-error learning methods also work iteratively.

DeepMind and other companies are currently working on other methods of learning, aside from backpropagation for DL networks. There has even been talk of doing one-shot learning. That is, being able to train a network on just a single image. Much like the way we humans can learn.

Now, it is often said that DL can be interpreted in many ways. As RL practitioners our interest in DL will be its use as an equation solver. You see fundamentally that is all DL does: solve equations; whether they are equations for classifying images, performing speech translation, or for RL. Deep reinforcement learning is about applying DL in order to solve the learning equations we looked at in the previous chapters and more. In fact, the addition of DL also provides many further capabilities in learning that we will explore in the rest of this book. In the next section, we cover a broad overview of the common DL frameworks used for DRL.

DL frameworks for DRL

There are a number of DL frameworks available for use, but only a few have been readily used in RL research or projects. Most of these frameworks share a number of similarities, so transferring knowledge from one to the other is relatively straightforward. The three most popular frameworks for RL in the past few years have been Keras, TensorFlow, and PyTorch.

A summary of the strengths and weaknesses of each framework is shown in the table here:

Framework	Keras	TensorFlow	PyTorch
Accessibility	Easiest to learn and use	Provides a high-level Keras interface and lower-level interface.	Medium to low-level interface
Scalability	Scales well for smaller projects	Scales to any size project and supported output network models may be run on many different platforms.	Well suited to large projects requiring scale
Performance/Power	Simple interface and limits customization	Powerful and great for performance	Excellent performance and provides the most control and additional interfaces for custom development
Popularity	Popularity decreasing	Consistently popular framework and considered state of the art.	Popularity increasing especially for DRL applications

If you review the table, the obvious choice for our DL framework will be PyTorch. PyTorch based on Torch is a relative newcomer but in just a few short years has gained incredible popularity as both a DL and DRL framework. Therefore, it will be our selected framework for this chapter. In the next section, we look at how to get started with PyTorch for DL.

Using PyTorch for DL

PyTorch provides both a low- and medium-level interface to building DL networks/computational graphs. As much as we build DL systems as networks with neurons connected in layers, the actual implementation of a neural network is through a computational graph. Computational graphs reside at the heart of all DL frameworks, and TensorFlow is no exception. However, Keras abstracts away any concept of computational graphs from the user, which makes it easier to learn but does not provide flexibility like PyTorch. Before we begin building computational graphs with PyTorch though, let's first install PyTorch in the next exercise:

1. Navigate your browser to `pytorch.org`, and scroll down to the **Run this Command** section, as shown in the following screenshot:

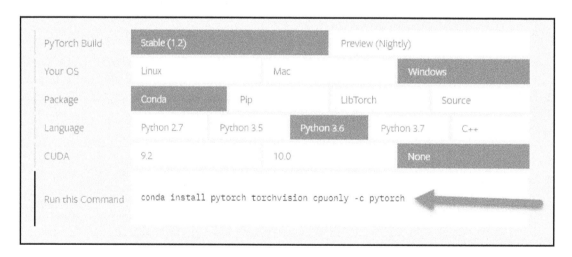

Generating a PyTorch installation command

2. Select the **Stable** version and then your specific **OS** (**Linux**, **Mac**, or **Windows**). Next select the **package** (**Conda**, **Pip**, **LibTorch**, or **Source**); our preference here is **Conda** for Anaconda, but if you have experience with others, use them.

3. Next, choose the **language** (Python 2.7, Python 3.5, Python 3.7, or C++); for our purposes, we will use **Python 3.6**.

4. The next option **CUDA** (**9.2, 10.0** or **None**) determines whether you have a **graphics processing unit** (**GPU**) that is capable of running **CUDA**. Currently, the only supported GPUs are built by NVIDIA. That's unlikely to change anytime soon. For our purposes, we will use **None**. **None** or CPU runs strictly on the CPU, which is slower, but will run across most devices.

5. Open a 64-bit Python console under administrative rights. If you are using **Conda**, launch the window as an admin.

6. Create a new virtual environment with the following commands:

```
conda create -n gameAI python=3.6
```

7. This creates the virtual environment using Python 3.6. PyTorch currently runs on Windows 64-bit. This may differ according to the OS. Then activate the environment with the following commands:

```
activate gameAI
```

8. Copy and paste the `install` command that was generated previously into the window, and execute it. An example of the command for Windows running Anaconda is shown here:

```
conda install pytorch torchvision cpuonly -c pytorch
```

9. This command should install PyTorch. If you saw any issues, such as errors claiming the libraries are not available for 32-bit, then make sure you are using a 64-bit version of Python.

The preceding process will install PyTorch and all the required dependencies we will need for now. If you have issues installing the framework, check the online documentation or one of the many online help forums. In most cases, installation issues will be resolved by making sure you are using 64-bit and running as an administrator.

All the code examples for this book have been prepared and tested with Visual Studio Professional or Visual Studio Code, both with the Python tools installed. VS Code is a good solid editor that is free and cross-platform. It is a relative newcomer for Python development but benefits from Microsoft's years of experience building **integrated development environments** (**IDEs**).

With PyTorch installed, we can move onto working with a simple example that creates a computational DL graph in the next section.

Computational graphs with tensors

At the core of all DL frameworks is the concept of a tensor or what we often think of as a multidimensional array or matrix. The computational graphs we construct will work on tensors using a variety of operations to linearly transform the inputs into final outputs. You can think of this as a kind of flow, and hence the reason TensorFlow has the name it does. In the following exercise, we are going to construct a two-layer DL network using a computation PyTorch graph and then train the network:

The concepts here assume an understanding of linear algebra and matrix multiplication and systems of linear equations. As such, it is recommended that any readers lacking in these skills or are in need of a quick refresher should do so. Of course, a quick refresher on calculus may also come in useful.

1. Open the `Chapter_6_1.py` code example. The example was derived from a PyTorch quickstart manual, with some of the variable names altered to be more contextual:

```python
import torch

dtype = torch.float
device = torch.device("cpu")
# device = torch.device("cuda:0") # Uncomment this to run on GPU

batch_size, inputs, hidden, outputs = 64, 1000, 100, 10
x = torch.randn(batch_size, inputs, device=device, dtype=dtype)
y = torch.randn(batch_size, outputs, device=device, dtype=dtype)

layer1 = torch.randn(inputs, hidden, device=device, dtype=dtype)
layer2 = torch.randn(hidden, outputs, device=device, dtype=dtype)
learning_rate = 1e-6

for t in range(500):
  h = x.mm(layer1)
  h_relu = h.clamp(min=0)
  y_pred = h_relu.mm(layer2)

  loss = (y_pred - y).pow(2).sum().item()
  if t % 100 == 99:
    print(t, loss)

  grad_y_pred = 2.0 * (y_pred - y)
  grad_layer2 = h_relu.t().mm(grad_y_pred)
  grad_h_relu = grad_y_pred.mm(layer2.t())
  grad_h = grad_h_relu.clone()
```

```
grad_h[h < 0] = 0
grad_layer1 = x.t().mm(grad_h)

layer1 -= learning_rate * grad_layer1
layer2 -= learning_rate * grad_layer2
```

2. We start by importing the PyTorch library with `import torch`. Then we set our preferred data type `dtype` variable to `torch.float`. Then we initialize the device variable by using `torch.device` and passing in `cpu` to denote a CPU only. The option to enable the example to run with CUDA on a GPU was left in, but installing CUDA is left up to you:

```
batch_size, inputs, hidden, outputs = 64, 1000, 100, 10
```

3. Next, we set up some variables to define how the data is processed and the architecture of the network. The `batch_size` parameter denotes how many items to train in an iteration. The `inputs` variable denotes the size of the input space into the network, whereas the `hidden` variable represents the number of hidden or middle-layer neurons in the network. The last `outputs` variable denotes the output space or the number of neurons in an output layer of a network:

```
x = torch.randn(batch_size, inputs, device=device, dtype=dtype)
y = torch.randn(batch_size, outputs, device=device, dtype=dtype)
```

4. After that, we set the inputs and outputs variables: x as the inputs, and y as the outputs, to be learned based on just a random sampling based on `batch_size`. The size of the `inputs` variable in this example is 1,000, so each element in the batch will have 1000 inputs for x. The outputs have a value of 10, so each sample of y will likewise have 10 items:

```
layer1 = torch.randn(inputs, hidden, device=device, dtype=dtype)
layer2 = torch.randn(hidden, outputs, device=device, dtype=dtype)
```

5. These two lines create our computational layers of a DL network defined by our previous `inputs`, `hidden`, and `outputs` parameters. The tensor contents of `layer1` and `layer2` at this point contain an initialized set of random weights the size of which is set by the number of inputs, hidden layers, and outputs.

6. You can visualize the size of these tensors by setting a breakpoint on the line after the layer setups and then running the file in debug mode *F5* on Visual Studio Code or Professional. When the breakpoint is hit, you can then use your mouse to hover over the variables to see information about the tensors as shown in the following screenshot:

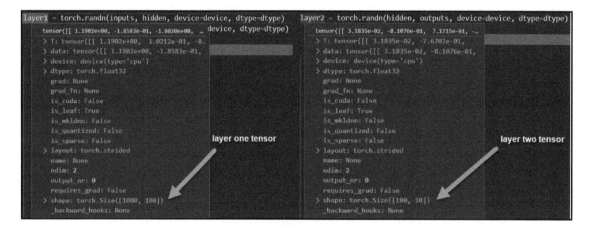

Inspecting the size of the layer weight tensors

7. Notice how the first layer dimensions are 1000 x 100 and the second layer dimensions are 100 x 10. Computationally, we transform the inputs by multiplying the weights of the first layer and then outputting the results to the second layer. Here, the second layer weights are multiplied by the output from the first layer. We will see how this functions shortly.

8. Next, we define a `learning_rate` parameter, or what we will clarify now as a hyperparameter. The learning rate is a multiplier by which we can scale the rate of learning and is not different than the learning rate alpha we previously explored:

```
learning_rate = 1e-6
```

 We will often use the terms `weight` and `parameter` to mean the same in DL. As such, other parameters such as `learning_rate`, epochs, batch size, and so on will be described as hyperparameters. Learning to tune hyperparameters will be an ongoing journey in building DL examples.

9. Before we get into the training loop, let's run the sample and observe the output. Run the sample as you normally would, in debug mode or not. The output of this example is shown in the following screenshot:

```
99 635.5177001953125
199 3.109295606613159
299 0.026640085503458977
399 0.0005209375522099435
499 6.454912363551557e-05
```

Output of example Chapter_6_1.py

The output basically shows how the error loss decreases over training iterations. At iteration 99, we can see in the preceding example the error is around 635, but decreases down to almost zero by iteration 499. While the inputs and outputs are all random, we can still see the network learns to identify a pattern in the data and thereby reduce errors. In the next section, we take a more detailed look at how this learning works.

Training a neural network – computational graph

In order to train a network or computational graph, we need to first feed it the input data, determine what the graph thinks is the answer, and then correct it iteratively using backpropagation. Let's go back to the Chapter_6_1.py code example, and follow the next exercise to learn how training works:

1. We will start at the beginning of the training loop that starts with the for loop, as shown in the following code:

```
for t in range(500):
    h = x.mm(layer1)
    h_relu = h.clamp(min=0)
    y_pred = h_relu.mm(layer2)
```

2. So, 500 in this example denotes the total number of training iterations or epochs. In each iteration, we calculate the predicted output using the next three lines. This step is called the forward pass through the graph or network. Where the first line does the matrix multiplication of the layer1 weights with the x inputs using x.mm. It then passes those output values through an activation function called **clamp**. Clamp sets limits on the output of the network, and in this case we use a clamp on 0. This also happens to correspond with the rectified linear unit or ReLU function.

We use many different forms of activation functions in DL. The ReLU function is currently one of the more popular functions, but we will use others along the way throughout this book.

3. After the output is activated through the ReLU function, it is then matrix multiplied by the second layer weights, `layer2`. The output of this result is `y_pred`, a tensor containing the output predictions.

4. From there we predict the loss or amount of error between what we want to actually predict in the `y` tensor and what our network just predicted as a tensor `y_pred` using the following code:

```
loss = (y_pred - y).pow(2).sum().item()
if t % 100 == 99:
    print(t, loss)
```

5. The `loss` value or total error is calculated using a method called **mean squared error** or **MSE**. Keep in mind that since `y_pred` and `y` are tensors, the subtraction operation is done tensor-wide. That is, all values of the 10 predictions are subtracted from the predicted `y` value and then squared and summed. We use the same output technique here to print out the total loss for every 99 iterations.

6. After computing the loss, we next need to compute the gradient of graph weights in order to determine how we push back and correct the errors in the graph. Calculating this gradient is outside the scope of this book, but the code is shown as follows:

```
grad_y_pred = 2.0 * (y_pred - y)
grad_layer2 = h_relu.t().mm(grad_y_pred)
grad_h_relu = grad_y_pred.mm(layer2.t())
grad_h = grad_h_relu.clone()
grad_h[h < 0] = 0
grad_layer1 = x.t().mm(grad_h)
```

7. We show the low-level code here to do GD against a simple network graph as an example of how the math works. Fortunately, automatic differentiation lets us for the most part ignore those finer, more painful details. The gradients calculated here now need to be applied back to the graph layer weights using the following code:

```
layer1 -= learning_rate * grad_layer1
layer2 -= learning_rate * grad_layer2
```

8. Notice how we are again using tensor subtraction to subtract the calculated gradients `grad_layer1` and `grad_layer2` scaled by the learning rate.

9. Run the sample again and you should see a similar output. It can be helpful to play with the `learning_rate` hyperparameter to see what effect this has on training.

This previous example was a low-level look at how we can implement a computational graph that represents a two-layer neural network. While this example was meant to show you the inner details of how things work in practice, we will use the higher-level neural network subset of PyTorch to build graphs. We will see how to construct an example in the next section.

Building neural networks with Torch

In the last section, we explored building computational graphs that resemble neural networks. This is a fairly common task as you may expect. So much so that PyTorch, as well as most DL frameworks, provides helper methods, classes, and functions to build DL graphs. Keras is essentially a wrapper around TensorFlow that does just that. Therefore, in this section, we are going to recreate the last exercise's example using the neural network helper functions in PyTorch. Open the `Chapter_6_2.py` code example and follow the next exercise:

1. The source code for the entire sample is as follows:

```
import torch

batch_size, inputs, hidden, outputs = 64, 1000, 100, 10

x = torch.randn(batch_size, inputs)
y = torch.randn(batch_size, outputs)

model = torch.nn.Sequential(
  torch.nn.Linear(inputs, hidden),
  torch.nn.ReLU(),
  torch.nn.Linear(hidden, outputs),
)

loss_fn = torch.nn.MSELoss(reduction='sum')
learning_rate = 1e-4

for t in range(500):
  y_pred = model(x)
  loss = loss_fn(y_pred, y)

  if t % 100 == 99:
    print(t, loss.item())

  model.zero_grad()
  loss.backward()
```

```
with torch.no_grad():
  for param in model.parameters():
    param -= learning_rate * param.grad
```

2. The code becomes greatly simplified, but not so much that it doesn't allow us to control the internals of the DL graph itself. This is not something you may appreciate entirely until working with other DL frameworks. However, it is not the simplicity but the flexibility that is pushing PyTorch to be the number one framework in DL:

```
model = torch.nn.Sequential(
  torch.nn.Linear(inputs, hidden),
  torch.nn.ReLU(),
  torch.nn.Linear(hidden, outputs),
)
```

3. There are a couple of big changes to the top section of the code, most notably with the setup of a model using `torch.nn.Sequential`. The setup of this model or graph is exactly the same as we did previously, except it describes each connection point more explicitly. We can see that the first layer is defined with `torch.nn.Linear` taking `inputs` and `hidden` as parameters. This gets connected to the activation function, again ReLU denoted by `torch.nn.ReLU`. After that, we create the final layer using `hidden` and `outputs` as the parameters. The `Sequential` term for the model denotes the whole graph is fully connected; the same as we looked at in the last example:

```
loss_fn = torch.nn.MSELoss(reduction='sum')
```

4. After the model definition, we can also see our `loss_fn` loss function is more descriptive by using `torch.nn.MSELoss` as the function. This lets us know explicitly what the `loss` function is and how it is going to be reduced, in this case, reducing the sum, denoted by `reduction='sum'`, or the sum of average squared errors:

```
for t in range(500):
  y_pred = model(x)
```

5. The start of the training loop remains the same but this time `y_pred` is taken from just inputting the entire `x` batch into the `model`. This operation is the same as the forward pass or where the network outputs the answer:

```
loss = loss_fn(y_pred, y)
```

6. After that, we calculate `loss` as a Torch tensor, using the `loss_fn` function. The next piece of code is the same loss output code as we have seen before:

```
model.zero_grad()
loss.backward()
```

7. Next, we zero any gradients in the model—this is essentially a reset. Then we calculate the gradients in the loss tensor using the `backward` function. This is essentially that nasty bit of code we previously looked at, which has now been simplified to a single line:

```
with torch.no_grad():
    for param in model.parameters():
        param -= learning_rate * param.grad
```

8. We finish off training the same way as before by adjusting the weights in the model using the calculated gradients of the `loss` tensor. While this section of code is more verbose than our last example, it explains better the actual learning process.

9. Run the example just like you did previously, and you should see very similar output to what we saw in the `Chapter_6_1.py` example.

Did you notice that the `learning_rate` variable in the second example was slightly lower? The reason for this is because the neural network model differs slightly in a few areas, including the use of another weight for each neuron called a **bias**. If you want to learn more about the bias, be sure to pick up a good course on DL.

With a good basic understanding of how we can use PyTorch, we will now look and see how we can apply our knowledge to RL in the next section.

Understanding DQN in PyTorch

Deep reinforcement learning became prominent because of the work of combining Q-learning with DL. The combination is known as deep Q-learning or **DQN** for **Deep Q Network**. This algorithm has powered some of the cutting edge examples of DRL, when Google DeepMind used it to make classic Atari games better than humans in 2012. There are many implementations of this algorithm, and Google has even patented it. The current consensus is that Google patented such a base algorithm in order to thwart patent trolls striking at little guys or developers building commercial applications with DQN. It is unlikely that Google would exercise this legally or that it would have to since this algorithm is no longer considered state of the art.

Patent trolling is a practice whereby an often less-than-ethical company will patent any and all manner of inventions just for the sake of securing patents. In many cases, these inventions don't even originate with the company but their efficient patent process allows them to secure intellectual property cheaply. These trolls often work primarily in software, since software start-ups and other innovators in this area often ignore filing a patent. Google and other big software companies now go out of their way to file these patents, but in essence suggest they would never enforce such a patent. Of course, it could change its mind—just look at Java.

DQN is like the Hello World of DRL, and almost every text or course on this subject will have a version demonstrated. The version we are going to look at here follows the standard pattern but is broken down in a manner that showcases our previous learning on TD and the temporal credit assignment. This will provide a good comparison between using DL and not using DL. In the next sections, we learn how to set up and run a DQN model.

Refreshing the environment

A major cause of a new user's frustration is often just setting up the examples. That is why we want to make sure that your environment has the proper components installed. If you recall earlier, you should have created a new virtual environment called `gameAI`. We are now going to install the other required modules we need for the next exercise:

1. You should be working with and in a new virtual environment now. As such, we will need to install the Gym and other required components again.
2. Make sure that you have a recent version of a Windows C++ compiler installed. For a list of supported compilers, check this site: `https://wiki.python.org/moin/WindowsCompilers`.

3. First let us install the required libraries for Windows, recall these steps are only required for Windows installations with the following commands:

```
conda install swig
pip install box2d-py
```

4. After you have installed the prerequisites on Windows, you do the remainder of the installation with the command to install Gym. This is the same command you will use on Mac and Linux installations:

```
pip install gym[all]
```

5. Next install `matplotlib` and `tqdm` with the following commands:

```
pip install matplotlib
pip install tqdm
```

6. Recall that those are the helper libraries we use to monitor training.

After installing those packages, make sure your IDE is configured to point to the `gameAI` virtual environment. Your particular IDE will have instructions to do this. In the next section, we look to some assumptions that allow us to solve infinite MDPs with DL such as DQN.

Partially observable Markov decision process

We have already seen how we can tackle a continuous or infinite observation space by discretizing it into buckets. This works well but as we saw computationally, it does not scale well to massive problems of observation state space. By introducing DL, we can effectively increase our state space inputs, but not nearly in the amount we need. Instead, we need to introduce the concept of a **partially observable Markov decision process (POMDP)**. That is, we can consider any problem that is an infinite MDP to be partially observable, meaning the agent or algorithm needs only observe the local or observed state in order to make actions. If you think about it, this is exactly the way you interact with your environment. Where you may consider your minute-to-minute activities as partially observable observations of the global infinite MDP or, in other words, the universe. Whereas your day-to-day actions and decisions occur at a higher observable state, you only ever have a partially observable view of the entire globally infinite MDP.

This concept of being able to switch from different partially observable views of the same infinite MDP is a center of much research. Currently, there are two main branches of DRL tackling this problem. They are **hierarchical reinforcement learning** (HRL), which attempts to describe a problem as a start to MDP hierarchies. The other branch is called **meta reinforcement learning** (MRL), and it takes a broader approach in an attempt to let the partially observable be learned in different time steps. By introducing time sequences here, we can also start to work with other forms of neural networks, called recurrent networks, that can learn time. We will revisit MRL in `Chapter 14`, *From DRL to AGI*.

In the next section, we finally look at how to build a DQN with PyTorch.

Constructing DQN

You can probably find a version of a DQN developed in every DL framework. The algorithm itself is an incredible achievement in learning, since it allows us now to learn continuous or infinite spaces/the infinite MDP. Open `Chapter_6_DQN.py`, and follow the next exercise to build the DQN sample:

> The source for this example was originally derived from this GitHub repository: `https://github.com/higgsfield/RL-Adventure/blob/master/1.dqn.ipynb`. It has been modified significantly in order to match the previous samples in this book.

1. At this time, the samples have become too large to list in a single listing. Instead, we will go through section by section as we normally would. As usual, it is helpful if you follow along with the code in an editor:

```
import math, random
import torch
import torch.nn as nn
import torch.optim as optim
import torch.autograd as autograd
import torch.nn.functional as F

import matplotlib.pyplot as plt
import gym
import numpy as np
from collections import deque
from tqdm import trange
```

2. These are are usual imports, but it should be mentioned that `torch` needs to load first before the other imports like `gym` or `numpy`. We are going to jump down past the first `ReplayBuffer` function until later:

```
env_id = "CartPole-v0"
env = gym.make(env_id)
epsilon_start = 1.0

epsilon_final = 0.01
epsilon_decay = 500
eps_by_episode = lambda epoch: epsilon_final + (epsilon_start -
epsilon_final) * math.exp(-1. * epoch / epsilon_decay)

plt.plot([eps_by_episode(i) for i in range(10000)])
plt.show()
```

3. The preceding code shows the typical setup for creating the RL environment and setting up our hyperparameters. Notice how we are generating`eps_by_episode` for the decaying `epsilon` using a lambda expression. This is a very Pythonic way of producing a decaying epsilon. The last couple lines of code plot the decaying epsilon in a chart and outputs something similar to the following graph:

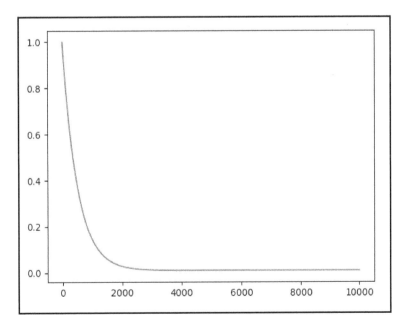

Plot showing decaying epsilon over training epochs

4. You can see from the preceding plot that epsilon more or less stabilizes around 2,000 iterations; this seems to suggest the agent should have learned enough by then. We will now scroll down to the next block of code not in a function:

```
model = DQN(env.observation_space.shape[0], env.action_space.n)
optimizer = optim.Adam(model.parameters())
replay_buffer = ReplayBuffer(1000)
```

5. These three lines of code set up the critical components—the model, which is of the DQN type, and a class we will get to shortly. The **optimizer**, in this case, is of the **Adam** type, defined by optim.Adam. The last line creates ReplayBuffer, another class we will get to shortly. We will again scroll down past all the code in functions and review the next section of main code:

```
episodes = 10000
batch_size = 32
gamma      = 0.99

losses = []
all_rewards = []
episode_reward = 0

state = env.reset()
tot_reward = 0
tr = trange(episodes+1, desc='Agent training', leave=True)
```

6. Most of this code should look familiar by now. Notice how we are now setting a new hyperparameter called batch_size. Basically, batch_size is the size of the number of items we push through a network at a single time. We prefer to do this in batches since it provides a better averaging mechanism. That means when we train the model, we will do so in batches:

```
for episode in tr:
  tr.set_description("Agent training (episode{}) Avg Reward
{}".format(episode+1,tot_reward/(episode+1)))
  tr.refresh()
  epsilon = eps_by_episode(episode)

  action = model.act(state, epsilon)
  next_state, reward, done, _ = env.step(action)

  replay_buffer.push(state, action, reward, next_state, done)
  tot_reward += reward

  state = next_state
```

```
episode_reward += reward

if done:
    state = env.reset()
    all_rewards.append(episode_reward)
    episode_reward = 0

if len(replay_buffer) > batch_size:
    loss = compute_td_loss(batch_size)
    losses.append(loss.item())

if epoch % 2000 == 0:
    plot(epoch, all_rewards, losses)
```

7. Once again, most of this code should feel quite familiar by now since it mirrors many of our previous examples. There are two highlighted sections of code that we will focus on. The first is the line that pushes the `state`, `action`, `reward`, `next_state`, and `done` functions onto `replay_buffer`. We have yet to look at the `replay` buffer, but just realize at this point all this information is getting stored for later. The other highlighted section has to do with the computation of loss using the `compute_td_loss` function. That function computes the loss using the TD error as we saw when covering TD and SARSA.

8. Before we explore the additional functions and classes, run the sample so that you can see the output. As the sample runs, you will need to repeatedly close the plotting window after every 2,000 iterations. The following graphs show the output from several thousand training iterations:

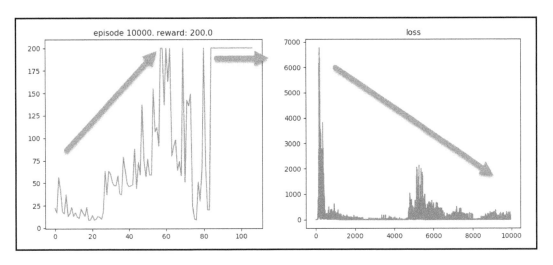

Example output after several thousand training iterations

The output in the graphs shows how the agent learns across episodes and is able to quickly maximize the reward as shown in the left plot. In comparison, the right plot shows a decreasing loss or total error in our agent's predictions. In fact, we can see around episode 8000 that the agent has indeed learned the problem and is able to consistently achieve the maximal reward. If you recall in `Chapter 5`, *Exploring SARSA*, we solved the CartPole environment, but just barely with discretized SARSA. Although, that still required almost 50,000 episodes of training. Now that we have observed this method is several times better than our previous attempts, in the next section we need to explore the details of how this works.

The replay buffer

Fundamental to the DL methods is the need for us to feed batches of observed agent events into the neural network. Remember, we do this in batches so the algorithm is able to average across errors or loss better. This requirement is more a function of DL than anything to do with RL. As such, we want to store a previous number of the observed state, action, next state, reward, and returns from our agent, taking an action into a container called `ReplayBuffer`. We then randomly sample those events from the replay buffer and inject them into the neural network for training. Let's see how the buffer is constructed again by reopening sample `Chapter_6_DQN.py` and following this exercise:

1. The entire code for the `ReplayBuffer` class is shown as follows:

```
class ReplayBuffer(object):
  def __init__(self, capacity):
    self.buffer = deque(maxlen=capacity)

  def push(self, state, action, reward, next_state, done):
    state       = np.expand_dims(state, 0)
    next_state = np.expand_dims(next_state, 0)
    self.buffer.append((state, action, reward, next_state, done))

  def sample(self, batch_size):
    state, action, reward, next_state, done
  = zip(*random.sample(self.buffer, batch_size))
    return np.concatenate(state), action,
  reward, np.concatenate(next_state), done

  def __len__(self):
    return len(self.buffer)
```

2. Internally the `ReplayBuffer` uses a class called `deque`, which is a class that can store any manner of objects. In the `init` function, we create the queue of the required specified size. The class has three functions `push`, `sample` and `len`. The `len` function is fairly self-explanatory, but the other functions we should look at:

```
def push(self, state, action, reward, next_state, done):
    state      = np.expand_dims(state, 0)
    next_state = np.expand_dims(next_state, 0)
    self.buffer.append((state, action, reward, next_state, done))
```

3. The `push` function pushes the `state`, `action`, `reward`, `next_state`, and `done` observations on to the queue for later processing:

```
def sample(self, batch_size):
    state, action, reward, next_state, done
      = zip(*random.sample(self.buffer, batch_size))
    return np.concatenate(state), action,
        reward, np.concatenate(next_state), done
```

4. The other function, `sample`, is where the buffer randomly samples events from the queue and zips them up using `zip`. It will then return this batch of random events to be fed into the network for learning.

5. Find the line of code that sets the size of the replay buffer and change it to the following:

```
replay_buffer = ReplayBuffer(3000)
```

6. Run the example again with the new buffer size, and observe the effect this has on training.

7. Now change the buffer size again with the following code:

```
replay_buffer = ReplayBuffer(333)
```

8. Run the example again, and observe the output closely. Notice the changes in the training performance.

We have effectively tried running the agent with 3 times, as well as 1/3 the buffer size. What you will find in this problem is that the smaller buffer size is more effective but perhaps not optimal. You can consider the buffer size as another one of those essential hyperparameters you will need to learn to set.

Replay buffers are a required component of our DL models, and we will see other similar classes in the future. In the next section, we will move on to building the DQN class.

The DQN class

Previously, we saw how the DQN class was used to construct the neural network model that we will use to learn the TD loss function. Reopen exercise `Chapter_6_DQN.py` again to review the construction of the DQN class:

1. The entire code for the DQN class is as follows:

```
class DQN(nn.Module):
    def __init__(self, num_inputs, num_actions):
        super(DQN, self).__init__()

        self.layers = nn.Sequential(
            nn.Linear(env.observation_space.shape[0], 128),
            nn.ReLU(),
            nn.Linear(128, 128),
            nn.ReLU(),
            nn.Linear(128, env.action_space.n))

    def forward(self, x):
        return self.layers(x)

    def act(self, state, epsilon):
        if random.random() > epsilon:
            state    =
autograd.Variable(torch.FloatTensor(state).unsqueeze(0),
                volatile=True)
            q_value = self.forward(state)
            action  = q_value.max(1)[1].item()
        else:
            action = random.randrange(env.action_space.n)
        return action
```

2. The `init` function initializes the network using the PyTorch `nn.Sequential` class to generate a fully connected network. We can see that the inputs into the first layer are set by `env.observation_space.shape[0]`, and the number of neurons is 128.

3. We can see there are three layers in this network, with the first layer consisting of 128 neurons connected by ReLU to a middle layer with 128 neurons. This layer is connected to the output layer, with the number of outputs defined by `env.action_space.n`. What we can see from this is that the network will be learning which action to select.

4. The `forward` function is just the forward pass or prediction by the network model.

5. Finally, the `act` function is quite similar to the other Q-learning samples we have built before. One thing we want to focus on is how the actual action is selected during non-exploration as the following code excerpt shows:

```
state    = autograd.Variable(torch.FloatTensor(state).unsqueeze(0),
           volatile=True)
q_value = self.forward(state)
action  = q_value.max(1)[1].item()
```

6. Calculating the `state` tensor in the first line with `autograd.Variable` is where the state is converted into a tensor so that it may be fed into the forward pass. It is the call to `self.forward` in the next line that calculates all the Q values, `q_value`, for that `state` tensor. We then use a greedy (max) selection strategy in the last line to choose the action.

7. Change the network size from 128 neurons to 32, 64, or 256 to see the effect this has on training. The following code shows the proper way to configure the example to use 64 neurons:

```
self.layers = nn.Sequential(
        nn.Linear(env.observation_space.shape[0], 64),
        nn.ReLU(),
        nn.Linear(64, 64),
        nn.ReLU(),
        nn.Linear(64, env.action_space.n))
```

8. Run the example again with various size changes, and see the effect this has on training performance.

Good news, we consider the number of neurons and number of layers in a network to be the additional training hyperparameters we need to observe while tackling problems. As you may have already noticed, these new inputs can have a dramatic effect on the training performance and need to be selected carefully.

We almost have all the pieces together to understand the entire algorithm. In the next section, we will cover the last piece, determining loss and training the network.

Calculating loss and training

Finally, we can see how all this comes together to train the agent to learn a policy. Open up `Chapter_6_DQN.py` again, and follow the next exercise to see how loss is calculated:

1. The function that calculates the loss in terms of TD errors is shown as follows:

```python
def compute_td_loss(batch_size):
  state, action, reward, next_state, done =
replay_buffer.sample(batch_size)

  state       =
autograd.Variable(torch.FloatTensor(np.float32(state)))
  next_state =
autograd.Variable(torch.FloatTensor(np.float32(next_state)),
    volatile=True)
  action      = autograd.Variable(torch.LongTensor(action))
  reward      = autograd.Variable(torch.FloatTensor(reward))
  done        = autograd.Variable(torch.FloatTensor(done))

  q_values       = model(state)
  next_q_values = model(next_state)
  q_value        = q_values.gather(1,
action.unsqueeze(1)).squeeze(1)

  next_q_value  = next_q_values.max(1)[0]
  expected_q_value = reward + gamma * next_q_value * (1 - done)

  loss = (q_value -
autograd.Variable(expected_q_value.data)).pow(2).mean()
  optimizer.zero_grad()
  loss.backward()
  optimizer.step()

  return loss
```

2. In the first line, we call `sample` from `replay_buffer` using `batch_size` as the input. This returns a randomly sampled set of events from a previous run. This returns `state`, `next_state`, `action`, `reward`, and `done`. These are then turned into tensors in the next five lines using the `autograd.Variable` function. This function is a helper for converting types into tensors of the appropriate type. Notice how the action is of the `long` type using `torch.LongTensor`, and the other variables are just floats.

3. The next section of code calculates the Q values:

```
q_values      = model(state)
next_q_values = model(next_state)
q_value       = q_values.gather(1, action.unsqueeze(1)).squeeze(1)
```

4. Remember that when we call `model(state)` that is the equivalent of doing a forward pass or prediction on the network. This now becomes the same as sampling from the policy in our previous examples.

5. We then go back to our previous defined Q Learning equation, and use that to determine what our best expected Q value should be, with the following code:

```
next_q_value   = next_q_values.max(1)[0]
expected_q_value = reward + gamma * next_q_value * (1 - done)
```

6. Calculating the `expected_q_value` value from earlier uses the Q Learning equation to determine what an expected value should be. Based on the expected value, we can determine the how much the network is in error and how much loss it needs to correct with the following line:

```
loss = (q_value -
autograd.Variable(expected_q_value.data)).pow(2).mean()
```

7. This line converts the value to a tensor and then determines the loss using our old friend MSE. Our final step is to optimize or reduce the loss of the network, using the following code:

```
optimizer.zero_grad()
loss.backward()
optimizer.step()
```

8. The code is quite similar to what we used before to optimize our neural network and computational graph examples. We first apply `zero_grad` to the optimizer in order to zero out any gradients as a reset. We then push the loss backward, and finally perform one step on the optimizer. That last part is new and has to do with the type of optimizer we are using.

We won't go heavily into the various optimizers you can use for DL until `Chapter 6`, *Going Deeper with DDQN*. In most cases, we will use the Adam optimizer or some derivation of it, depending on the environment.

9. Feel free to run the code sample yet again in order to better observe all the details in training.

Hopefully by now, even with the inclusion of DL, these samples are starting to feel consistently familiar. In some ways, DL makes these algorithms much simpler than our previous examples. Fortunately, that is a good thing because our agents will need to get more complicated and robust as we evolve to harder and harder environments.

Up until now, we have only been able to view our agent training and see no actual update in performance. Since that is essential to our understanding of how an agent trains, in the next section we are going to add that to the last example.

Exercising DQN

As we have progressed through this book, we have spent time making sure we can see how our agents our progressing in their respective environments. In this section, we are aiming to add rendering to the agent environment during training using our last DQN example. Then we can see how the agent is actually performing and perhaps try out another couple of new environments along the way.

Adding the ability to watch the agent play in the environment is not that difficult, and we can implement this as we have done with other examples. Open the `Chapter_6_DQN_wplay.py` code example, and follow the next exercise:

1. The code is almost identical to the DQN sample earlier, so we won't need to review the whole code. However, we do want to introduce two new variables as hyperparameters; this will allow us to better control the network training and observer performance:

    ```
    buffer_size = 1000
    neurons = 128
    ```

2. We will use `buffer_size` to denote the size of the buffer. This value will also come in handy when we determine whether our model has some amount of training. DQN will not start training the model until the replay buffer or what we often refer to as the experience buffer is full. Notice that we also added a new hyperparameter for neurons; this will allow us to quickly tweak the network as we need.

3. Next we will look at how the code to render the agent playing the game is injected into the training loop:

    ```
    if done:
      if episode > buffer_size:
        play_game()
    ```

```
state = env.reset()
all_rewards.append(episode_reward)
episode_reward = 0
```

4. The highlighted lines represent the new code that will check whether the current episode is larger than `buffer_size`. If it is then we render the agent playing the game using the model/policy.

5. Next we will look at the new `play_game` function, as follows:

```
def play_game():
  done = False
  state = env.reset()
  while(not done):
    action = model.act(state, epsilon_final)
    next_state, reward, done, _ = env.step(action)
    env.render()
    state = next_state
```

6. This code is quite similar to other `play_game` functions we crafted previously. Notice the highlighted line showing where we predict the next action using the `model.act` function. Passed into this function is the state and our minimum value for epsilon, called `epsilon_final`. We set the minimum value here since we choose the agent performing minimal exploration and the actions are selected entirely from the policy/model.

7. Run this example, and you can watch the agent play the CartPole environment successfully as shown in the following diagram:

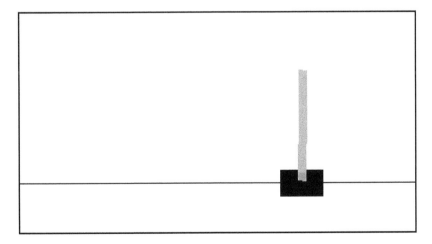

Example rendering of an agent playing CartPole successfully

With a new agent able to tackle the CartPole environment far easier, in the next section we will now look to throw our failed example from the last chapter, the LunarLander environment.

Revisiting the LunarLander and beyond

Now with our solid example of DQN, we can move on to solve more difficult environments, like LunarLander. In this exercise, we set up the DQN agent to solve the LunarLander environment in order to compare our previous attempts with discretized SARSA:

1. Open the `Chapter_6_DQN_lunar.py` example, and note the change in the `env_id` environment ID and creation of the environment shown as follows:

   ```
   env_id = 'LunarLander-v2'
   env = gym.make(env_id)
   ```

2. We also adjust a couple of the hyperparameters to account for the increased complexity of the environment:

   ```
   epsilon_decay = 1000
   buffer_size = 3000
   neurons = 192
   ```

3. We increase `epsilon_decay` in order to encourage the agent to explore longer. Exploration is a trade-off we always need to balance with the environment. Note `buffer_size` is also increased to a value of 3,000 to account for the increase in environment complexity, again. As well, we also increase the size of the network to 192 neurons across the board.

4. You may also need to increase the number of total training episodes from 10,000 to a higher value. We will leave that decision up to you.

5. From here, you can run the example and visualize the agent landing the lander as shown in the following screen image:

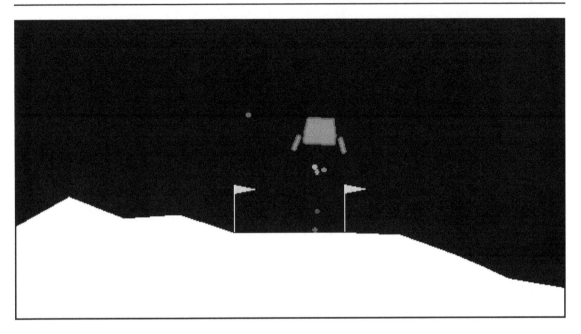

Agent playing the LunarLander environment

That completes our exploration of DQN, and you are encouraged to follow the exercises in the next section to practice those new skills.

Exercises

As we progress through the book, I hope you can see the value of performing these additional hands-on exercises. Learning how to tune hyperparameters will be essential in building DRL models that can tackle difficult environments. Use the following exercises to reinforce your learning of the material:

1. Modify the `batch_size`, `inputs`, `hidden`, and `outputs` hyperparameters from `Chapter_6_1.py` and see what effect these have on the output loss.
2. Alter the number of training iterations in the `Chapter_6_1.py` example in conjunction with other hyperparameters in order to evaluate the impact this has on training.
3. Modify the `batch_size`, `inputs`, `hidden` , and `outputs` hyperparameters from `Chapter_6_2.py`, and see what effect these have on the output loss.

4. Alter the number of training iterations in the `Chapter_6_2.py` example in conjunction with other hyperparameters in order to evaluate the impact this has on training.

5. Tune the hyperparameters in the `Chapter_6_DQN.py` example to improve training performance on the CartPole environment. Create any additional hyperparameters you may need.

6. Tune the hyperparameters in the `Chapter_6_DQN_wplay.py` example to improve training performance on the CartPole environment. Create any additional hyperparameters you may need.

7. Tune the hyperparameters in the `Chapter_6_DQN_lunar.py` example to improve training performance on the LunarLander environment. Create any additional hyperparameters you may need.

8. Tune the `batch_size` hyperparameter to low values of 8 or 16 all the way up to 256, 512, and 1,024 to see what effect this has on any and all the DQN examples.

9. Introduce a main function that will take command-line arguments that will allow you to configure the various hyperparameters at runtime. You will likely need to use a helper library (`argparse`) to do this.

10. Add the ability to render the training performance without blocking the training execution.

Doing two or three of these exercises can greatly improve your grasp of this knowledge, and there really is no better way to learn than doing, just ask one of your agents. Alas, we have come to the end of this chapter, and in the next section we have the summary.

Summary

In this chapter, we looked at the Hello World of DRL, the DQN algorithm, and applying DL to RL. We first looked at why we need DL in order to tackle more complex continuous observation state environments like CartPole and LunarLander. Then we looked at the more common DL environments you may use for DL and the one we use, PyTorch. From there, we installed PyTorch and set up an example using computational graphs as a low-level neural network. Following that, we built a second example with the PyTorch neural network interface in order to see the difference between a raw computational graph and neural network.

With that knowledge, we then jumped in and explored DQN in detail. We looked at how DQN uses experience replay or a replay buffer to replay events when training the network/policy in DQN. As well, we looked at how the TD loss was calculated based on the difference between the predicted and expected value. We used our old friend the Q Learning equation in order to calculate the expected value and feed back the difference as a loss to the model. By doing so, we were able to train the model/policy so the agent could solve CartPole and the LunarLander environments, given sufficient iterations.

In the next chapter, we again extend our knowledge from this chapter and explore the next level of DQN, the Double DQN or DDQN. Along with this, we will explore advances in network image processing with CNN so that we can tackle even more complex environments, such as the classic Atari.

7
Going Deeper with DDQN

Deep learning is the evolution of raw computational learning and it is quickly evolving and starting to dominate all areas of data science, **machine learning** (**ML**), and **artificial intelligence** (**AI**) in general. In turn, these enhancements have brought about incredible innovation in **deep reinforcement learning** (**DRL**) that have allowed it to play games, previously thought to be impossible. DRL is now able to tackle game environments such as the classic Atari 2600 series and play them better than a human. In this chapter, we'll look at what new features in DL allow DRL to play visual state games, such as Atari games. First, we'll look at how a game screen can be used as a visual state. Then, we'll understand how DL can consume a visual state with a new component called **convolutional neural networks** (**CNNs**). After, we'll use that knowledge to build a modified DQN agent to tackle the Atari environment. Building on that, we'll look at an enhancement of DQN called **DDQN**, or **double (dueling) DQN**. Finally, we'll finish the chapter by playing other visual environments.

In summary, in this chapter we'll look at how extensions to DL, called CNNs, can be used to observe visual states. Then, we'll use that knowledge to play Atari games and implement further enhancements as we go. The following is what we will cover in this chapter:

- Understanding visual state
- Introducing CNNs
- Working with a DQN on Atari
- Introducing DDQN
- Extending replay with prioritized experience replay

We will continue using the same virtual environment we constructed in Chapter 6, *Going Deep with DQN*, in this chapter. You will need that environment set up and configured properly in order to use the examples in this chapter.

Understanding visual state

Up until now, we have observed state as an encoded value or values. These values may have been the cell number in a grid or the x,y location in an area. Either way, these values have been encoded with respect to some reference. In the case of the grid environment, we may use a number to denote the square or a pair of numbers. For x,y coordinates, we still need to denote an origin, and examples of these three types of encoding mechanism are as follows:

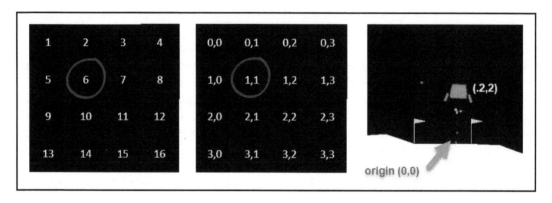

Three types of encoding state for an agent

In the preceding diagram, there are three examples of encoding state for an environment. For the first example, which is on the left, we just use a number to represent that state. Moving right to the next grid, the state is now represented as a pair of digits, row by column. On the far right, we can see our old friend the Lunar Lander and how part of its state, the location, is taken with respect to the landing pad, which is the origin. With all these cases, the state is always represented as some form of encoding, whether a single-digit or eight like in the Lander environment. By encoding, we mean that we are using a value, that is, a number, to represent that state of the environment. In Chapter 5, *Exploring SARSA*, we learned how discretization of state is a type of transformation of that encoding into simpler forms but that transforming this encoding would need to be tweaked or learned and we realized there needed to be a better way to do this. Fortunately, we did devise a better way, but before we get to that, let's consider what state it is itself.

State is just a numeric representation or index of our policy that lets our agent determine its choice of next actions. The important thing to remember here is that state needs to be an index into the policy or, in the case of DRL, the model. Therefore, our agent will always need to transform that state into a numeric index in that model. This is made substantially simpler with DL, as we have already seen. What would be ideal is for the agent to be able to visually consume the same visible state – the game area – as we humans do and learn to encode the state on its own. 10 years ago, that statement would have sounded like science fiction. Today, it is a science fact, and we will learn how that is done in the next section.

Encoding visual state

Fortunately for DRL, the concept of learning from an image has been the center of ongoing research into DL for over 30 years. DL has taken this concept from being able to recognize handwritten digits to being able to detect object position and rotation to understanding the human pose. All of this is done by feeding raw pixels into a deep learning network and it being taught (or teaching itself) how to encode those images to some answer. We will use these same tools in this chapter, but before we do, let's understand the fundamentals of taking an image and feeding it into a network. An example of how you may do this is shown in the following diagram:

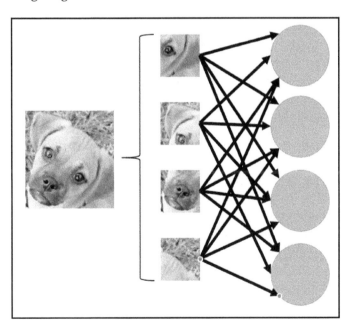

Dissecting an image for input into DL

In the preceding diagram, the image was split into four sections and each section was fed as a piece into the network. One thing to note is how each piece is fed into each neuron on the input layer. Now, we could use four pieces, like in the preceding diagram, or 100 pieces, perhaps breaking the image apart pixel by pixel. Either way, we are still blindly discretizing the space, that is, an image, and trying to make sense of it. Funnily enough, this problem that we recognized in RL with discretization is the same type of problem we encounter in deep learning. It is perhaps further compounded in DL because we would often just flatten the image, a 2D matrix of data, into a 1D vector of numbers. In the preceding example, for instance, we can see two eyes being entered into the network but no indication of a relationship, such as spacing and orientation, between them. This information is completely lost when we flatten an image and is more significant the more we discretize the input image. What we need, and what DL discovered, was a way to extract particular features from a set of data, such as an image, and preserve those features in order to classify the entire image in some manner. DL did, in fact, solve this problem very well and we will discover how in the next section.

Introducing CNNs

In September 2012, a team supervised by Dr. Geoffrey Hinton from the University of Toronto, considered the godfather of deep learning, competed to build AlexNet. AlexNet was training against a behemoth image test set called ImageNet. ImageNet consisted of more than 14 million images in over 20,000 different classes. AlexNet handily beat its competition, a non-deep learning solution, by more than 10 points that year and achieved what many thought impossible – that is, the recognition of objects in images done as well or perhaps even better than humans. Since that time, the component that made this possible – CNN – has in some cases surpassed human cognition levels in image recognition.

The component that made this possible, CNN, works by dissecting an image into features – features that it learns to detect by learning to detect those features. This sounds a bit recursive and it is, but it is also the reason it works so well. So, let's repeat that again. CNN works by detecting features in an image, except we don't specify those features – what we specify is whether the answer is right or wrong. By using that answer, we can then use backpropagation to push any errors back through the network and correct the way the network detects those features.

In order to detect features, we use filters, much the same way you may use a filter in Photoshop. These filters are the pieces that we now train and do so by introducing them in a new type of layer called CNN, convolution, or CONV. What we find is that we can then also stack those layers on top of each other to extract further features. These concepts likely still remain abstract. Fortunately, there are plenty of great tools that we can use to explore these concepts in the next exercise. Let's take a look at one:

1. Open and point a web browser to `tensorspace.org`.
2. Find the link for the **Playground** and click on it.
3. On the **TensorSpace Playground** page, note the various model names on the left-hand side. Click on the **AlexNet** example, as shown in the following screenshot:

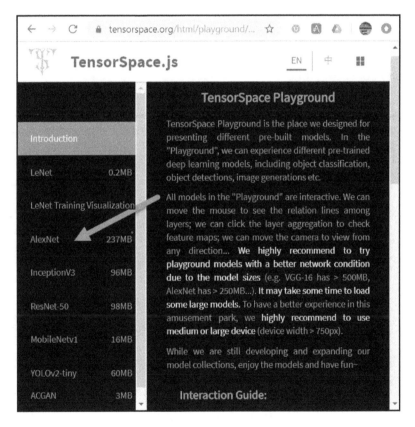

TensorSpace Playground – AlexNet

Playground allows you to interactively explore the various deep learning models, such as AlexNet, right down to the layer.

4. Move through and click on the various layers in the diagram. You can zoom in and out and explore the model in 3D. You will be able to look at all the layers in the network model. Each layer type is color coded. This includes CNN layers (yellow), as well as special pooling layers (blue).

> Pooling layers, which are layers that collect the learned features from a CNN layer, allow a network to learn quicker since the layers essentially reduce the size of the learning space. However, that reduction eliminates any spatial relationship between features. As such, we typically avoid using pooling layers in DRL and games.

5. If you zoom in, you can look at the way the image is broken by each color channel (red, green, and blue) and then fed into the network. The following screenshot shows this:

Inspecting the image separation and filter extraction

6. From the way the image is separated, we can see how the first layer of CNN, the filters, are extracting features. By doing this, it is possible to recognize the entire dog, but as you go through the layer, the features get smaller and smaller.

7. Finally, there is a final pooling layer in blue, followed by a green layer, which is a single line. This single line layer represents the input data being flattened so that it can be fed into further layers of your typical deep learning network.

Of course, feel free to explore many of the other models in the Playground. Understanding how layers extract features is import to understanding how CNN works. In the next section, we'll look at upgrading our DQN agent so that it can play Atari games using CNN.

Working with a DQN on Atari

Now that we've looked at the output CNNs produce in terms of filters, the best way to understand how this works is to look at the code that constructs them. Before we get to that, though, let's begin a new exercise where we use a new form of DQN to solve Atari:

1. Open this chapter's sample code, which can be found in the `Chapter_7_DQN_CNN.py` file. The code is fairly similar to `Chapter_6_lunar.py` but with some critical differences. We will just focus on the differences in this exercise. If you need a better explanation of the code, review `Chapter 6`, *Going Deep with DQN*:

   ```
   from wrappers import *
   ```

2. Starting at the top, the only change is a new import from a local file called `wrappers.py`. We will examine what this does by creating the environment:

   ```
   env_id = 'PongNoFrameskip-v4'
   env = make_atari(env_id)
   env = wrap_deepmind(env)
   env = wrap_pytorch(env)
   ```

3. We create the environment quite differently here for a few reasons. The three functions, `make_atari`, `wrap_deepmind`, and `wrap_pytorch`, are all located in the new `wrappers.py` file we imported earlier. These wrappers are based on the OpenAI specification for creating wrappers around the Gym environment. We will spend more time on wrappers later but for now, the three functions do the following:
   - `make_atari`: This prepares the environment so that we can capture visual input in a form we can encode with CNN. We are setting this up so we can take screenshots of the environment at set intervals.

- `wrap_deepmind`: This is another wrapper that allows for some helper tools. We will look at this later.
- `wrap_pytorch`: This is a helper library that converts the visual input image we load into the CNN network into a special form for PyTorch. The various deep learning frameworks have different input styles for CNN layers, so until all the DL frameworks are standardized, you have to be aware of which way the channels appear in your input image. In PyTorch, image channels need to be first. For other frameworks, such as Keras, it is the exact opposite.

4. After that, we need to alter some of the other code that sets the hyperparameters, as follows:

```
epsilon_start = 1.0
epsilon_final = 0.01
epsilon_decay = 30000

epsilon_by_episode = lambda episode: epsilon_final + (epsilon_start
- epsilon_final) * math.exp(-1. * episode / epsilon_decay)

plt.plot([epsilon_by_episode(i) for i in range(1000000)])
plt.show()
```

5. The highlighted lines show the changes we made. The main thing we are changing is just increasing values – a lot. The Pong Atari environment is the simplest and still may require 1 million iterations to solve. On some systems, that may take days:

```
model = CnnDQN(env.observation_space.shape, env.action_space.n)
optimizer = optim.Adam(model.parameters(), lr=0.00001)

replay_start = 10000
replay_buffer = ReplayBuffer(100000)
```

6. In the preceding block of code, we can see that we are constructing a new class called `CnnDQN`. We will get to that shortly. After that, the code is mostly the same except for a new variable, `replay_start`, and how large the replay buffer is now set to. Our buffer has increased in size 100 times from 1,000 to 100,000 entries. However, we want to be able to train the agent before the entire buffer fills now. After all, that is a lot of entries. Due to this, we're using `replay_start` to denote a training starting point for when the buffer will be used to train the agent:

```
episodes = 1400000
```

7. Next, we update the episode count to a much higher number. This is because we can expect this environment requires at least a million episodes to train an agent:

```
if episode % 200000 == 0:
    plot(episode, all_rewards, losses)
```

8. All of the other code remains the same aside from the last part of the training loop, which can be seen in the preceding code. This code shows that we plot iterations every 200,000 episodes. Previously, we did this every 2,000 episodes. You can, of course, increase this or remove it altogether if it gets annoying when training for long hours.

This environment and many of the others we will look at may now take hours or days to train. In fact, DeepMind recently estimated that it would take a regular desktop system somewhere near 45 years to train its top RL algorithms. And in case you are wondering, most of the other environments take 40 million iterations to converge. Pong is the easiest at 1 million iterations.

9. Run the example as you normally do. Wait for a while and perhaps move on to the rest of this book. This sample will take hours to train, so we will continue exploring other sections of code while it runs. To confirm the sample is running correctly though, just confirm that the environment is rendering, as shown in the following image:

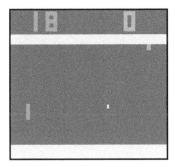

Running the code example

Keep the sample running. In the next section, we will look at how the CNN layers are built into the new model.

Adding CNN layers

Now that we understand the basic premise behind CNN layers, it's time to take an in-depth look at how they work. Open up code example, which can be found in the `Chapter_7_DQN_CNN.py` file, and follow these steps:

1. At this point, the only code we need to focus on is for a new class called `CnnDQN`, as shown here:

```python
class CnnDQN(nn.Module):
  def __init__(self, input_shape, num_actions):
    super(CnnDQN, self).__init__()

    self.input_shape = input_shape
    self.num_actions = num_actions

    self.features = nn.Sequential(
      nn.Conv2d(input_shape[0], 32, kernel_size=8, stride=4),
      nn.ReLU(),
      nn.Conv2d(32, 64, kernel_size=4, stride=2),
     nn.ReLU(),
      nn.Conv2d(64, 64, kernel_size=3, stride=1),
      nn.ReLU())
    self.fc = nn.Sequential(
      nn.Linear(self.feature_size(), 512),
      nn.ReLU(),
      nn.Linear(512, self.num_actions))

  def forward(self, x):
    x = self.features(x)
    x = x.view(x.size(0), -1)
    x = self.fc(x)
    return x

  def feature_size(self):
    return self.features(autograd.Variable(torch.zeros(1,
      *self.input_shape))).view(1, -1).size(1)

  def act(self, state, epsilon):
    if random.random() > epsilon:
      state = autograd.Variable(torch.FloatTensor(
        np.float32(state)).unsqueeze(0), volatile=True)
      q_value = self.forward(state)
      action = q_value.max(1)[1].data[0]
    else:
      action = random.randrange(env.action_space.n)
    return action
```

2. The preceding class replaces our previous vanilla DQN version. A number of key differences exist between both, so let's start with the network setup and building the first convolution layer, as shown here:

```
self.features = nn.Sequential(
    nn.Conv2d(input_shape[0], 32, kernel_size=8, stride=4),
```

3. The first thing to notice is that we are constructing a new model and putting it in `self.features`. `features` will be our model for performing convolution and separating features. The first layer is constructed by passing in `input_shape`, the number of filters (32), `kernel_size` (8), and the `stride` (4). All of these inputs are described in more detail here:

- `input_shape[0]`: The input shape refers to the observation space. With the wrappers we looked at earlier, we transformed the input space to (1, 84,84). Remember that we needed to order the channels first. With 1 channel, we can see our image is grayscale (no RGB). 1 channel is also the number we input as the first value into `Conv2d`.
- **The** number of filters (`32`): The next input represents the number of filter patches we want to construct in this layer. Each filter is applied across the image and is determined by a window size (kernel size) and movement (stride). We observed the results of these patches earlier when we used TensorSpace Playground to view CNN models in detail.
- `kernel_size` (8): This represents the window size. In this case, since we are using a 2D convolution, Conv2d, that size actually represents a value of 8x8. Passing the window or kernel over the image and applying the learned filter is the convolving operation.
- `stride` (4): Stride indicates how much the window or kernel moves between operations. A stride of 4 means that the window is moved 4 pixels or units which, as it turns out, is half the window size of 8.

4. An example of how convolution works can be seen in the following image. The upper area is a single output patch. Each element in the kernel, that is, the 3x3 patch in the following image, is the part that is being learned:

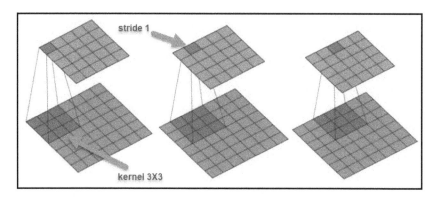

The strided convolution process explained

5. The process of applying the kernel on the image is done by simply multiplying the values in the patch with each value in the image. All these values are summed and then output as a single element in the resulting output filter operation:

```
self.fc = nn.Sequential(
    nn.Linear(self.feature_size(), 512),
```

6. Using the code that constructs the model for the convolution layers, we build another Linear model, just like we constructed in our previous examples. This model will flatten the output from the convolution layers and use that flattened model to predict actions from. We end up with two models for the network in this case but note that we will pass the output from one to the other, as well as backpropagate errors back from one model to the other. The `feature_size` function is just a helper so that we can calculate the input from the CNN model to the `Linear` model:

```
def forward(self, x):
    x = self.features(x)
    x = x.view(x.size(0), -1)
    x = self.fc(x)
    return x
```

7. Inside the `forward` function, we can see that the prediction of our model has changed. Now, we will break up the prediction by passing it to the `self.features` or the CNN part of our model. Then, we need to flatten the data and feed it into the Linear portion with `self.fc`.

8. The `action` function remains the same as our previous DQN implementation.

If the agent is still running, see if you can wait for it to finish. It can take a while but it can be both rewarding and interesting to see the final results. Like almost anything in RL, there have been various improvements to the DQN model and we will look at those in the next section.

Introducing DDQN

DDQN stands for **dueling DQN** and is different from the double DQN, although people often confuse them. Both variations assume some form of duality, but in the first case, the model is assumed to be split at the base, while in the second case, double DQN, the model is assumed to be split into two entirely different DQN models.

The following diagram shows the difference between DDQN and DQN, which is not to be confused with dueling DQN:

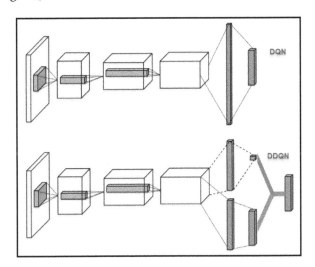

The difference between DQN and DDQN

In the preceding diagram, CNN layers are being used in both models but in the upcoming exercises, we will just use linear fully connected layers instead, just to simplify things.

Notice how the DDQN network separates into two parts that then converge back to an answer. This is the dueling part of the DDQN model we will get to shortly. Before that, though, let's explore the double DQN model.

Double DQN or the fixed Q targets

In order to understand why we may use two networks in combination, or dueling, we first need to understand why we would need to do that. Let's go back to how we calculated the TD loss and used that as our way to estimate actions. As you may recall, we calculated loss based on estimations of the target. However, in the case of our DQN model, that target is now continually changing. The analogy we can use here is that our agent may chase its own tail at times, trying to find a target. Those of you who have been very observant may have viewed this during previous training by seeing an oscillating reward. What we can do here is create another target network that we will aim for and update as we go along. This sounds way more complicated than it is, so let's look at an example:

1. Open the code example in the `Chapter_7_DoubleDQN.py` file. This example was built from the `Chapter_6_DQN_lunar.py` file that we looked at earlier. There are a number of subtle changes here, so we will review each of those in detail, starting with model construction:

```
current_model = DQN(env.observation_space.shape[0],
env.action_space.n)
target_model = DQN(env.observation_space.shape[0],
env.action_space.n)

optimizer = optim.Adam(current_model.parameters())
```

2. As its name suggests, we now construct two DQN models: one for online use and one as a target. We train the `current_model` value and then swap back to the target model every *x* number of iterations using the following code:

```
def update_target(current_model, target_model):
  target_model.load_state_dict(current_model.state_dict())

update_target(current_model, target_model)
```

3. The `update_target` function updates `target_model` so that it uses the `current_model` model. This assures us that the target Q values are always sufficiently enough ahead or behind since we are using skip traces and looking back.

4. Right after that is the `compute_td_loss` function, which needs to be updated as follows:

```
def compute_td_loss(batch_size):
  state, action, reward, next_state, done =
replay_buffer.sample(batch_size)

  state = autograd.Variable(torch.FloatTensor(np.float32(state)))
  next_state =
autograd.Variable(torch.FloatTensor(np.float32(next_state)),
    volatile=True)
  action = autograd.Variable(torch.LongTensor(action))
  reward = autograd.Variable(torch.FloatTensor(reward))
  done = autograd.Variable(torch.FloatTensor(done))

  q_values = current_model(state)
  next_q_values = current_model(next_state)
  next_q_state_values = target_model(next_state)

  q_value = q_values.gather(1, action.unsqueeze(1)).squeeze(1)
  next_q_value = next_q_state_values.gather(1,
    torch.max(next_q_values, 1)[1].unsqueeze(1)).squeeze(1)
  expected_q_value = reward + gamma * next_q_value * (1 - done)

  loss = (q_value -
autograd.Variable(expected_q_value.data)).pow(2).mean()

  optimizer.zero_grad()
  loss.backward()
  optimizer.step()

  return loss
```

5. The highlighted lines in the function show the lines that were changed. Notice how the new models, `current_model` and `target_model`, are used to predict the loss now and not just the individual model itself. Finally, in the training or trial and error loop, we can see a couple of final changes:

```
action = current_model.act(state, epsilon)
```

6. The first change is that we are now taking the action from the `current_model` model:

```
if episode % 500 == 0:
 update_target(current_model, target_model)
```

7. The second change is updating `target_model` with the weights from `current_model` using `update_target`:

```
def play_game():
 done = False
 state = env.reset()
 while(not done):
    action = current_model.act(state, epsilon_final)
    next_state, reward, done, _ = env.step(action)
    env.render()
    state = next_state
```

8. We also need to update the `play_game` function so that we can take the action from `current_model`. It may be interesting to see what happens if you change that to the target model instead.

9. At this point, run the code as you normally would and observe the results.

Now that we understand why we may want to use a different model, we will move on and learn how we can use dueling DQN or DDQN to solve the same environment.

Dueling DQN or the real DDQN

Dueling DQN or DDQN extends the concept of a fixed target or fixed Q target and extends that to include a new concept called advantage. Advantage is a concept where we determine what additional value or advantage we may get by taking other actions. Ideally, we want to calculate advantage so that it includes all the other actions. We can do this with computational graphs by separating the layers into a calculation of state value and another that calculates the advantage from all the permutations of state and action.

This construction can be seen in the following diagram:

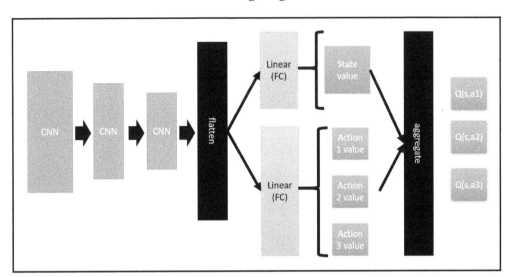

DDQN visualized in detail

The preceding diagram once again shows CNN layers, but our example will just start with the linear flattened model. What we can see is how the model is split into two parts after it is flattened. The first part calculates the state value or value and the second lower part calculates the advantage or action values. This is then aggregated to output the Q values. This setup works because we can push the loss back through the entire network using optimization, also known as backpropagation. Therefore, the network learns how to calculate the advantage of each action. Let's look at how this comes together in a new code example. Open the same in the Chapter_7_DDQN.py file and follow these steps:

1. This example uses the previous example as a source but differs in terms of a number of important details:

```
class DDQN(nn.Module):
  def __init__(self, num_inputs, num_outputs):
    super(DDQN, self).__init__()

    self.feature = nn.Sequential(
      nn.Linear(num_inputs, 128),
      nn.ReLU())

    self.advantage = nn.Sequential(
      nn.Linear(128, 128),
      nn.ReLU(),
      nn.Linear(128, num_outputs))
```

```
      self.value = nn.Sequential(
        nn.Linear(128, 128),
        nn.ReLU(),
        nn.Linear(128, 1))

  def forward(self, x):
    x = self.feature(x)
    advantage = self.advantage(x)
    value = self.value(x)
    return value + advantage - advantage.mean()

  def act(self, state, epsilon):
    if random.random() > epsilon:
      state =
autograd.Variable(torch.FloatTensor(state).unsqueeze(0),
        volatile=True)
      q_value = self.forward(state)
      action = q_value.max(1)[1].item()
    else:
      action = random.randrange(env.action_space.n)
    return action
```

2. The DDQN class is almost entirely new aside from the `act` function. Inside the init function, we can see the construction of the three submodels: `self.feature`, `self.value`, and `self.advantage`. Then, inside the `forward` function, we can see how the input, **x** is transformed by the first **feature** submodel, then fed into the advantage and value submodels. The outputs, `advantage` and `value`, are then used to calculate the predicted value, as follows:

```
return value + advantage - advantage.mean()
```

3. What we can see is that the predicted value is the state value denoted by value. This is added to the advantage or combined state-action values and subtracted from the mean or average. The result is a prediction of the best advantage or what the agent learns may be an advantage:

```
current_model = DDQN(env.observation_space.shape[0],
env.action_space.n)
target_model = DDQN(env.observation_space.shape[0],
env.action_space.n)
```

4. The next change is that we now construct two instances of the DDQN model instead of a DQN in our last double DQN example. This means that we also continue to use two models in order to evaluate our targets. After all, we don't want to go backward.

5. The next major change occurs in the `compute_td_loss` function. The updated lines are as follows:

```
q_values = current_model(state)
next_q_values = target_model(next_state)

q_value = q_values.gather(1, action.unsqueeze(1)).squeeze(1)
next_q_value = next_q_values.max(1)[0]
expected_q_value = reward + gamma * next_q_value * (1 - done)

loss = (q_value - expected_q_value.detach()).pow(2).mean()
```

6. This actually simplifies the preceding code. Now, we can clearly see that our next_q_values are being taken from the `target_model`.

7. Run the code example as you always do and watch the agent play the Lander. Make sure you keep the agent training until it reaches some amount of positive reward. This may require you to increase the number of training iterations or episodes.

 As a reminder, we use the term episode to mean one training observation or iteration for one time step. Many examples will use the word frame and frames to denote the same thing. While frame can be appropriate in some contexts, it is less so in others, especially when we start to stack frames or input observations. If you find the name confusing, an alternative may be to use training iteration.

You will see that this algorithm does indeed converge faster, but as you may expect, there are improvements we can make to this algorithm as well. We will look at how we can improve on this in the next section.

Extending replay with prioritized experience replay

So far, we've seen how using a replay buffer or experience replay mechanism allows us to pull values back in batches at a later time in order to train the network graph. These batches of data were composed of random samples, which works well, but of course, we can do better. Therefore, instead of storing just everything, we can make two decisions: what data to store and what data is a priority to use. In order to simplify things, we will just look at prioritizing what data we extract from the experience replay. By prioritizing the data we extract, we can hope this will dramatically improve the information we do feed to the network for learning and thus the whole performance of the agent.

Unfortunately, the idea behind prioritizing the replay buffer is quite simple to grasp but far more difficult in practice to derive and estimate. What we can do, though, is prioritize the return events by the TD error or loss from the prediction and the actual expected target of that event. Thus, we prioritize the values the agent predicts where the most amount of error is or where the agent is wrong the most. Another way to think of this is that we prioritize the events that surprised the agent the most. The replay buffer is structured so that it prioritizes those events by surprise level and then returns a sample of those, except it doesn't necessarily order the events by surprise. Here, it's better to randomly sample the events from a bucket or distribution ordered by surprise. This means the agent would then be more inclined to choose samples from the more average surprising events.

In this section, we'll use a Prioritized Experience Replay mechanism, which was first introduced in this paper: `https://arxiv.org/pdf/1511.05952.pdf`. It was then coded in PyTorch from this repository: `https://github.com/higgsfield/RL-Adventure/blob/master/4.prioritized%20dqn.ipynb`. Our implementation has been modified to run outside a notebook and for Python 3.6 (`https://github.com/higgsfield/RL-Adventure/blob/master/4.prioritized%20dqn.ipynb`).

We will work with an entirely new sample. Open up `Chapter_7_DDQN_wprority.py` and follow these steps:

1. The first big change in this sample is an upgrade from the `ReplayBuffer` class to `NaivePrioritizedBuffer`, as shown here:

```
class NaivePrioritizedBuffer(object):
  def __init__(self, capacity, prob_alpha=0.6):
    self.prob_alpha = prob_alpha
    self.capacity = capacity
    self.buffer = []
```

```
        self.pos = 0
        self.priorities = np.zeros((capacity,), dtype=np.float32)

    def push(self, state, action, reward, next_state, done):
        assert state.ndim == next_state.ndim
        state = np.expand_dims(state, 0)
        next_state = np.expand_dims(next_state, 0)
        max_prio = self.priorities.max() if self.buffer else 1.0

        if len(self.buffer) < self.capacity:
            self.buffer.append((state, action, reward, next_state, done))
        else:
            self.buffer[self.pos] = (state, action, reward, next_state,
done)

        self.priorities[self.pos] = max_prio
        self.pos = (self.pos + 1) % self.capacity

    def sample(self, batch_size, beta=0.4):
        if len(self.buffer) == self.capacity:
            prios = self.priorities
        else:
            prios = self.priorities[:self.pos]

        probs = prios ** self.prob_alpha
        probs /= probs.sum()

        indices = np.random.choice(len(self.buffer), batch_size,
p=probs)
        samples = [self.buffer[idx] for idx in indices]

        total = len(self.buffer)
        weights = (total * probs[indices]) ** (-beta)
        weights /= weights.max()
        weights = np.array(weights, dtype=np.float32)

        batch = list(zip(*samples))
        states = np.concatenate(batch[0])
        actions = batch[1]
        rewards = batch[2]
        next_states = np.concatenate(batch[3])
        dones = batch[4]

        return states, actions, rewards, next_states, dones, indices,
weights

    def update_priorities(self, batch_indices, batch_priorities):
        for idx, prio in zip(list(batch_indices), [batch_priorities]):
```

```
                self.priorities[idx] = prio

            def __len__(self):
                return len(self.buffer)
```

2. This code naively assigns priorities based on observed error prediction. Then, it sorts those values based on priority order. It then randomly samples those events back. Again, since the sampling is random, but the samples are aligned by priority, random sampling will generally take the samples with an average error.

3. What happens is that by reordering the samples, we reorder to expected actual distribution of data. Therefore, to account for this, we introduce a new factor called **beta**, or **importance-sampling**. **Beta** allows us to control the distribution of events and essentially reset them to their original placement:

```
beta_start = 0.4
beta_episodes = episodes / 10
beta_by_episode = lambda episode: min(1.0,
   beta_start + episode * (1.0 - beta_start) / beta_episodes)

plt.plot([beta_by_episode(i) for i in range(episodes)])
```

4. Now, we will define a function to return an increasing beta over episodes using the preceding code. Then, the code plots beta much like we plot epsilon, as shown here:

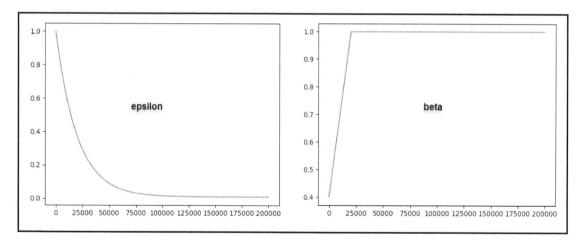

Example of beta and epsilon plots

5. After modifying the sample function in the replay buffer, we also need to update the `compute_td_loss` function, as shown here:

```
def compute_td_loss(batch_size, beta):
    state, action, reward, next_state, done, indices,
      weights = replay_buffer.sample(batch_size, beta)

    state = autograd.Variable(torch.FloatTensor(np.float32(state)))
    next_state =
autograd.Variable(torch.FloatTensor(np.float32(next_state)))
    action = autograd.Variable(torch.LongTensor(action))
    reward = autograd.Variable(torch.FloatTensor(reward))
    done = autograd.Variable(torch.FloatTensor(done))
    weights = autograd.Variable(torch.FloatTensor(weights))

    q_values = current_model(state)
    next_q_values = target_model(next_state)

    q_value = q_values.gather(1, action.unsqueeze(1)).squeeze(1)
    next_q_value = next_q_values.max(1)[0]
    expected_q_value = reward + gamma * next_q_value * (1 - done)

    loss = (q_value - expected_q_value.detach()).pow(2).mean()
    prios = loss + 1e-5
    loss = loss.mean()

    optimizer.zero_grad()
    loss.backward()
    replay_buffer.update_priorities(indices,
prios.data.cpu().numpy())
    optimizer.step()

    return loss
```

6. Only the preceding highlighted lines are different from what we have seen already. The first difference is the return of two new values: `indices` and `weights`. Then, we can see that `replay_buffer` calls `update_priorities` based on the previously returned `indices`:

```
if done:
    if episode > buffer_size and avg_reward > min_play_reward:
        play_game()
    state = env.reset()
    all_rewards.append(episode_reward)
    episode_reward = 0
```

7. Next, inside the training loop, we update the call to `play_game` and introduce a new `min_play_reward` threshold value. This allows us to set some minimum reward threshold before rendering the game. Rendering the game can be quite time-consuming and this will also speed up training:

```
if len(replay_buffer) > batch_size:
    beta = beta_by_episode(episode)
    loss = compute_td_loss(batch_size, beta)
    losses.append(loss.item())
```

8. Continuing inside the training loop, we can see how we extract `beta` and use that in the `td_compute_loss` function.

9. Run the sample again. This time, you may have to wait to see the agent drive the Lander but when it does, it will do quite well, as shown here:

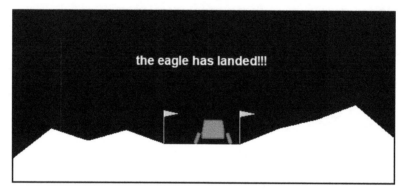

The agent landing the Lander

Typically, in a reasonably short amount of time, the agent will be able to consistently land the Lander. The algorithm should converge to landing within 75,000 iterations. You can, of course, continue to tweak and play with the hyperparameters, but that is what our next section is for.

Exercises

The further we progress in this book, the more valuable and expensive each of these exercises will become. By expensive, we mean the amount of time you need to invest in each will increase. That may mean you are inclined to do fewer exercises, but please continue to try and do two or three exercises on your own:

1. Revisit TensorSpace Playground and see if you can understand the difference pooling makes in those models. Remember that we avoid the use of pooling in order to avoid losing spatial integrity.
2. Open `Chapter_7_DQN_CNN.py` and alter some of the convolutional layer inputs such as the kernel or stride size. See what effect this has on training.
3. Tune the hyperparameters or create new ones for `Chapter_7_DoubleDQN.py`.
4. Tune the hyperparameters or create new ones for `Chapter_7_DDQN.py`.
5. Tune the hyperparameters or create new ones for `Chapter_7_DoubleDQN_wprority.py`.
6. Convert `Chapter_7_DoubleDQN.py` so that it uses convolutional layers and then upgrade the sample so that it works with an Atari environment such as Pong.
7. Convert `Chapter_7_DDQN.py` so that it uses convolutional layers and then upgrade the sample so that it works with an Atari environment such as Pong.
8. Convert `Chapter_7_DDQN_wprority.py` so that it uses convolutional layers and then upgrade the sample so that it works with an Atari environment such as Pong.
9. Add a Pooling layer in-between the convolutional layers in one of the examples. You will likely need to consult the PyTorch documentation to learn how to do this.
10. How else could you improve the experience replay buffer in the preceding example? Are there other forms of replay buffers you could use?

As always, have fun working through the samples. After all, if you are not happy watching your code play the Lunar Lander or an Atari game, when will you be?

In the next section, we'll wrap up this chapter and look at what we'll learn about next.

Summary

Extending from where we left off with DQN, we looked at ways of extending this model with CNN and adding additional networks to create double DQN and dueling DQN, or DDQN. Before exploring CNN, we looked at what visual observation encoding is and why we need it. Then, we briefly introduced CNN and used the TensorSpace Playground to explore some well-known, state-of-the-art models. Next, we added CNN to a DQN model and used that to play the Atari game environment Pong. After, we took a closer look at how we could extend DQN by adding another network as the target and adding another network to duel against or to contradict the other network, also known as the dueling DQN or DDQN. This introduced the concept of advantage in choosing an action. Finally, we looked at extending the experience replay buffer so that we can prioritize events that get captured there. Using this framework, we were able to easily land the Lander with just a short amount of agent training.

In the next chapter, we'll look at new ways of selecting policy methods and no longer look at global averages. Instead, we will sample distributions using policy gradient methods.

8
Policy Gradient Methods

Previously, our **reinforcement learning** (**RL**) methods have focused on finding the maximum or best value for choosing a particular action in any given state. While this has worked well for us in previous chapters, it certainly is not without its own problems, one of which is always determining when to actually take the max or best action, hence our exploration/exploitation trade-off. As we have seen, the best action is not always the best and it can be better to take the average of the best. However, mathematically averaging is dangerous and tells us nothing about what the agent actually sampled in the environment. Ideally, we want a method that can learn the distribution of actions for each state in the environment. This introduces a new class of methods in RL known as **Policy Gradient** (**PG**) methods and this will be our focus in this chapter.

In this chapter, we will take a look at PG methods and how they improve on our previous attempts in many different ways. We first look at understanding the intuition behind PG methods and then look to the first method, REINFORCE. After that, we will explore the class of advantage functions and introduce ourselves to actor-critic methods. From there, we will move on to looking at **Deep Deterministic Policy Gradient** methods and how they can be used to solve Lunar Lander. Then, we will progress to an advanced method known as **Trust Region Policy Optimization** and how it estimates returns based on regions of trust.

Following is a summary of the main topics we will focus on in this chapter:

- Understanding policy gradient methods
- Introducing REINFORCE
- Using advantage actor-critic
- Building a deep deterministic policy gradient
- Exploring trust region policy optimization

PG methods are mathematically far more complex than our previous attempts and go deeper into statistical and probabilistic methods. While we will focus on understanding the intuition and not the mathematics behind these methods, it may still be confusing to some readers. If you find this, you may find a refresher on statistics and probability will help. In the next section, we look to begin our understanding of the intuition behind PG methods.

 All of the code for this entire chapter was originally sourced from this GitHub repository: `https://github.com/seungeunrho/minimalRL`. The original author did an excellent job of sourcing the original collection. As per usual, the code has been significantly modified to fit the style of this book and the other code to be consistent.

Understanding policy gradient methods

One thing we need to understand about PG methods is why we need them and what the intuition is behind them. Then, we can cover some of the mathematics very briefly before diving into the code. So, let's cover the motivation behind using PG methods and what they hope to achieve beyond the other previous methods we have looked at. I have summarized the main points of why/what PG methods do and try to solve:

- **Deterministic versus stochastic functions**: We often learn early in science and mathematics that many problems require a single or deterministic answer. In the real world, however, we often equate some amount of error to deterministic calculations to quantify their accuracy. This quantification of how accurate a value is can be taken a step further with stochastic or probabilistic methods.

  Stochastic methods are often used to quantify expectation of risk or uncertainty and they do this by finding the distribution that describes a range of values. Whereas previously we used a value function to find the optimum state-value that described an action, now we want to understand the distribution that generated that value. The following diagram shows an example of a deterministic versus stochastic function output, a distribution next to the mean, median, mode, and max values:

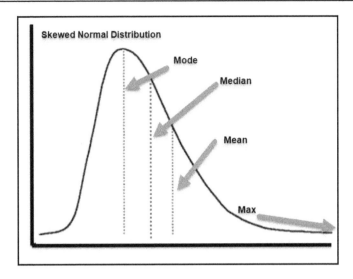

A skewed normal distribution

Previously, we assumed that our agent was always sampling from a perfectly normal distribution. This assumption allowed us to use the max or even mean (average) values. However, a normal distribution is never just normal and in most cases, an environment may not even be distributed close to normal.

- **Deterministic versus stochastic environments**: The other problem we have with our assumption of everything being normally distributed is that it often isn't and, in the real world, we often need to interpret an environment as random or stochastic. Our previous environments have been for the most part static, meaning they change very little between episodes. Real-world environments are never entirely static and, in games, that is certainly the case. So, we need an algorithm that can respond to random changes in the environment.

- **Discrete versus continuous action spaces**: We have already spent some time considering discrete versus continuous observation spaces and learned how to handle these environments with discretization and deep learning, except real-world environments and/or games are not always discrete. That is, instead of discrete actions such as up, down, left, and right, we now need to consider continuous actions such as left 10-80%, right 10-90%, up 10-90%, and so on. Fortunately, PG methods provide a mechanism that makes continuous actions easier to implement. Reciprocally, discrete action spaces are doable but don't train as well as continuous.

PG methods work much better in continuous action spaces due to the nature of the algorithm itself. They can be used to solve discrete action space environments but they generally will not perform as well as the other methods we will cover later.

Now that we understand why we need PG methods, we need to move on to the how in the next section.

Policy gradient ascent

The basic intuition behind PG methods is we move from finding a value function that describes a deterministic policy to a stochastic policy with parameters used to define a policy distribution. Thinking this way, we can now assume that our policy function needs to be defined so that our policy, π, can be set by adjusting parameters θ so that we understand the probability of taking a given action in a state. Mathematically, we can simply define this like so:

$$\pi_\theta(a|s)$$

You should consider the mathematics we cover in this chapter the minimum you need to understand the code. If you are indeed serious about developing your own extensions to PG methods, then you likely want to spend some time exploring the mathematics further using *An Introduction to Reinforcement Learning* (Barto/Sutton, 2nd edition, 2017).

π denotes the policy determined by parameters θ, where we plan to find those parameters easily enough with a deep learning network. Now, we have seen previously how we used deep learning to minimize the loss of a network with gradient descent and we will now turn the problem upside down. We now want to find the parameters that give us the best probability of taking an action for a given state that should maximize an action to 1.0 or 100%. That means instead of reducing a number, we now need to maximize it using gradient ascent. This also transforms our update from a value to a parameter that describes the policy and we rewrite our update equations like so:

$$\theta_{t+1} = \theta_t + \alpha \nabla \pi_{\theta_t}(a^*|s)$$

In the equation, we have the following:

- θ_t = The parameter's value at the previous time step
- α = The learning rate
- $\nabla \pi_{\theta_t}(a^*|s)$ = The calculated update gradient for action a^*, or the optimal action

The intuition here is that we are pushing toward the action that will yield the best policy. However, what we find is that making a further assumption of assuming all pushes are equal is just as egregious. After all, we should be able to introduce those deterministic predictions of value back into the preceding equation as a further guide to the real value. We can do this by updating the last equation like so:

$$\theta_{t+1} = \theta_t + \alpha Q(\hat{s}, a) \nabla \pi_{\theta_t}(a^*|s)$$

Here, we now introduce the following:

$Q(\hat{s}, a)$: This becomes our guess at a Q value for the given state and action pair.

Hence, state-action pairs with higher estimated Q values will benefit more than those that do not, except, we now have to take a step back and reconsider our old friend the exploration/exploitation dilemma and consider how our algorithm/agent needs to select actions. We no longer want our agent to take just the best or random action but, instead, use the learnings of the policy itself. That means a couple of things. Our agent now needs to continually sample and learn off of the same policy meaning PG is on policy but it also means we need to update our update equation to account for this like so:

$$\theta_{t+1} = \theta_t + \alpha \frac{Q(\hat{s}, a) \nabla \pi_{\theta_t}(a^*|s)}{\pi_\theta(a|s)}$$

Here, we now introduce the following:

$\pi_\theta(a|s)$: This is the probability of a given action in a given state—essentially, what the policy itself predicts.

Dividing by the policy's probability of taking an action in a given state accounts for how frequently that action may be taken. Hence, if an action is twice as popular as another, it will be updated only half as much, but likely for twice the number of times. Again, this tries to eliminate skewing of actions that get sampled more often and allow for the algorithm to weight those rare but beneficial actions more accordingly.

Now that you understand the basic intuition of our new update and process, we can see how this works in practice. Implementing PG methods in practice is more difficult mathematically but fortunately, deep learning alleviates that for us by providing gradient ascent as we will see when we tackle our first practical algorithm in the next section.

Introducing REINFORCE

The first algorithm we will look at is known as **REINFORCE**. It introduces the concept of PG in a very elegant manner, especially in PyTorch, which masks many of the mathematical complexities of this implementation. REINFORCE also works by solving the optimization problem in reverse. That is, instead of using gradient ascent, it reverses the mathematics so we can express the problem as a loss function and hence use gradient descent. The update equation now transforms to the following:

$$\theta_{t+1} = \theta_t + \alpha\hat{A}(s,a)\nabla_\theta log\pi_\theta(a|s)$$

Here, we now assume the following:

- $\hat{A}(s,a) =$ This is the advantage over the baseline expressed by $\hat{Q}(s,a)$; we will get to the advantage function in more detail shortly.
- $\nabla_\theta log\pi_\theta(a|s) =$ This is the gradient now expressed as a loss and is equivalent to $\frac{\pi_{\theta_t}(a^*|s)}{\pi_\theta(a|s)}$, assuming with the chain rule and the derivation of $1/x = log\ x$.

Essentially, we flip the equation using the chain rule and the property $1/x = log\ x$. Again, breaking down the mathematics in detail is outside the scope of this book, but the critical intuition here is the use of the log function as a derivation trick to invert our equation into a loss function combined with the advantage function.

REINFORCE stands for **REward Increment = Non-negative Factor *x* Offset Reinforcement *x* Characteristic Eligibility**. The acronym attempts to describe the mathematical intuition of the algorithm itself, where the non-negative factor represents the advantage function, $\hat{A}$. Offset reinforcement is the gradient itself denoted by ∇. Then, we introduce characteristic eligibility, which reverts back to our learning of TD and eligibility traces using π_θ. Scaling this whole factor by α or the learning rate allows us to adjust how quickly the algorithm/agent learns.

Being able to intuitively tune the hyperparameters, the learning rate (alpha) and discount factor (gamma), should be a skill you have already started to master. However, PG methods bring a different intuition into how an agent wants/needs to learn. As such, be sure to spend an equal amount of time understanding how tuning these values has changed.

Of course, as game programmers, the best way for us to understand this is to work with the code and that is exactly what we will do in the next exercise. Open example `Chapter_8_REINFORCE.py` and follow the exercise here:

1. REINFORCE in PyTorch becomes a nice compact algorithm and the entire code listing is shown here:

```python
import gym
import torch
import torch.nn as nn
import torch.nn.functional as F
import torch.optim as optim
from torch.distributions import Categorical

#Hyperparameters
learning_rate = 0.0002
gamma = 0.98

class REINFORCE(nn.Module):
    def __init__(self, input_shape, num_actions):
        super(REINFORCE, self).__init__()
        self.data = []

        self.fc1 = nn.Linear(input_shape, 128)
        self.fc2 = nn.Linear(128, num_actions)
        self.optimizer = optim.Adam(self.parameters(),
lr=learning_rate)

    def act(self, x):
        x = F.relu(self.fc1(x))
        x = F.softmax(self.fc2(x), dim=0)
        return x

    def put_data(self, item):
        self.data.append(item)

    def train_net(self):
        R = 0
        for r, log_prob in self.data[::-1]:
            R = r + gamma * R
            loss = -log_prob * R
```

```
          self.optimizer.zero_grad()
          loss.backward()
          self.optimizer.step()
        self.data = []

env = gym.make('LunarLander-v2')
pi = REINFORCE(env.observation_space.shape[0], env.action_space.n)
score = 0.0
print_interval = 100
iterations = 10000
min_play_reward = 20

def play_game():
  done = False
  state = env.reset()
  its = 500
  while(not done and its > 0):
    its -= 1
    prob = pi.act(torch.from_numpy(state).float())
    m = Categorical(prob)
    action = m.sample()
    next_state, reward, done, _ = env.step(action.item())
    env.render()
    state = next_state

for iteration in range(iterations):
  s = env.reset()
  for t in range(501):
    prob = pi.act(torch.from_numpy(s).float())
    m = Categorical(prob)
    action = m.sample()
    s_prime, r, done, info = env.step(action.item())
    pi.put_data((r,torch.log(prob[action])))

    s = s_prime
    score += r
    if done:
      if score/print_interval > min_play_reward:
        play_game()
      break
  pi.train_net()
  if iteration%print_interval==0 and iteration!=0:
    print("# of episode :{}, avg score : {}".format(iteration,
score/print_interval))
    score = 0.0

env.close()
```

2. As usual, we start with our usual imports with one new addition from `torch.distributions` called `Categorical`. Now, `Categorical` is used to sample our action space from a continuous probability back to discrete action value. After that, we initialize our base hyperparameters, `learning_rate` and `gamma`.

3. Next, we come to a new class called `REINFORCE`, which encapsulates the functionality of our agent algorithm. We have seen most of this code before in DQN and DDQN configurations. However, we want to focus on the training function, `train_net`, shown here:

```
def train_net(self):
    R = 0
    for r, log_prob in self.data[::-1]:
        R = r + gamma * R
        loss = -log_prob * R
        self.optimizer.zero_grad()
        loss.backward()
        self.optimizer.step()
    self.data = []
```

4. `train_net` is where we use the loss calculation to push back (backpropagate) errors in the policy network. Notice, in this class, we don't use a replay buffer but instead, just use a list called `data`. It should also be clear that we push all of the values in the list back through the network.

5. After the class definition, we jump to creating the environment and setting up some additional variables, shown here:

```
env = gym.make('LunarLander-v2')
pi = REINFORCE(env.observation_space.shape[0], env.action_space.n)
score = 0.0
print_interval = 100
iterations = 10000
min_play_reward = 20
```

6. You can see we are back to playing the Lunar Lander environment. The other variables are similar to ones we used before to control the amount of training and how often we output results. If you change this to a different environment, you will most likely need to adjust these values.

7. Again, the training iteration code is quite similar to our previous examples with one keen difference and that is how we sample and execute actions in the environment. Here is the code that accomplishes this part:

```
prob = pi.act(torch.from_numpy(s).float())
m = Categorical(prob)
action = m.sample()
s_prime, r, done, info = env.step(action.item())
pi.put_data((r,torch.log(prob[action])))
```

8. The main thing to notice here is we are extracting the probability of an action from the policy generated by REINFORCE using `pi.act`. After that, we convert this probability into a categorical or discrete bin of values with `Categorical`. We then extract the discrete action value using `m.sample()`. This conversion is necessary for a discrete action space such as the Lunar Lander v2 environment.

   Later, we will see how we can use this in a continuous space environment without the conversion. If you scroll up to the `play_game` function, you will note that the same code block is used to extract the action from the policy when playing the game. Pay special attention to the last line where `pi.put_data` is used to store the results and notice how we are using `torch.log` on the `prop[action]` value. Remember, by using the log function here, we convert or reverse the need to use gradient ascent to maximize an action value. Instead, we can use gradient descent and `backprop` on our policy network.

9. Run the code as you normally do and observe the results. This algorithm will generally train quickly.

The elegance of this algorithm especially in PyTorch obfuscates the complex mathematics here beautifully. Unfortunately, that may not be a good thing unless you understand the intuition. In the next section, we explore the advantage function we mentioned earlier in the last exercise and look at how this relates to actor-critic methods.

Using advantage actor-critic

We have already discussed the concept of advantage a few times throughout a few previous chapters including the last exercise. Advantage is often thought of as understanding the difference between applying different agents/policies to the same problem. The algorithm learns the advantage and, in turn, the benefits it provides to enhancing reward. This is a bit abstract so let's see how this applies to one of our previous algorithms like DDQN. With DDQN, advantage was defined by understanding how to narrow the gap in moving to a known target or goal. Refer back to Chapter 7, *Going Deeper with DDQN*, if you need a refresher.

The concept of advantage can be extended to what we refer to as actor-critic methods. With actor-critic, we define advantage by training two networks, one as an actor; that is, it makes decisions on the policy, and another network critiques those decisions based on expected returns. The goal now will not only be to optimize the actor and critic but to do so in a manner to reduce the number of surprises. You can think of a surprise as a time when the agent may expect some reward but instead doesn't or possibly receives more reward. With AC methods, the goal is to minimize surprises and it does this by using a value-based approach (DQN) as the critic and a PG (REINFORCE) method as the actor. See the following diagram to see how this comes together:

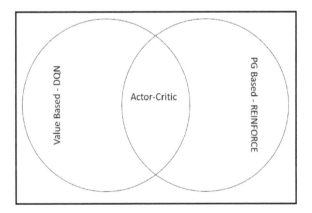

Explaining actor-critic methods

In the next section, we jump in and see how AC can be applied to our previous PG example.

Actor-critic

AC methods use a combination of networks to predict the output of the value and policy functions, where our value function network resembles DQN and our policy function is defined using a PG method such as REINFORCE. Now, for the most part, this is as simple as it sounds; however, there are several details in the way in which we code these implementations that require some attention. We will, therefore, cover the details of this implementation as we review the code. Open `Chapter_8_ActorCritic.py` and follow the next exercise:

1. As this code follows the same pattern as previous examples, we will only need to cover a few sections in detail. The first section of importance is the new `ActorCritic` class at the top of the file and shown here:

```python
class ActorCritic(nn.Module):
  def __init__(self, input_shape, num_actions):
    super(ActorCritic, self).__init__()
    self.data = []
    self.fc1 = nn.Linear(input_shape,256)
    self.fc_pi = nn.Linear(256,num_actions)
    self.fc_v = nn.Linear(256,1)
    self.optimizer = optim.Adam(self.parameters(), lr=learning_rate)

  def pi(self, x, softmax_dim = 0):
    x = F.relu(self.fc1(x))
    x = self.fc_pi(x)
    prob = F.softmax(x, dim=softmax_dim)
    return prob

  def v(self, x):
    x = F.relu(self.fc1(x))
    v = self.fc_v(x)
    return v

  def put_data(self, transition):
    self.data.append(transition)

  def make_batch(self):
    s_lst, a_lst, r_lst, s_prime_lst, done_lst = [], [], [], [], []
    for transition in self.data:
      s,a,r,s_prime,done = transition
      s_lst.append(s)
      a_lst.append([a])
      r_lst.append([r/100.0])
      s_prime_lst.append(s_prime)
      done_mask = 0.0 if done else 1.0
```

```
            done_lst.append([done_mask])
        s_batch, a_batch, r_batch, s_prime_batch, done_batch
            = torch.tensor(s_lst, dtype=torch.float),
            torch.tensor(a_lst), \
            torch.tensor(r_lst, dtype=torch.float),
            torch.tensor(s_prime_lst,   dtype=torch.float), \
            torch.tensor(done_lst, dtype=torch.float)

        self.data = []
        return s_batch, a_batch, r_batch, s_prime_batch, done_batch

    def train_net(self):
        s, a, r, s_prime, done = self.make_batch()
        td_target = r + gamma * self.v(s_prime) * done
        delta = td_target - self.v(s)
        pi = self.pi(s, softmax_dim=1)
        pi_a = pi.gather(1,a)
        loss = -torch.log(pi_a) * delta.detach()
            + F.smooth_l1_loss(self.v(s), td_target.detach())
        self.optimizer.zero_grad()
        loss.mean().backward()
        self.optimizer.step()
```

2. Starting at the init function, we can see that we construct three Linear network layers: fc1 and fc_pi for policy and fc_v for value. Then, right after init, we see the pi and v functions. These functions do the forward pass for each network (pi and v). Notice how both networks share fc1 as an input layer. That means that the first layer in our network will be used to encode network state in a form both the actor and critic networks will share. Sharing layers like this is common in more advanced network configurations.

3. Next, we see the put_data function, which just puts memories into a replay or experience buffer.

4. After that, we have an imposing function called make_batch, which just builds the batches of data we use in experience replay.

5. We will skip over the ActorCritic training function, train_net, and jump down to the iteration training code shown here:

```
for iteration in range(iterations):
 done = False
 s = env.reset()
 while not done:
   for t in range(n_rollout):
     prob = model.pi(torch.from_numpy(s).float())
     m = Categorical(prob)
     a = m.sample().item()
```

```
            s_prime, r, done, info = env.step(a)
            model.put_data((s,a,r,s_prime,done))

            s = s_prime
            score += r
            if done:
              if score/print_interval > min_play_reward:
                play_game()
              break

        model.train_net()

        if iteration%print_interval==0 and iteration!=0:
          print("# of episode :{},
            avg score : {:.1f}".format(iteration,
    score/print_interval))
            score = 0.0

    env.close()
```

6. You may not have noticed, but our last exercise used episodic training or what we refer to as Monte Carlo or off-policy training. This time, our training takes place on-policy, and that means our agent acts as soon as it receives new updates. Otherwise, the code is quite similar to many other examples we have and will run.

7. Run the example as you normally would. Training may take a while, so start it running and jump back to this book.

Now that we understand the basic layout of the example code, it is time to get into the details of training in the next section.

Training advantage AC

Using advantage and training multiple networks to work together as you may imagine is not trivial. Therefore, we want to focus a whole exercise on understanding how training works in AC. Open up `Chapter_8_ActorCritic.py` again and follow the exercise:

1. Our main focus will be the `train_net` function in the `ActorCritic` class we saw before. Starting with the first two lines, we can see this is where the training batch is first made and we calculate `td_target`. Recall we covered the form of TD error calculation check when we implemented DDQN:

```
s, a, r, s_prime, done = self.make_batch()
td_target = r + gamma * self.v(s_prime) * done
```

2. Next, we calculate the change or delta between our target and the value function. Again, this was covered in DDQN and the code to do this is shown here:

```
delta = td_target - self.v(s)
```

3. After that, we do a forward pass over the π network with `self.pi` and then gather the results. The gather function essentially aligns or gathers data. Interested readers should consult the PyTorch site for further documentation on `gather`. The code for this step is here:

```
pi = self.pi(s, softmax_dim=1)
pi_a = pi.gather(1,a)
```

4. Then, we calculate the loss with the following code:

```
loss = -torch.log(pi_a) * delta.detach()
    + F.smooth_l1_loss(self.v(s), td_target.detach())
```

5. Loss is calculated using the updated policy method where we use log to inverse optimize for our actions. Recall, in our previous discussion, the introduction of the $\hat{A}$ function. This function denotes the advantage function where we take the negative log of the policy and add it to the output of the L1 squared errors from the value function, v, and `td_target`. The `detach` function on the tensors just allows for the network to not update those values when training.

6. Finally, we push the loss back through the network with the following code:

```
self.optimizer.zero_grad()
loss.mean().backward()
self.optimizer.step()
```

7. There's nothing new here. The code first zeroes out the gradients, then calculates the mean loss of the batch and pushes that backward with a call to `backward`, finishing with stepping the optimizer using `step`.

You will need to tune the hyperparameters in this example to train an agent to complete the environment. Of course, you are more than up to the challenge by now. In the next section, we will move up and look at another class of PG methods.

Building a deep deterministic policy gradient

One of the problems we face with PG methods is that of variability or too much randomness. Of course, we might expect that from sampling from a stochastic or random policy. The **Deep Deterministic Policy Gradient** (**DDPG**) method was introduced in a paper titled *Continuous control with deep reinforcement learning*, in 2015 by Tim Lillicrap. It was meant to address the problem of controlling actions through continuous action spaces, something we have avoided until now. Remember that a continuous action space differs from a discrete space in that the actions may indicate a direction but also an amount or value that expresses the effort in that direction whereas, with discrete actions, any action choice is assumed to always be at 100% effort.

So, why does this matter? Well, in our previous chapter exercises, we explored PG methods over discrete action spaces. By using these methods in discrete spaces, we essentially buffered or masked the problem of variability by converting action probabilities into discrete values. However, in environments with continuous control or continuous action spaces, this does not work so well. Enter DDPG. The answer is in the name: deep deterministic policy gradient, which, in essence, means we are introducing determinism back into a PG method to rectify the problem of variability.

The last two PG methods we will cover in this chapter, DDPG and TRPO, are generally considered need-specific and in some cases too complex to implement effectively. Therefore, in the past few years, these methods have not seen much use in more state-of-the-art development. The code for these methods has been provided for completeness but the explanations may be rushed.

Let's see how this looks in code by opening `Chapter_8_DDPG.py` and following the next exercise:

1. The full source code for this example is too large to list in full. Instead, we will go through the relevant sections in the exercise, starting with the hyperparameters, here:

```
lr_mu = 0.0005
lr_q = 0.001
gamma = 0.99
batch_size = 32
buffer_limit = 50000
tau = 0.005
```

2. It looks like we have introduced a few new hyperparameters but we really only introduce one new one called `tau`. The other variables, `lr_mu` and `lr_q`, are learning rates for two different networks.

3. Next, we jump past the `ReplayBuffer` class, which is something we have seen before for storing experiences, then past the other code until we come to the environment setup and more variable definitions, as shown here:

```
env = gym.make('Pendulum-v0')
memory = ReplayBuffer()

q, q_target = QNet(), QNet()
q_target.load_state_dict(q.state_dict())
mu, mu_target = MuNet(), MuNet()
mu_target.load_state_dict(mu.state_dict())

score = 0.0
print_interval = 20
min_play_reward = 0
iterations = 10000

mu_optimizer = optim.Adam(mu.parameters(), lr=lr_mu)
q_optimizer = optim.Adam(q.parameters(), lr=lr_q)
ou_noise = OrnsteinUhlenbeckNoise(mu=np.zeros(1))
```

4. First, we see the setup of a new environment, `Pendulum`. Now, `Pendulum` is a continuous control environment that requires learning continuous space actions. After that, `memory` and `ReplayBuffer` are created, followed by the creation of a couple of classes called `QNet` and `MuNet`. Next, more control/monitoring parameters are initialized. Just before the last line, we see the creation of two optimizers, `mu_optimizer` and `q_optimizer`, for the `MuNet` and `QNet` networks respectively. Finally, on the last line, we see the creation of a new tensor called `ou_noise`. There is a lot of new stuff going on here but we will see how this all comes together shortly:

```
for iteration in range(iterations):
  s = env.reset()
  for t in range(300):
```

5. Next, move down to the top of the train loop shown in the preceding lines. We make sure that the algorithm can loop entirely through an episode. Hence, we set the range in the inner loop to a value higher than the iterations the agent is given in the environment:

```
a = mu(torch.from_numpy(s).float())
a = a.item() + ou_noise()[0]
s_prime, r, done, info = env.step([a])
memory.put((s,a,r/100.0,s_prime,done))
score +=r
s = s_prime
```

6. Next comes the trial and error training code. Notice that the a action is taken from the network called mu. Then, in the next line, we add the ou_noise value to it. After that, we let the agent take a step, put the results in memory, and update the score and state. The noise value we use here is based on the Ornstein-Uhlenbeck process and is generated by the class of the same name. This process generates a moving stochastic value that tends to converge to the value μ or mu.

Recall that we initialized this value to zeroes in the earlier instantiation of the OrnsteinUhlenbeckNoise class. The intuition here is that we want the noise to converge to 0 over the experiment. This has the effect of controlling the amount of exploration the agent performs. More noise yields more uncertainty in the actions it selects and hence the agent selects more randomly. You can think of noise in an action now as the amount of uncertainty an agent has in that action and how much more it needs to explore to reduce that uncertainty.

 The Ornstein-Uhlenbeck process is used for noise here because it converges in a random but predictable manner, in that it always converges. You could, of course, use any value you like here for the noise, even something more deterministic.

7. Staying inside the training loop, we jump to the section that performs the actual training using the following code:

```
if memory.size()>2000:
  for i in range(10):
    train(mu, mu_target, q, q_target, memory, q_optimizer,
mu_optimizer)
    soft_update(mu, mu_target)
    soft_update(q, q_target)
```

8. We can see here that once the memory `ReplayBuffer` is above `2000`, the agent begins training in loops of 10. First, we see a call to the `train` function with the various networks/models constructed, `mu`, `mu_target`, `q`, and `q_target`; `memory`; and the `q_optimizer` and `mu_optimizer` optimizers. Then, there are two calls to the `soft_update` function with the various models. `soft_update`, shown here, just converges the input model to the target in an iterative fashion using `tau` to scale the amount of change per iteration:

```
def soft_update(net, net_target):
  for param_target, param in zip(net_target.parameters(),
net.parameters()):
    param_target.data.copy_(param_target.data * (1.0 - tau) +
param.data * tau)
```

9. This convergence from some acting model to a target is not new but, with the introduction of AC, it does complicate things. Before we get to that though, let's run the sample and see it in action. Run the code as you normally would and wait: this one can take a while. If your agent reaches a high enough score, you will be rewarded with the following:

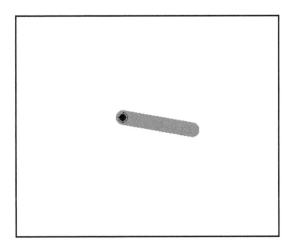

An example of the Pendulum environment

As the sample runs pay particular attention to how the score is being updated on the screen. Try and get a sense of how this may look graphically. In the next section, we will explore the finer details of this last example.

Training DDPG

Now, as you may have noticed in the last example, `Chapter_8_DDPG.py` is using four networks/models to train, using two networks as actors and two as critics, but also using two networks as targets and two as current. This gives us the following diagram:

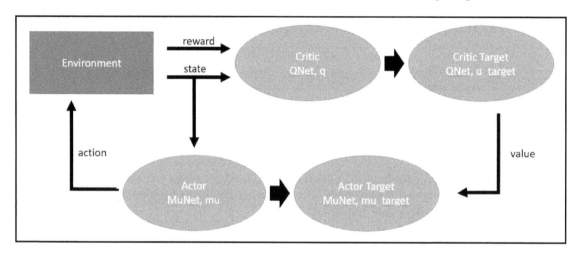

Diagram of actor-critic target-current networks

Each oval in the preceding diagram represents a complete deep learning network. Notice how the critic, the value or Q network implementation, is taking both environment outputs reward and state. The critic then pushes a value back to the actor or policy target network.

Open example `Chapter_8_DDPG.py` back up and follow the next exercise to see how this comes together in code:

1. We will first look at our definition of the critic or the `QNet` network class shown here:

```python
class QNet(nn.Module):
    def __init__(self):
        super(QNet, self).__init__()

        self.fc_s = nn.Linear(3, 64)
        self.fc_a = nn.Linear(1,64)
        self.fc_q = nn.Linear(128, 32)
        self.fc_3 = nn.Linear(32,1)

    def forward(self, x, a):
        h1 = F.relu(self.fc_s(x))
```

```
h2 = F.relu(self.fc_a(a))
cat = torch.cat([h1,h2], dim=1)
q = F.relu(self.fc_q(cat))
q = self.fc_3(q)
return q
```

2. The construction of this network is also a little different and what happens here is the `fc_s` layer encodes the state, then `fc_a` encodes the actions. These two layers are joined in the forward pass to create a single Q layer, `fc_q`, which is then output through the last layer, `fc_3`.

If you need help picturing these types of networks, it can be and is often helpful to draw them out. The key here is to look at the code in the train function, which describes how the layers are joined.

3. Moving from the critic, we move to the actor network as defined by the `MuNet` class and shown here:

```
class MuNet(nn.Module):
    def __init__(self):
        super(MuNet, self).__init__()
        self.fc1 = nn.Linear(3, 128)
        self.fc2 = nn.Linear(128, 64)
        self.fc_mu = nn.Linear(64, 1)

    def forward(self, x):
        x = F.relu(self.fc1(x))
        x = F.relu(self.fc2(x))
        mu = torch.tanh(self.fc_mu(x))*2
        return mu
```

4. `MuNet` is a fairly simple implementation of a network that encodes the state from 3 values to 128 input neurons, `fc1`, followed by 64 hidden layer neurons, `fc2`, and then finally output to a single value on the output layer, `fc_mu`. The only note of interest is the way we translate `fc_mu`, the output layer in the `forward` function, into the `mu` output value. This is done to account for the control range in the `Pendulum` environment, which takes action values in the range -2 to 2. If you convert this sample into another environment, be sure to account for any change in action space values.

5. Next, we will move down to the start of the `train` function, as shown here:

```
def train(mu, mu_target, q, q_target, memory, q_optimizer,
mu_optimizer):
    s,a,r,s_prime,done_mask = memory.sample(batch_size)
```

6. The `train` function takes all of the networks, memory, and optimizer as inputs. In the first line, it extracts the s state, a action, r reward, s_prime next state, and done_mask from the replayBuffer memory:

```
target = r + gamma * q_target(s_prime, mu_target(s_prime))
q_loss = F.smooth_l1_loss(q(s,a), target.detach())
q_optimizer.zero_grad()
q_loss.backward()
q_optimizer.step()
```

7. The first block of code inside the function calculates the target value based on the output of the q_target network, which takes as input the last state, s_prime, and mu_target output from the last state. Then, we calculate the q_loss loss based on the output of the q network with an input state and action using the target values as the target. This somewhat abstract conversion is to convert the value from stochastic into deterministic. On the last three lines, we see the typical optimizer code for zeroing the gradient and doing a backprop pass:

```
mu_loss = -q(s,mu(s)).mean()
mu_optimizer.zero_grad()
mu_loss.backward()
mu_optimizer.step()
```

8. Calculating the mu_loss policy loss is much simpler and all we do is take the output of the q network using the state and output action from the mu network. A couple of things to note is that we make the loss negative and take the mean or average. Then, we finish the function with a typical optimizer backprop on mu_loss.

9. If the agent is still running from the previous exercise, examine the results with this newfound knowledge. Consider how or what hyperparameters you could tune to improve the results of this example.

For some, the pure code explanation of DDPG may be a bit abstract but hopefully not. Hopefully, by this point, you can read the code and assume the mathematics or intuition you need to understand the concepts. In the next section, we will look to what is considered one of the more complicated methods in DRL, the **Trust Region Policy Optimization (TRPO)** method.

Exploring trust region policy optimization

PG methods suffer from several technical issues, some of which you may have already noticed. These issues manifest themselves in training and you may have already observed this in lack of training convergence or wobble. This is caused by several factors we can summarize here:

- **Gradient ascent versus gradient descent**: In PG, we use gradient ascent to assume the maximum action value is at the top of a hill. However, our chosen optimization methods (SGD or ADAM) are tuned for gradient descent or looking for values at the bottom of hills or flat areas, meaning they work well finding the bottom of a trough but do poorly finding the top of a ridge, especially if the ridge or hill is steep. A comparison of this is shown here:

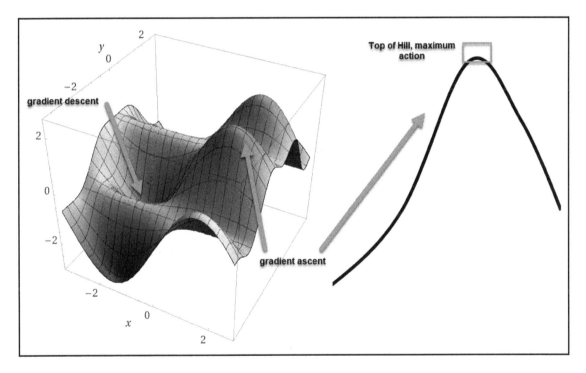

A comparison of gradient descent and ascent

Finding the peak, therefore, becomes the problem, especially in environments that require fine control or narrow discrete actions. This often appears as training wobble, where the agent keeps increasing in score but then falls back several steps every so often.

- **Policy versus parameter space mapping**: By its very nature, we will often be required to map a policy to some known action space either through continuous or discretization transformation. This step, unsurprisingly, is not without issue. Discretizing action space can be especially problematic and further compounds the hill-climbing problem from earlier.

- **Static versus dynamic learning rate**: In part due to the optimizer problem we mentioned earlier, we also tend to find that using a static learning rate is problematic. That is, we often find that we need to decrease the learning rate as the agent continues to find the peak of those maximum action hills.

- **Policy sampling efficiency**: PG methods restrict us from updating the policy more than once per trajectory. If we try to update more frequently, after x number of steps, for instance, we see training diverge. Therefore, we are restricted to one update per trajectory or episode. This can provide for very poor sample efficiency especially in training environments with multiple steps.

TRPO and another PG method called **proximal policy optimization**, which we will look at in Chapter 9, *Asynchronous Action and the Policy*, attempt to resolve all of the previous issues using several common strategies.

The code for this TRPO implementation was sourced directly from https://github.com/ikostrikov/pytorch-trpo and, at the time of writing, the code was only modified slightly to allow for easier running. This is a great example and worthy of further exploration and enhancements.

Before we get to reviewing each of these strategies, let's open the code for and follow the next exercise:

1. TRPO is a hefty algorithm not easily run in a single file. We will start by looking at the code structure by opening the TRPO folder in the source folder for this chapter. This example covers code in several files and we will only review small snippets here. It is recommended you quickly review the source fully before continuing.

2. Refer to the main.py file; this is the startup file. main takes several parameters defined within this file as inputs when running.

3. Scroll to about the middle and you will see where the environment is constructed on the main policy and value networks, as shown here:

```
env = gym.make(args.env_name)

num_inputs = env.observation_space.shape[0]
num_actions = env.action_space.shape[0]
```

```
env.seed(args.seed)
torch.manual_seed(args.seed)

policy_net = Policy(num_inputs, num_actions)
value_net = Value(num_inputs)
```

4. Next, scroll down further until you come to that familiar training loop. For the most part, this should look similar to other examples, except for the introduction of another `while` loop, shown here:

```
while num_steps < args.batch_size:
```

5. This code assures that one agent episode consists of a given number of steps determined by `batch_size`. However, we still don't break the inner training loop until the environment says the episode is done. However, now, an episode or trajectory update is not done until the provided `batch_size` is reached. This attempts to solve the PG method sampling problem we talked about earlier.

6. Do a quick review of each of the source files; the list here summarizes the purpose of each:

   - `main.py`: This is the startup source file and main point of agent training.
   - `conjugate_gradients.py`: This is a helper method to conjugate or join gradients.
   - `models.py`: This file defines the network class Policy (actor) and value (the critic). The construction of these networks is a little unique so be sure to see how.
   - `replay_memory.py`: This is a helper class to contain replay memory.
   - `running_state.py`: This is a helper class to compute the running variance of the state, essentially, running estimates of mean and standard deviation. This can be beneficial for an arbitrary sampling of a normal distribution.
   - `trpo.py`: This is the code specific to TRPO and is meant to address those PG problems we mentioned earlier.
   - `utils.py`: This provides some helper methods.

7. Use the default start parameters and run `main.py` as you normally would a Python file and watch the output, as shown here:

```
C:\ProgramData\Anaconda3\envs\game\python.exe                                    —    □    ×
fval before -2.056834235095027e-17
a/e/r 0.004196146307487529 0.004245106934584498 0.988466573904631
fval after -0.00419614630748755
Episode 91      Last reward: -912.6011060549151 Average reward -973.64
('lagrange multiplier:', tensor(0.2289), 'grad_norm:', tensor(0.0912))
fval before 7.105427357601002e-17
a/e/r 0.004674936250927307 0.0045777398718830084 1.021232394536284
fval after -0.004674936250927236
Episode 92      Last reward: -1011.7306568770845        Average reward -998.55
('lagrange multiplier:', tensor(0.2264), 'grad_norm:', tensor(0.1863))
fval before -9.349246523159213e-18
a/e/r 0.004193475940531191 0.0045323531795798495 0.925231502131069
fval after -0.0041934759405312
Episode 93      Last reward: -998.7409040861277 Average reward -1002.09
('lagrange multiplier:', tensor(0.1980), 'grad_norm:', tensor(0.1286))
fval before 1.6828643741686585e-17
a/e/r 0.0036979960207453337 0.003958261570809577 0.9342475110832528
fval after -0.0036979960207453168
Episode 94      Last reward: -903.6812992964333 Average reward -1006.95
('lagrange multiplier:', tensor(0.2623), 'grad_norm:', tensor(0.2498))
fval before -4.113668470190054e-17
a/e/r 0.005604256367298496 0.005227386032703227 1.0720953708483585
fval after -0.005604256367298536
Episode 95      Last reward: -1004.4161781600075        Average reward -1010.09
('lagrange multiplier:', tensor(0.2762), 'grad_norm:', tensor(0.3254))
fval before 1.3088945132422898e-17
a/e/r 0.005118301075806763 0.005511908796890441 0.9285895802002869
fval after -0.00511830107580675
Episode 96      Last reward: -1017.8063539769834        Average reward -1003.34
```

The output of the TRPO sample

The output from this particular implementation is more verbose and displays factors that monitor performance over the issues we mentioned PG methods suffer from. In the next few sections, we will walk through exercises that show how TRPO tries to address these problems.

 Jonathan Hui (`https://medium.com/@jonathan_hui`) has several excellent posts on Medium.com that discuss various implementations of DRL algorithms. He does an especially good job of explaining the mathematics behind TRPO and other more complex methods.

Conjugate gradients

The fundamental problem we need to address with policy methods is the conversion to a natural gradient form of gradient ascent. Previously, we handled conjugating this gradient by simply applying the log function. However, this does not yield a natural gradient. Natural gradients are not susceptible to model parameterization and provide an invariant method to compute stable gradients. Let's look at how this is done in code by opening up our IDE to the TRPO example again and following the next exercise:

1. Open the `trpo.py` file in the TRPO folder. The three functions in this file are meant to address the various problems we encounter with PG. The first problem we encounter is to reverse the gradient and the code to do that is shown here:

```python
def conjugate_gradients(Avp, b, nsteps, residual_tol=1e-10):
    x = torch.zeros(b.size())
    r = b.clone()
    p = b.clone()
    rdotr = torch.dot(r, r)
    for i in range(nsteps):
        _Avp = Avp(p)
        alpha = rdotr / torch.dot(p, _Avp)
        x += alpha * p
        r -= alpha * _Avp
        new_rdotr = torch.dot(r, r)
        betta = new_rdotr / rdotr
        p = r + betta * p
        rdotr = new_rdotr
        if rdotr < residual_tol:
            break
    return x
```

2. The `conjugate_gradients` function is used iteratively to produce a natural more stable gradient we can use for the ascent.

3. Scroll down to the `trpo_step` function and you will see how this method is used as shown in the code here:

```python
stepdir = conjugate_gradients(Fvp, -loss_grad, 10)
```

4. This outputs a `stepdir` tensor denoting the gradient used to step the network. We can see by the input parameters the output conjugate gradient will be solved over 10 iterations using an approximation function, `Fvp`, and the inverse of the loss gradient, `loss_grad`. This is entangled with some other optimizations so we will pause here for now.

Conjugate gradients are one method we can use to better manage the gradient descent versus gradient ascent problem we encounter with PG methods. Next, we will look at further optimization again to address problems with gradient ascent.

Trust region methods

A further optimization we can apply to gradient ascent is using trust regions or controlled regions of updates. These methods are of course fundamental to TRPO given the name but the concept is further extended to other policy-based methods. In TRPO, we extend regions of trust over the approximation functions using the **Minorize-Maximization** or **MM** algorithm. The intuition of MM is that there is a lower bound function that we can always expect the returns/reward to be higher than. Hence, if we maximize this lower bound function, we also attain our best policy. Gradient descent by default is a line search algorithm but this again introduces the problem of overshooting. Instead, we can first approximate the step size and then establish a region of trust within that step. This trust region then becomes the space we optimize for.

The analogy we often use to explain this involves asking you to think of yourself climbing a narrow ridge. You run the risk of falling off either side of the ridge so using normal gradient descent or line search becomes dangerous. Instead, you decide that to avoid falling you want to step on the center of the ridge or the center region you trust. The following screenshot taken from a blog post by Jonathan Hui shows this concept further:

Line search
(like gradient ascent)

Trust region

A comparison of line search versus Trust region

We can see how this looks in code by opening up the TRPO folder and following the next exercise:

1. Open up `trpo.py` again and scroll down to the following block of code:

```
def linesearch(model, f, x, fullstep, expected_improve_rate,
  max_backtracks=10, accept_ratio=.1):
fval = f(True).data
print("fval before", fval.item())
for (_n_backtracks, stepfrac) in
enumerate(.5**np.arange(max_backtracks)):
    xnew = x + stepfrac * fullstep
    set_flat_params_to(model, xnew)
    newfval = f(True).data
    actual_improve = fval - newfval
    expected_improve = expected_improve_rate * stepfrac
    ratio = actual_improve / expected_improve
    print("a/e/r", actual_improve.item(), expected_improve.item(),
     ratio.item())

if ratio.item() > accept_ratio and actual_improve.item() > 0:
  print("fval after", newfval.item())
  return True, xnew

return False, x
```

2. The `linesearch` function is used to find how far up the ridge we want to locate the next region of trust. This function is used to indicate the distance to the next region of trust and is executed with the following code:

```
success, new_params = linesearch(model, get_loss, prev_params,
fullstep,
    neggdotstepdir / lm[0])
```

3. Notice the use of `neggdotstepdir`. This value is calculated from the step direction, `stepdir`, we calculated in the last exercise with the following code:

```
neggdotstepdir = (-loss_grad * stepdir).sum(0, keepdim=True)
```

4. Now that we have a direction with `neggdotstepdir` and an amount with `linesearch`, we can determine the trust region with the following code:

```
set_flat_params_to(model, new_params)
```

5. The `set_flat_params_to` function is in `utils.py` and the code is shown here:

```
def set_flat_params_to(model, flat_params):
  prev_ind = 0
  for param in model.parameters():
    flat_size = int(np.prod(list(param.size())))
    param.data.copy_(
      flat_params[prev_ind:prev_ind +
flat_size].view(param.size()))
    prev_ind += flat_size
```

6. This code essentially flattens the parameters into the trust region. This is the trust region we test to determine whether the next step is within, using the `linesearch` function.

Now we understand the concept of trust regions and the need to properly control step size, direction, and amount when using PG methods. In the next section, we will look at the step itself.

The TRPO step

As you can see now, taking a step or update with TRPO is not trivial and things are still going to get more complicated. The step itself requires the agent to learn several factors from updating the policy and value function to also attain an advantage, also known as actor-critic. Understanding the actual details of the step function is beyond the scope of this book and you are again referred to those external references. However, it may be helpful to review what constitutes a step in TRPO and how this may compare complexity wise to other methods we look at in the future. Open up the sample TRPO folder again and follow the next exercise:

1. Open up the `main.py` file and find the following line of code, around line 130:

```
trpo_step(policy_net, get_loss, get_kl, args.max_kl, args.damping)
```

2. This last line of code is within the `update_params` function, which is where the bulk of the training takes place.
3. You can further see at almost the bottom of the `main.py` file a call to the `update_params` function with `batch`, `batch` being a sample from `memory`, as shown in the following code:

```
batch = memory.sample()
update_params(batch)
```

4. Scroll back up to the `update_params` function and notice the first loop that builds `returns`, `deltas,` and `advantages` with the following code:

```
for i in reversed(range(rewards.size(0))):
    returns[i] = rewards[i] + args.gamma * prev_return * masks[i]
    deltas[i] = rewards[i] + args.gamma * prev_value *
        masks[i] - values.data[i]
    advantages[i] = deltas[i] + args.gamma * args.tau *
        prev_advantage * masks[i]
```

5. Notice how we reverse the rewards and then loop through them to build our various lists `returns`, `deltas,` and `advantages`.

6. From there, we flatten the parameters and set the value network, the critic. Then, we calculate the advantages and actions mean and standard deviation. We do this as we are working with distributions and not deterministic values.

7. After that, we use the `trpo_step` function to take a training step or update in the policy.

You may have noticed the use of `kl` in the source code. This stands for KL divergence and is something we will explore in a later chapter.

Keep the example running for around 5,000 training iterations. This may take some time so be patient. It is worth running to completion, if not just once. The TRPO example in this section is meant to be experimented with and used with various control environments. In the next section, be sure to review the experiments you can play with to explore more about this method.

Exercises

Use the exercises for your enjoyment and learning and to gain additional experience. Deep learning and deep reinforcement learning are very much areas where your knowledge will only improve by working with the examples. Don't expect to be a natural with training agents; it takes a lot of trial and error. Fortunately, the amount of experience we need is not as much as our poor agents require but still expect to put some time in.

1. Open example `Chapter_8_REINFORCE.py` back up and alter the hyperparameters to see what effect this has on training.

2. Open example `Chapter_8_ActorCritic.py` back up and alter the hyperparameters to see what effect this has on training.

3. Open example `Chapter_8_DDPG.py` back up and alter the hyperparameters to see what effect this has on training.

4. How can you convert the **REINFORCE** or `ActorCritic` examples to use continuous action spaces? Attempt to do this for new environments such as `LunarLanderContinous-v2`.

5. Set up example `Chapter_8_DDPG.py` to use the `LunarLanderContinuous-v2` or another continuous environment. You will need to modify the action state from 3 to the environment you choose.

6. Tune the hyperparameters for the `Chapter_8_DDPG.py` example. This will require you to learn and understand that new parameter, `tau`.

7. Tune the hyperparameters for the **TRPO** example. This will require you to learn how to set the hyperparameters from the command line and then tweak those parameters. You should not be modifying any code to complete this exercise.

8. Enable the MuJoCo environments and run one of these environments with the TRPO example.

9. Add plotting output to the various examples.

10. Convert one of the single-file examples into use a main method that takes arguments and allows a user to train hyperparameters dynamically, instead of modifying source code.

Be sure to complete from 1-3 of the preceding exercises before moving on to the next section and end of this chapter.

Summary

In this chapter, we introduced policy gradient methods, where we learned how to use a stochastic policy to drive our agent with the REINFORCE algorithm. After that, we learned that part of the problem of sampling from a stochastic policy is the randomness of sampling from a stochastic policy. We found that this could be corrected using dual agent networks, with one that represents the acting network and another as a critic. In this case, the actor is the policy network that refers back to the critic network, which uses a deterministic value function. Then, we saw how PG could be improved upon by seeing how DDPG works. Finally, we looked at what is considered one of the more complex methods in DRL, TRPO, and saw how it tries to manage the several shortcomings of PG methods.

Continuing with our look at PG methods, we will move on to explore next-generation methods such as PPO, AC2, AC2, and ACER in the next chapter.

9
Optimizing for Continuous Control

Up until now, we have considered most of the training/challenge environments we've looked at as being episodic; that is, the game or environment has a beginning and an end. This is good since most games have a beginning and an end – it is, after all, a game. However, in the real world, or for some games, an episode could last days, weeks, months, or even years. For these types of environment, we no longer think of an episode; rather we work with the concept of an environment that requires continuous control. So far, we have looked at a subset of algorithms that can solve this type of problem but they don't do so very well. So, like most things in RL, we have a special class of algorithms devoted to those types of environment, and we'll explore them in this chapter.

In this chapter, we'll look at improving the policy methods we looked at previously for performing continuous control of advanced environments. We'll start off by setting up and installing the Mujoco environment, a specialized area we can use to test these new algorithms, the first of which will be the proximal policy optimization or PPO method. After that, we'll look at a novel improvement called recurrent networks for capturing context and learn how that is applied on top of PPO. Then, we'll get back into actor-critic and this time look at asynchronous actor-critic in a couple of different configurations. Finally, we'll look at ACER and actor-critic with experience replay.

Here is a summary of the main topics we will cover in this chapter:

- Understanding continuous control with Mujoco
- Introducing proximal policy optimization
- Using PPO with recurrent networks
- Deciding on synchronous and asynchronous actors
- Building actor-critic with experience replay

In this chapter, we'll look at a class of RL methods that attempts to deal specifically with real-world problems of robotics or other control systems. Of course, this doesn't mean these same algorithms couldn't be used in gaming – they are. In the next section, we'll begin by looking at the specialized Mujoco environment.

Understanding continuous control with Mujoco

The standard environment for building continuous control agents is the Mujoco environment. **Mujoco** stands for **Multi-Joint dynamics with Contract** and it is a full physics environment for training robotic or simulation agents. This environment provides a number of simulations that challenge some form of robotic control agent to perform a task, such as walking, crawling, and implementing several other physics control-based tasks. An example of the diversity of these environments is summarized well in the following image, which has been extracted from the Mujoco home page:

Extract of example environments from the Mujoco home page

Obviously, we will want to use this cool environment. However, this package is not free and requires a license, but note that a 30-day trial is provided. Now for the bad news. The package is extremely difficult to set up, install, and train, especially if you are using Windows. In fact, it is so difficult that, although we strongly suggest using Mujoco as an environment, we won't be using it for the remaining exercises in this chapter. Why? Again, it is extremely difficult and we don't want to exclude people who are unable to install the Mujoco environment.

There are plenty of blog posts or Stack Overflow articles available that walk through various installations of the various versions of Mujoco for Windows. Mujoco's support for Windows was stopped after version 1.5. While it is still possible to install Mujoco on Windows, it is not trivial and is likely to change often. As such, if you are inclined to use Windows with Mujoco, your best bet is to look to the most recent blogs or forum posts discussing this for help.

In this exercise, we'll walk through the basic installation of Mujoco (not for Windows):

1. The first thing we need is a license. Open your browser, go to `mujoco.org`, and locate the **License** button at the top of the page. Then, click it.
2. On the page, you will see an entry for **Computer id**. This will require you to download a key generator from the blue links shown to the right. Click one of the links to download the key generator.
3. Run the key generator on your system and enter the key in the **Computer id** field.
4. Fill in the rest of the license information with your name and email and click **Submit**, as shown in the following screenshot:

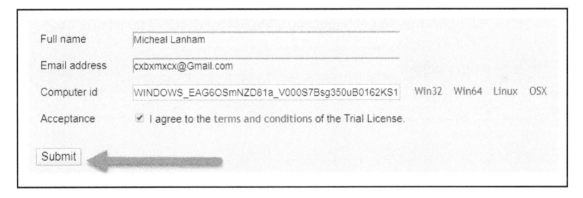

Submitting for a Mujoco license

5. You should get a key emailed to you in a few minutes with directions as to where to put the key. Then, you need to download the binaries for your platform. Click on the **Products** link at the top of the page to be taken to the downloads. Download the version you need for your OS.

6. Unzip the files into your root user folder, `~/.mujoco/mujoco%version%`, where `%version%` denotes the version of the software. On Windows, your user folder is `C:\Users\%username%`, where `%username%` denotes the logged in user's name.

7. Now, you need to build the Mujoco package and set up the `mujoco-py` scripts. This varies widely by installation. Use the following commands to build and install Mujoco:

```
pip3 install -U 'mujoco-py<2.1,>=2.0'  #use the version appropriate
for you
cd path/to/mujoco-py/folder
python -c "import mujoco_py" #force compile mujoco_py
python setup.py install
```

8. To test the installation and check for dependencies, run the following command to reinstall the entire Gym again:

```
pip install gym[all]
```

If you run this command and still see errors, you likely need more help. Consult online resources for the most current search on `mujoco install` and try those instructions. Again, at the time of writing, Windows is no longer supported and you may be better off using another platform. Fortunately, setting up a VM or Cloud service for this can now be quite easy and you may have more luck there.

9. You can test the Mujoco installation and ensure that the license is all set up by running `Chapter_9_Mujoco.py` as you normally would. The listing is shown here:

```
import gym
from gym import envs

env = gym.make('FetchReach-v1')

env.reset()
for _ in range(1000):
 env.render()
 env.step(env.action_space.sample()) # take a random action
env.close()
```

If you have everything installed correctly, then you should see something similar to the following image, which has been taken from the Mujoco environment:

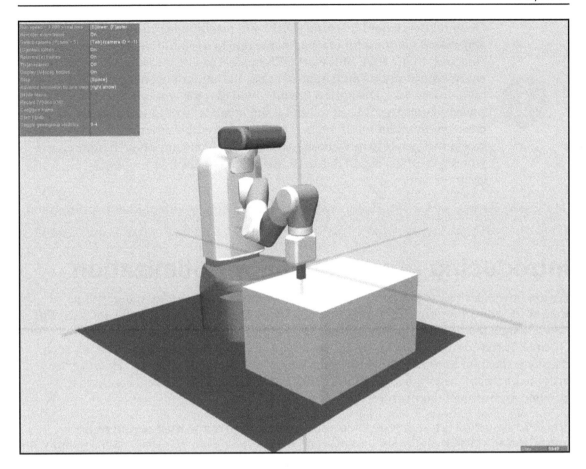

The fetch reach Mujoco environment

If you are able to install the Mujoco environments, then great – have fun exploring a whole new world of environments. For those of you who are not able to install Mujoco, don't fret. We will learn how to create our own physics-based environments when we start using Unity in Chapter 10, *Exploiting ML-Agents*. Rest assured that, while Mujoco is indeed cool, much like the Atari games we have seen before, it is also not trivial to train. Not unlike Atari, Mujoco environments can take millions of training iterations. Therefore, to keep things simple and also remain energy-conscious, we will use the regular old Gym environments. The additional plus now is that we have a better comparison between various algorithms across a single environment.

Deep reinforcement learning (DRL) and **machine learning** (ML) in general are getting a bit of a bad name due to the additional energy they consume. Many state-of-the-art DRL models can be measured in terms of energy consumption and, in most cases, the amount of energy is quite high. In one case, DeepMind has admitted that the amount of processing/energy it used to train a single model would run a single desktop computer for 45 years. That is an incredible amount of energy in a world that needs to be cautious about energy consumption. Therefore, wherever applicable, in this book we will favor cheaper training environments.

In the next section, we look at advancing these policy methods with gradient optimization.

Introducing proximal policy optimization

We are now entering areas where we will start looking at state-of-the-art algorithms, at least at the time of writing. Of course, that will likely change and things will advance. For now, though, the **proximal policy optimization** algorithm (**PPO**), was introduced by OpenAI, is considered a state-of-the-art deep reinforcement learning algorithm. As such, the sky is the limit as to what environments we can throw at this problem. However, in order to quantify our progress and for a variety of other reasons, we will continue to baseline against the Lunar Lander environment.

The PPO algorithm is just an extension and simplification of the **trust region policy optimization** (**TRPO**) algorithm we covered in Chapter 8, *Policy Gradient Methods*, but with a few key differences. PPO is also much simpler to understand and follow. For these reasons, we will review each feature that makes policy optimization with trust regions in the case of TRPO and clipping with PPO so powerful.

The code for this chapter was originally sourced from the following repository: https://github.com/seungeunrho/minimalRL. A number of modifications have been made to the code so that it fits the examples in this book.

Since we have already gone over the major intuition behind this improvement, let's jump into the next coding exercise by opening Chapter_9_PPO.py. Perform the following steps:

1. The code for this listing is quite similar to many of the other listings we have reviewed. As such, we will limit our review to critical sections:

```
for iteration in range(iterations):
  s = env.reset()
```

```
done = False
while not done:
    for t in range(T_horizon):
        prob = model.pi(torch.from_numpy(s).float())
        m = Categorical(prob)
        a = m.sample().item()
        s_prime, r, done, info = env.step(a)

        model.put_data((s, a, r/100.0, s_prime, prob[a].item(),done))
        s = s_prime

        score += r
        if done:
            if score/print_interval > min_play_reward:
                play_game()
            break

    model.train_net()
    if iteration%print_interval==0 and iteration!=0:
        print("# of episode :{}, avg score : {:.1f}".format(iteration,
            score/print_interval))
        score = 0.0

env.close()
```

2. Scrolling right to the bottom, we can see that the training code is almost identical to our most recent examples in the previous chapters. One key thing to notice is the inclusion of a new hyperparameter, `T_horizon`, which we will define shortly:

```
learning_rate = 0.0005
gamma = 0.98
lmbda = 0.95
eps_clip = 0.1
K_epoch = 3
T_horizon = 20
```

3. If we scroll back to the top, you will see the definition of new hyperparameters for `T_horizon`, `K_epoch`, `eps_clip`, and `lambda`. Just note these new variables for now – we will get to their purpose shortly.

4. Let's jump to some of the other important differences, such as the network definition, which can be seen in the `init` method of the `PPO` class as follows:

```
def __init__(self, input_shape, num_actions):
    super(PPO, self).__init__()
    self.data = []
```

```
self.fc1 = nn.Linear(input_shape,256)
self.fc_pi = nn.Linear(256,num_actions)
self.fc_v = nn.Linear(256,1)
self.optimizer = optim.Adam(self.parameters(), lr=learning_rate)
```

5. What we can see is that the network comprises a first input state `Linear` layer called `fc1` that is composed of 256 neurons. Then, we can see that the `fc_pi` or policy network is defined as `Linear` with 256 neurons and outputs the `num_actions` or number of actions. Following that is the definition of `fc_v`, which is the value layer. Again, this has 256 neurons and one output, that is, the expected value.

6. The rest of the code for the PPO class is almost the same as in the previous examples and we won't need to cover it here.

7. Run the code as normal. This example will take a while to run but not as long as previous versions. We'll leave it up to you whether you want to wait for the example to complete before continuing.

One thing you should quickly notice is how much faster the algorithm trains. Indeed, the agent gets good quite fast and could actually solve the environment in fewer than 10,000 iterations, which is quite impressive. Now that we have seen how impressive policy optimization can be, we will look at how this is possible in the next section.

The hows of policy optimization

In `Chapter 8`, *Policy Gradient Methods*, we covered how policy gradient methods can fail and then introduced the TRPO method. Here, we talked about the general strategies TRPO uses to address the failings in PG methods. However, as we have seen, TRPO is quite complex and seeing how it works in code was not much help either. This is the main reason we minimized our discussion of the details when we introduced TRPO and instead waited until we got to this section to tell

the full story in a concise manner.

That said, let's review how policy optimization with TRPO or PPO can do what it does:

*   **Minorize-Maximization MM algorithm**: Recall that this is where we find the minimum of an upper bound function by finding the maximum of a lower bound function that is constrained to be within the upper bound function.

*   **Line search**: We have seen this being used to define in which direction and by what amount we could optimize our function (deep learning network). This allows our algorithm to avoid overshooting the target of optimization.

- **Trust region**: Along with MM and Line Search, we also want the policy function to have a stable base or platform to move along on. You can think of this stable base as a region of trust or safety. In PPO, this is defined differently, as we will see.

PPO and TRPO share all these improvements as a way of finding a better policy. PPO improves on this by also understanding how much we want to change the policy's distribution over each iteration. This understanding also allows us to limit the amount of change during each iteration. We have seen how TRPO does this to a certain extent with KL divergence, but PPO takes this one step further by adjusting or adapting to the amount of change. In the next section, we'll look at how this adaptation works.

PPO and clipped objectives

Before we get into the finer details of how PPO works, we need to step back and understand how we equate the difference in distributed data distributions or just distributions. Remember that PG methods look to understand the returns-based sampling distribution and then use that to find the optimum action or the probability of the optimum action. Due to this, we can use a method called **KL Divergence** to determine how different the two distributions are. By understanding this, we can determine how much room or area of trust we can allow our optimization algorithm to explore with. PPO improves on this by clipping the objective function by using two policy networks.

Jonathan Hui has a number of insightful blog posts on the mathematics behind various RL and PG methods. In particular, his post on PPO (`https://medium.com/@jonathan_hui/rl-proximal-policy-optimization-ppo-explained-77f014ec3f12`) is quite good. Be warned that they do assume a very sophisticated level of mathematics knowledge. If you are serious about RL, you will want to be able to read and understand this content at some point. However, you can get quite far in DRL by intuitively understanding most algorithms, like we're doing here.

Let's learn how this works in code by opening up `Chapter_9_PPO.py` and performing the following steps:

1. Having looked through the bulk of the main code, we only want to focus on the training code here and, in particular, the `train_net` function from the `PPO` class, as shown here:

```
def train_net(self):
  s, a, r, s_prime, done_mask, prob_a = self.make_batch()

  for i in range(K_epoch):
   td_target = r + gamma * self.v(s_prime) * done_mask
   delta = td_target - self.v(s)
   delta = delta.detach().numpy()

   advantage_lst = []
   advantage = 0.0
   for delta_t in delta[::-1]:
      advantage = gamma * lmbda * advantage + delta_t[0]
      advantage_lst.append([advantage])
   advantage_lst.reverse()
   advantage = torch.tensor(advantage_lst, dtype=torch.float)

   pi = self.pi(s, softmax_dim=1)
   pi_a = pi.gather(1,a)
   ratio = torch.exp(torch.log(pi_a) - torch.log(prob_a))

   surr1 = ratio * advantage
   surr2 = torch.clamp(ratio, 1-eps_clip, 1+eps_clip) * advantage
   loss = -torch.min(surr1, surr2) + F.smooth_l1_loss(self.v(s) ,
      td_target.detach())

   self.optimizer.zero_grad()
   loss.mean().backward()
   self.optimizer.step()
```

2. After the initial `make_batch` function call, in order to build the lists, we come to the iteration loop controlled by `K_epoch`. `K_epoch` is a new hyperparameter that controls the number of iterations we use to optimize the advantage convergence:

```
td_target = r + gamma * self.v(s_prime) * done_mask
delta = td_target - self.v(s)
delta = delta.detach().numpy()
```

3. The first block of code inside the `K_epoch` iteration is the calculation of `td_target` using the reward `r`, plus the discount factor `gamma` times the output of the v or value network and `done_mask`. Then, we take the `delta` or TD change and convert it into a `numpy` tensor:

```
for delta_t in delta[::-1]:
    advantage = gamma * lmbda * advantage + delta_t[0]
    advantage_lst.append([advantage])
```

4. Next, using the delta, we build a list of advantages using the `advantage` function, as follows:

```
pi = self.pi(s, softmax_dim=1)
pi_a = pi.gather(1,a)
ratio = torch.exp(torch.log(pi_a) - torch.log(prob_a))
```

5. Then, we push the state **s** into the policy network, `pi`. Next, we gather the axis along the first dimension and then take the ratio using the equation $\epsilon^{(log(pi_a)-log(prob_a))}$, which is used to calculate a possible ratio for the clipping region or area we want to use for trust:

```
surr1 = ratio * advantage
surr2 = torch.clamp(ratio, 1-eps_clip, 1+eps_clip) * advantage
loss = -torch.min(surr1, surr2) + F.smooth_l1_loss(self.v(s) ,
    td_target.detach())
```

6. We use the `ratio` value to calculate the `surr1` value, which defines the surface or clipping region. The next line calculates a second version of the surface, `surr2`, by clamping this ratio and using the bounds of our clipping region set by `eps_clip` to define the area. Then, it takes the minimum area of either surface and uses that to calculate the loss.

We use the term `surface` here to understand that the calculation of loss is over a multi-dimensional array of values. Our optimizer works across this surface to find the best global minimum or lowest area on the surface.

7. The last section of code is our typical gradient descent optimization and is shown next for completeness:

```
self.optimizer.zero_grad()
loss.mean().backward()
self.optimizer.step()
```

8. There's nothing new here. Go ahead and run the sample again or review the output from the previous exercise. An example of the training output is shown here:

```
C:\ProgramData\Anaconda3\envs\game\python.exe                    —    □    ×
# of episode :740, avg score : 31.4
# of episode :760, avg score : -1.4
# of episode :780, avg score : -38.4
# of episode :800, avg score : -61.1
# of episode :820, avg score : -95.9
# of episode :840, avg score : -120.6
# of episode :860, avg score : -6.4
# of episode :880, avg score : 12.4
# of episode :900, avg score : 7.5
# of episode :920, avg score : -93.8
# of episode :940, avg score : -152.1
# of episode :960, avg score : -122.7
# of episode :980, avg score : -77.0
# of episode :1000, avg score : -69.9
# of episode :1020, avg score : -4.5
# of episode :1040, avg score : -55.6
# of episode :1060, avg score : -114.5
# of episode :1080, avg score : -19.3
# of episode :1100, avg score : 63.3
# of episode :1120, avg score : -114.9
# of episode :1140, avg score : -118.9
# of episode :1160, avg score : -122.5
# of episode :1180, avg score : -156.1
# of episode :1200, avg score : -133.7
# of episode :1220, avg score : -144.2
# of episode :1240, avg score : -106.1
# of episode :1260, avg score : 10.5
# of episode :1280, avg score : -46.7
# of episode :1300, avg score : -133.6
```

Example output from Chapter_9_PPO.py

A couple of things to note is that we are stilling using discrete action spaces and not continuous ones. Again, our primary reason for doing this is to continue using a baseline-consistent environment, Lunar Lander v2. Lunar Lander does have a continuous action environment that you can try, but you will need to convert the sample so that you can use continuous actions. On the second item of note, PPO and other PG methods actually perform better on continuous action environments, which means you aren't really seeing their full potential. So, why are we continuing to use discrete action spaces? Well, in almost all cases, games and interactive environments will use discrete spaces. Since this is a book on games and AI and not robotics and AI, we will stick to discrete spaces.

There are various research initiatives on other PG methods but you should consider PPO to be a milestone in DRL, not unlike DQN. For those of you who are curious, PPO made its name by beating human players in the DOTA2 strategy game. In the next section, we'll look at other methods that have been layered on top of PG and other methods to improve DRL.

Using PPO with recurrent networks

In `Chapter 7`, *Going Deeper with DDQN*, we saw how we could interpret visual state using a concept called **convolutional neural networks** (**CNNs**). CNN networks are used to detect features in visual environments such as Atari games. While this technique allowed us to play any of a number of games with the same agent, the added CNN layers took much more time to train. In the end, the extra training time wasn't worth the cool factor of playing Atari games. However, there are other network structures we can put on top of our networks in order to make better interpretations of state. One such network structure is called recurrent networks. Recurrent network layers allow us to add the concept of context or time in our model's interpretation of state. This can work very well in any problem where context or memory is important.

Recurrent network layers are a form of deep learning perceptron that essentially feeds back its state to previous neurons. This, in effect, gives the network the ability to understand time or context. It does this so well that recurrent networks are now at the heart of all text and language processing networks. Language is especially contextual and recurrent layers, in various configurations, make short work of understanding the context. There are various configurations of recurrent network layers but the only one we'll focus on here is called **long short term memory** (**LSTM**).

Recurrent networks and LSTM layers are worthy of in-depth study on their own. These powerful network layers have been responsible for some very interesting discoveries in the last few years. While recurrent layers have turned out to have limited use in DRL, it is believed they should have more. After all, understanding context in a trajectory must be important.

LSTM layers for the purposes of DRL are quite simple to put in place. Open `Chapter_9_PPO_LSTM.py` and follow these steps to see how this works:

1. This sample is virtually identical to `Chapter_9_PPO.py` but with the few key differences, all of which we will look at here.

2. Skip to the `PPO` class definition, as shown here:

```
class PPO(nn.Module):
    def __init__(self, input_shape, num_actions):
        super(PPO, self).__init__()
        self.data = []
        self.fc1 = nn.Linear(input_shape,64)
        self.lstm = nn.LSTM(64,32)
        self.fc_pi = nn.Linear(32,num_actions)
        self.fc_v = nn.Linear(32,1)
        self.optimizer = optim.Adam(self.parameters(),
lr=learning_rate)
```

3. The only new part here is the definition of a new layer, `lstm`, which is of the `LSTM(64.32)` type. The LSTM layer that's injected at the top of the state encoding allows the network to learn the context in actions or memory. Now, instead of understanding which state-actions provide the best trajectory, our agent is learning which state-action sets are providing the best outcome. In gaming, this may be analogous to learning that a special move unlocks a sequence to get some special reward.

4. Next, we will move down to the policy pi function and value v function network definitions and look at how it has been modified:

```
def pi(self, x, hidden):
        x = F.relu(self.fc1(x))
        x = x.view(-1, 1, 64)
        x, lstm_hidden = self.lstm(x, hidden)
        x = self.fc_pi(x)
        prob = F.softmax(x, dim=2)
        return prob, lstm_hidden

def v(self, x, hidden):
        x = F.relu(self.fc1(x))
```

```
x = x.view(-1, 1, 64)
x, lstm_hidden = self.lstm(x, hidden)
v = self.fc_v(x)
return v
```

5. The `pi` and `v` functions take a hidden layer but only `pi`, or the policy function, is used as the output of a hidden layer. We will see how these hidden LSTM layers work shortly.

6. Then, at the top of the `train_net` function, we can see where the layers are extracted from the batching process, `make_batch`:

```
def train_net(self):
        s,a,r,s_prime,done_mask, prob_a, (h1_in, h2_in), (h1_out,
h2_out) = self.make_batch()
        first_hidden = (h1_in.detach(), h2_in.detach())
        second_hidden = (h1_out.detach(), h2_out.detach())
```

7. We use two hidden or middle LSTM layers between our actor-critics, where `second_hidden` denotes the output and `first_hidden` denotes the input. Below that, in the `for` loop, we can see the calculation of delta using the LSTM input and output:

```
v_prime = self.v(s_prime, second_hidden).squeeze(1)
td_target = r + gamma * v_prime * done_mask
v_s = self.v(s, first_hidden).squeeze(1)
delta = td_target - v_s
delta = delta.detach().numpy()
```

8. The calculation of delta here is done by applying the difference between the before and after the LSTM layer was applied, which allows the delta to encapsulate the effect the LSTM has on the calculation of value `v`.

9. Run the sample as you normally would and observe the output, as shown here:

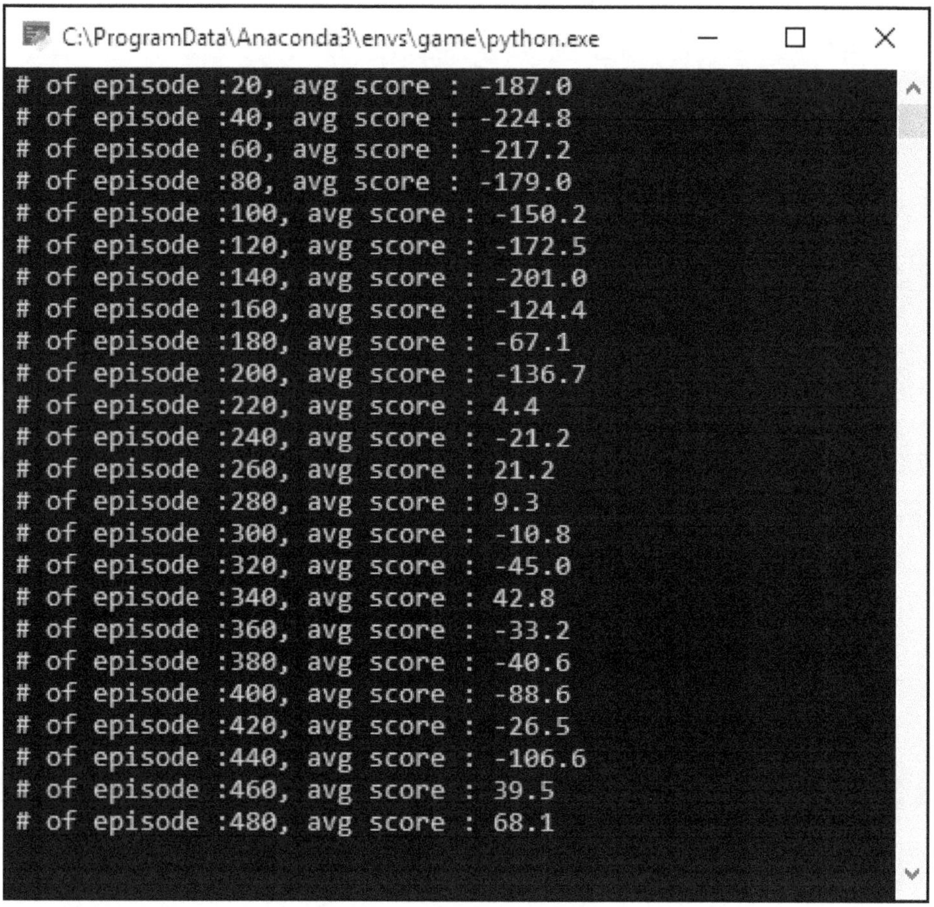

```
C:\ProgramData\Anaconda3\envs\game\python.exe                  —    □    ×
# of episode :20, avg score : -187.0
# of episode :40, avg score : -224.8
# of episode :60, avg score : -217.2
# of episode :80, avg score : -179.0
# of episode :100, avg score : -150.2
# of episode :120, avg score : -172.5
# of episode :140, avg score : -201.0
# of episode :160, avg score : -124.4
# of episode :180, avg score : -67.1
# of episode :200, avg score : -136.7
# of episode :220, avg score : 4.4
# of episode :240, avg score : -21.2
# of episode :260, avg score : 21.2
# of episode :280, avg score : 9.3
# of episode :300, avg score : -10.8
# of episode :320, avg score : -45.0
# of episode :340, avg score : 42.8
# of episode :360, avg score : -33.2
# of episode :380, avg score : -40.6
# of episode :400, avg score : -88.6
# of episode :420, avg score : -26.5
# of episode :440, avg score : -106.6
# of episode :460, avg score : 39.5
# of episode :480, avg score : 68.1
```

Example output of Chapter_9_PPO_LSTM.py

Notice how this slight improvement increased training performance significantly from the vanilla PPO example we looked at in the previous exercise. In the next section, we'll improve PPO further by applying parallel environments.

Deciding on synchronous and asynchronous actors

We started off this book with a simple discussion of what **artificial general intelligence** (**AGI**) is. In short, AGI is our attempt at generalizing an intelligent system to solve multiple tasks. RL is often thought of as a stepping stool to AGI primarily because it tries to generalize state-based learning. While both RL and AGI take deep inspiration from how we think, be it rewards or possibly consciousness itself, the former tends to incorporate direct analogies. The actor-critic concept in RL is an excellent example of how we use an interpretation of human psychology to create a form of learning. For instance, we humans often consider the consequences of our actions and determine the advantages they may or may not give us. This example is perfectly analogous to actor-critic and advantage methods we use in RL. Take this further and we can consider another human thought process: asynchronous and synchronous thought.

A direct example of asynchronous/synchronous thought is when an answer to a problem **pops** into your head after being asked a question several hours earlier. Perhaps you didn't have the answer then but then it came to you a few hours later. Were you thinking about the question all that time? Not likely, and more than likely the answer just came to you – it popped into your head. But were you thinking of it all the time in some background process or did some process just fire up and provide the answer? The animal brain thinks like this all the time and it is what we would call in computerese parallel processing. So, could our agents not also benefit from this same thought process? As it turns out, yes.

This inspiration likely came in part from the preceding analogy but also has a mathematical background in how we can evaluate advantage. The direct evaluation of how our brains think is still a big answer but we can assume our thoughts to be synchronous or asynchronous. So, instead of just considering one thought process, what if we consider several? We can take this analogy a step further and apply this back to DRL – in particular, actor-critic. Here, we have a single thought process or global network that is fed the output of several worker thought processes. An example of this is shown here:

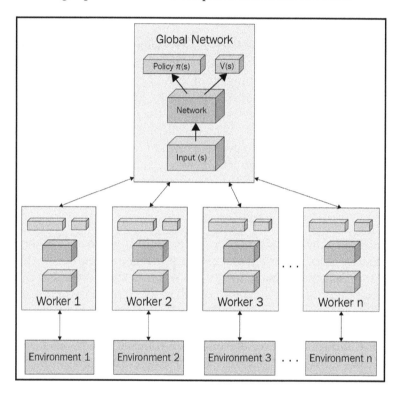

Example of asynchronous AC by Dr. Arthur Juliani

What we can see here is the basic intuition behind the advantage of the actor-critic architecture, A2C, and the asynchronous advantage actor-critic architecture, A3C. Notice how each worker brain/agent has its own copy of a separate environment. All of these worker agents feed their learning into a master brain. Each worker brain is then updated iteratively to coincide with the master, not unlike our earlier advantage calculations. In the next section, we will see how this is put into practice by implementing A2C.

Using A2C

To avoid any confusion, it is important to understand that A2C and A3C both use AC, but it is the fashion in which they update their models that differ. In A2C, the method is synchronous, so each brain is feeding thoughts into the main brain.

Let's see how this looks in code by opening the `Chapter_9_A2C.py` file and reviewing the hyperparameters inside it:

```
n_train_processes = 3
learning_rate = 0.0002
update_interval = 5
gamma = 0.98
max_train_steps = 60000
PRINT_INTERVAL = update_interval * 100
environment = "LunarLander-v2"
```

Keep the sample open and follow these steps to continue with this exercise:

1. This is a large code example, so we will limit the sections we show here. The main thing of note here is the hyperparameters that are listed at the top of the file. The only thing new to note is `n_train_processes`, which sets the number of worker processes:

```
class ActorCritic(nn.Module):
    def __init__(self, input_shape, num_actions):
        super(ActorCritic, self).__init__()
        self.fc1 = nn.Linear(input_shape, 256)
        self.fc_pi = nn.Linear(256, num_actions)
        self.fc_v = nn.Linear(256, 1)

    def pi(self, x, softmax_dim=1):
        x = F.relu(self.fc1(x))
        x = self.fc_pi(x)
        prob = F.softmax(x, dim=softmax_dim)
        return prob

    def v(self, x):
        x = F.relu(self.fc1(x))
        v = self.fc_v(x)
        return v
```

2. Next comes the `ActorCritic` class, which is the same class that we used previously:

```
def worker(worker_id, master_end, worker_end):
    master_end.close()
    env = gym.make(environment)
    env.seed(worker_id)

    while True:
        cmd, data = worker_end.recv()
        if cmd == 'step':
            ob, reward, done, info = env.step(data)
            if done:
                ob = env.reset()
            worker_end.send((ob, reward, done, info))
        elif cmd == 'reset':
            ob = env.reset()
            worker_end.send(ob)
        elif cmd == 'reset_task':
            ob = env.reset_task()
            worker_end.send(ob)
        elif cmd == 'close':
            worker_end.close()
            break
        elif cmd == 'get_spaces':
            worker_end.send((env.observation_space,
env.action_space))
        else:
            raise NotImplementedError
```

3. Then comes the definition of the `worker` function. This function is where the worker's brain sends messages between the worker and master brains:

```
class ParallelEnv:
    def __init__(self, n_train_processes):
        self.nenvs = n_train_processes
        self.waiting = False
        self.closed = False
        self.workers = list()

        master_ends, worker_ends = zip(*[mp.Pipe() for _ in
range(self.nenvs)])
        self.master_ends, self.worker_ends = master_ends,
worker_ends

        for worker_id, (master_end, worker_end) in
enumerate(zip(master_ends, worker_ends)):
            p = mp.Process(target=worker,
```

```
                                    args=(worker_id, master_end,
    worker_end))
                p.daemon = True
                p.start()
                self.workers.append(p)

            # Forbid master to use the worker end for messaging
            for worker_end in worker_ends:
                worker_end.close()
```

4. After those functions is the big `ParallelEnv` class. The preceding code just shows the `init` function from that class since it's quite large. This class merely coordinates activities between the masters and workers:

```
    def compute_target(v_final, r_lst, mask_lst):
        G = v_final.reshape(-1)
        td_target = list()

        for r, mask in zip(r_lst[::-1], mask_lst[::-1]):
            G = r + gamma * G * mask
            td_target.append(G)

        return torch.tensor(td_target[::-1]).float()
```

5. Scrolling down past the `test` function, or the `play_game` function in our other examples, we can see the `compute_target` function. This is the calculation of the TD loss and the difference here is the use of the `mask` variable. `mask` is just a flag or filter that removes any calculation of discounted G on 0 returns:

```
    if __name__ == '__main__':
        envs = ParallelEnv(n_train_processes)
        env = gym.make(environment)
        state_size = env.observation_space.shape[0]
        action_size = env.action_space.n
        model = ActorCritic(state_size, action_size)
        optimizer = optim.Adam(model.parameters(), lr=learning_rate)
```

6. After that, we get into an `if` function, which determines whether the current process is `'__main__'`. We do this to avoid having additional worker processes trying to run this same block of code. After that, we can see the typical environment and model setup being completed:

```
    for _ in range(update_interval):
        prob = model.pi(torch.from_numpy(s).float())
        a = Categorical(prob).sample().numpy()
        s_prime, r, done, info = envs.step(a)
```

```
s_lst.append(s)
a_lst.append(a)
r_lst.append(r/100.0)
mask_lst.append(1 - done)

s = s_prime
step_idx += 1
```

7. The interval training loop code is virtually identical to those from the previous examples and should be self-explanatory at this point, for the most part. Something to note is the `env.steps` function call. This represents a step in all the worker environments, synchronously. Remember that the worker agents are running synchronously in A2C:

```
s_final = torch.from_numpy(s_prime).float()
v_final = model.v(s_final).detach().clone().numpy()
td_target = compute_target(v_final, r_lst, mask_lst)

td_target_vec = td_target.reshape(-1)
s_vec = torch.tensor(s_lst).float().reshape(-1, state_size)
a_vec = torch.tensor(a_lst).reshape(-1).unsqueeze(1)
mod = model.v(s_vec)
advantage = td_target_vec - mod.reshape(-1)

pi = model.pi(s_vec, softmax_dim=1)
pi_a = pi.gather(1, a_vec).reshape(-1)
loss = -(torch.log(pi_a) * advantage.detach()).mean() +\
            F.smooth_l1_loss(model.v(s_vec).reshape(-1),
td_target_vec)

optimizer.zero_grad()
loss.backward()
optimizer.step()
```

8. Then, we come to the outer training loop. In this example, we can see how the training targets are pulled from the lists constructed by the workers, where `s_lst` is for the state, `a_lst` is for actions, `r_lst` is for rewards, and `mask_lst` is for done. Aside from torch tensor manipulation, the calculations are the same as in PPO.

9. Run the code as you normally would and visualize the output, an example of which is as follows:

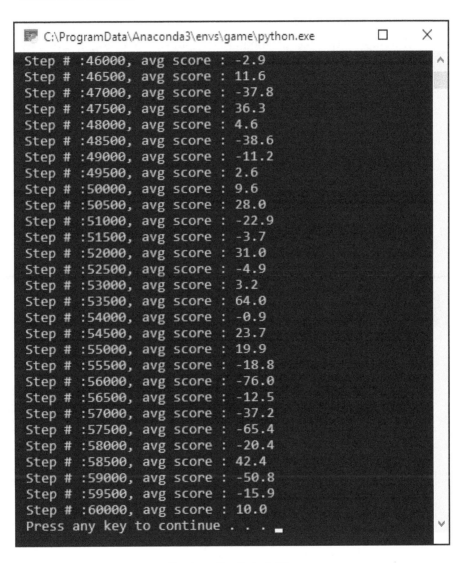

Example output from Chapter_9_A2C.py

You will need to tune the hyperparameters to get this example to run perfectly. Now, we will move on and look at the asynchronous version of A2C—A3C.

Using A3C

Synchronous actor-critic workers provide a training advantage by essentially providing more sampling variations that should, in turn, reduce the amount of expected error and thus improve training performance. Mathematically, all we are doing is providing a larger sampling space which, as any statistician will tell you, just reduces the sampling error. However, if we assume that each worker is asynchronous, meaning it updates the global model in its own time, this also provides us with more statistical variability in our sampling across the entire trajectory space. This can also happen along the sampling space at the same time. In essence, we could have workers sampling the trajectory at many different points, as shown in the following diagram:

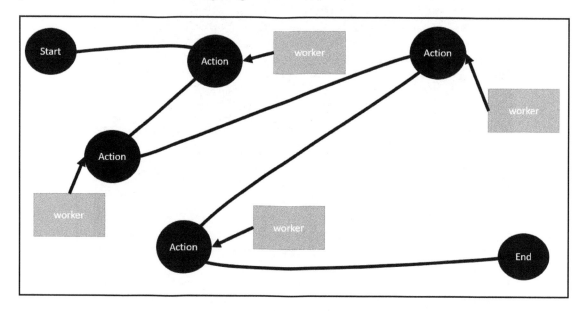

Multiple workers sampling across a trajectory space

With A3C and asynchronous actor-critic workers, we can get a much better picture of the entire trajectory space sooner, which allows our agent to make clearer and better decisions. It does this by sampling across the trajectory space asynchronously with multiple workers. Let's see how this works by opening up `Chapter_9_A3C.py` and performing the following steps:

1. We will start by looking at typical hyperparameters and setup code, as follows:

    ```
    n_train_processes = 6
    learning_rate = 0.0002
    update_interval = 6
    ```

```
gamma = 0.98
max_train_ep = 3000
max_test_ep = 400
environment = "LunarLander-v2"

env = gym.make(environment)
state_size = env.observation_space.shape[0]
action_size = env.action_space.n
```

2. Here, we can see the inclusion of two new hyperparameters, `max_train_ep` and `max_test_ep`. The first variable, `max_train_ep`, sets the maximum number of training episodes, while the second variable, `max_text_ep`, is used to evaluate performance.

3. The next section is the `ActorCritic` class and is identical to our previous couple of examples, so we won't need to review it here. After that is the `train` function, as shown here:

```
def train(global_model, rank):
    local_model = ActorCritic(state_size, action_size)
    local_model.load_state_dict(global_model.state_dict())

    optimizer = optim.Adam(global_model.parameters(),
lr=learning_rate)

    env = gym.make(environment)

    for n_epi in range(max_train_ep):
        done = False
        s = env.reset()
        while not done:
            s_lst, a_lst, r_lst = [], [], []
            for t in range(update_interval):
                prob = local_model.pi(torch.from_numpy(s).float())
                m = Categorical(prob)
                a = m.sample().item()
                s_prime, r, done, info = env.step(a)

                s_lst.append(s)
                a_lst.append([a])
                r_lst.append(r/100.0)

                s = s_prime
                if done:
                    break

            s_final = torch.tensor(s_prime, dtype=torch.float)
            R = 0.0 if done else local_model.v(s_final).item()
```

```
                td_target_lst = []
                for reward in r_lst[::-1]:
                    R = gamma * R + reward
                    td_target_lst.append([R])
                td_target_lst.reverse()

                s_batch, a_batch, td_target = torch.tensor(s_lst,
        dtype=torch.float), torch.tensor(a_lst), \
                    torch.tensor(td_target_lst)
                advantage = td_target - local_model.v(s_batch)

                pi = local_model.pi(s_batch, softmax_dim=1)
                pi_a = pi.gather(1, a_batch)
                loss = -torch.log(pi_a) * advantage.detach() + \
                    F.smooth_l1_loss(local_model.v(s_batch),
        td_target.detach())

                optimizer.zero_grad()
                loss.mean().backward()
                for global_param, local_param in
        zip(global_model.parameters(), local_model.parameters()):
                    global_param._grad = local_param.grad
                optimizer.step()
                local_model.load_state_dict(global_model.state_dict())

            env.close()
            print("Training process {} reached maximum
        episode.".format(rank))
```

4. The `train` function is quite similar to our previous training code. However, notice how we are passing in a `global_model` input. This global model is used as the clone for the local model, which we then train on experiences learned by the worker agent. One of the keys things to observe about this code is the last section, which is where we update the global model using the local model we have been training independently.

5. Next comes the test function. This is where `global_model` is evaluated using the following code:

```
def test(global_model):
    env = gym.make(environment)
    score = 0.0
    print_interval = 20

    for n_epi in range(max_test_ep):
        done = False
        s = env.reset()
        while not done:
```

```
        prob = global_model.pi(torch.from_numpy(s).float())
        a = Categorical(prob).sample().item()
        s_prime, r, done, info = env.step(a)
        s = s_prime
        score += r

    if n_epi % print_interval == 0 and n_epi != 0:
        print("# of episode :{}, avg score : {:.1f}".format(
            n_epi, score/print_interval))
        score = 0.0
        time.sleep(1)
env.close()
```

6. All this code does is evaluate the model by using it to play the game and evaluate the score. This would certainly be a great place to render the environment for visuals while training.

7. Finally, we have the main block of processing code. This block of code is identified with the name if statement, as follows:

```
if __name__ == '__main__':
    global_model - ActorCritic(state_size, action_size)
    global_model.share_memory()

    processes = []
    for rank in range(n_train_processes + 1): # + 1 for test
process
        if rank == 0:
            p = mp.Process(target=test, args=(global_model,))
        else:
            p = mp.Process(target=train, args=(global_model,
rank,))
        p.start()
        processes.append(p)
    for p in processes:
        p.join()
```

8. As we can see, this is where the global_model model is constructed with shared memory. Then, we start up the subprocesses using the first or rank 0 process as the test or evaluation process. Finally, we can see that the code ends when we join back up all the processes with p.join.

9. Run the code as you normally would and take a look at the results, an example of which is as follows:

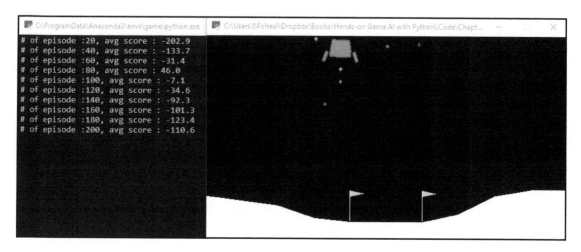

Example output from Chapter_9_A3C.py

Building actor-critic with experience replay

We have come to a point in this book where we have learned about all the major concepts of DRL. There will be more tools we will throw at you in later chapters, such as the one we showed in this section, but if you have made it this far, you should consider yourself knowledgeable of DRL. As such, consider building your own tools or enhancements to DRL, not unlike the one we'll show in this section. If you are wondering if you need to have the math worked out first, then the answer is no. It can often be more intuitive to build these models in code first and then understand the math later.

Actor-critic with experience replay (ACER) provides another advantage by adjusting sampling based on past experiences. This concept was originally introduced by DeepMind in a paper titled *Sample Efficient Actor-Critic with Experience Replay* and developed the concept for ACER. The intuition behind ACER is that we develop dual dueling stochastic networks in order to reduce the bias and variance and update the trust regions we select in PPO. In the next exercise, we'll explore actor-critic combined with experience replay.

The math behind ACER is best understood by reviewing the aforementioned paper or searching for blog posts. It is strongly suggested that you understand the math behind TRPO and PPO first, before tackling the paper.

Open `Chapter_9_ACER.py` and follow these steps to complete this exercise:

1. The first thing you will notice in this example is the `ReplayBuffer` class, as shown here:

```python
class ReplayBuffer():
    def __init__(self):
        self.buffer = collections.deque(maxlen=buffer_limit)

    def put(self, seq_data):
        self.buffer.append(seq_data)
    def sample(self, on_policy=False):
        if on_policy:
            mini_batch = [self.buffer[-1]]
        else:
            mini_batch = random.sample(self.buffer, batch_size)

        s_lst, a_lst, r_lst, prob_lst, done_lst, is_first_lst = [], [], [], [], [], []
        for seq in mini_batch:
            is_first = True
            for transition in seq:
                s, a, r, prob, done = transition

                s_lst.append(s)
                a_lst.append([a])
                r_lst.append(r)
                prob_lst.append(prob)
                done_mask = 0.0 if done else 1.0
                done_lst.append(done_mask)
                is_first_lst.append(is_first)
                is_first = False

        s,a,r,prob,done_mask,is_first = torch.tensor(s_lst, dtype=torch.float), torch.tensor(a_lst), \
                                            r_lst,
        torch.tensor(prob_lst, dtype=torch.float), done_lst, \
                                            is_first_lst
        return s,a,r,prob,done_mask,is_first
    def size(self):
        return len(self.buffer)
```

2. This is an updated version of the `ReplayBuffer` class we looked at in previous chapters.

3. The bulk of the code should be self-explanatory, aside from new sections in the `train` function, starting with the first few blocks of code:

```
q = model.q(s)
q_a = q.gather(1,a)
pi = model.pi(s, softmax_dim = 1)
pi_a = pi.gather(1,a)
v = (q * pi).sum(1).unsqueeze(1).detach()
rho = pi.detach()/prob
rho_a = rho.gather(1,a)
rho_bar = rho_a.clamp(max=c)
correction_coeff = (1-c/rho).clamp(min=0)
```

4. The new code is the calculation of `rho` from taking the ratio of `pi` over the action probability, `prob`. Then, the code gathers the tensor to 1, clamps it, and calculates a correction coefficient called `correction_coeff`.

5. Scrolling past some of the other familiar code, we come to a new section where the calculation of loss has been updated with the values `rho_bar` and `correction_coeff`, as follows:

```
loss1 = -rho_bar * torch.log(pi_a) * (q_ret - v)
loss2 = -correction_coeff * pi.detach() * torch.log(pi) *
(q.detach()-v) loss = loss1 + loss2.sum(1) + F.smooth_l1_loss(q_a,
q_ret)
```

6. Here, we can see that the inverse of `rho_bar` and `correction_coeff` are both used to skew the calculations of loss. `rho`, the original value we used to calculate these coefficients from, is based on the ratio between previous actions and predicted actions. The effect that's produced by applying this bias is narrowing the search along the trajectory path. This is a very good thing when it's applied to continuous control tasks.

7. Finally, let's skip to the training loop code and see where the data is appended to `ReplayBuffer`:

```
seq_data.append((s, a, r/100.0, prob.detach().numpy(), done))
```

8. What we can see here is that the action probability, `prob`, is entered by detaching from the PyTorch tensor using `detach()` and then converting it into a `numpy` tensor. This value is what we use to calculate `rho` later in the `train_net` function.

9. Run the code as you normally would and observe the output, an example of which is as follows:

```
C:\ProgramData\Anaconda3\envs\game\python.exe                    —    □    ×
# of episode :80, avg score : -205.5, buffer size : 840
# of episode :100, avg score : -204.8, buffer size : 1063
# of episode :120, avg score : -214.8, buffer size : 1294
# of episode :140, avg score : -240.3, buffer size : 1532
# of episode :160, avg score : -179.0, buffer size : 1791
# of episode :180, avg score : -169.1, buffer size : 2054
# of episode :200, avg score : -124.0, buffer size : 2427
# of episode :220, avg score : -209.3, buffer size : 2806
# of episode :240, avg score : -176.4, buffer size : 3161
# of episode :260, avg score : -141.7, buffer size : 3469
# of episode :280, avg score : -123.3, buffer size : 3834
# of episode :300, avg score : -75.7, buffer size : 4509
# of episode :320, avg score : -58.7, buffer size : 5365
# of episode :340, avg score : -2.9, buffer size : 6000
# of episode :360, avg score : -32.5, buffer size : 6000
# of episode :380, avg score : 45.0, buffer size : 6000
# of episode :400, avg score : 75.0, buffer size : 6000
# of episode :420, avg score : 30.6, buffer size : 6000
# of episode :440, avg score : 87.6, buffer size : 6000
# of episode :460, avg score : 75.5, buffer size : 6000
# of episode :480, avg score : 63.8, buffer size : 6000
# of episode :500, avg score : 29.6, buffer size : 6000
# of episode :520, avg score : 68.5, buffer size : 6000
# of episode :540, avg score : 72.6, buffer size : 6000
# of episode :560, avg score : 73.6, buffer size : 6000
# of episode :580, avg score : 55.7, buffer size : 6000
# of episode :600, avg score : 54.9, buffer size : 6000
# of episode :620, avg score : 29.8, buffer size : 6000
# of episode :640, avg score : 45.1, buffer size : 6000
```

Example output from Chapter_9_ACER.py

Here, we can see how the buffer size increases and that the agent becomes smarter. This is because we are using those experiences in the replay buffer to adjust the understanding of bias and variance from the policy distribution, which, in turn, reduces the size or clipping area of the trust regions we use. As we can see from this exercise, which is the most impressive one in this chapter, it does indeed learn the environment in a more convergent manner than our previous attempts in this chapter.

That's all for optimizing PG methods. In the next section, we'll look at some exercises that you can carry out on your own.

Exercises

The exercises in this section are for you to explore on your own. Substantially advancing any of the techniques we cover from this point forward is an accomplishment, so the work you do here could morph into something beyond just learning. Indeed, the environments and examples you work on now will likely indicate your working preference going forward. As always, try to complete two to three of the following exercises:

1. Tune the hyperparameters for `Chapter_9_PPO.py` and/or `Chapter_9_PPO_LSTM.py`.
2. Tune the hyperparameters for `Chapter_9_A2C.py` and/or `Chapter_9_A3C.py`.
3. Tune the hyperparameters for `Chapter_9_ACER.py`.
4. Apply LSTM layers to the A2C and/or A3C examples.
5. Apply LSTM layers to the ACER example.
6. Add a `play_game` function to the A2C and/or A3C examples.
7. Add a `play_game` function to the ACER example.
8. Adjust the buffer size in the ACER example and see how that improves training.
9. Add synchronous and/or asynchronous workers to the ACER example.
10. Add the ability to output results to matplot or TensorBoard. This is quite advanced but is something we will cover in later chapters.

These exercises are intended to reinforce what we learned in this chapter. In the next section, we will summarize this chapter.

Summary

In this chapter, we learned how PG methods are not without their own faults and looked at ways to fix or correct them. This led us to explore more implementation methods that improved sampling efficiency and optimized the objective or clipped gradient function. We did this by looking at the PPO method, which uses clipped objective functions to optimize the region of trust we use to calculate the gradient. After that, we looked at adding a new network layer configuration to understand the context in state.

Then, we used the new layer type, an LSTM layer, on top of PPO to see the improvements it generated. Then, we looked at improving sampling using parallel environments and synchronous or asynchronous workers. We did this by implementing synchronous workers by building an A2C example, followed by looking at an example of using asynchronous workers on A3C. We finished this chapter by looking at another improvement we can make to sampling efficiency through the use of ACER, or actor-critic with experience replay.

In the next chapter, we'll improve upon our knowledge by looking at different methods that are more applicable to gaming. PG methods have been shown to be very successful in gaming tasks, but in the next chapter we'll go back to DQN and see how it can be made state-of-the-art with varying improvements.

All about Rainbow DQN **10**

Throughout this book, we have learned how the various threads in **Reinforcement Learning** (**RL**) combined to form modern RL and then advanced to **Deep Reinforcement Learning** (**DRL**) with the inclusion of **Deep Learning** (**DL**). Like most other specialized fields from this convergence, we now see a divergence back to specialized methods for specific classes of environments. We started to see this in the chapters where we covered **Policy Gradient** (**PG**) methods and the environments it specialized on are continuous control. The flip side of this is the more typical episodic game environment, which is episodic with some form of discrete control mechanism. These environments typically perform better with DQN but the problem then becomes about DQN. Well, in this chapter, we will look at how smart people solved that by introducing Rainbow DQN.

In this chapter, we will introduce Rainbow DQN and understand the problems it works to address and the solutions it provides. Since we have already covered a majority of those solutions in other chapters, we will cover the few that make Rainbow special, by first looking at noisy or fuzzy networks for a better understanding of sampling and exploration. Then, we will look at distributed RL and how it can be used to improve value estimates by predicting distributions, not unlike our policy networks from PG, combining these improvements and others into Rainbow and seeing how well that performs. Finally, we will look at hierarchical DQN for understanding tasks and sub-tasks for possible training environments, with the plan to use this advanced DQN on more sophisticated environments later.

Here are the main topics we will cover in this chapter:

- Rainbow – combining improvements in deep reinforcement learning
- Using TensorBoard
- Introducing distributional RL
- Understanding noisy networks
- Unveiling Rainbow DQN

Be sure to brush up on your understanding of probability, statistics, stochastic processes, and/or Bayesian inference and variational inference methods. This is something you should have already been doing in previous chapters but that knowledge will now be essential as we move to some of the more advanced content in DRL—and DL, for that matter.

In the next section, we will look to understand what is Rainbow DQN and why it was needed.

Rainbow – combining improvements in deep reinforcement learning

The paper that introduced Rainbow DQN, *Rainbow: Combining Improvements in Deep Reinforcement Learning*, by DeepMind in October 2017 was developed to address several failings in DQN. DQN was introduced by the same group at DeepMind, led by David Silver to beat Atari games better than humans. However, as we learned over several chapters, while the algorithm was groundbreaking, it did suffer from some shortcomings. Some of these we have already addressed with advances such as DDQN and experience replay. To understand what encompasses all of Rainbow, let's look at the main elements it contributes to RL/DRL:

- **DQN**: This is, of course, the core algorithm, something we should have a good understanding of by now. We covered DQN in `Chapter 6`, *Going Deep with DQN*.
- **Double DQN**: This is not to be confused with DDQN or dueling DQN. Again, we already covered this in `Chapter 7`, *Going Deeper with DDQN*.
- **Prioritized Experience Replay:** This is another improvement we already covered in `Chapter 6`, *Going Deep with DQN*.
- **Dueling Network Architecture** (**DDQN**): This is an element we have covered already and is mentioned previously.
- **Multi-step returns**: This is our calculation of TD lambda and estimations of expectation or advantage.
- **Distributional RL**: This tries to understand the value distribution, not unlike our policy model in actor-critic except, in this case, we use values. This enhancement will be covered in its own section in this chapter.

- **Noisy Nets**: Noisy or fuzzy networks are DL networks that learn to balance a distribution of weight parameters rather than actual discriminant values of network weights. These advanced DL networks have been used to better understand data distributions and hence data by modeling the weights it uses as distributions. We will cover these advanced DL networks in a further section in this chapter.

Many of these improvements we have already covered in previous chapters, apart from distributional RL and noisy nets. We will cover both of these improvements in this chapter starting with distributional RL in a future section. Before we do that though, let's take a step back and improve our logging output capabilities with TensorBoard in the next section.

Using TensorBoard

At this point in this book, we need to move beyond building toy examples and look to building modules or frameworks you can use to train your own agents in the future. In fact, we will use the code in this chapter for training agents to solve other challenge environments we present in later chapters. That means we need a more general way to capture our progress, preferably to log files that we can view later. Since building such frameworks is such a common task to machine learning as a whole, Google developed a very useful logging framework called TensorBoard. TensorBoard was originally developed as a subset of the other DL framework we mentioned earlier, TensorFlow. Fortunately, for us, PyTorch includes an extension that supports logging to TensorBoard. So, in this section, we are going to set up and install TensorBoard for use as a logging and graphing platform.

In the next exercise, we will install TensorBoard for use with PyTorch. If you have only ever used PyTorch, you likely need to follow these instructions. For those of you that have already installed TensorFlow previously, you will already be good to go and can skip this exercise:

1. Open an Anaconda or Python shell and switch to your virtual environment. You likely already have one open. You may want to create an entirely separate clean virtual environment for TensorBoard. This minimizes the amount of code that can or will break in that environment. TensorBoard is a server application and is best treated as such, meaning the environment it runs on should be pristine.

2. Then, we need to install TensorBoard with the following command run from your Anaconda or Python shell:

```
pip install tensorboard --upgrade
```

This installs TensorBoard into your virtual environment.

3. Next, to avoid dependency issues that may arise, we need to run the following command:

   ```
   pip install future
   ```

4. After that is all installed, we can run TensorBoard with the following command:

   ```
   tensorboard --logdir runs
   ```

5. This will start a server application on port 6006, by default, and pull logs generated from a folder called runs, the default used by PyTorch. If you need to customize the port or input log folder, you can use the following command options:

   ```
   tensorboard --logdir=/path_to_log_dir/ --port 6006
   ```

6. TensorBoard is a server application with a web interface. This is quite common for applications that we always want on and pulling from some output log or other data processing folder. The following diagram shows TensorBoard running in the shell:

```
2019-11-02 11:40:20.756778: I T:\src\github\tensorflow\tensorflow\core\platform\cpu_feature_guard.cc:140] Your CPU
    instructions that this TensorFlow binary was not compiled to use: AVX2
TensorBoard 1.7.0 at http://DESKTOP-V2J9HRG:6006
```

TensorBoard starting up

7. When TB first runs, it will output the address that you can use in your browser to see the interface. Copy the URL as shown in the diagram and paste it to your favorite web browser. Note that if you have trouble accessing the page, it may be a binding issue, meaning your computer may be preventing this access. A couple of things to try are using a localhost:6006 or 127.0.0.1:6006 address and/or use the bind all option for TB.

8. When your browser opens and assuming you have not run TensorBoard before or put output in the data folder, you will see something like the following:

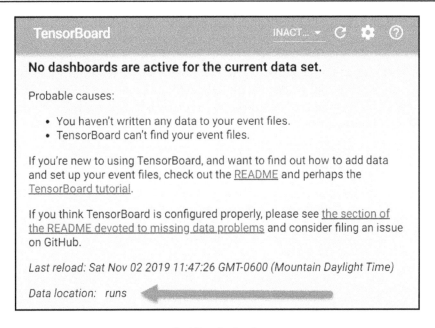

Empty TensorBoard running

The one important point to note when running TB for the first time is that it is using the right data folder. You should see the `Data location: runs` label designating the folder that will contain the logging output.

With TB set up, we can now move on to exploring the innovations that made Rainbow DQN so much better than vanilla DQN. While we have already used and explored a few of those innovations already, we can now move on to understanding the remaining two innovations that were included in Rainbow. We start with distributional RL in the next section.

Introducing distributional RL

The name distributional RL can be a bit misleading and may conjure up images of multilayer distributed networks of DQN all working together. Well, that indeed may be a description of distributed RL, but distribution RL is where we try and find the value distribution that DQN is predicting, that is, not just find the maximum or mean value but understanding the data distribution that generated it. This is quite similar to both intuition and purpose for PG methods. We do this by projecting our known or previously predicted distribution into a future or future predicted distribution.

This definitely requires us to review a code example, so open `Chapter_10_QRDQN.py` and follow the next exercise:

1. The entire code listing is too big to drop here, so we will look at sections of importance. We will start with the **QRDQN** or **Quantile Regressive DQN**. Quantile regression is a technique to predict distributions from observations. The QRDQN listing follows:

```python
class QRDQN(nn.Module):
    def __init__(self, num_inputs, num_actions, num_quants):
        super(QRDQN, self).__init__()
        self.num_inputs = num_inputs
        self.num_actions = num_actions
        self.num_quants = num_quants
        self.features = nn.Sequential(
            nn.Linear(num_inputs, 32),
            nn.ReLU(),
            nn.Linear(32, 64),
            nn.ReLU(),
            nn.Linear(64, 128),
            nn.ReLU(),
            nn.Linear(128, self.num_actions * self.num_quants)
        )
        self.num_quants, use_cuda=USE_CUDA)
    def forward(self, x):
        batch_size = x.size(0)
        x = self.features(x)
        x = x.view(batch_size, self.num_actions, self.num_quants)
        return x
    def q_values(self, x):
        x = self.forward(x)
        return x.mean(2)
    def act(self, state, epsilon):
        if random.random() > epsilon:
            state =
autograd.Variable(torch.FloatTensor(np.array(state,
dtype=np.float32)).unsqueeze(0), volatile=True)
            qvalues = self.forward(state).mean(2)
            action = qvalues.max(1)[1]
            action = action.data.cpu().numpy()[0]
        else:
            action = random.randrange(self.num_actions)
        return action
```

2. Most of this code looks the same as before, but one thing to note and not get confused by is `qvalues` denotes a Q value (state-action) and not a Q policy value as we saw with PG methods.

3. Next, we will scroll down to the `projection_distribution` function, as shown here:

```
def projection_distribution(dist, next_state, reward, done):
    next_dist = target_model(next_state)
    next_action = next_dist.mean(2).max(1)[1]
    next_action =
next_action.unsqueeze(1).unsqueeze(1).expand(batch_size, 1,
num_quant)
    next_dist = next_dist.gather(1,
next_action).squeeze(1).cpu().data

    expected_quant = reward.unsqueeze(1) + 0.99 * next_dist * (1 -
done.unsqueeze(1))
    expected_quant = autograd.Variable(expected_quant)

    quant_idx = torch.sort(dist, 1, descending=False)[1]

    tau_hat = torch.linspace(0.0, 1.0 - 1./num_quant, num_quant) +
0.5 / num_quant
    tau_hat = tau_hat.unsqueeze(0).repeat(batch_size, 1)
    quant_idx = quant_idx.cpu().data
    batch_idx = np.arange(batch_size)
    tau = tau_hat[:, quant_idx][batch_idx, batch_idx]
    return tau, expected_quant
```

4. This code is quite mathematical and outside the scope of this book. It essentially just extracts what it believes to be the distribution of Q values.

5. After that, we can see the construction of our two models, denoting that we are building a DDQN model here using the following code:

```
current_model = QRDQN(env.observation_space.shape[0],
env.action_space.n, num_quant)
target_model = QRDQN(env.observation_space.shape[0],
env.action_space.n, num_quant)
```

6. After that, we get the computation of the TD loss with the `computer_td_loss` function, shown here:

```python
def compute_td_loss(batch_size):
    state, action, reward, next_state, done =
replay_buffer.sample(batch_size)

    state = autograd.Variable(torch.FloatTensor(np.float32(state)))
    next_state =
autograd.Variable(torch.FloatTensor(np.float32(next_state)),
volatile=True)
    action = autograd.Variable(torch.LongTensor(action))
    reward = torch.FloatTensor(reward)
    done = torch.FloatTensor(np.float32(done))

    dist = current_model(state)
    action = action.unsqueeze(1).unsqueeze(1).expand(batch_size, 1,
num_quant)
    dist = dist.gather(1, action).squeeze(1)
    tau, expected_quant = projection_distribution(dist, next_state,
reward, done)
    k = 1
    huber_loss = 0.5 * tau.abs().clamp(min=0.0, max=k).pow(2)
    huber_loss += k * (tau.abs() - tau.abs().clamp(min=0.0, max=k))
    quantile_loss = (tau - (tau < 0).float()).abs() * huber_loss
    loss = torch.tensor(quantile_loss.sum() / num_quant,
requires_grad=True)
    optimizer.zero_grad()
    loss.backward()
    nn.utils.clip_grad_norm(current_model.parameters(), 0.5)
    optimizer.step()
    return loss
```

7. This loss calculation function is similar to other DQN implementations we have seen before although this one does expose a few twists and turns. Most of the twists are introduced by using **Quantile Regression** (**QR**). QR is essentially about predicting the distribution using quants or quantiles, that is, slices of the probability to iteratively determine the predicted distribution. This predicted distribution is then used to determine the network loss and train it back through the DL network. If you scroll back up, you can note the introduction of the three new hyperparameters that allow us to tune that search. These new values, shown here, allow us to define the number iterations, num_quants, and search range, Vmin and Vmax:

```
num_quant = 51
Vmin = -10
Vmax = 10
```

8. Finally, we can see how the training code is run by scrolling to the bottom of the code and reviewing it here:

```
state = env.reset()
for iteration in range(1, iterations + 1):
    action = current_model.act(state, epsilon_by_frame(iteration))
    next_state, reward, done, _ = env.step(action)
    replay_buffer.push(state, action, reward, next_state, done)
    state = next_state
    episode_reward += reward
    if done:
        state = env.reset()
        all_rewards.append(episode_reward)
        episode_reward = 0
    if len(replay_buffer) > batch_size:
        loss = compute_td_loss(batch_size)
        losses.append(loss.item())
    if iteration % 200 == 0:
        plot(iteration, all_rewards, losses, episode_reward)
    if iteration % 1000 == 0:
        update_target(current_model, target_model)
```

9. We have seen very similar code in Chapters 6 and 7 when we previously looked at DQN so we won't review it here. Instead, familiarize yourself with the DQN model again if you need to. Note the differences between it and PG methods. When you are ready, run the code as you normally would. The output of running the sample is shown here:

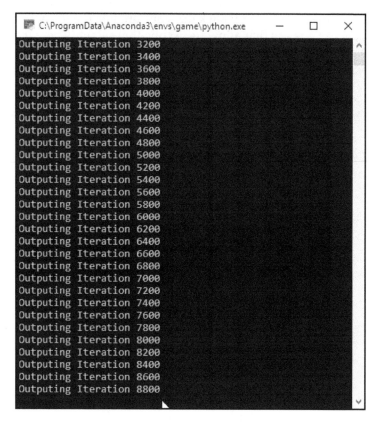

Example output from Chapter_10_QRDQN.py

The output generated from this sample is just a reminder that we have more information being output to a log folder. To see that log folder, we need to run TensorBoard again and we will do that in the next section.

Back to TensorBoard

With the sample from the last exercise still running, we want to return to TensorBoard and now see the output from our sample running. To do that, open a new Python/Anaconda command shell and follow the next exercise:

1. Open the shell to the same folder you are running your previous exercise code example in. Switch to your virtual environment or a special one just for TB and then run the following command to start the process:

```
tensorboard --logdir=runs
```

2. This will start TB in the current folder using that `runs` folder as the data dump directory. After the sample is running for a while, you may see something like the following when you visit the TB web interface now:

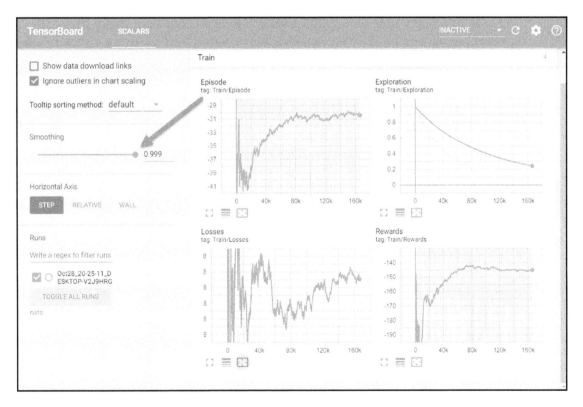

TensorBoard output from Chapter_10_QRDQN.py

3. Turn up the **Smoothing** control as shown in the screenshot to see the visual trend of the data. Seeing a general trend in the data allows you to extrapolate if or when your agent may be fully trained.

4. Now, we need to go back to the `Chapter_10_QRDQN.py` example code and see how we generated this output data. First, notice the new `import` and declaration of a new variable, `writer`, of the `SummaryWriter` class imported from `torch.utils.tensorboard` and shown here:

```
from common.replay_buffer import ReplayBuffer
from torch.utils.tensorboard import SummaryWriter

env_id = "LunarLander-v2"
env = gym.make(env_id)
writer = SummaryWriter()
```

5. The `writer` object is used to output to the log files that get constructed in the `run` folder. Every time we run this example piece of code now, this writer will output to the `run` folder. You can alter this behavior by inputting a directory into the `SummaryWriter` constructor.

6. Next, scroll down to the revised `plot` function. This function, shown here, now generates the log output we can visualize with TB:

```
def plot(iteration, rewards, losses, ep_reward):
    print("Outputing Iteration " + str(iteration))
    writer.add_scalar('Train/Rewards', rewards[-1], iteration)
    writer.add_scalar('Train/Losses', losses[-1], iteration)
    writer.add_scalar('Train/Exploration',
epsilon_by_frame(iteration), iteration)
    writer.add_scalar('Train/Episode', ep_reward, iteration)
    writer.flush()
```

7. This updated block of code now outputs results using TB `writer` and not `matplotlib plot`, as we did before. Each `writer.add_scalar` call adds a value to the data plot we visualized earlier. There are plenty of other functions you can call on to add many different types of output. Considering the ease with which we can generate impressive output, you likely may ever find a need to use `matplotlib` again.

8. Go back to your TB web interface and observe the continued training output.

This code sample may need some tuning to be able to tune the agent to a successful policy. However, you now have at your disposal even more powerful tools TensorBoard to assist you in doing that. In the next section, we will look at the last improvement introduced by Rainbow, noisy networks.

Understanding noisy networks

Noisy networks are not those networks that need to know everything—those would be nosey networks. Instead, noisy networks introduce the concept of noise into the weights used to predict the output through the network. So, instead of having a single scalar value to denote the weight in a perceptron, we now think of weights as being pulled from some form of distribution. Obviously, we have a common theme going on here and that is going from working with numbers as single scalar values to what is better described as a distribution of data. If you have studied the subject of Bayesian or variational inference, you will likely understand this concept concretely.

For those without that background, let's look at what a distribution could be in the following diagram:

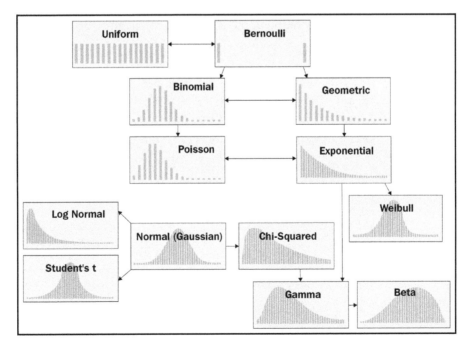

Example of different data distributions

The source for the preceding diagram comes from a blog post by Akshay Sharma (`https://medium.com/mytake/understanding-different-types-of-distributions-you-will-encounter-as-a-data-scientist-27ea4c375eec`). What is shown in the diagram is a sampling pattern of various well-known data distributions. Basic statistics assumes that all data is always evenly or normally distributed. In statistics, you will learn of other distributions you use to define various tests of variance or fit such as the Chi or Student's t. You are also likely quite familiar with a uniform distribution if you have ever sampled a random number in a computer program. Most computer programs always assume a uniform distribution, which in some ways is the problem we have in machine learning and hence the move to better understanding how real data or actions/events are distributed.

Variational inference or quantitative risk analysis is a technique whereby we use typical equations of engineering, economics, or other disciplines and assume their inputs are distributions rather that discriminant values. By using distributions of data as input we, therefore, assume our output is also a distribution in some form. That distribution can then be used to evaluate terms of risk or reward.

It's time for another exercise, so open `Chapter_10_NDQN.py` and follow the next exercise:

1. This is another big example so we will only focus on what is important. Let's start by scrolling down and looking at the `NoisyDQN` class here:

```python
class NoisyDQN(nn.Module):
    def __init__(self, num_inputs, num_actions):
        super(NoisyDQN, self).__init__()
        self.linear = nn.Linear(env.observation_space.shape[0],
128)
        self.noisy1 = NoisyLinear(128, 128)
        self.noisy2 = NoisyLinear(128, env.action_space.n)
    def forward(self, x):
        x = F.relu(self.linear(x))
        x = F.relu(self.noisy1(x))
        x = self.noisy2(x)
        return x
    def act(self, state):
        state =
autograd.Variable(torch.FloatTensor(state).unsqueeze(0),
volatile=True)
        q_value = self.forward(state)
        action = q_value.max(1)[1].item()
        return action
    def reset_noise(self):
        self.noisy1.reset_noise()
        self.noisy2.reset_noise()
```

2. This is quite similar to our previous DQN samples but with a key difference: the addition of a new specialized DL network layer type called `NoisyLinear`.

3. Scrolling down further, we can see the `td_compute_loss` function updated to handle the noisy or fuzzy layers:

```
def compute_td_loss(batch_size, beta):
    state, action, reward, next_state, done, weights, indices =
replay_buffer.sample(batch_size, beta)

    state = autograd.Variable(torch.FloatTensor(np.float32(state)))
    next_state =
autograd.Variable(torch.FloatTensor(np.float32(next_state)))
    action = autograd.Variable(torch.LongTensor(action))
    reward = autograd.Variable(torch.FloatTensor(reward))
    done = autograd.Variable(torch.FloatTensor(np.float32(done)))
    weights = autograd.Variable(torch.FloatTensor(weights))

    q_values = current_model(state)
    next_q_values = target_model(next_state)

    q_value = q_values.gather(1, action.unsqueeze(1)).squeeze(1)
    next_q_value = next_q_values.max(1)[0]
    expected_q_value = reward + gamma * next_q_value * (1 - done)
    loss = (q_value - expected_q_value.detach()).pow(2) * weights
    prios = loss + 1e-5
    loss = loss.mean()
    optimizer.zero_grad()
    loss.backward()
    optimizer.step()
    replay_buffer.update_priorities(indices,
prios.data.cpu().numpy())
    current_model.reset_noise()
    target_model.reset_noise()
    return loss
```

4. This function is quite close to our previous vanilla DQN examples and that is because all of the work/difference is going on in the new noisy layers, which we will get to shortly.

5. Scroll back up the definition of the `NoisyLinear` class, as seen here:

```
class NoisyLinear(nn.Module):
    def __init__(self, in_features, out_features, std_init=0.4):
        super(NoisyLinear, self).__init__()
        self.in_features = in_features
        self.out_features = out_features
        self.std_init = std_init
        self.weight_mu =
```

```
nn.Parameter(torch.FloatTensor(out_features, in_features))
        self.weight_sigma =
nn.Parameter(torch.FloatTensor(out_features, in_features))
        self.register_buffer('weight_epsilon',
torch.FloatTensor(out_features, in_features))
        self.bias_mu =
nn.Parameter(torch.FloatTensor(out_features))
        self.bias_sigma =
nn.Parameter(torch.FloatTensor(out_features))
        self.register_buffer('bias_epsilon',
torch.FloatTensor(out_features))
        self.reset_parameters()
        self.reset_noise()
    def forward(self, x):
        if self.training:
            weight = self.weight_mu +
self.weight_sigma.mul(autograd.Variable(self.weight_epsilon))
            bias = self.bias_mu +
self.bias_sigma.mul(autograd.Variable(self.bias_epsilon))
        else:
            weight = self.weight_mu
            bias = self.bias_mu
        return F.linear(x, weight, bias)
    def reset_parameters(self):
        mu_range = 1 / math.sqrt(self.weight_mu.size(1))
        self.weight_mu.data.normal_(-mu_range, mu_range)
        self.weight_sigma.data.fill_(self.std_init /
math.sqrt(self.weight_sigma.size(1)))
        self.bias_mu.data.normal_(-mu_range, mu_range)
        self.bias_sigma.data.fill_(self.std_init /
math.sqrt(self.bias_sigma.size(0)))
    def reset_noise(self):
        epsilon_in = self._scale_noise(self.in_features)
        epsilon_out = self._scale_noise(self.out_features)
        self.weight_epsilon.copy_(epsilon_out.ger(epsilon_in))
self.bias_epsilon.copy_(self._scale_noise(self.out_features))
    def _scale_noise(self, size):
        x = torch.randn(size)
        x = x.sign().mul(x.abs().sqrt())
        return x
```

6. The `NoisyLinear` class is a layer that uses a normal distribution to define each of the weights in the layers. This distribution is assumed to be normal, which means it is defined by a mean, mu, and standard variation, sigma. So, if we assumed 100 weights in a layer previously, we would now have two values (mu and sigma) that now define how the weight is sampled. In turn, the values for mu and sigma also become the values we train the network on.

With other frameworks, building in the ability to apply variational weights to layers is quite difficult and often requires more code. Fortunately, this is one of the strengths with PyTorch and it boosts a built-in probabilistic framework designed to predict and handle distributional data.

7. Different distributions may use different descriptive values to define them. The normal or Gaussian distribution is defined by mu and sigma, while the uniform distribution is often just defined by a min/max values and the triangle would be min/max and peak value for instance. We almost always prefer to use a normal distribution for most natural events.

8. Scroll down to the training code and you will see virtually the same code as the last exercise with one key difference. Instead of epsilon for exploration, we introduce a term called beta. Beta becomes our de-facto exploration term and replaces epsilon.

9. Run the application as you normally would and observe the training in TensorBoard, as shown in the screenshot here:

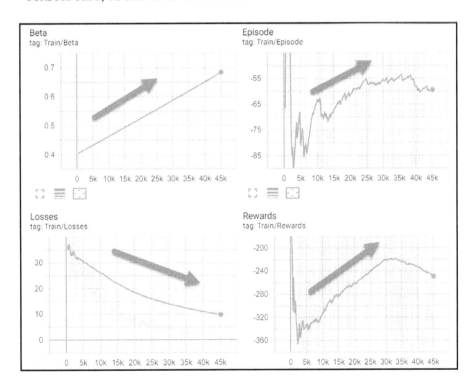

TensorBoard output from sample Chapter_10_NDQN.py

The arrows and the direction the arrow is pointing denotes the direction in which we want our agent/algorithm to move. We get these trend plots by increasing the **Smoothing** parameter to the max, .99. By doing this, it is easier to see the general or median trend.

One thing we need to revisit before moving on to Rainbow is how exploration is managed when using noisy networks. This will also help to explain the use of that the new beta parameter for z.

Noisy networks for exploration and importance sampling

Using noisy networks also introduces fuzziness in our action prediction. That is, since the weights of the network are now being pulled from a distribution that also means that they equally becoming distributional. We can also say they are stochastic and that stochasticity is defined by a distribution, basically meaning that the same input could yield two completely different results, which means we can no longer take just the max or best action because that is now just fuzzy. Instead, we need a way to decrease the size of the sampling distributions we use for weights and therefore the uncertainty we have in the actions the agent selects.

 Decreasing the size of a distribution is more or less the same as reducing the uncertainty in that data. This is a cornerstone of data science and machine learning.

We reduce this uncertainty by introducing a factor called beta that is increased over time. This increase is not unlike epsilon but just in reverse. Let's see how this looks in code by opening `Chapter_10_NDQN.py` back up and follow the exercise here:

1. We can see how beta is defined by looking at the main code here:

```
beta_start = 0.4
beta_iterations = 50000
beta_by_iteration = lambda iteration: min(1.0, beta_start +
iteration * (1.0 - beta_start) / beta_iterations)
```

2. This setup and equation are again not unlike how we defined epsilon previously. The difference here is that beta increases gradually.

3. Beta is used to correct the weights being trained and hence introduces the concept of importance sampling. Importance sampling is about how much importance we have on the weights before correcting/sampling them. Beta then becomes the importance sampling factor where a value of 1.0 means 100% important and 0 means no importance.

4. Open up the `replay_buffer.py` file found in the `common` folder in the same project. Scroll down to the `sample` function and notice the code, as shown here:

```
assert beta > 0

idxes = self._sample_proportional(batch_size)

weights = []
p_min = self._it_min.min() / self._it_sum.sum()
max_weight = (p_min * len(self._storage)) ** (-beta)

for idx in idxes:
    p_sample = self._it_sum[idx] / self._it_sum.sum()
    weight = (p_sample * len(self._storage)) ** (-beta)
    weights.append(weight / max_weight)
weights = np.array(weights)
encoded_sample = self._encode_sample(idxes)
return tuple(list(encoded_sample) + [weights, idxes])
```

5. The `sample` function is part of the `PrioritizedExperienceReplay` class we are using to hold experiences. There's no need for us to review this whole class other than to realize it orders experiences in terms of priority. Sampling weights for the network based on the importance factor, `beta`.

6. Finally, jump back to the sample code and review the plot function. The line that generates our plot of beta in TensorBoard now looks like this:

```
writer.add_scalar('Train/Beta', beta_by_iteration(iteration),
iteration)
```

7. At this point, you can review more of the code or try and tune the new hyperparameters before continuing.

That completes our look at noisy and not nosey networks for exploration. We saw how we could introduce distributions to be used as the weights for our DL network. Then, we saw how, to compensate for that, we needed to introduce a new training parameter, beta. In the next section, we see how all these pieces come together in Rainbow DQN.

Unveiling Rainbow DQN

The author of *Rainbow: Combining Improvements in Deep Reinforcement Learning*, Matteo Hessel (`https://arxiv.org/search/cs?searchtype=authoramp;query=Hessel%2C+M`), did several comparisons against other state-of-the-art models in DRL, many of which we have already looked at. They performed these comparisons against the standard 2D classic Atari games with impressive results. Rainbow DQN outperformed all of the current state-of-the-art algorithms. In the paper, they used the familiar classic Atari environment. This is fine since DeepMind has a lot of data for that environment that is specific to applicable models to compare with. However, many have observed that the paper lacks a comparison between PG methods, such as PPO. Of course, PPO is an OpenAI advancement and it may have been perceived by Google DeepMind to be an infringement or just wanting to avoid acknowledgment by comparing it at all. Unfortunately, this also suggests that even a highly intellectual pursuit such as DRL cannot be removed from politics.

 Methods such as PPO have been used to beat or best some of the biggest challenges in DRL currently. PPO was in fact responsible for taking the 100 thousand dollar grand prize in the Unity Obstacle Tower Challenge. For that reason, you should not discount PG methods anytime soon.

Given that previous plot, we should be expecting some big things from Rainbow. So, let's open up `Chapter_10_Rainbow.py` and follow the next exercise:

1. This example will be very familiar by now and we will limit ourselves to looking at just the differences, starting with the main implementation of the `RainbowDQN` class itself here:

```
class RainbowDQN(nn.Module):
    def __init__(self, num_inputs, num_actions, num_atoms, Vmin,
Vmax):
        super(RainbowDQN, self).__init__()
        self.num_inputs = num_inputs
        self.num_actions = num_actions
        self.num_atoms = num_atoms
```

```
        self.Vmin = Vmin
        self.Vmax = Vmax
        self.linear1 = nn.Linear(num_inputs, 32)
        self.linear2 = nn.Linear(32, 64)
        self.noisy_value1 = NoisyLinear(64, 64, use_cuda=False)
        self.noisy_value2 = NoisyLinear(64, self.num_atoms,
use_cuda=False)
        self.noisy_advantage1 = NoisyLinear(64, 64, use_cuda=False)
        self.noisy_advantage2 = NoisyLinear(64, self.num_atoms *
self.num_actions, use_cuda=False)
    def forward(self, x):
        batch_size = x.size(0)
        x = F.relu(self.linear1(x))
        x = F.relu(self.linear2(x))
        value = F.relu(self.noisy_value1(x))
        value = self.noisy_value2(value)
        advantage = F.relu(self.noisy_advantage1(x))
        advantage = self.noisy_advantage2(advantage)
        value = value.view(batch_size, 1, self.num_atoms)
        advantage = advantage.view(batch_size, self.num_actions,
self.num_atoms)
        x = value + advantage - advantage.mean(1, keepdim=True)
        x = F.softmax(x.view(-1, self.num_atoms)).view(-1,
self.num_actions, self.num_atoms)
        return x
    def reset_noise(self):
        self.noisy_value1.reset_noise()
        self.noisy_value2.reset_noise()
        self.noisy_advantage1.reset_noise()
        self.noisy_advantage2.reset_noise()
    def act(self, state):
        state =
autograd.Variable(torch.FloatTensor(state).unsqueeze(0),
volatile=True)
        dist = self.forward(state).data.cpu()
        dist = dist * torch.linspace(self.Vmin, self.Vmax,
self.num_atoms)
        action = dist.sum(2).max(1)[1].numpy()[0]
        return action
```

2. The preceding code defines the network structure for the RainbowDQN. This network is a bit complicated so we have put the major elements in the diagram here:

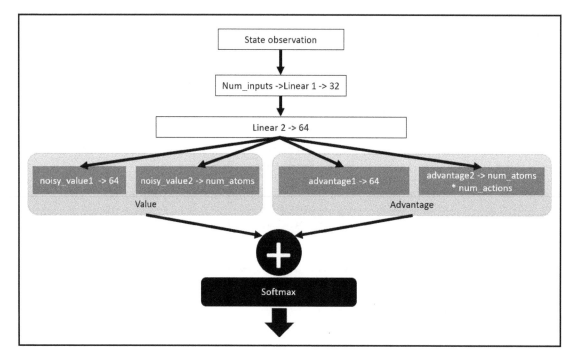

Rainbow Network Architecture

3. If you go over the `init` and `forward` functions, you should be able to see how this diagram was built.

4. We can't leave the preceding code just yet and we need to review the act function again and shown here:

```
def act(self, state):
        state =
autograd.Variable(torch.FloatTensor(state).unsqueeze(0),
volatile=True)
        dist = self.forward(state).data.cpu()
        dist = dist * torch.linspace(self.Vmin, self.Vmax,
self.num_atoms)
        action = dist.sum(2).max(1)[1].numpy()[0]
        return action
```

5. The `act` function shows how the agent selects an action. We have refined the action selection strategy here and now use the values for Vmin, Vmax, and num_atoms . We use these values as inputs into `torch.linspace` as a way to create a discrete distribution ranging in value from Vmin to Vmax and in steps defined by num_atoms. This outputs scaling values within the min/max ranges that are then multiplied by the original distribution, `dist`, output from the `forward` function. This multiplying a distribution returned by the `forward` function and the one generated from `torch.linspace` applies a type of scaling.

You may have noticed that the hyperparameters, num_atoms, Vmin, and Vmax, now perform dual purposes in tuning parameters in the model. This is generally a bad thing. That is, you always want the hyperparameters you define to be single-purpose.

6. Next, we will scroll down and look at the differences in the `projection_distribution` function. Remember this function is what performs the distributional part of finding the distribution rather than a discrete value:

```
def projection_distribution(next_state, rewards, dones):
    batch_size = next_state.size(0)
    delta_z = float(Vmax - Vmin) / (num_atoms - 1)
    support = torch.linspace(Vmin, Vmax, num_atoms)
    next_dist = target_model(next_state).data.cpu() * support
    next_action = next_dist.sum(2).max(1)[1]
    next_action =
next_action.unsqueeze(1).unsqueeze(1).expand(next_dist.size(0), 1,
next_dist.size(2))
    next_dist = next_dist.gather(1, next_action).squeeze(1)
    rewards = rewards.unsqueeze(1).expand_as(next_dist)
    dones = dones.unsqueeze(1).expand_as(next_dist)
    support = support.unsqueeze(0).expand_as(next_dist)
    Tz = rewards + (1 - dones) * 0.99 * support
```

```
        Tz = Tz.clamp(min=Vmin, max=Vmax)
        b = (Tz - Vmin) / delta_z
        l = b.floor().long()
        u = b.ceil().long()
        offset = torch.linspace(0, (batch_size - 1) * num_atoms,
    batch_size).long()\
                            .unsqueeze(1).expand(batch_size, num_atoms)

        proj_dist = torch.zeros(next_dist.size())
        proj_dist.view(-1).index_add_(0, (l + offset).view(-1),
    (next_dist * (u.float() - b)).view(-1))
        proj_dist.view(-1).index_add_(0, (u + offset).view(-1),
    (next_dist * (b - l.float())).view(-1))
        return proj_dist
```

7. This code is quite different than the quantile regression code we looked at previously. The primary difference here is the use of the PyTorch libraries here whereas before, the code was more low-level. Using the libraries is a bit more verbose but hopefully, you can appreciate how more explanatory the code is now compared to the previous example.

8. One thing to note here is that we continue to use epsilon for exploration, as the following code shows:

```
epsilon_start = 1.0
epsilon_final = 0.01
epsilon_decay = 50000

epsilon_by_frame = lambda iteration: epsilon_final + (epsilon_start
- epsilon_final) * math.exp(-1. * iteration / epsilon_decay)
```

9. Run the example as you normally would and observe the output.

Keep in mind that since this example lacks a prioritized replay buffer, it fails to be a complete RainbowDQN implementation. However, it does cover the 80/20 rule and implementing a prioritized replay buffer is left as an exercise to the reader. Let the sample keep running while we jump to the next section on observing training.

When does training fail?

One thing that trips any newcomer to DL and certainly deep reinforcement learning is when to know whether your model is failing, is just being a bit stubborn, or is not ever going to work. It is a question that causes frustration and angst in the AI field and often leaves you to wonder: *what if I let that agent train a day longer*? Unfortunately, if you speak to experts, they will often say just be patient and keep training, but this perhaps builds on those frustrations. After all, what if what you built has no hope of ever doing anything—are you wasting time and energy to keep it going?

Another issue that many face is that the more complex an algorithm/model gets, the more time it takes to train, except you never know how long that is unless you trained it before or read a really well-written paper that uses the exact same model. Even with the same exact model, the environment may also differ perhaps being more complex as well. With all of these factors at play, as well as the pain of tuning hyperparameters, it is a wonder why anyone of sane mind would want to work in DRL at all.

 The author hosts a Deep Learning Meetup support group for RL and DRL. One of the frequent discussions in this group is how DL researchers can keep their sanity and/or reduce their stress levels. If you work in AI, you understand the constant need to live up to the hype overcoming the world. This hype is a good thing but can also be a bad thing when it involves investors or impatient bosses.

Fortunately, with advanced tools such as TensorBoard, we can gain insights into how are agent trains or hopes to train.

Open up TensorBoard and follow the next exercise to see how to effectively diagnose training problems:

1. The output from TB is shown in the following screenshot:

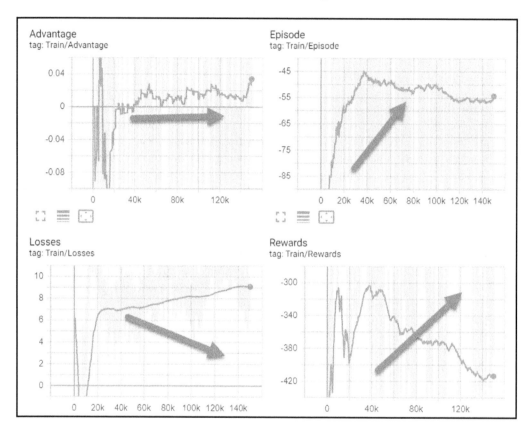

TensorBoard output from Rainbow DQN

2. From the preceding screenshot, where the **Smoothing** has been upped to .99, we can see training is failing. Remember, the graphs in the screenshot are annotated to show the preferred direction. For all of those plots, that is not the case. However, don't assume that if the plot is going in the opposite direction that it is necessarily bad—it isn't. Instead, any movement is a better indication of some training activity. This is also the reason we smooth these plots so highly.

3. The one key plot that often dictates future training performance is the **Losses** plot. An agent will be learning when losses are decreasing and will be forgetting/confused if the losses are increasing. If losses remain constant, then the agent is stagnant and could be confused or stuck. A helpful summary of this is shown in the screenshot here:

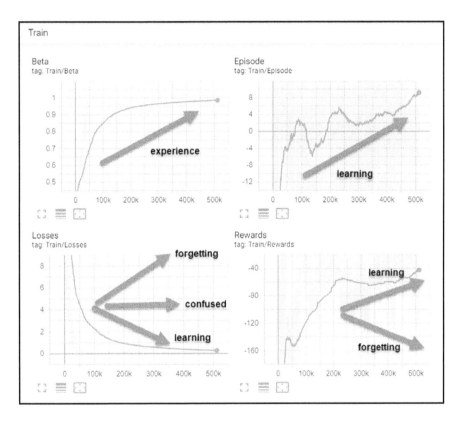

The Losses plot summarized

4. The preceding screenshot shows the ideal training over 500 thousand episodes and for this environment, you can expect to train double or triple that amount. As a general rule, it is best to consider no movement, positive or negative, over 10% or the training time to be a failure. For example, if you are training an agent for 1 million iterations, then your 10% window would be about 100 thousand iterations. If your agent is training constantly or flat-lining in any plot, aside from **Advantage**, over a period equal to or larger than the 10% window size, it may be best to tune hyperparameters and start again.

5. Again, pay special attention to the **Losses** plot as this provides the strongest indicator for training problems.

6. You can run view the results of multiple training efforts side by side by just running the sample repeatedly for the same number of iterations, as the screenshot here shows:

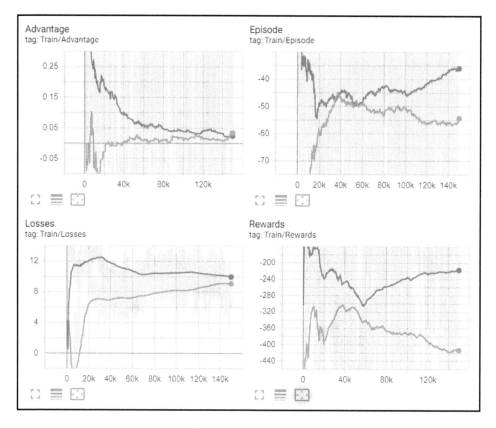

Examples of multiple training outputs on the same graph

7. Stop the current sample change some hyperparameters and run it again to see the preceding example.

These simple rules will hopefully help you to avoid frustrations on building/training your own models on new or different environments. Fortunately, we have several more chapters to work through and that includes plenty of more exercises like those featured in the next section.

Exercises

When it comes to working in the real world, the experience you build from doing these exercises may mean the difference between not getting that job and certainly keeping it. As a programmer, you don't have the luxury of just understanding how something works; you're a mechanic/engineer that needs to get their hands dirty and actually do the work:

1. Tune the hyperparameters for `Chapter_10_QRDQN.py` and see what effect this has on training.

2. Tune the hyperparameters for `Chapter_10_NDQN.py` and see what effect this has on training.

3. Tune the hyperparameters for `Chapter_10_Rainbow.py` and see what effect this has on training.

4. Run and tune the hyperparameters for any of this chapter's samples on another environment such as CartPole or FrozenLake or something more complex such as Atari. Reducing the complexity of an environment is also helpful if your computer is older and needs to work harder training agents.

5. This chapter also includes sample code for Hierarchical DQNs and Categorical DQNs in the `Chapter_10_HDQN.py` and `Chapter_10_C51.py` samples. Run these examples, review the code, and do some investigation on your own on what improvements these samples bring to DRL.

6. Add the ability to save/load the trained model from any of the examples. Can you now use the trained model to show the agent playing the game?

7. Add the ability to output other training values to TensorBoard that you may think are important to training an agent.

8. Add `NoisyLinear` layers to the `Chapter_10_QRDQN.py` example. There may already be code that is just commented out in the example.

9. Add a prioritized replay buffer to the `Chapter_10_Rainbow.py` example. You can use the same method found in the `Chapter_10_NDQN.py` example.

10. TensorBoard allows you to output and visualize a trained model. Use TensorBoard to output the trained model from one of the examples.

Obviously, the number of exercises has increased to reflect your increasing skill level and/or interest in DRL. You certainly don't need to complete all of these exercises but 2-3 will go a long way. In the next section, we will summarize the chapter.

Summary

In this chapter, we looked specifically at one of the more state-of-the-art advances in DRL from DeepMind called Rainbow DQN. Rainbow combines several improvements layered on top of DQN that allow dramatic increases in training performance. As we have already covered many of these improvements, we only needed to review a couple of new advances. Before doing that though, we installed TensorBoard as a tool to investigate training performance. Then, we looked at the first advancement in distributional RL and how to model the action by understanding the sampling distribution. Continuing with distributions, we then looked at noisy network layers—network layers that don't have individual weights but rather individual distributions to describe each weight. Building on this example, we moved onto Rainbow DQN with our last example, finishing off with a quick discussion on when to determine whether an agent is not trainable or flat-lining.

For the next chapter, we will move from building DRL algorithms/agents to building environments with Unity and constructing agents in those environments with the ML-Agents toolkit.

11
Exploiting ML-Agents

At some point, we need to move beyond building and training agent algorithms and explore building our own environments. Building your own environments will also give you more experience in making good reward functions. We have virtually omitted this important question in **Reinforcement Learning** (**RL**) and **Deep Reinforcement Learning** (**DRL**) and that is what makes a good reward function.

In this chapter, we will look to answer the question of what makes a good reward function or what a reward function is. We will talk about reward functions by building new environments with the Unity game engine. We will start by installing and setting up Unity ML-Agents, an advanced DRL kit for building agents and environments. From there, we will look at how to build one of the standard Unity demo environments for our use with our PyTorch models. Conveniently, this leads us to working with the ML-Agents toolkit for using a Unity environment from Python and PyTorch with our previously explored Rainbow DQN model. After that, we will look at creating a new environment, and then finish this chapter by looking at advances Unity has developed for furthering RL.

Here are the main topics we will cover in this chapter:

- Installing ML-Agents
- Building a Unity environment
- Training a Unity environment with Rainbow
- Creating a new environment
- Advancing RL with ML-Agents

Unity is the largest and most frequently used game engine for game development. You likely already know this if you are a game developer. The game engine itself is developed with C++ but it provides a scripting interface in C# that 99% of its game developers use. As such, we will need to expose you to some C# code in this chapter, but just a tiny amount.

In the next section, we'll install Unity and the ML-Agents toolkit.

Installing ML-Agents

Installing Unity, the game engine itself, is not very difficult, but when working with ML-Agents, you need to be careful when you pick your version. As such, the next exercise is intended to be more configurable, meaning you may need to ask/answer questions while performing the exercise. We did this to make this exercise longer lasting since this toolkit has been known to change frequently with many breaking changes.

Unity will run on any major desktop computer (Windows, Mac, or Linux), so open your development computer and follow along with the next exercise to install Unity and the ML-Agents toolkit:

1. Before installing Unity, check the ML-Agents GitHub installation page (`https://github.com/Unity-Technologies/ml-agents/blob/master/docs/Installation.md`) and confirm which version of Unity is currently supported. At the time of writing, this is 2017.4, and we will prefer to use only that version even though the documentation suggests later versions are supported.

 You can download and install Unity directly or through the Unity Hub. Since managing multiple versions of Unity is so common, Unity built a management app, the Unity Hub, for this purpose.

2. Download and install the required minimum version of Unity. If you have never installed Unity, you will need to create a user account and verify their license agreement. After you create a user account, you will be able to run the Unity editor.

3. Open a Python/Anaconda command shell and make sure to activate your virtual environment with the following command:

```
conda activate gameAI
--- or ---
activate gameAI
```

4. Install the Unity Gym wrapper with the following command:

```
pip install gym_unity
```

5. Change to a root working folder, preferably `C:` or `/`, and create a directory for cloning the ML-Agents toolkit into with the following command:

```
cd /
mkdir mlagents
cd mlagents
```

6. Then, assuming you have `git` installed, use `git` to pull down the ML-Agents toolkit with this:

```
git clone https://github.com/Unity-Technologies/ml-agents.git
```

The reason we prefer a root folder is that the ML-Agents directory structure can get quite deep and this may cause too long filename errors on some operating systems.

7. Testing the entire installation is best done by consulting the current Unity docs and using their most recent guide. A good place to start is the first example environment, the 3D Balance Ball. You can find this document at `https://github.com/Unity-Technologies/ml-agents/blob/master/docs/Getting-Started-with-Balance-Ball.md`.

Take some time and explore the ML-Agents toolkit on your own. It is meant to be quite accessible and if your only experience in DRL is this book, you should have plenty of background by now to understand the general gist of running Unity environments. We will review some of these procedures but there are plenty of other helpful guides out there that can help you run ML-Agents in Unity. Our priority here will be using Unity to build environments and possibly new environments we can use to test our models on. While we won't use the ML-Agents toolkit to train agents, we will use the Gym wrappers, which do require knowledge of what a brain or academy is.

Adam Kelly has an excellent blog, Immersive limit (`http://www.immersivelimit.com/tutorials/tag/Unity+ML+Agents`), devoted to machine learning and DRL with a specialization of creating very cool ML-Agents environments and projects.

ML-Agents currently uses PPO and Soft Actor-Critic methods to train agents. It also provides several helpful modules for state encoding using convolutional and recurrent networks, hence allowing for visual observation encoding and memory or context. Additionally, it provides methods for defining discrete or continuous action spaces, as well as enabling mixing action or observation types. The toolkit is extremely well done but, with the rapidly changing landscape of ML, it has become quickly outdated and/or perhaps just out-hyped. In the end, it also appears that most researchers or serious practitioners of DRL just want to build their own frameworkll for now.

While DRL is quite complicated, the amount of code to make something powerful is still quite small. Therefore, we will likely see a plethora of RL frameworks trying to gain a foothold on the space. Whether you decide to use one of these frameworks or build your own is up to you. Just remember that frameworks come and go, but the more underlying knowledge you have on a topic, the better your ability to guide future decisions.

Regardless of whether you decide to use the ML-Agents framework for training DRL agents, use another framework, or build your own, Unity provides you with an excellent opportunity to build new and more exciting environments. We learn how to build a Unity environment we can train with DRL in the next section.

Building a Unity environment

The ML-Agents toolkit provides not only a DRL training framework but also a mechanism to quickly and easily set up AI agents within a Unity game. Those agents can then be externally controlled through a Gym interface—yes, that same interface we used to train most of our previous agent/algorithms. One of the truly great things about this platform is that Unity provides several new demo environments that we can explore. Later, we will look at how to build our own environments for training agents.

The exercises in this section are meant to summarize the setup steps required to build an executable environment to train with Python. They are intended for newcomers to Unity who don't want to learn all about Unity to just build a training environment. If you encounter issues using these exercises, it is likely the SDK may have changed. If that is the case, then just revert back and consult the full online documentation.

Building a Unity environment for agent training requires a few specialized steps we will cover in this exercise:

1. First, open the Unity editor, either through the Unity Hub or just Unity itself. Remember to use a version that supports the ML-Agents toolkit.
2. Using the Unity Hub, we can add the project using the **Add** button, as shown in the following screenshot:

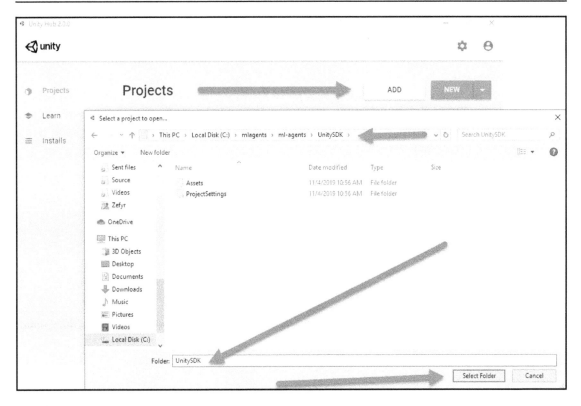

Adding a project in the Unity Hub

3. After you click **Add**, you will be prompted to locate the project folder. Use the dialog to find and select the UnitySDK project folder we pulled down with git in the previous exercise. This folder should be located in your /mlagents/ml-agents/UnitySDK folder.

4. When the project has been added, it will also be added to the top of the list of projects. You will likely see a warning icon indicating you need to select the version number. Select a version of Unity that coincides with the ML-Agents toolkit and then select the project to launch it in the editor.

5. You may be prompted to **Upgrade** the project. If you are prompted, then select **Yes** to do so. If the upgrade fails or the project won't run right, then you can just delete all of the old files and try again with a different version of Unity. Loading this project may take some time, so be patient, grab a drink, and wait.

6. After the project finishes loading and the editor opens, open the scene for the `3DBall` environment located in the `Assets/ML-Agents/Examples/Hallway/Scenes` folder by double-clicking on the `3DBall` scene file.

7. We need to set the Academy to control the brain, that is, allow the brain to be trained. To do that, select the **Academy**, then locate the **Hallway Academy** component in the **Inspector** window, and select the **Control** option, as shown in the following screenshot:

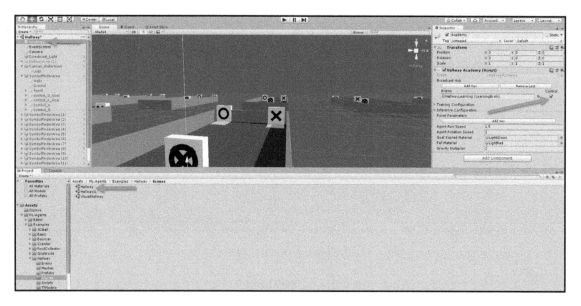

Setting the academy to control the brain

8. Next, we need to modify the run parameters for the environment. The idea here is that we will build the Unity environment as an executable game that we can then use the wrappers on to train an agent to play. However, to do that, we need to make some assumptions about the game:

   - The game is windowless and runs in the background.
   - Any player actions need to be controlled by the agent. A dialog prompts for warnings, errors, or anything else that must be avoided.
   - Make sure that the training scene is loaded first.

9. Before finishing that though, turn the **Control** option back off or on for the academy and run the scene by pressing the **Play** button at the top of the interface. You will be able to observe an already trained agent play through the scene. Make sure to turn the **Control** option back on when you are done viewing the agent play.

Now, the ML-Agents toolkit will allow you to train directly from here by just running a separate Python command shell and script controlling the editor. As of yet, this is not possible and our only way to run an environment is with wrappers. In the next section, we will finish setting up the environment by setting some final parameters and building them.

Building for Gym wrappers

Configuring the setup of an environment just requires setting a few additional parameters. We will learn how to do this in the following exercise:

1. From the editor menu, select **Edit** | **Project Settings...** to open the **Project Settings** window. You can anchor this window or close it after you've finished editing.

2. Select the **Player** option. Player, in this case, denotes the player or game runner—not to be confused with an actual human player. Change the text in the **Company Name** and **Product Name** fields to `GameAI`.

3. Open the **Resolution and Presentation** section and then be sure that **Run In Background*** is checked and **Display Resolution Dialog** is set to **Disabled**, as shown in the following screenshot:

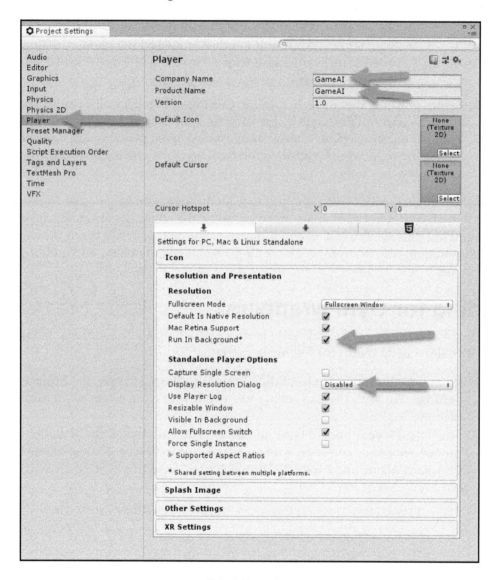

Setting the Player settings

4. Close the dialog or anchor it and then, from the menu, select **File** | **Build Settings**.

5. Click the **Add Open Scene** button and be sure to select your default platform for training. This should be a desktop environment you can easily run with Python. The following screenshot shows the Windows option by default:

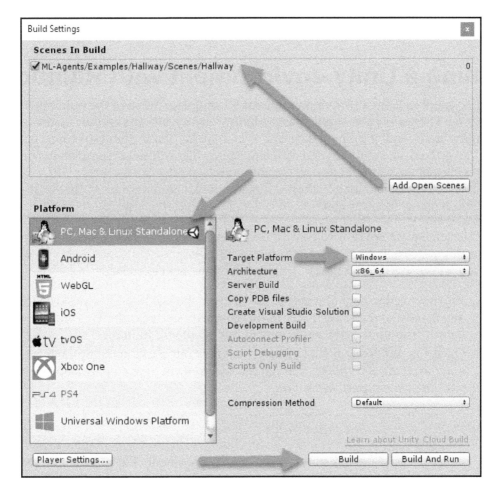

Building the scene into a game environment

6. Click the **Build** button at the bottom of the dialog to build the executable environment.

7. You will be prompted to save the output to a folder. Be sure to note the location of this folder and/or save it someplace accessible. A good suggested location is the `mlagents` root folder in `/mlagents`. Create a new folder called `desktop` and save the output there.

The environment should be built and runnable now as a Gym environment. We will set up this environment and start training it as an environment in the next section.

Training a Unity environment with Rainbow

Training an agent to learn a Unity environment is not unlike much of the training we have already done. There are a few slight changes to the way we interact and set up the environment but overall it is much the same, which makes it a further plus for us because now we can go back and train several different agents/algorithms on completely new environments that we can even design. Furthermore, we now can use other DRL frameworks to train agents with Python— outside the ML-Agents agents, that is. We will cover more on using other frameworks in `Chapter 12`, *DRL Frameworks*.

In the next exercise, we see how to convert one of our latest and most state-of-the-art samples, `Chapter_10_Rainbow.py`, and turn it into `Chapter_11_Unity_Rainbow.py`. Open `Chapter_11_Unity_Rainbow.py` and follow the next exercise:

1. We first need to copy the output folder from the last build, the desktop folder, and place it in the same folder as this chapter's source code. This will allow us to launch that build as the environment our agent will train on.

2. Since you will likely want to convert a few of our previous samples to run Unity environments, we will go through the required changes step by step, starting first with the new import, as follows:

```
from unityagents import UnityEnvironment
```

3. This imports the `UnityEnviroment` class, which is a Gym adapter to Unity. We next use this class to instantiate the `env` environment, like so; note that we have placed commented lines for other operating systems:

```
env = UnityEnvironment(file_name="desktop/gameAI.exe") # Windows
#env = UnityEnvironment(file_name="desktop/gameAI.app") # Mac
#env = UnityEnvironment(file_name="desktop/gameAI.x86") # Linux x86
#env = UnityEnvironment(file_name="desktop/gameAI.x86_64") # Linux
x86_64
```

4. Next, we get `brain` and `brain_name` from the environment. Unity uses the concept of a brain to control agents. We will explore agent brains in a later section. For now, realize that we just take the first available brain with the following code:

```
brain_name = env.brain_names[0]
brain = env.brains[brain_name]
```

5. Then, we extract the action (`action_size`) and state size (`state_size`) from the brain and use these as inputs to construct our `RainbowDQN` models, like so:

```
action_size = brain.vector_action_space_size
state_size = brain.vector_observation_space_size

current_model = RainbowDQN(state_size, action_size, num_atoms,
Vmin, Vmax)
target_model = RainbowDQN(state_size, action_size, num_atoms, Vmin,
Vmax)
```

6. The last part we need to worry about is down in the training code and has to do with how the environment is reset. Unity allows for multiple agents/brains to run in concurrent environments concurrently, either as a way mechanism for A2C/A3C or other mechanisms. As such, it requires a bit more care as to which specific brain and mode we want to reset. The following code shows how we reset the environment when training Unity:

```
env_info = env.reset(train_mode=True)[brain_name]
state = env_info.vector_observations[0]
```

7. As mentioned, the purpose of the slightly confusing indexing has to do with which brain/agent you want to pull the state from. Unity may have multiple brains training multiple agents in multiple sub-environments, all either working together or against each other. We will cover more about training multiple agent environments in Chapter 14, *From DRL to AGI*.

8. We also have to change any other occurrences of when the environment may reset itself like in the following example when the algorithm checks whether the episode is done, with the following code:

```
if done:
        #state = env.reset()
        env_info = env.reset(train_mode=True)[brain_name]
        state = env_info.vector_observations[0]
        all_rewards.append(episode_reward)
        episode_reward = 0
```

9. Run the code and watch the agent train. You won't see any visuals other than TensorBoard output, assuming you go through the steps and run TB in another shell, which you can likely do on your own by now.

 This example may be problematic to run due to API compatibility issues. If you encounter problems when running the sample, then try and set up a whole new virtual environment and install everything again. If the issue continues, then check online for help in places such as Stack Overflow or GitHub. Be sure to also refer to the latest Unity documentation on ML-Agents.

The real benefit of plugging in and using Unity is the ability to construct your own environments and then use those new environments with your own or another RL framework. In the next section, we will look at the basics of building your own RL environment with Unity ML-Agents.

Creating a new environment

The great thing about the ML-Agents toolkit is the ability it provides for creating new agent environments quickly and simply. You can even transform existing games or game projects into training environments for a range of purposes, from building full robotic simulations to simple game agents or even game agents that play as non-player characters. There is even potential to use DRL agents for game quality assurance testing. Imagine building an army of game testers that learn to play your game with just trial and error. The possibilities are endless and Unity is even building a full cloud-based simulation environment for running or training these agents in the future.

In this section, we will walk through using a game project as a new training environment. Any environment you create in Unity would be best tested with the ML-Agents toolkit before you set up your own Python code. DRL agents are masters at finding bugs and/or cheats. As such, you will almost always want to test the environment first with ML-Agents before training it with your own code. I already recommended that you go through the process of setting up and running the ML-Agents Python code to train agents. Remember that once you export an environment for Gym training, it becomes windowless and you will not have any knowledge of how well the agent trains or performs in the environment. If there are any cheats or bugs to be found, the agent will most assuredly find them. After all, your agent will attempt millions of different trial and error combinations trying to find how to play the game.

We are going to look at the **Basic** ML-Agents environment as a way of understanding how to build our own extended or new environment. The ML-Agents documentation is an excellent source to fall back on if the information here is lacking. This exercise is intended to get you up to speed building your own environments quickly:

1. Open up the **Unity Editor** to the **UnitySDK** ML-Agents project we previously had open. Locate and open (double-click) the **Basic** scene at `Assets/ML-Agents/Examples/Basic/Scenes`.

2. At the center of any environment is the Academy. Locate and select the **Academy** object in the **Hierarchy** window and then view the properties in the **Inspector** window, as shown in the screenshot:

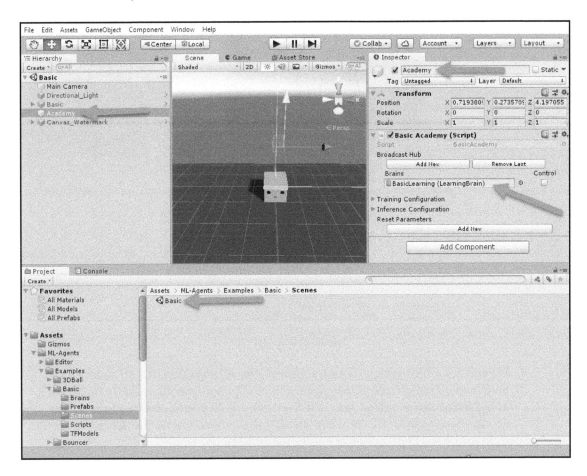

Inspecting the Academy

3. Click on and select the **BasicLearning (LearningBrain)** brain in the **Basic Academy | Broadcast Hub | Brains** entry. This will highlight the entry in the **Project** window. Select the **BasicLearning** brain in the **Project** window and view the brain setup in the **Inspector** window, as shown in the screenshot:

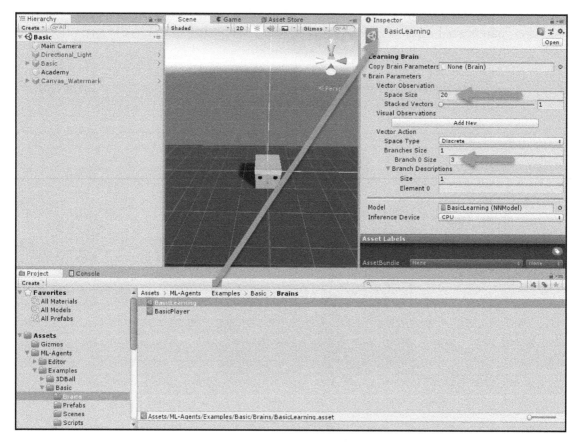

Inspecting the Learning Brain

4. We can see a few things about the brain here. A brain controls an agent so the brain's observation and action space effectively become the same as the agent's. In the **Inspector** window, you can see there are 20 vector observations and an action space of three discrete actions. For this environment, the actions are left or right and null. The 0 action becomes a null or pause action.

5. Next, we want to inspect the agent itself. Click on and expand the **Basic** object in the **Hierarchy** window. Select the **BasicAgent** object and then review the **Inspector** window, as the screenshot shows:

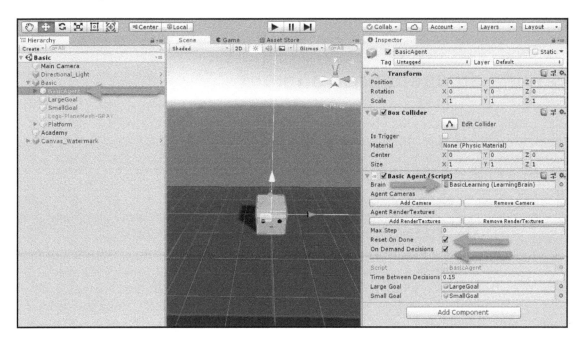

Inspecting the Basic Agent

6. Inspect the Basic Agent component and you can see the **Brain** is set to the **BasicLearning** brain and there are other properties displayed here. Note how the **Reset On Done** and **On Demand Decisions** are both checked. **Reset On Done** enables the environment to reset itself when an episode is complete—what you would expect is the default behavior but is not. **On Demand Decisions** equate to using on- versus off-policy models and is more relevant when training with ML-Agents toolkit.

7. Pressing **Play** will show you the agent playing the game. Watch how the agent plays and while the agent moves around, be sure to select and inspect objects in the editor. Unity is great for seeing how your game mechanics work and this comes in especially handy when building your own agent environments.

The academy, brain, and agent are the main elements you will need to consider when building any new environment. As long as you follow this basic example, you should be able to construct a simple working environment quickly. The other tricky part of building your own environment is the special coding you may have to do and we will cover that in the next section.

Coding an agent/environment

Unity provides an excellent interface for prototyping and building commercial games. You can actually get quite far with very little coding. Unfortunately, that is currently not the case when building new ML-Agents environments.

As such, we will explore the important coding parts in the next exercise:

1. Next, locate and open the **Scripts** folder under `Assets/ML-Agents/Examples/Basic` and inside that double-click to open `BasicAgent.cs`. This is a C# (CSharp) file and it will open in the default editor.

2. At the top of the file, you will note that this `BasicAgent` class is extended from `Agent` and not `MonoBehaviour`, which is the Unity default. `Agent` is a special class in Unity, which as you likely guessed, defines an agent that is capable of exploring the environment. However, in this case, agent refers more to a worker as in a worker in asynchronous or synchronous actor-critic. This means a single brain may control multiple agents, which is often the case:

   ```
   using UnityEngine;
   using MLAgents;

   public class BasicAgent : Agent
   ```

3. Skipping down past the fields, we will jump to the method definitions starting with `CollectObservations`, shown here:

   ```
   public override void CollectObservations()
   {
     AddVectorObs(m_Position, 20);
   }
   ```

4. Inside this method, we can see how the agent/brain collects observations from the environment. In this case, the observation is added using `AddVectorObs`, which adds the observation as a one-hot encoded vector of the required size. In this case, the vector size is 20, the same as the brain's state size.

One-hot encoding is a method by which we encode can encode class information in terms of binary values inside a vector. Hence, if a one-hot encoded vector denoting class or position 1 was active, it would be written as [0,1,0,0].

5. The main action method is the `AgentAction` method. This where the agent performs actions in the environment, be these actions moving or something else:

```
public override void AgentAction(float[] vectorAction, string
textAction)
{
  var movement = (int)vectorAction[0];
  var direction = 0;
  switch (movement)
  {
    case 1:
      direction = -1;
      break;
    case 2:
      direction = 1;
      break;
  }

  m_Position += direction;
  if (m_Position < m_MinPosition) { m_Position = m_MinPosition; }
  if (m_Position > m_MaxPosition) { m_Position = m_MaxPosition; }

  gameObject.transform.position = new Vector3(m_Position - 10f, 0f,
0f);

  AddReward(-0.01f);

  if (m_Position == m_SmallGoalPosition)
  {
    Done();
    AddReward(0.1f);
  }

  if (m_Position == m_LargeGoalPosition)
  {
    Done();
    AddReward(1f);
  }
}
```

6. The first part of this code just determines how the agent moves based on the action it has taken. You can see how the code adjusts the agent's position based on its move. Then, we see the following line of code:

```
AddReward(-0.01f);
```

7. This line adds a step reward, meaning it always adds this reward every step. It does this as a way of limiting the agent's moves. Hence, the longer the agent takes to make the wrong decisions, the less the reward. We sometimes use a step reward but it can also have negative effects and it often makes sense to eliminate a step reward entirely.

8. At the bottom of the `AgentAction` method, we can see what happens when the agent reaches the small or large goal. If the agent reaches the large goal it gets a reward of 1 and .1 if it makes the small goal. With that, we can also see that, when it reaches a goal, the episode terminates using a call to `Done()`:

```
Done();
AddReward(0.1f);  //small goal
// or
Done();
AddReward(1f);  //large goal
```

9. Reverse the numbers for the rewards, save the code, and return to the editor. Set the **Academy** to **Control the brain** and then train the agent with the ML-Agents or the code we developed earlier. You should very clearly see the agent having a preference for the smaller goal.

Extending these concepts and building your own environment now will be up to you. The sky really is the limit and Unity provides several excellent examples to work with and learn from. In the next section, we will take the opportunity to look at the advances ML-Agents provides as mechanisms to enhance your agents or even explore new ways to train.

Advancing RL with ML-Agents

The ML-Agents toolkit, the part that allows you to train DRL agents, is considered one of the more serious and top-end frameworks for training agents. Since the framework was developed on top of Unity, it tends to perform better on Unity-like environments. However, not unlike many others who spend time training agents, the Unity developers realized early on that some environments present such difficult challenges as to require us to assist our agents.

Now, this assistance is not so much direct but rather indirect and often directly relates to how easy or difficult it is for an agent to find rewards. This, in turn, directly relates to how well the environment designer can build a reward function that an agent can use to learn an environment. There are also the times when an environment's state space is so large and not obvious that creating a typical reward function is just not possible. With all that in mind, Unity has gone out of its way to enhance the RL inside ML-Agents with the following new forms of learning:

- Curriculum learning
- Behavioral cloning (imitation learning)
- Curiosity learning
- Training generalized RL agents

We will cover each form of learning in a quick example using the Unity environment.

Curriculum learning

Curriculum learning allows you to train an agent by increasing the complexity of the task as the agent learns. This is fairly intuitive and likely very similar to the way we learn various tasks from math to programming.

Follow the exercise to quickly see how you can set up for curriculum learning:

1. Open the `WallJump` scene located in the `Assets/ML-Agents/Examples/WallJump/Scenes` folder.

2. Select the **Academy** in the scene and review the settings of the **Wall Jump Academy** component in the **Inspector** window and as shown in the screenshot:

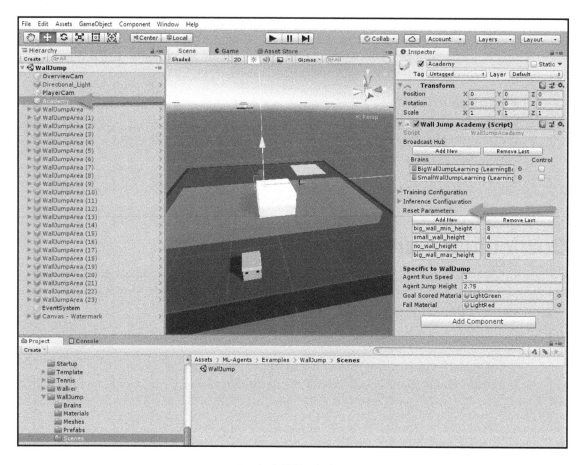

Inspecting the WallJump Academy

3. Inside the academy is an expanded section called **Reset Parameters**. These parameters represent training level parameters for various training states we want to put the agent through.

4. These parameters now need to be configured in a configuration file the ML-Agents toolkit will use to train the agent with curriculum. The contents of this file can be found or created at `config/curricula/wall-jump/` and consist of the following:

```
{
    "measure" : "progress",
    "thresholds" : [0.1, 0.3, 0.5],
    "min_lesson_length" : 100,
    "signal_smoothing" : true,
    "parameters" :
    {
        "big_wall_min_height" : [0.0, 4.0, 6.0, 8.0],
        "big_wall_max_height" : [4.0, 7.0, 8.0, 8.0]
    }
}
```

5. Understanding these parameters can be best done by referring back to the ML-Agents docs. Basically, the idea here is that these parameters control the wall height which is increased over time. Hence, the agent needs to learn to move the block over to jump over the wall as it gets harder and harder.

6. Set the **Control** flag on the **Academy** brains and then run an ML-Agents session in a Python shell with the following:

```
mlagents-learn config/trainer_config.yaml --
curriculum=config/curricula/wall-jump/ --run-id=wall-jump-
curriculum --train
```

7. Assuming the configuration files are in the correct place, you will be prompted to run the editor and watch the agent train in the environment. The results of this example are shown here:

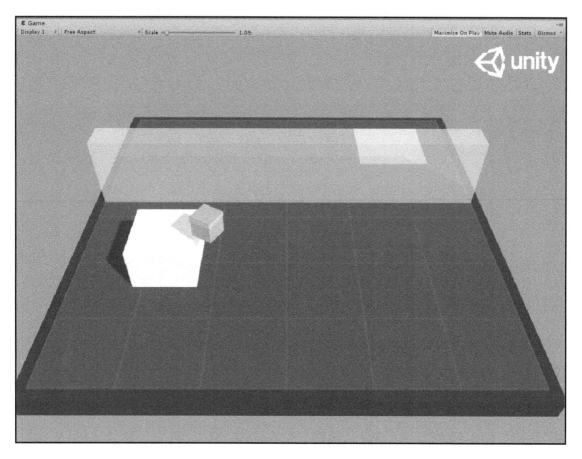

The output of curriculum training example

Curriculum learning solves the problem of an environment not having an obvious answer in a novel way. In this case, the agent's goal is to make the target square. However, if the wall started out very high and the agent needed to move the block there to jump over it, it likely won't even understand it needs to get to a block. Therefore, we help it to train by first allowing it to get to the goal but then make it gradually harder to do so. As the difficulty increases, the agent learns how to use the block to jump over the wall.

In the next section, we look to another method that helps agents to solve tasks with difficult to find or what we call sparse rewards.

Behavioral cloning

Behavioral cloning is sometimes also referred to as imitation learning. While not exactly both the same, we will use the terms interchangeably here. In RL, we use the term sparse rewards or rewards sparsity for any environment where it is difficult for an agent to just finish a task by trial and error and perhaps luck. The larger an environment is, the more sparse the rewards and in many cases, the observation space can be so large that any hope of training an agent at all is extremely difficult. Fortunately, a method called behavioral cloning or imitation learning can solve the problem of sparse rewards by using the observations of humans as previous sampled observations. Unity provides three methods to generate previous observations and they are as follows:

- **Generative Adversarial Imitation Learning** (**GAIL**): You can use something called the GAIL reward signal to enhance learning rewards from a few observations.
- **Pretraining**: This allows you to use prerecorded demonstrations likely from a human and use those to bootstrap the learning of the agent. If you use pretraining, you also need to provide a configuration section in your ML-Agents config file like so:

```
pretraining:
        demo_path: ./demos/Tennis.demo
        strength: 0.5
        steps: 10000
```

- **Behavioral Cloning** (**BC**): In this training, setup happens directly in the Unity editor. This is great for environments where small demonstrations can help to increase an agent's learning. BC does not work so well on larger environments with a large observation state space.

These three methods can be combined in a variety of configurations and used together in the case of pretraining and GAIL with other methods such as curiosity learning, which we will see later.

It can be especially entertaining to train an agent in real time with BC, as we'll see in the next exercise. Follow the next exercise to explore using the BC method of demonstrating to an agent:

1. Open the **TennisIL** scene located in the `Assets/ML-Agents/Examples/Tennis/Scenes` folder.

2. This environment is an example of a sparse rewards environment, whereby the agent needs to find and hit the ball back to its opponent. This environment makes for an excellent example to test BC with on.

3. Select the **Academy** object in the **Hierarchy** window and then check the **Control** option of **TennisLearning (LearningBrain)** in the **Inspector** window, as shown in the screenshot here:

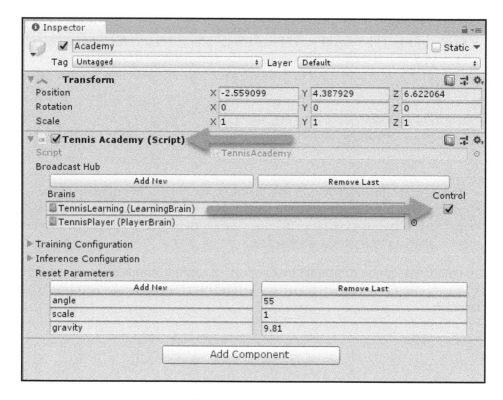

Turning on the learning brain to control

4. As you can see, there are two brains in this scene: one student brain— the learning brain, and one teacher brain—the player brain. The teacher brain, controlled by the human player, won't control an actual agent but rather just take direct inputs from the player. The student brain observes the teacher's actions and uses those as samples in its policy. In a basic sense, this becomes the teacher working from the human policy that the target policy, the agent, needs to learn. This is really no different than us having current and target networks.

5. The next thing we have to do is customize the ML-Agents hyperparameters config file. We customize the file by adding the following entry for `StudentBrain`:

```
StudentBrain:
  trainer: imitation
  max_steps: 10000
  summary_freq: 1000
  brain_to_imitate: TeacherBrain
  batch_size: 16
  batches_per_epoch: 5
  num_layers: 4
  hidden_units: 64
  use_recurrent: false
  sequence_length: 16
  buffer_size: 128
```

6. The highlighted elements in the preceding configuration show the `trainer:` set to `imitation` and `brain_to_imitate:` as `TeacherBrain`. Plenty of more information about setting up the configuration for ML-Agents can be found with the online docs.

7. Next, you need to open a Python/Anaconda shell and change to the `mlagents` folder. After that, run the following command to start training:

```
mlagents-learn config/trainer_config.yaml --run-id=tennis1 --train
```

8. This will start the trainer and in short while you will be prompted to start the Unity editor in **Play** mode.

9. Press **Play** to put the editor in play mode and use the *WASD* controls to maneuver the paddle to play tennis against the agent. Assuming you do well, the agent will also improve. A screenshot of this training is shown here:

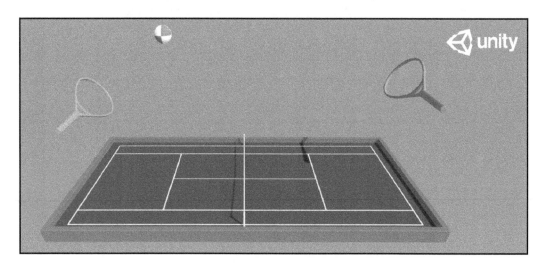

Training the tennis agent with BC

Imitation learning was a key ingredient in training the agent, AlphaStar. AlphaStar was shown to beat human players at a very complex real-time strategy game called *StarCraft 2*. It has many keen benefits in getting agents past the sparse rewards problem. However, there are many in the RL community that want to avoid IL or BC because it can introduce human bias. Human bias has been shown to decrease agent performance when compared to agents trained entirely without BC. In fact, AlphaStar was trained to a sufficient enough level of playability before it was trained on itself. It was this self-training that is believed to be responsible for the innovation that allowed it to beat human players.

In the next section, we look at another exciting way Unity has tried to capture a method to counter sparse reward problems.

Curiosity learning

Up until now, we have only ever considered external rewards given to the agent from the environment. Yet, we and other animals receive a wide variety of external and internal rewards. Internal rewards are often characterized by emotion or feeling. An agent could have an internal reward that gives it +1 every time it looks to some face, perhaps denoting some internal love or infatuation reward. These types of rewards are called intrinsic rewards and they represent rewards that are internal or self-derived by the agent. This has some powerful capabilities for everything from creating interesting motivated agents to enhancing an agent's learning ability.

It is the second way in which Unity introduced curiosity learning or the internal curiosity reward system as a way of letting agents explore more when they get surprised. That is, whenever an agent is surprised by an action, its curiosity increases and hence it needs to explore the state actions in the space that surprised it.

Unity has produced a very powerful example of curiosity learning in an environment called Pyramids. It is the goal of the agent in this environment to find a pile of yellow blocks with a gold block on top. Knock over the pile of blocks and then get the gold block. The problem is that there are piles of boxes in many rooms at the start but none start yellow. To turn the blocks yellow, that agent needs to find and press a button. Finding this sequence of tasks using straight RL could be problematic and/or time-consuming. Fortunately, with CL, we can improve this performance dramatically. We will look at how to use CL in the next section to train the Pyramids environment:

1. Open the **Pyramids** scene located in the `Assets/ML-Agents/Examples/Pyramids/Scenes` folder.

2. Press **Play** to run the default agent; this will be one trained with Unity. When you run the agent, watch it play through the environment and you will see the agent first find the button, press it, then locate the pile of blocks it needs to knock over. It will knock over the boxes as shown in the sequence of screenshots here:

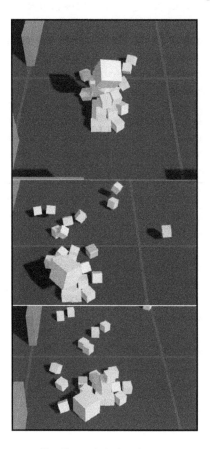

Pyramids agent playing the environment

3. Training an agent with curiosity just requires setting the Academy to control the brain and running the ML-Agents trainer with the proper configuration. This documentation to drive CL has changed several times over the course of ML-Agents development. Therefore, it is recommended you consult the ML-Agents docs for the most recent documentation.

CL can be very powerful and the whole concept of intrinsic rewards has some fun and interesting application towards games. Imagine being able to power internal reward systems for enemy agents that may play to greed, power, or some other evil trait. In the next section, we finish out this chapter with a look at training generalized reinforcement learning agents.

Training generalized reinforcement learning agents

We often have to remind ourselves that RL is just a derivation of data science best practices and we often have to consider how could you fix a training issue with data science. In the case of RL, we see the same issues we see in data science and machine learning only at different scales and exposed in another manner. One example of this is when an agent is overfitted to an environment that we then try to apply to other general variations of that environment. For instance, imagine the Frozen Lake environment that could be various sizes or even provide random starting points or other variations. By introducing these types of variations, we allow our agent to better generalize to a wider variety of similar environments. It is this generalization that we want to introduce into our environment.

 AGI or **Artificial General Intelligence** is the concept of generalized training agents to the nth degree. It is expected that a truly AGI agent would be able to be placed in any environment and learn to solve the task. This could take an amount of training but ideally, no other hyperparameters or other human intervention should be required.

By making the environment stochastic, we are essentially increasing the likelihood of our methods that use distributional RL and noisy networks will also become more powerful. Unfortunately, enabling these types of parameters with other training code, or our PyTorch code, is not currently available. In the next exercise, we'll learn how to set up a generalized training environment:

1. Open the **WallJump** scene located in the `Assets/ML-Agents/Examples/WallJump/Scenes` folder.

2. **WallJump** is already set up and configured with several reset parameters we looked at earlier when we reviewed curriculum learning. This time, instead of progressively changing those parameters, we are going to have the environment sample them randomly.

3. The parameters we want to resample are based on this sample. We can create a new generalized YAML file called `walljump_generalize.yaml` in the config folder.

4. Open and put the following text in this file and then save it:

```
resampling-interval: 5000

big_wall_min_height:
    sampler-type: "uniform"
    min_value: 5
    max_value: 8

big_wall_max_height:
    sampler-type: "uniform"
    min_value: 8
    max_value: 10

small_wall_height:
    sampler-type: "uniform"
    min_value: 2
    max_value: 5

no_wall_height:
    sampler-type: "uniform"
    min_value: 0
    max_value: 3
```

5. This sets up the sampling distributions for how we will sample the values. The values for the environment can then be sampled with the following code:

```
SamplerFactory.register_sampler(*custom_sampler_string_key*,
*custom_sampler_object*)
```

6. We can also define new sampler types or ways of sampling data values using a custom sampler that our classes place in the `sample_class.py` file in the ML-Agents code. The following is an example of a custom sampler:

```
class CustomSampler(Sampler):
    def __init__(self, argA, argB, argC):
        self.possible_vals = [argA, argB, argC]

    def sample_all(self):
        return np.random.choice(self.possible_vals)
```

7. Then, you can configure the config file to run this sampler like so:

```
height:
    sampler-type: "custom-sampler"
    argB: 1
    argA: 2
    argC: 3
```

8. Remember that you still need to sample the values and modify the environment's configuration when the agent resets. This will require modifying the code to sample the inputs using the appropriate samplers.

9. You can then run the Unity ML-Agents trainer code with the following command:

```
mlagents-learn config/trainer_config.yaml --
sampler=config/walljump_generalize.yaml
--run-id=walljump-generalization --train
```

Being able to train agents in this manner allows your agents to be more robust and able to tackle various incarnations of your environments. If you are building a game that needs a practical agent, you will most likely need to train your agents in a generalized manner. Generalized agents will generally be able to adapt to unforeseen changes in the environment far better than an agent trained otherwise.

That about does it for this chapter and, in the next section, we'll look at gaining further experience with the sample exercises for this chapter.

Exercises

The exercises in this section are intended to introduce you to Unity ML-Agents in more detail. If your preference is not to use ML-Agents as a training framework, then move on to the next section and the end of this chapter. For those of you still here, ML-Agents on its own is a powerful toolkit for quickly exploring DRL agents. The toolkit hides most of the details of DRL but that should not be a problem for you to figure out by now:

1. Set up and run one of the Unity ML-Agents sample environments in the editor to train an agent. This will require that you consult the Unity ML-Agents documentation.
2. Tune the hyperparameters of a sample Unity environment.
3. Start TensorBoard and run it so that it collects logs from the Unity runs folder. This will allow you to watch the training performance of the agents being trained with ML-Agents.

4. Build a Unity environment and train it with the Rainbow DQN example.

5. Customize one of the existing Unity environments by changing the setup, parameters, reset parameters, and/or reward function. That is, change the reward feedback the agent receives when completing actions or tasks.

6. Set up and train an agent with pretrained data. This will require you to set up a player brain to record demonstrations. Play the game to record those demonstrations and then set the game for training with a learning brain.

7. Train an agent with behavioral cloning using the tennis environment.

8. Train an agent with curiosity learning using the Pyramids scene.

9. Set up and run a Unity environment for generalized training. Use the sampling to pull stochastic values from distributions for the environment. What effect do different distributions have on the agent's training performance?

10. Convert a PG method example such as PPO so that you can run a Unity environment. How does the performance compare with Rainbow DQN?

Use these examples to familiarize yourself with Unity ML-Agents and more advanced concepts in RL. In the next section, we will summarize and complete this chapter.

Summary

In this chapter, we took a diversion and built our own DRL environments for training with our own code, or another framework, or using the ML-Agents framework from Unity. At first, we looked at the basics of installing the ML-Agents toolkit for the development of environments, training, and training with our own code. Then, we looked at how to build a basic Unity environment for training from a Gym interface like we have been doing throughout this whole book. After that, we learned how our RainbowDQN sample could be customized to train an agent. From there, we looked at how we can create a brand new environment from the basics. We finished this chapter by looking at managing rewards in environments and the set of tools ML-Agents uses to enhance environments with sparse rewards. There, we looked at several methods Unity has added to ML-Agents to assist with difficult environments and sparse rewards.

Moving on from this chapter, we will continue to explore other DRL frameworks that can be used to train agents. ML-Agents is one of many powerful frameworks that can be used to train agents, as we will soon see.

12
DRL Frameworks

Working through and exploring the code in this book is meant to be a learning exercise in how **Reinforcement Learning** (**RL**) algorithms work but also how difficult it can be to get them to work. It is because of this difficulty that so many open source RL frameworks seem to pop up every day. In this chapter, we will explore a couple of the more popular frameworks. We will start with why you would want to use a framework and then move on to exploring the more popular frameworks such as Dopamine, Keras-RL, TF-Agents, and RL Lib.

Here is a quick summary of the main topics we will cover in this chapter:

- Choosing a framework
- Introducing Google Dopamine
- Playing with Keras-RL
- Exploring RL Lib
- Using TF agents

We will use a combination of notebook environments on Google Colab and virtual environments depending on the complexity of the examples in this chapter. Jupyter Notebooks, which Colab is based on, is an excellent way to demonstrate code. It is generally not the preferred way to develop code and this is the reason we avoided this method until now.

In the next section, we look at why you would want to choose a framework.

Choosing a framework

As you may have surmised by now, writing your own RL algorithms and functions on top of a deep learning framework, such as PyTorch, is not trivial. It is also important to remember that the algorithms in this book go back about 30 years over the development of RL. That means that any serious new advances in RL take substantial effort and time—yes, for both development and especially training. Unless you have the time, resources, and incentive for developing your own framework, then it is highly recommended to graduate using a mature framework. However, there is an ever-increasing number of new and comparable frameworks out there, so you may find that you are unable to choose just one. Until one of these frameworks achieves true AGI, then you may also need separate frameworks for different environments or even different tasks.

Remember, **AGI** stands for **Artificial General Intelligence** and it really is the goal of any RL framework to be AGI. An AGI framework can be trained on any environment. An advanced AGI framework may be able to transfer learning across tasks. Transfer learning is where an agent can learn one task and then use those learnings to accomplish another similar task.

We are going to look at the current most popular frameworks that have the most promise, in later sections. It is important to compare the various current frameworks to see whether one may be a better choice for you and your team. Therefore, we will look at a comparison of the various RL frameworks currently available in the following list.

This list features the current most popular frameworks ordered by current popularity (by Google), but this list is expected to change with time:

- **OpenAI Gym and Baselines**: OpenAI Gym is the framework we have used for most of the environments we have explored in this book. This library also has a companion called Baselines that provides several agents for, you guessed it, baselining the Gym environments. Baselines is also a very popular and good RL framework but we have omitted it here in favor of looking at other libraries.
- **Google Dopamine**: This is a relatively new framework that has gained popularity very quickly. This is likely due, in part, to its implementation of the RainbowDQN agent. The framework is well developed but has been described as being clunky and not very modular. We showcase it here because it is popular and you will likely want a closer look at it anyway.

- **ML-Agents**: We have more or less already covered a whole chapter on this framework, so we won't need to explore it here. Unity has developed a very solid but not very modular framework. The implementation currently only supports PG methods such as PPO and Soft Actor-Critic. ML-Agents on its own, however, it can be a great and recommended way to demonstrate RL to development teams or even introduce concepts to clients.

- **RL Lib with the ray-project**: This has strange origins in that it started as a parallelization project for Python and evolved into a training platform for RL. As such, it tends to favor training regimes that use asynchronous agents such as A3C, and it is well suited to complex environments. Not to mention, this project is based on PyTorch so it will be worth a look.

- **Keras-RL**: Keras itself is another deep learning framework that is very popular on its own. The deep learning library itself is quite concise and easy to use—perhaps in some ways, too easy. However, it can be an excellent way to prototype an RL concept or environment and deserves a closer look by us.

- **TRFL**: This library, not unlike Keras-RL, is an extension of the TensorFlow framework to incorporate RL. TensorFlow is another low-level deep learning framework. As such, the code to build any working agent also needs to be quite a low level and using this library likely won't be for you, especially if you enjoy PyTorch.

- **Tensorforce**: This is another library focused on extending TensorFlow for RL. The benefit of using a TF-based solution is cross-compatibility and even the ability to port your code to web or mobile. However, building low-level computational graphs is not for everyone and does require a higher level of mathematics than we covered in this book.

- **Horizon**: This framework is from Facebook and is developed on top of PyTorch. Unfortunately, the benefits of this framework fall short in several areas including not having a `pip` installer. It also lacks tight integration with Gym environments so, unless you work at Facebook, you will likely want to avoid this framework.

- **Coach**: This is one of those sleeper frameworks that could build a substantial following of its own someday. There are many useful and powerful features to Coach, including a dedicated dashboard and direct support for Kubernetes. This framework also currently boasts the largest implementation of RL algorithms and will give you plenty of room to explore. Coach is a framework worth exploring on your own.

- **MAgent**: This project is similar to RLLib (Ray) in that it specializes in training multiple agents asynchronously or in various configurations. It is developed on top of TensorFlow and uses its own grid-world designed environments for what is coined as real-life simulations. This is a very specialized framework for developers or real-life RL solutions.

- **TF-Agents**: This is another RL implementation from Google developed on top of TensorFlow. As such, it is a more low-level framework but is more robust and capable than the other TF frameworks mentioned here. This framework appears to be a strong contender for more serious research and/or production implementations and worth a further look from readers looking to do such work.

- **SLM-Lab**: This is another PyTorch-based framework that is actually based on top of Ray (RLLib), although it is designed more for pure research. As such, it lacks a `pip` installer and assumes the user is pulling code directly from a repository. It is likely best to leave this framework to the researchers for now.

- **DeeR**: This is another library that is integrated with Keras and is intended to be more accessible. The library is well kept and the documentation is clear. However, this framework is intended for those learning RL and if you made it this far, you likely already need something more advanced and robust.

- **Garage**: This is another TF-based framework that has some excellent functionality but lacks documentation and any good installation procedures, which makes this another good research framework but may be better avoided by those interested in developing working agents.

- **Surreal**: This framework is designed more for robotics applications and, as such, is more closed. Robotics RL with environments such as Mujoco have been shown to be commercially viable. As such, this branch of RL is seeing the impact of those trying to take their share. This means that this framework is currently free but not open source and the free part is likely to change soon. Still, if you are specializing in robotics applications, this may be worth a serious look.

- **RLgraph**: This is perhaps another sleeper project to keep your eye on. This library is currently absorbing a ton of commits and changing quickly. It is also built with both PyTorch and TensorFlow mappings. We will spend some time looking at using this framework in a later section.

- **Simple RL**: This is perhaps as simple as you can get with an RL framework. The project is intended to be very accessible and examples with multiple agents can be developed in less than eight lines of code. It can actually be as simple as the following block of code taken from the example documentation:

```
from simple_rl.agents import QLearningAgent, RandomAgent, RMaxAgent
from simple_rl.tasks import GridWorldMDP
from simple_rl.run_experiments import run_agents_on_mdp

# Setup MDP.
mdp = GridWorldMDP(width=4, height=3, init_loc=(1, 1),
goal_locs=[(4, 3)], lava_locs=[(4, 2)], gamma=0.95, walls=[(2, 2)],
slip_prob=0.05)

# Setup Agents.
```

```
ql_agent = QLearningAgent(actions=mdp.get_actions())
rmax_agent = RMaxAgent(actions=mdp.get_actions())
rand_agent = RandomAgent(actions=mdp.get_actions())

# Run experiment and make plot.
run_agents_on_mdp([ql_agent, rmax_agent, rand_agent], mdp,
instances=5, episodes=50, steps=10)
```

With so many frameworks to choose from, we only have time to go over the most popular frameworks in this chapter. While frameworks become popular because they are well written and tend to work well in a wide variety of environments, until we reach AGI, you may still need to explore various frameworks to find an algorithm/agent that works for you and your problem.

To see how this has evolved over time, we can use Google Trends to perform a search comparison analysis. Doing this can often give us an indication of how popular a particular framework is trending in search terms. More search terms means more interest in the framework, which in turn, leads to more development and better software.

The following Google Trends plot shows a comparison of the top five listed frameworks:

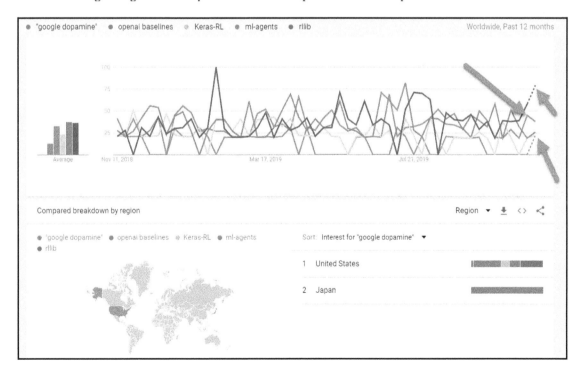

Google trends comparison of RL frameworks

You can see in the plot the trending increase for RL Lib and Google Dopamine. It is also interesting to note that the primary interest in RL development is the current greatest in the US and Japan, with Japan taking a special interest in ML-Agents.

ML-Agents' popularity lends itself to several factors, one of which being the VP of AI and ML at Unity, Dr. Danny Lange. Dr. Lange lived in Japan for several years and is fluent in Japanese and this has likely contributed to this specific popularity.

It is interesting to note the absence of China in this area, at least for these types of frameworks. China's interest in RL is currently very specific to planning applications popularized by the defeat of the game of Go by an RL agent. That RL agent was developed using an algorithm called Monte Carlo Tree Search, which is intended to do a full exploration of complex but finite state spaces. We started looking at finite state spaces but took a turn to explore continuous or infinite state spaces. These types of agents also transition well to general games and robotics, which is not a major interest by the Chinese. Therefore, it remains to be seen how or what interest China shows in this area but that will most likely influence this space as well when that happens.

In the next section, we look at our first framework and one that we may find the most familiar, Google Dopamine.

Introducing Google Dopamine

Dopamine was developed at Google as a platform to showcase the company's latest advances in DRL. Of course, there are also other groups at Google doing the same thing, so it is perhaps a testament to how varied these platforms still are and need to be. In the next exercise, we will use Google Colab to build an example that uses Dopamine on the cloud to train an agent.

 To access all of the features on Colab, you will likely need to create a Google account with payment authorized. This likely means entering a credit or debit card. The plus here is that Google provides $300 US in credits to use the GCP platform, of which Colab is one small part.

Open your browser to `colab.research.google.com` and follow the next exercise:

1. We will first start by creating a new **Python 3 Notebook**. Be sure to choose this by the prompt dialog or through the Colab **File** menu.

This notebook is based on a variation by the Dopamine authors and the original may be found in the following link: https://github.com/google/dopamine/blob/master/dopamine/colab/agents.ipynb.

2. We first need to install several packages to support the training. On a Colab notebook, we can pass any command to the underlying shell by prefixing it with !. Enter the following code in a cell and then run the cell:

```
!pip install --upgrade --no-cache-dir dopamine-rl
!pip install cmake
!pip install atari_py
!pip install gin-config
```

3. Then, we do some imports and set up some global strings in a new cell:

```
import numpy as np
import os
from dopamine.agents.dqn import dqn_agent
from dopamine.discrete_domains import run_experiment
from dopamine.colab import utils as colab_utils
from absl import flags
import gin.tf

BASE_PATH = '/tmp/colab_dope_run'  # @param
GAME = 'Asterix'  # @param
```

4. The @param function denotes the value as a parameter and this provides a helpful textbox on the interface for changing this parameter later. This is a cool notebook feature:

```
!gsutil -q -m cp -R gs://download-dopamine-rl/preprocessed-
benchmarks/* /content/
experimental_data = colab_utils.load_baselines('/content')
```

5. Then, we run the preceding command and code in another new cell. This loads the data we will use to run the agent on:

```
LOG_PATH = os.path.join(BASE_PATH, 'random_dqn', GAME)

class MyRandomDQNAgent(dqn_agent.DQNAgent):
  def __init__(self, sess, num_actions):
    """This maintains all the DQN default argument values."""
    super(MyRandomDQNAgent, self).__init__(sess, num_actions)
  def step(self, reward, observation):
    """Calls the step function of the parent class, but returns a
random action.
```

```
"""
    _ = super(MyRandomDQNAgent, self).step(reward, observation)
    return np.random.randint(self.num_actions)

def create_random_dqn_agent(sess, environment,
summary_writer=None):
  """The Runner class will expect a function of this type to create
an agent."""
  return MyRandomDQNAgent(sess,
num_actions=environment.action_space.n)

random_dqn_config = """
import dopamine.discrete_domains.atari_lib
import dopamine.discrete_domains.run_experiment
atari_lib.create_atari_environment.game_name = '{}'
atari_lib.create_atari_environment.sticky_actions = True
run_experiment.Runner.num_iterations = 200
run_experiment.Runner.training_steps = 10
run_experiment.Runner.max_steps_per_episode = 100
""".format(GAME)
gin.parse_config(random_dqn_config, skip_unknown=False)

random_dqn_runner = run_experiment.TrainRunner(LOG_PATH,
create_random_dqn_agent)
```

6. Create a new cell and enter the preceding code and run it. This creates a random DQN agent for more or less blindly exploring an environment.

7. Next, we want to train the agent by creating a new cell and entering the following code:

```
print('Will train agent, please be patient, may be a while...')
random_dqn_runner.run_experiment()
print('Done training!')
```

8. This can take a while, so if you have authorized payment enabled, you can run this example on a GPU instance by just changing the notebook type. You can do this by selecting from the menu **Runtime** | **Change runtime type**. A dialog will pop up; change the runtime type and close the dialog, as shown in the following screenshot:

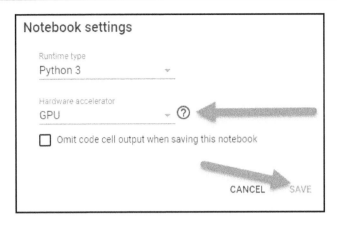

Changing the runtime type on Colab

9. After you change the runtime type, you will need to run the whole notebook again. To do this, select from the menu **Runtime | Run all** to run all of the cells again. You will still need to wait a while for the training to run; it is, after all, running an Atari environment but that is the point.

The agent we just built is using a random DQN agent running on the classic Atari game, *Asterix*. Dopamine is a powerful framework that is easy to use as we have just seen. You can find much more about the library from the source itself, including how to output the results from the last example exercise.

In the next section, we will move away from Colab and explore another framework, Keras-RL with regular Python.

Playing with Keras-RL

Keras is a very popular deep learning framework on its own and it is heavily used by newcomers looking to learn about the basics of constructing networks. The framework is considered very high-level and abstracts most of the inner details of constructing networks. It only goes to assume that an RL framework built with Keras would attempt to do the same thing.

This example is dependent on the version of Keras and TensorFlow and may not work correctly unless the two can work together. If you encounter trouble, try installing a different version of TensorFlow and try again.

To run this example, we will start by doing the installation and all of the setup in this exercise:

1. To install Keras, you should create a new virtual environment using Python 3.6 and use `pip` to install it along with the `keras-rl` framework. The commands to do all of this on Anaconda are shown here:

```
conda create -n kerasrl python=3.6
conda activate kerasrl
pip install tensorflow==1.7.1  #not TF 2.0 at time of writing
pip install keras
pip install keras-rl
pip install gym
```

2. After all of the packages are installed, open the sample code file, `Chapter_12_Keras-RL.py`, as shown here:

```
import numpy as np
import gym

from keras.models import Sequential
from keras.layers import Dense, Activation, Flatten
from keras.optimizers import Adam

from rl.agents.dqn import DQNAgent
from rl.policy import BoltzmannQPolicy
from rl.memory import SequentialMemory

ENV_NAME = 'CartPole-v0'

env = gym.make(ENV_NAME)
np.random.seed(123)
env.seed(123)
nb_actions = env.action_space.n

model = Sequential()
model.add(Flatten(input_shape=(1,) + env.observation_space.shape))
model.add(Dense(16))
model.add(Activation('relu'))
model.add(Dense(16))
model.add(Activation('relu'))
model.add(Dense(16))
```

```
model.add(Activation('relu'))
model.add(Dense(nb_actions))
model.add(Activation('linear'))
print(model.summary())

memory = SequentialMemory(limit=50000, window_length=1)
policy = BoltzmannQPolicy()
dqn = DQNAgent(model=model, nb_actions=nb_actions, memory=memory,
nb_steps_warmup=10,
                target_model_update=1e-2, policy=policy)
dqn.compile(Adam(lr=1e-3), metrics=['mae'])
dqn.fit(env, nb_steps=50000, visualize=True, verbose=2)

dqn.save_weights('dqn_{}_weights.h5f'.format(ENV_NAME),
overwrite=True)

dqn.test(env, nb_episodes=5, visualize=True)
```

3. We haven't covered any Keras code but hopefully, the simple nature of the code makes it fairly self-explanatory. If anything, the code should feel quite familiar, although missing a training loop.

4. Notice in the proceeding code block how the model is constructed using something called a `Sequential` class. The class is a container for network layers, which we then add next interspersed with appropriate activation functions. Note at the end of the network, how the last layer uses a linear activation function.

5. Next, we will take a closer look at the construction of memory, policy, and agent itself. See the following code:

```
memory = SequentialMemory(limit=50000, window_length=1)
policy = BoltzmannQPolicy()
dqn = DQNAgent(model=model, nb_actions=nb_actions, memory=memory,
nb_steps_warmup=10,
                target_model_update=1e-2, policy=policy)
```

6. The interesting thing to note here is how we construct the network model outside the agent and feed it as an input to the agent along with the memory and policy. This is very powerful and provides for some interesting extensibility.

7. At the end of the file, we can find the training code. The training function called `fit` is used to iteratively train the agent. All of the code to do this is encapsulated in the `fit` function, as the following code shows:

```
dqn.fit(env, nb_steps=50000, visualize=True, verbose=2)
```

8. The last section of code saves the model and then runs a test on the agent with the following code:

```
dqn.save_weights('dqn_{}_weights.h5f'.format(ENV_NAME),
overwrite=True)

dqn.test(env, nb_episodes=5, visualize=True)
```

9. Run the code as you normally would and watch the visual training output and testing as shown in the following diagram:

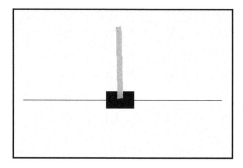

Example output from Chapter_12_Keras-RL.py

Keras-RL is a light powerful framework for testing concepts or other ideas quickly. The performance of Keras itself is not as powerful as TensorFlow or PyTorch, so any serious development should be done using one of those platforms. In the next section, we will look at another RL platform based on PyTorch called RLLib.

Exploring RL Lib

RL Lib is based on the Ray project, which is essentially a Python job-based system. RL Lib is more like ML-Agents, where it exposes functionality using config files although, in the case of ML-Agents, the structure is completely run on their platform. Ray is very powerful but requires a detailed understanding of the configuration parameters and setup. As such, the exercise we show here is just to demonstrate the power and flexibility of Ray but you are directed to the full online documentation for further discovery on your own.

Open your browser to `colab.research.google.com` and follow the next exercise:

1. The great thing about using Colab is it can be quite easy to run and set up. Create a new Python 3 notebook and enter the following commands:

    ```
    !pip uninstall -y pyarrow
    !pip install tensorflow ray[rllib] > /dev/null 2>&1
    ```

2. These commands install the framework on the Colab instance. After this is installed, you need to restart the runtime by selecting from the menu: **Runtime |**
    Restart runtime.

3. After the runtime restarts, create a new cell and enter the following code:

    ```
    import ray
    from ray import tune

    ray.init()
    ```

4. That block of code imports the framework and the tune class for hyperparameter tuning.

5. Create a new cell and enter the following code:

    ```
    tune.run("DQN", stop={"episode_reward_mean": 100},
        config={
                "env": "CartPole-v0",
                "num_gpus": 0,
                "num_workers": 1,
                "lr": tune.grid_search([0.01, 0.001, 0.0001]),
                "monitor": False,     },)
    ```

6. Believe it or not, that's it. That is the remainder of the code to build a DQN agent to run and train on the `CartPole` environment. Not to mention the `tune` class is set to tune the learning rate hyperparameter, `lr` (alpha), using the `tune.grid_search` function.

7. Run the last cell and observe the output. The output is extremely comprehensive and an example is shown here:

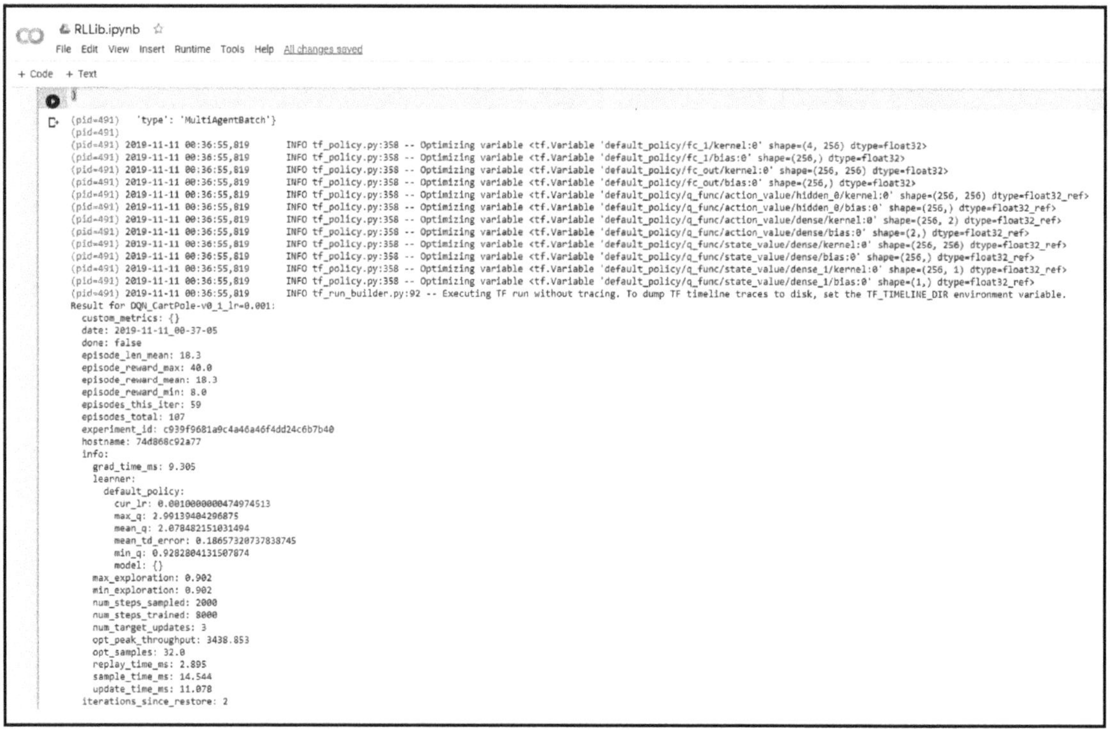

Training RLLib on Google Colab

As you can see in the preceding screenshot, this is a very powerful framework designed to optimize hyperparameter tuning and it provides plenty of options to do so. It also allows for multiagent training in various configurations. This framework is a must-study for anyone doing serious work or research in RL. In the next section, we will look at the last framework, TF-Agents.

Using TF-Agents

The last framework we are going to look at is TF-Agents, a relatively new but up-and-coming tool, again, from Google. It seems Google's approach to building RL frameworks is a bit like RL itself. They are trying multiple trial and error attempts/actions to get the best reward—not entirely a bad idea for Google, and considering the resources they are throwing at RL, it may not unexpected to see more RL libraries come out.

TF-Agents, while newer, is typically seen as more robust and mature. It is a framework designed for notebooks and that makes it perfect for trying out various configurations, hyperparameters, or environments. The framework is developed on TensorFlow 2.0 and works beautifully on Google Colab. It will likely become the de-facto platform to teach basic RL concepts and demo RL in the future.

There are plenty of notebook examples to show how to use TF-Agents at the TF-Agents Colab repository (`https://github.com/tensorflow/agents/tree/master/tf_agents/colabs`). The whole repository is a great resource but this section itself can be especially useful for those of us that want to see working code examples.

Open your browser up to the TF-Agents Colab page at the preceding link and follow the next exercise:

1. For this exercise, we are going to modify the training environment for one of the samples. That should give us enough of an overview of what the code looks like and how to make changes yourself later on. Locate `1_dqn_tutorial.ipynb` and click on it to open the page. Note that `.ipynb` stands for **I-Python Notebook**; I-Python is a server platform for hosting notebooks.

2. Click the link at the top that says **Run in Google Colab**. This will open the notebook in Colab.

3. From the menu, select **Runtime** | **Change runtime type to GPU** and then click **Save**. We are going to convert this example to use the Lunar Lander from Cart Pole. As we know, this will take more compute cycles.

4. First, we will want to modify the initial `pip install` commands to import the full `gym` package by updating the commands in the first cell to the following:

```
!apt-get install xvfb
!pip install gym[all]
!pip install 'imageio==2.4.0'
!pip install PILLOW
!pip install 'pyglet==1.3.2'
!pip install pyvirtualdisplay
!pip install tf-agents-nightly
try:
  %%tensorflow_version 2.x
except:
  pass
```

5. Next, we will want to locate the two cells that refer to the **CartPole** environment. We want to change all mentions of **CartPole** to **LunarLander**, as shown in the following code:

```
env_name = 'LunarLander-v2'
env = suite_gym.load(env_name)

# -- and --

example_environment =
tf_py_environment.TFPyEnvironment(uite_gym.load('LunarLander-v2'))
```

6. The algorithm this example uses is a simple DQN model. As we know from experience, we can't just run the same hyperparameters for `LunarLander`; therefore, we will change them to the following:
    - `num_iterations`: 500000 from 20000
    - `initial_collect_steps`: 20000 from 1000
    - `collect_steps_per_iteration`: 5 from 1
    - `replay_buffer_max_length`: 250000 from 100000
    - `batch_size`: 32 from 64
    - `learning_rate`: 1e-35 from 1e-3
    - `log_interval`: 2000 from 200
    - `num_eval_episodes`: 15 from 10
    - `eval_interval`: 500 from 1000

7. Let's move on to adjusting the network size. Locate the following line of code and change it as shown:

```
fc_layer_params = (100,)

# change to

fc_layer_params = (256,)
```

8. Feel free to change other parameters as you like. If you have done your homework, working with this example should be very straightforward. One of the great things about TF-Agents and Google Colab, in general, is how interactive sample and the training output is.

This book was almost entirely written with Google Colab notebooks. However, as good as they are, notebooks still lack a few good elements needed for larger samples. They also make it difficult for several reasons to use later in other examples. Therefore a preference was given to keep the samples in Python files.

9. From the menu, select **Runtime** | **Run all**, to run the sample and then wait patiently for the output. This may take a while so grab a beverage and relax for a while.

On the page, you will be able to see several other algorithm forms that we have covered and that we did not get time to cover in this book. The following is a list of the agent types TF-Agents currently supports and a brief description about each:

- **DQN**: This is the standard deep Q-learning network agent we have already looked at plenty of times. There isn't a DDQN agent so it looks like you may need to just put two DQN agents together.
- **REINFORCE**: This is the first policy gradient method we looked at.
- **DDPG**: This is a PG method, more specifically, the deep deterministic policy gradient method.
- **TD3**: This is best described as a clipped double Q-learning model that uses Actor-Critic to better describe the advantages in discrete action spaces. Typically, PG methods can perform poorly in discrete action spaces.
- **PPO**: This is our old friend proximal policy optimization, another PG method.
- **SAC**: This is based on soft Actor-Critic—an off-policy maximum entropy deep reinforcement learning with a stochastic actor. The basic reasoning here is the agent maximizes expected rewards by being as random as possible.

TF-Agents is a nice stable platform that allows you to build up intuitive samples that you can train in the cloud very easily. This will likely make it a very popular framework for building proof-of-concept models for a variety of problems. In the next section, we will wrap up this chapter with the usual additional exercises.

Exercises

The exercises in this section are a bit wider in scope in this chapter in hopes you look through several frameworks on your own:

1. Take some time and look at one of the frameworks listed earlier but not reviewed in this chapter.
2. Use SimpleRL to solve a grid-world MDP that is different than the one in the example. Be sure to take the time to tune hyperparameters.
3. Use Google Dopamine to train an agent to play the LunarLander environment. The best choice is likely RainbowDQN or a variation of that.
4. Use Keras-RL to train an agent to play the Lunar Lander environment; make sure to spend time tuning hyperparameters.
5. Use RL Lib to train an agent to play the Lunar Lander environment; make sure to spend time tuning hyperparameters.
6. Modify the Keras-RL example and modify the network structure. Change the number of neurons and layers.
7. Modify the RL Lib example and change some of the hyperparameters such as the num workers and the number of GPUs, as shown in the following tune code:

```
tune.run("DQN", stop={"episode_reward_mean": 100},
    config={
            "env": "CartPole-v0",
            "num_gpus": 0,
            "num_workers": 1,
            "lr": tune.grid_search([0.01, 0.001, 0.0001]),
            "monitor": False,     },)
```

8. Modify the RLLib example and use a different agent type. You will likely have to check the documentation for RLLib to see what other agents are supported.
9. Use TD3 from TF-Agents to train an agent to complete the Lunar Lander environment.
10. Use SAC from TF-Agents and use it train the Lunar Lander environment.

Feel free to perform these exercises with Google Colab or in your favorite IDE. If you do use an IDE, you may need to take extra care to install some dependencies. In the next and last section of this chapter, we will finish up with the summary.

Summary

This was a short but intense chapter in which we spent time looking at various third-party DRL frameworks. Fortunately, all of these frameworks are all still free and open source, and let's hope they stay that way. We started by looking at the many growing frameworks and some pros and cons. Then, we looked at what are currently the most popular or promising libraries. Starting with Google Dopamine, which showcases RainbowDQN, we looked at how to run a quick sample of Google Colab. After that, Keras-RL was next, and we introduced ourselves to the Keras framework as well as how to use the Keras-RL library. Moving on to RLLib, we looked at the powerful automation of the DRL framework that has many capabilities. Finally, we finished up this chapter with another entry from Google, TF-Agents, where we ran a complete DQN agent using TF-Agents on a Google Colab notebook.

We have spent plenty of time learning about and using RL and DRL algorithms. So much so, we should be fairly comfortable with training and looking to move on to more challenging environments.

In the next chapter, we will move on to training agents in more complex environments such as the real world. However, instead of the real world, we are going to use the next best thing: 3D worlds.

Section 3: Reward Yourself 3

We have come to the end of this book. We started by first exploring the basics of RL, and then exploiting and enhancing that knowledge in the second section. Finally, we will complete the third and final section by rewarding you by exploring more challenging environments for fun or profit.

This section contains the following chapters:

- Chapter 13, *3D Worlds*
- Chapter 14, *From DRL to AGI*

13
3D Worlds

We are almost nearing the end of our journey into what **artificial general intelligence (AGI)** is and how **deep reinforcement learning (DRL)** can be used to help us get there. While it is still questionable whether DRL is indeed the right path to AGI, it is what appears to be our current best option. However, the reason we are questioning DRL is because of its ability or inability to master diverse 3D spaces or worlds, the same 3D spaces we humans and all animals have mastered but something we find very difficult to train RL agents on. In fact, it is the belief of many an AGI researcher that solving the 3D state-space problem could go a long way to solving true general artificial intelligence. We will look at why that is the case in this chapter.

For this chapter, we are going to look at why 3D worlds pose such a unique problem to DRL agents and the ways we can train them to interpret state. We will look at how typical 3D agents use vision to interpret state and we will look to the type of deep learning networks derived from that. Then we look to a practical example of using 3D vision in an environment and what options we have for processing state. Next, sticking with Unity, we look at the Obstacle Tower Challenge, an AI challenge with a $100,000 prize, and what implementation was used to win the prize. Moving to the end of the chapter, we will look at another 3D environment called Habitat and how it can be used for developing agents.

Here is a summary of the main points we will discuss this chapter:

- Reasoning on 3D worlds
- Training a visual agent
- Generalizing 3D vision
- Challenging the Unity Obstacle Tower Challenge
- Exploring habitat—embodied agents by FAIR

The examples in this chapter can take an especially long time to train, so please either be patient or perhaps just choose to do one. This not only saves you time but reduces energy consumption. In the next chapter, we explore why 3D worlds are so special.

Reasoning on 3D worlds

So, why are 3D worlds so important, or are at least believed to be so? Well, it all has to come down to state interpretation, or what we in DRL like to call state representation. A lot of work is being done on better representation of state for RL and other problems. The theory is that being able to represent just key or converged points of state allow us to simplify the problem dramatically. We have looked at doing just that using various techniques over several chapters. Recall how we discretized the state representation of a continuous observation space into a discrete space using a grid mesh. This technique is how we solved more difficult continuous space problems with the tools we had at the time. Over the course of several chapters since then, we saw how we could input that continuous space directly into our deep learning network. That included the ability to directly input an image as the game state, a screenshot, using convolutional neural networks. However, 3D worlds, ones that represent the real world, pose a unique challenge to representing state.

So what is the difficulty in representing the state space in a 3D environment? Could we not just give the agent sensors, as we did in other environments? Well, yes and no. The problem is that giving the agent sensors is putting our bias on what the agent needs to use in order to interpret the problem. For example, we could give the agent a sensor that told it the distance of an object directly in front of it, as well as to its left and right. While that would likely be enough information for any driving agent, would it work for an agent that needed to climb stairs? Not likely. Instead, we would likely need to give the height of the stairs as another sensor input, which means our preferred method of introducing state to an agent for a 3D world is using vision or an image of the environment. The reason for this, of course, is to remove any bias on our part (us humans) and we can best do that by just feeding the environment state as an image directly to the agent.

We have already seen how we could input game state using an image of the playing area when we looked at playing Atari games. However, those game environments were all 2D, meaning the state space was essentially flattened or converged. The word **converged** works here because this becomes the problem when tackling 3D environments and the real world. In 3D space, one vantage point could potentially yield to multiple states, and likewise, multiple state spaces can be observed by one single vantage point.

We can see how this works in the following diagram:

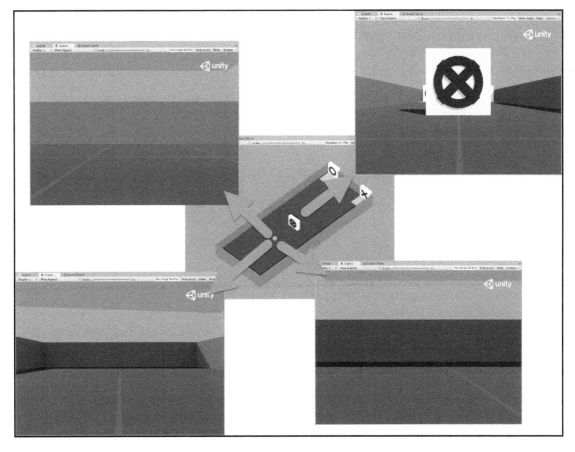

Examples of agent state in a 3D world

In the diagram, we can see the agent, the blue dot in the center of Visual Hallway environment in Unity with the ML-Agents toolkit. We will review an example of this environment shortly, so don't worry about reviewing it just yet. You can see from the diagram how the agent is observing different observations of state from the same physical position using an agent camera. An agent camera is the vision we give to the agent to observe the world.

From this camera, the agent ingests the state as a visual observation that is fed as an image into a deep learning network. This image is broken up with 2D convolutional neural network layers into features, which the agent learns. The problem is that we are using 2D filters to try and digest 3D information. In Chapter 7, *Going Deeper with DDQN*, we explored using CNNs to ingest the image state from Atari games and, as we have seen, this works very well.

You will need the ML-Agents toolkit installed and should have opened the **UnitySDK** test project. If you need assistance with this, return to Chapter 11, *Exploiting ML-Agents*, and follow some of the exercises there first.

Unity does the same thing for its agent camera setup, and in the next exercise we will see how the following looks:

1. Locate the folder at `ml-agents/ml-agents/mlagents/trainers` located in the ML-Agents repository. If you need help pulling the repository, follow the previous information tip given.
2. From this folder, locate and open the `models.py` file in a text or Python IDE. ML-Agents is written in TensorFlow, which may be intimidating at first, but the code follows many of the same principles as PyTorch.
3. Around line 250 a `create_visual_observation_encoder` function from the `LearningModel` base class is created. This is the base class model that ML-Agents, the PPO, and SAC implementations use.

ML-Agents was originally developed in Keras and then matured to TensorFlow in order to improve performance. Since that time, PyTorch has seen a huge surge in popularity for academic researchers, as well as builders. At the time of writing, PyTorch is the fastest growing DL framework. It remains to be seen if Unity will also follow suit and convert the code to PyTorch, or just upgrade it to TensorFlow 2.0.

4. The `create_visual_observation_encoder` function is the base function for encoding state, and the full definition of the function (minus comments) is shown here:

```
def create_visual_observation_encoder(
        self,
        image_input: tf.Tensor,
        h_size: int,
        activation: ActivationFunction,
        num_layers: int,
        scope: str,
```

```
        reuse: bool,
) -> tf.Tensor:
    with tf.variable_scope(scope):
        conv1 = tf.layers.conv2d(
            image_input,
            16,
            kernel_size=[8, 8],
            strides=[4, 4],
            activation=tf.nn.elu,
            reuse=reuse,
            name="conv_1",
        )
        conv2 = tf.layers.conv2d(
            conv1,
            32,
            kernel_size=[4, 4],
            strides=[2, 2],
            activation=tf.nn.elu,
            reuse=reuse,
            name="conv_2",
        )
        hidden = c_layers.flatten(conv2)

    with tf.variable_scope(scope + "/" + "flat_encoding"):
        hidden_flat = self.create_vector_observation_encoder(
            hidden, h_size, activation, num_layers, scope,
reuse
        )
    return hidden_flat
```

5. While the code is in TensorFlow, there are a few obvious indicators of common terms, such as layers and conv2d. With that information, you can see that this encoder uses two CNN layers: one with a kernel size of 8 x 8, a stride of 4 x 4, and 16 filters; followed by a second layer that uses a kernel size of 4 x 4, a stride of 2 x 2, and 32 filters.

Notice again the use of no pooling layers. This is because spatial information is lost when we use pooling between CNN layers. However, depending on the depth of the network, a single pooling layer near the top can be beneficial.

6. Notice the return from the function is a hidden flat layer denoted by `hidden_flat`. Recall that our CNN layers are being used to learn state that is then fed into our learning network as the following diagram shows:

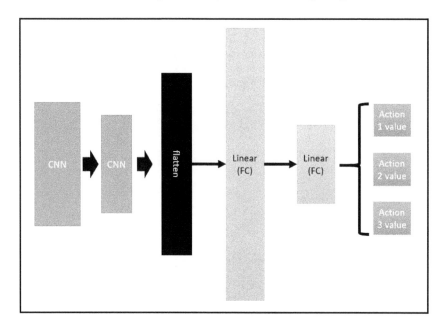

Example network diagram

7. The preceding diagram is a simplified network diagram showing that the CNN layers flatten as they feed into the hidden middle layer. Flattening is converting that convolutional 2D data into a one-dimensional vector and then feeding that into the rest of the network.

8. We can see how the image source is defined by opening up the Unity editor to the **ML-Agents UnitySDK** project to the **VisualHallway** scene located in the `Assets/ML-Agents/Examples/Hallway/Scenes` folder.

9. Expand the first **VisualSymbolFinderArea** and select the **Agent** object in the **Hierarchy** window. Then, in the **Inspector** window, locate and double-click on the **Brain** to bring it up in the following window:

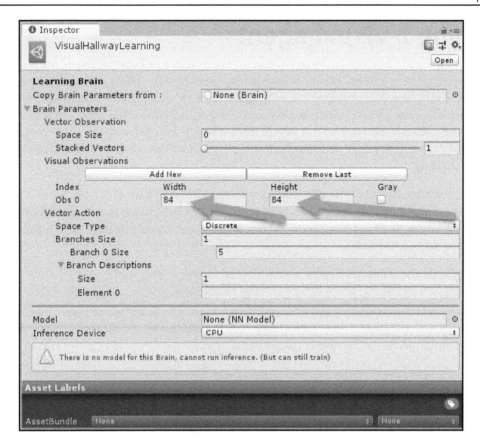

Inspecting the VisualHallwayLearning Brain

The important thing to note here is that the agent is set up to accept an image of size 84 x 84 pixels. That means the agent camera is sampled down to an image size matching the same pixel area. A relatively small pixel area for this environment works because of the lack of detail in the scene. If the detail increased, we would likely also need to increase the resolution of the input image.

In the next section, we look at training the agent visually using the ML-Agents toolkit.

Training a visual agent

Unity develops a 2D and 3D gaming engine/platform that has become the most popular platform for building games. Most of these games are the 3D variety, hence the specialized interest by Unity in mastering the task of agents that can tackle more 3D natural worlds. It naturally follows then that Unity has invested substantially into this problem and has/is working with DeepMind to develop this further. How this collaboration turns out remains to be seen, but one thing is for certain is that Unity will be our go-to platform for exploring 3D agent training.

In the next exercise, we are going to jump back into Unity and look at how we can train an agent in a visual 3D environment. Unity is arguably the best place to set up and build these type of environments as we have seen in the earlier chapters. Open the Unity editor and follow these steps:

1. Open the **VisualHallway** scene located in the `Assets/ML-Agents/Examples/Hallway/Scenes` folder.

2. Locate the **Academy** object in the scene hierarchy window and set the **Control** option to enabled on the **Hallway Academy** component **Brains** section and as shown in the following screenshot:

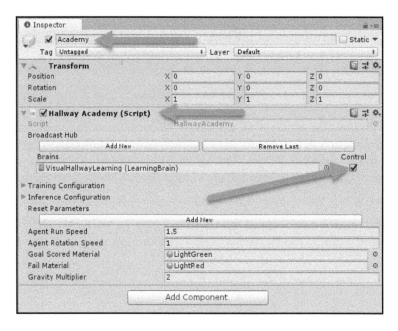

Setting the academy to control the learning brain

3. This sets the Academy to control the Brain for the agent.

4. Next, select all the **VisualSymbolFinderArea** objects from **(1)** to **(7)** and then make sure to enable them all by clicking the object's **Active** option in the Inspector window, as shown in the following screenshot:

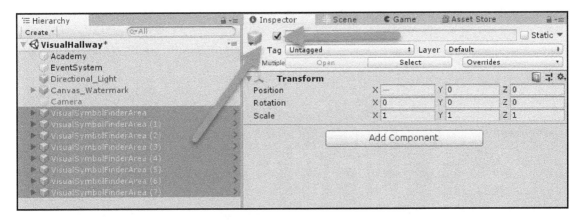

Enabling all the sub-environments in the scene

5. This enables all the sub environment areas and allows us to run an additional seven agents when training. As we have seen when using actor-critic methods, being able to sample more efficiently from the environment has many advantages. Almost all the example ML-Agents environments provide for multiple sub-training environments. These multiple environments are considered separate environments but allow for the brain to be trained synchronously with multiple agents.

6. Save the scene and the project file from the **File** menu.

7. Open a new Python or Anaconda shell and set the virtual environment to use the one you set up earlier for ML-Agents. If you need help, refer to Chapter 11, *Exploiting ML-Agents*.

8. Navigate to the Unity `ml-agents` folder and execute the following command to start training:

```
mlagents-learn config/trainer_config.yaml --run-id=vishall_1 --
train
```

9. This will start the Python trainer, and after a few seconds, will prompt you to click Play in the editor. After you do that, the agents in all the environments will begin training and you will be able to visualize this in the editor. An example of how this looks in the command shell is shown in the following screenshot:

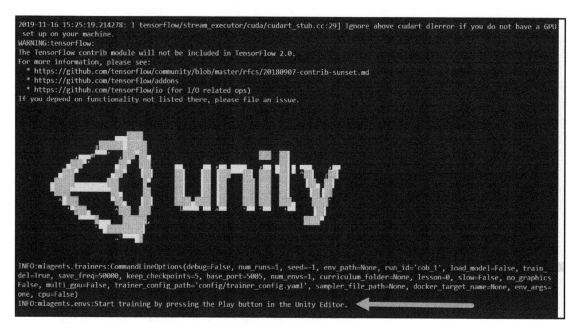

Running the ML-Agents trainer

Now that we have reviewed how to train an agent in Unity with ML-Agents, we can move on to explore some other undocumented training options in the next section.

If you encounter problems training the Hallway environment, you can always try one of the other various environments. It is not uncommon for a few of the environments to become broken because of releases or version conflicts.

Generalizing 3D vision

As previously mentioned in Chapter 11, *Exploiting ML-Agents*, we saw how the team at Unity is one of the leaders in training agents for 3D worlds. After all, they do have a strong vested interest in providing an AI platform that developers can just plug into and build intelligent agents. Except, the very agents that fit this broad type of application are now considered the first step to AGI because if Unity can successfully build a universal agent to play any game, it will have effectively built a first-level AGI.

The problem with defining AGI is trying to understand how broad or general an intelligence has to be as well as how we quantify the agent's understanding of that environment and possible ability to transfer knowledge to other tasks. We really won't know how best to define what that is until someone has the confidence to stand up and claim to have developed an AGI. A big part of that claim will depend on how well an agent can generalize environmental state and a big part of that will be generalizing 3D vision itself.

Unity has an undocumented way to alter the type of visual encoder you can use in training on an environment (at least at time of writing).

In the next exercise, we look at how the hyperparameter can be added to the configuration and set for different visual encoders by following these steps:

1. Locate the trainer_config.yaml configuration file located in the mlagents/ml-agents/config folder and open it in an IDE or text editor.

 YAML is an acronym that stands for for **YAML ain't markup language**. The format of the ML-Agents configuration markup files is quite similar to Windows INI configuration files of old.

2. This file defines the configuration for the various learning brains. Locate the section for the VisualHallwayLearning brain as shown here:

```
VisualHallwayLearning:
    use_recurrent: true
    sequence_length: 64
    num_layers: 1
    hidden_units: 128
    memory_size: 256
    beta: 1.0e-2
    num_epoch: 3
    buffer_size: 1024
    batch_size: 64
```

```
max_steps: 5.0e5
summary_freq: 1000
time_horizon: 64
```

3. These hyperparameters are additional to a set of base values set in a default brain configuration at the top of the config file and shown as follows:

```
idefault:
    trainer: ppo
    batch_size: 1024
    beta: 5.0e-3
    buffer_size: 10240
    epsilon: 0.2
    hidden_units: 128
    lambd: 0.95
    learning_rate: 3.0e-4
    learning_rate_schedule: linear
    max_steps: 5.0e4
    memory_size: 256
    normalize: false
    num_epoch: 3
    num_layers: 2
    time_horizon: 64
    sequence_length: 64
    summary_freq: 1000
    use_recurrent: false
    vis_encode_type: simple
    reward_signals:
        extrinsic:
            strength: 1.0
            gamma: 0.99
```

4. The hyperparameter of interest for us is the `vis_encode_type` value set to simple highlighted in the preceding code example. ML-Agents supports two additional types of visual encoding by changing that option like so:

- `vis_enc_type`: Hyperparameter to set type of visual encoding:
    - `simple`: This is the default and the version we already looked at.
    - `nature_cnn`: This defines a CNN architecture proposed by a paper in Nature, we will look at this closer shortly.
    - `resnet`: ResNet is a published CNN architecture that has been shown to be very effective at image classification.

5. We will change the default value in our `VisualHallwayLearning` brain by adding a new line to the end of the brain's configuration:

```
VisualHallwayLearning:
    use_recurrent: true
    sequence_length: 64
    num_layers: 1
    hidden_units: 128
    memory_size: 256
    beta: 1.0e-2
    num_epoch: 3
    buffer_size: 1024
    batch_size: 64
    max_steps: 5.0e5
    summary_freq: 1000
    time_horizon: 64
    vis_enc_type: nature_cnn --or-- resnet
```

6. Now that we know how to set these, let's see what they look like by opening the `models.py` code like we did earlier from the `ml-agents/trainers` folder. Scroll down past the `create_visual_observation_encoder` function to the `create_nature_cnn_observation_encoder` function shown here:

```
def create_nature_cnn_visual_observation_encoder(
        self,
        image_input: tf.Tensor,
        h_size: int,
        activation: ActivationFunction,
        num_layers: int,
        scope: str,
        reuse: bool,
    ) -> tf.Tensor:
        with tf.variable_scope(scope):
            conv1 = tf.layers.conv2d(
                image_input,
                32,
                kernel_size=[8, 8],
                strides=[4, 4],
                activation=tf.nn.elu,
                reuse=reuse,
                name="conv_1",
            )
            conv2 = tf.layers.conv2d(
                conv1,
                64,
                kernel_size=[4, 4],
                strides=[2, 2],
```

```
                        activation=tf.nn.elu,
                        reuse=reuse,
                        name="conv_2",
                    )
                    conv3 = tf.layers.conv2d(
                        conv2,
                        64,
                        kernel_size=[3, 3],
                        strides=[1, 1],
                        activation=tf.nn.elu,
                        reuse=reuse,
                        name="conv_3",
                    )
                    hidden = c_layers.flatten(conv3)

                with tf.variable_scope(scope + "/" + "flat_encoding"):
                    hidden_flat = self.create_vector_observation_encoder(
                        hidden, h_size, activation, num_layers, scope,
    reuse
                    )
                return hidden_flat
```

7. The main difference with this implementation is the use of a third layer called conv3. We can see this third layer has a kernel size of 3 x 3, a stride of 1 x 1 and 64 filters. With a smaller kernel and stride size, we can see this new layer is being used to extract finer features. How useful that is depends on the environment.

8. Next, we want to look at the third visual encoding implementation listed just after the last function. The next function is create_resent_visual_observation_encoder and is shown as follows:

```
    def create_resnet_visual_observation_encoder(
            self,
            image_input: tf.Tensor,
            h_size: int,
            activation: ActivationFunction,
            num_layers: int,
            scope: str,
            reuse: bool,
        ) -> tf.Tensor:
            n_channels = [16, 32, 32]
            n_blocks = 2
            with tf.variable_scope(scope):
                hidden = image_input
                for i, ch in enumerate(n_channels):
                    hidden = tf.layers.conv2d(
                        hidden,
                        ch,
```

```
                        kernel_size=[3, 3],
                        strides=[1, 1],
                        reuse=reuse,
                        name="layer%dconv_1" % i,
                    )
                    hidden = tf.layers.max_pooling2d(
                        hidden, pool_size=[3, 3], strides=[2, 2],
        padding="same"
                    )
                    for j in range(n_blocks):
                        block_input = hidden
                        hidden = tf.nn.relu(hidden)
                        hidden = tf.layers.conv2d(
                            hidden,
                            ch,
                            kernel_size=[3, 3],
                            strides=[1, 1],
                            padding="same",
                            reuse=reuse,
                            name="layer%d_%d_conv1" % (i, j),
                        )
                        hidden = tf.nn.relu(hidden)
                        hidden = tf.layers.conv2d(
                            hidden,
                            ch,
                            kernel_size=[3, 3],
                            strides=[1, 1],
                            padding="same",
                            reuse=reuse,
                            name="layer%d_%d_conv2" % (i, j),
                        )
                        hidden = tf.add(block_input, hidden)
                hidden = tf.nn.relu(hidden)
                hidden = c_layers.flatten(hidden)

            with tf.variable_scope(scope + "/" + "flat_encoding"):
                hidden_flat = self.create_vector_observation_encoder(
                    hidden, h_size, activation, num_layers, scope,
        reuse
                )
            return hidden_flat
```

9. You can now go back and update the `vis_enc_type` hyperparameter in the config file and retrain the visual agent. Note which encoder is more successful if you have time to run both versions.

We have seen what variations of visual encoders that ML-Agents supports and the team at Unity has also included a relatively new variant called ResNet. ResNet is an important achievement, and thus far, has shown to be useful for training agents in some visual environments. Therefore, in the next section, we will spend some extra time looking at ResNet.

ResNet for visual observation encoding

Convolutional layers have been used in various configurations for performing image classification and recognition tasks successfully for some time now. The problem we encounter with using straight 2D CNNs is we are essentially flattening state representations, but generally not in a good way. This means that we are taking a visual observation of a 3D space and flattening it to a 2D image that we then try and extract important features from. This results in an agent thinking it is in the same state if it recognizes the same visual features from potentially different locations in the same 3D environment. This creates confusion in the agent and you can visualize this by watching an agent just wander in circles.

The same type of agent confusion can often be seen happening due to vanishing or exploding gradients. We haven't encountered this problem very frequently because our networks have been quite shallow. However, in order to improve network performance, we often deepen the network by adding additional layers. In fact, in some vision classification networks, there could be 100 layers or more of convolution trying to extract all manner of features. By adding this many additional layers, we introduce the opportunity for vanishing gradients. A vanishing gradient is a term we use for a gradient that becomes so small as to appear to vanish, or really have no effect on training/learning. Remember that our gradient calculation requires a total loss that is then transferred back through the network. The more layers the loss needs to push back through the network, the smaller it becomes. This is a major issue in the deep CNN networks that we use for image classification and interpretation.

ResNet or residual CNN networks were introduced as a way of allowing for deeper encoding structures without suffering vanishing gradients. Residual networks are so named because they carry forth a residual identity called an **identity shortcut connection**. The following diagram, sourced from the *Deep Residual Learning for Image Recognition* paper, shows the basic components in a residual block:

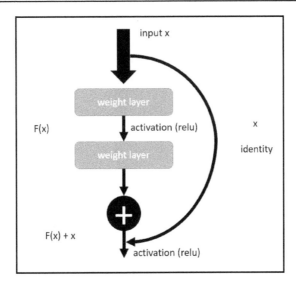

A residual block

The intuition from the authors in the paper is that stacked layers shouldn't degrade network performance just because they are stacked. Instead, by pushing the output of the last layer to the layer ahead, we are effectively able to isolate training to individual layers. We refer to this as an **identity** because the size of the output from the last layer will likely not match the input of the next layer, since we are bypassing the middle layer. Instead, we multiply the output of the last layer with an identity input tensor in order to match the output to the input.

Let's jump back to the ResNet encoder implementation back in ML-Agents and see how this is done in the next exercise:

1. Open the `models.py` file located in the `mlagents/ml-agents/trainers` folder.
2. Scroll down to the `create_resnet_visual_observation_encoder` function again. Look at the first two lines that define some variables for building up the residual network as shown here:

   ```
   n_channels = [16, 32, 32] # channel for each stack
   n_blocks = 2 # number of residual blocks
   ```

3. Next, scroll down a little more to where we enumerate the number of channels listed to build up each of the input layers. The code is shown as follows:

```
for i, ch in enumerate(n_channels):
    hidden = tf.layers.conv2d(
        hidden,
        ch,
        kernel_size=[3, 3],
        strides=[1, 1],
        reuse=reuse,
        name="layer%dconv_1" % i,)
        hidden = tf.layers.max_pooling2d(
            hidden, pool_size=[3, 3], strides=[2, 2],
padding="same")
```

4. The `n_channels` variable represents the number of channels or filters used in each of the input convolution layers. Thus, we are creating three groups of residual layers with an input layer and blocks in between. The blocks are used to isolate the training to each of the layers.

5. Keep scrolling down, and we can see where the blocks are constructed between the layers with the following code:

```
for j in range(n_blocks):
    block_input = hidden
    hidden = tf.nn.relu(hidden)
    hidden = tf.layers.conv2d(
        hidden,
        ch,
        kernel_size=[3, 3],
        strides=[1, 1],
        padding="same",
        reuse=reuse,
        name="layer%d_%d_conv1" % (i, j),)
    hidden = tf.nn.relu(hidden)
    hidden = tf.layers.conv2d(
        hidden,
        ch,
        kernel_size=[3, 3],
        strides=[1, 1],
        padding="same",
        reuse=reuse,
        name="layer%d_%d_conv2" % (i, j),)
    hidden = tf.add(block_input, hidden)
```

6. This code creates a network structure similar to what is shown in the following diagram:

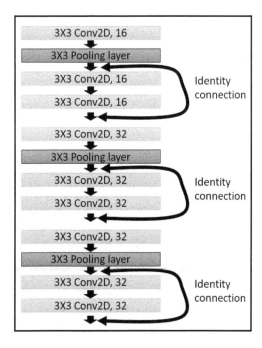

Diagram of the ResNet architecture in ML-Agents

7. In essence, we still only have three distinct convolutional layers extracting features, but each of those layers can now be trained independently. Furthermore, we can likely increase the depth of this network several times and expect an increase in visual encoding performance.
8. Go back and, if you have not already done so, train a visual agent with residual networks for visual observation encoding.

What you will likely find if you went back and trained another visual agent with residual networks is the agent performs marginally better, but they still can get confused. Again, this is more of a problem with the visual encoding system than the DRL itself. However, it is believed that once we can tackle visual encoding of visual environments, real AGI will certainly be a lot closer.

In the next section, we look at a special environment that the team at Unity put together (with the help of Google DeepMind) in order to challenge DRL researchers, which is the very problem of visual encoding 3D worlds.

Challenging the Unity Obstacle Tower Challenge

In late 2018, Unity, with the help of DeepMind, began development of a challenge designed to task researchers in the most challenging areas of DRL. The challenge was developed with Unity as a Gym interface environment and featured a game using a 3D first-person perspective. The 3D perspective is a type of game interface made famous with the likes of games such as Tomb Raider and Resident Evil, to name just a couple of examples. An example of the game interface is shown in the following screenshot:

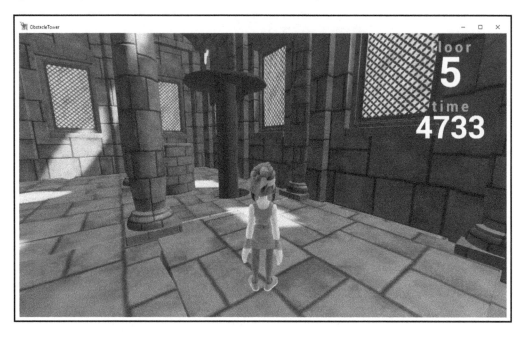

Example the obstacle tower challenge

The Obstacle Tower Challenge is not only in 3D, but the patterns and materials in the rooms and on the walls change over the levels. This makes vision generalization even more difficult. Furthermore, the challenge poses multiple concurrent steps to complete tasks. That is, each level requires the character to find a door and open it. On more advancing levels, the doors require a special key to be activated or acquired, which makes this almost a multi-task RL problem—not a problem we have considered solving previously. Fortunately, as we demonstrated using ML-Agents Curiosity Learning, multi-step RL can be accomplished, provided the tasks are linearly connected. This means there is no branching or tasks that require decisions.

Multi-task reinforcement learning is quickly advancing in research but it is still a very complicated topic. The current preferred method to solve MTRL is called **meta reinforcement learning**. We will cover Meta Reinforcement Learning in `Chapter 14`, *From DRL to AGI,* where we will talk about the next evolutions of DRL in the coming months and/or years.

For the next exercise, we are going to closely review the work of the winner of the Unity Obstacle Tower Challenge, Alex Nichol. Alex won the $100,000 challenge by entering a modified PPO agent that was pre-trained on classified images and human recorded demonstrations (behavioural cloning). He essentially won by better generalizing the agent's observations of state using a number of engineered solutions.

Open up your Anaconda prompt and follow the next example:

1. It is recommended that you create a new virtual environment before installing any new code and environments. This can easily be done with Anaconda using the following commands:

```
conda create -n obtower python=3.6
conda activate obstower
```

2. First, you will need to download and install the Unity Obstacle Tower Challenge from this repository (`https://github.com/Unity-Technologies/obstacle-tower-env`) or just use the following commands from a new virtual environment:

```
git clone git@github.com:Unity-Technologies/obstacle-tower-env.git
cd obstacle-tower-env
pip install -e .
```

3. Running the OTC environment is quite simple and can be done with this simple block of code that just performs random actions in the environment:

```
from obstacle_tower_env import ObstacleTowerEnv,
ObstacleTowerEvaluation
def run_episode(env):
    done = False
    episode_return = 0.0
    while not done:
        action = env.action_space.sample()
        obs, reward, done, info = env.step(action)
        episode_return += reward
    return episode_return

if __name__ == '__main__':
    eval_seeds = [1001, 1002, 1003, 1004, 1005]
    env = ObstacleTowerEnv('./ObstacleTower/obstacletower')
```

```
env = ObstacleTowerEvaluation(env, eval_seeds)
while not env.evaluation_complete:
    episode_rew = run_episode(env)
print(env.results)
env.close()
```

4. The code to run the OTC environment should be quite familiar by now, but does have one item to note. The agent cycles through episodes or lives, but the agent only has a certain number of lives. This environment simulates a real game, and hence, the agent only has a limited number of tries and time to complete the challenge.

5. Next, pull down the repository from Alex Nichol (`unixpickle`) here: `https://github.com/unixpickle/obs-tower2.git`, or check the `Chapter_13/obs-tower2` source folder.

6. Navigate to the folder and run the following command to install the required dependencies:

   `pip install -e .`

7. After that, you need to configure some environment variables to the following:

   ```
    `OBS_TOWER_PATH` - the path to the obstacle tower binary.
    `OBS_TOWER_RECORDINGS` - the path to a directory where
   demonstrations are stored.
    `OBS_TOWER_IMAGE_LABELS` - the path to the directory of labeled
   images.
   ```

8. How you set these environment variables will depend on your OS and at what level you want them set. For Windows users, you can set the environment variable using the **System Environment Variables** setup panel as shown here:

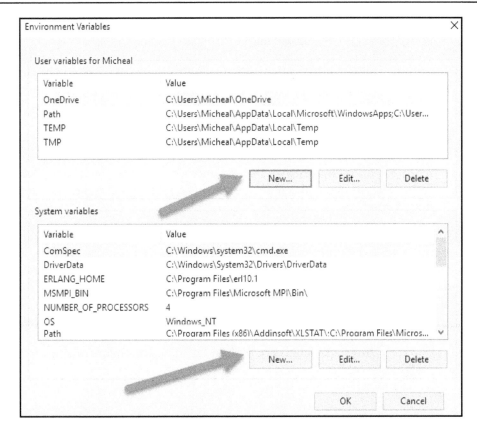

Setting the environment variables (Windows)

Now with everything set up, it is time to move on to pre-training the agent. We will cover that training in the next section.

Pre-training the agent

We have already covered a number of ways to manage training performance often caused by low rewards or rewards sparsity. This covered using a technique called behavioural cloning, whereby a human demonstrates a set of actions leading to a reward and those actions are then fed back into the agent as a pre-trained policy. The winning implementation here used a combination of behavioural cloning with pre-trained image classification.

We will continue from where we left off in the last exercise and learn what steps we need to perform in order to pre-train a classifier first:

1. Firstly, we need to capture images of the environment in order to pre-train a classifier. This requires you to run the `record.py` script located at the `obs_tower2/recorder/record.py` folder. Make sure when running this script that your environment variables are configured correctly.

The documentation or `README.md` on the repository is good but is only really intended for advanced users who are very interested in replicating results. If you do encounter issues in this walkthrough, refer back to that documentation.

2. Running the script will launch the Unity OTC and allow you as a player to interact with the game. As you play the game, the `record.py` script will record your moves as images after every episode. You will need to play several games in order to have enough training data. Alternatively, Alex has provided a number of recordings online at this location: `http://obstower.aqnichol.com/`.

Note:
The recordings and labels are both in tar files with the recordings weighing in at 25 GB.

3. Next, we need to label the recorded images in order to assist the agent in classification. Locate and run the `main.py` script located in the `obs_tower2/labeler/` folder. This will launch a web application. As long as you have your paths set correctly, you can now open a browser and go to `http://127.0.0.1:5000` (localhost, port `5000`).

4. You will now be prompted to label images by using the web interface. For each image, classify the state as shown in the following screenshot:

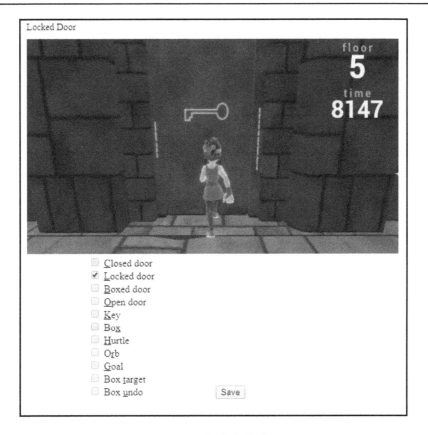

Labeling image data for classification

5. Alex notes in his original documentation that he could label 20-40 images per second after some practice. Again, if you want to avoid this step, just download the tar files containing his example recordings and labels.

6. Next, you will need to run that classifier with the training input images and labels you either just generated or downloaded. Run the classified by executing the following commands:

```
cd obs_tower2/scripts
python run_classifier.py
```

7. After the classification is done, the results will be output to a `save_classifier.pk1` file periodically. The whole process may take several hours to train completely.

8. With the pre-classifier built, we can move to behavioral cloning using the human sample playing. This means you will used the saved and pre-labelled sessions as inputs for later agent training. You can start the process by running the following:

```
python run_clone.py
```

9. Running this script generates periodic output to a save_clone.pkl file and the whole script can take a day or more to run. When the script is complete, copy the output to a save_prior.pkl file like so:

```
cp save_clone.pkl save_prior.pkl
```

This creates a prior set of recordings or memories we will use to train the agent in the next section.

Prierarchy – implicit hierarchies

Alex used the notion of hierarchical reinforcement learning in order to tackle the problem of multi-task agent learning that OTC requires you to solve. HRL is another method outside Meta-RL that has been used to successfully solve multi-task problems. Prierarchy-RL refines this by building a prior hierarchy that allows an action or action-state to be defined by entropy or uncertainty. High entropy or highly uncertain actions become high level or top-based actions. This is someone abstract in concept, so let's look at a code example to see how this comes together:

1. The base agent used to win the challenge was PPO; following is a full source listing of that agent and a refresher to PPO:

```
import itertools

import numpy as np
import torch
import torch.nn.functional as F
import torch.optim as optim
from .util import atomic_save

class PPO:
    def __init__(self, model, epsilon=0.2, gamma=0.99, lam=0.95,
lr=1e-4, ent_reg=0.001):
        self.model = model
        self.epsilon = epsilon
        self.gamma = gamma
        self.lam = lam
```

```
            self.optimizer = optim.Adam(model.parameters(), lr=lr)
            self.ent_reg = ent_reg

    def outer_loop(self, roller, save_path='save.pkl', **kwargs):
        for i in itertools.count():
            terms, last_terms = self.inner_loop(roller.rollout(),
**kwargs)
            self.print_outer_loop(i, terms, last_terms)
            atomic_save(self.model.state_dict(), save_path)

    def print_outer_loop(self, i, terms, last_terms):
        print('step %d: clipped=%f entropy=%f explained=%f' %
              (i, last_terms['clip_frac'], terms['entropy'],
terms['explained']))

    def inner_loop(self, rollout, num_steps=12, batch_size=None):
        if batch_size is None:
            batch_size = rollout.num_steps * rollout.batch_size
        advs = rollout.advantages(self.gamma, self.lam)
        targets = advs + rollout.value_predictions()[:-1]
        advs = (advs - np.mean(advs)) / (1e-8 + np.std(advs))
        actions = rollout.actions()
        log_probs = rollout.log_probs()
        firstterms = None
        lastterms = None
        for entries in rollout.batches(batch_size, num_steps):
            def choose(values):
                return self.model.tensor(np.array([values[t, b] for
t, b in entries]))
            terms = self.terms(choose(rollout.states),
                               choose(rollout.obses),
                               choose(advs),
                               choose(targets),
                               choose(actions),
                               choose(log_probs))
            self.optimizer.zero_grad()
            terms['loss'].backward()
            self.optimizer.step()
            lastterms = {k: v.item() for k, v in terms.items() if k
!= 'model_outs'}
            if firstterms is None:
                firstterms = lastterms
            del terms
        return firstterms, lastterms

    def terms(self, states, obses, advs, targets, actions,
log_probs):
        model_outs = self.model(states, obses)
```

```
            vf_loss = torch.mean(torch.pow(model_outs['critic'] -
targets, 2))
            variance = torch.var(targets)
            explained = 1 - vf_loss / variance

            new_log_probs = -F.cross_entropy(model_outs['actor'],
actions.long(), reduction='none')
            ratio = torch.exp(new_log_probs - log_probs)
            clip_ratio = torch.clamp(ratio, 1 - self.epsilon, 1 +
self.epsilon)
            pi_loss = -torch.mean(torch.min(ratio * advs, clip_ratio *
advs))
            clip_frac = torch.mean(torch.gt(ratio * advs, clip_ratio *
advs).float())

            all_probs = torch.log_softmax(model_outs['actor'], dim=-1)
            neg_entropy = torch.mean(torch.sum(torch.exp(all_probs) *
all_probs, dim=-1))
            ent_loss = self.ent_reg * neg_entropy

            return {
                'explained': explained,
                'clip_frac': clip_frac,
                'entropy': -neg_entropy,
                'vf_loss': vf_loss,
                'pi_loss': pi_loss,
                'ent_loss': ent_loss,
                'loss': vf_loss + pi_loss + ent_loss,
                'model_outs': model_outs,
            }
```

2. Familiarize yourself with the differences between this implementation and what we covered for PPO. Our example was simplified for explanation purposes but follows the same patterns.

3. Pay particular attention to the code in `inner_loop` and understand how this works:

```
def inner_loop(self, rollout, num_steps=12, batch_size=None):
```

4. Open the `prierarchy.py` file located in the root `obs_tower2` folder and as shown here:

```
import numpy as np
import torch
import torch.nn.functional as F

from .ppo import PPO
```

```
class Prierarchy(PPO):
    def __init__(self, prior, *args, kl_coeff=0, **kwargs):
        super().__init__(*args, **kwargs)
        self.prior = prior
        self.kl_coeff = kl_coeff

    def print_outer_loop(self, i, terms, last_terms):
        print('step %d: clipped=%f entropy=%f explained=%f kl=%f' %
              (i, last_terms['clip_frac'], last_terms['entropy'],
terms['explained'],
               terms['kl']))

    def inner_loop(self, rollout, num_steps=12, batch_size=None):
        if batch_size is None:
            batch_size = rollout.num_steps * rollout.batch_size
        prior_rollout = self.prior.run_for_rollout(rollout)
        prior_logits = prior_rollout.logits()
        rollout = self.add_rewards(rollout, prior_rollout)
        advs = rollout.advantages(self.gamma, self.lam)
        targets = advs + rollout.value_predictions()[:-1]
        actions = rollout.actions()
        log_probs = rollout.log_probs()
        firstterms = None
        lastterms = None
        for entries in rollout.batches(batch_size, num_steps):
            def choose(values):
                return self.model.tensor(np.array([values[t, b] for
t, b in entries]))
            terms = self.extended_terms(choose(prior_logits),
                                        choose(rollout.states),
                                        choose(rollout.obses),
                                        choose(advs),
                                        choose(targets),
                                        choose(actions),
                                        choose(log_probs))
            self.optimizer.zero_grad()
            terms['loss'].backward()
            self.optimizer.step()
            lastterms = {k: v.item() for k, v in terms.items() if k
!= 'model_outs'}
            if firstterms is None:
                firstterms = lastterms
            del terms
        return firstterms, lastterms

    def extended_terms(self, prior_logits, states, obses, advs,
targets, actions, log_probs):
        super_out = self.terms(states, obses, advs, targets,
```

```
actions, log_probs)
        log_prior = F.log_softmax(prior_logits, dim=-1)
        log_posterior =
F.log_softmax(super_out['model_outs']['actor'], dim=-1)
        kl = torch.mean(torch.sum(torch.exp(log_posterior) *
(log_posterior - log_prior), dim=-1))
        kl_loss = kl * self.ent_reg
        super_out['kl'] = kl
        super_out['kl_loss'] = kl_loss
        super_out['loss'] = super_out['vf_loss'] +
super_out['pi_loss'] + kl_loss
        return super_out

    def add_rewards(self, rollout, prior_rollout):
        rollout = rollout.copy()
        rollout.rews = rollout.rews.copy()

        def log_probs(r):
            return
F.log_softmax(torch.from_numpy(np.array([m['actor'] for m in
r.model_outs])),
                                dim=-1)

        q = log_probs(prior_rollout)
        p = log_probs(rollout)
        kls = torch.sum(torch.exp(p) * (p - q), dim=-1).numpy()

        rollout.rews -= kls[:-1] * self.kl_coeff

        return rollout
```

5. What we see here is the `Pierarchy` class, an extension to `PPO`, which works by extending the `inner_loop` function. Simply, this code refines the KL-Divergence calculation that allowed us to secure that spot on the hill without falling off. Recall this was our discussion of the clipped objective function.

6. Notice the use of the `prior` policy or the policy that was generated based on the pre-training and behavioral cloning done earlier. This prior policy defines if actions are high or low in uncertainty. That way, an agent can actually use the prior hierarchy or prierarchy to select a series of high and then lower entropy/uncertain actions. The following diagram illustrates how this effectively works:

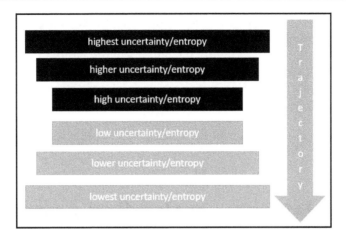

Agent selecting action based on entropy hierarchy

7. Thus, instead of deciding when and if to explore, the agent decides random actions based on their hierarchy or uncertainty. This means that higher-level actions can be reduced in uncertainty quickly because each successive action has less uncertainty.

A helpful example when trying to understand Priercarchy is the movie *Groundhog Day*, starring Bill Murray. In the movie, the character continually cycles through the same day, attempting by trial and error to find the optimum path to break out of the path. In the movie, we can see the character try thousands, perhaps millions, of different combinations, but we see this done in hierarchical steps. We first see the character wildly going about his day never accomplishing anything, until he learns through past hierarchical actions what are the best possible rewards. He learns that by improving on himself, his time in eternity becomes more pleasant. In the end, we see the character try to live their best life, only to discover they solved the game and can move on to the next day.

8. You can train the agent by running the following command on the first 10 levels:

```
cp save_prior.pkl save.pkl
python run_tail.py --min 0 --max 1 --path save.pkl
```

9. Then, to train the agent on floors greater than 10, you can use the following:

```
cp save_prior.pkl save_tail.pkl
python run_tail.py --min 10 --max 15 --path save_tail.pkl
```

Every 10 levels in the OTC, the game theme changes. This means the wall color and textures will change as well as the tasks that need to get completed. As we mentioned earlier, this visual change, combined with 3D, will make the Unity OTC one of the most difficult and benchmark challenges to beat when we first get smart/bold and/or brave enough to tackle AGI. AGI and the road to more general intelligence with DRL will be our focus for `Chapter 14`, *From DRL to AGI.*

In the next section, we look at 3D world Habitat by Facebook, which is more difficult but equally fun.

Exploring Habitat – embodied agents by FAIR

Habitat is a relatively new entry by Facebook AI Research for a new form of embodied agents. This platform represents the ability to represent full 3D worlds displayed from real-world complex scenes. The environment is intended for AI research of robots and robotic-like applications that DRL will likely power in the coming years. To be fair though, pun intended, this environment is implemented to train all forms of AI on this type of environment. The current Habitat repository only features some simple examples and implementation of PPO.

The Habitat platform comes in two pieces: the Habitat Sim and Habitat API. The simulation environment is a full 3D powered world that can render at thousands of frames per second, which is powered by photogrammetry RGBD data. RGBD is essentially RGB color data plus depth. Therefore, any image taken will have a color value and depth. This allows the data to be mapped in 3D as a hyper-realistic representation of the real environment. You can explore what one of these environments look like by using Habitat itself in your browser by following the next quick exercise:

1. Navigate your browser to `https://aihabitat.org/demo/`.

 Habitat will currently only run in Chrome or on your desktop.

2. It may take some time to load the app so be patient. When the app is loaded, you will see something like the following screenshot:

Example of Habitat running in the browser

3. Use the WASD keys to move around in the environment.

Habitat supports importing from the following three vendors: MatterPort3D, Gibson, and Replica, who produce tools and utilities to capture RGBD data and have libraries of this data. Now that we understand what Habitat is, we will set it up in the next section.

Installing Habitat

At the time of writing, Habitat was still a new product, but the documentation worked well to painlessly install and run an agent for training. In our next exercise, we walk through parts of that documentation to install and run a training agent in Habitat:

1. Open an Anaconda command prompt and navigate to a clean folder. Use the following commands to download and install the Habitat:

```
git clone --branch stable git@github.com:facebookresearch/habitat-sim.git
cd habitat-sim
```

2. Then, create a new virtual environment and install the required dependencies with the following:

```
conda create -n habitat python=3.6 cmake=3.14.0
conda activate habitat
pip install -r requirements.txt
```

3. Next, we need to build the Habitat Sim with the following:

```
python setup.py install
```

4. Download the test scenes from the following link: http://dl.fbaipublicfiles.com/habitat/habitat-test-scenes.zip.

5. Unzip the scene files into a familiar path, one that you can link to later. These files are sets of RGBD data that represent the scenes.

 RGBD image capture is not new, and traditionally, it has been expensive since it requires moving a camera equipped with a special sensor around a room. Thankfully, most modern cell phones also feature this depth sensor. This depth sensor is often used to build augmented reality applications now. Perhaps in a few years, agents themselves will be trained to capture these types of images using just a simple cell phone.

6. After everything is installed, we can test the Habitat installation by running the following command:

```
python examples/example.py --scene
/path/to/data/scene_datasets/habitat-test-scenes/skokloster-
castle.glb
```

7. That will launch the Sim in non-interactive fashion and play some random moves. If you want to see or interact with the environment, you will need to download and install the interactive plugin found in the repository documentation.

After the Sim is installed, we can move on to installing the API and training an agent in the next section.

Training in Habitat

At the time of writing, Habitat was quite new but showed amazing potential, especially for training agents. This means the environment currently only has a simple and PPO agent implementation in which you can quickly train agents. Of course, since Habitat uses PyTorch, you could probably implement one of the other algorithms we have covered. In the next exercise, we finish off by looking at the PPO implementation in Habitat and how to run it:

1. Download and install the Habitat API with the following commands:

```
git clone --branch stable git@github.com:facebookresearch/habitat-
api.git
cd habitat-api
pip install -r requirements.txt
python setup.py develop --all
```

2. At this point, you can use the API in a number of ways. We will first look at a basic code example you could write to run the Sim:

```
import habitat

# Load embodied AI task (PointNav) and a pre-specified virtual
robot
env = habitat.Env(
    config=habitat.get_config("configs/tasks/pointnav.yaml")
)

observations = env.reset()

# Step through environment with random actions
while not env.episode_over:
    observations = env.step(env.action_space.sample())
```

3. As you can see, the Sim allows us to program an agent using the same familiar Gym style interface we are used to.

4. Next, we need to install the Habitat Baselines package. This package is the RL portion and currently provides an example of PPO. The package is named Baselines after the OpenAI testing package of the same name.

5. Install the Habitat Baselines package using the following commands:

```
# be sure to cd to the habitat_baselines folder
pip install -r requirements.txt
python setup.py develop --all
```

6. After the installation, you can run the `run.py` script in order to train an agent with the following command:

```
python -u habitat_baselines/run.py --exp-config
habitat_baselines/config/pointnav/ppo_pointnav.yaml --run-type
train
```

7. Then, you can test this agent with the following command:

```
python -u habitat_baselines/run.py --exp-config
habitat_baselines/config/pointnav/ppo_pointnav.yaml --run-type eval
```

Habitat is a fairly recent development and opens the door to training agents/robots in real-world environments. While Unity and ML-Agents are great platforms for training agents in 3D game environments, they still do not compare to the complexity of the real world. In the real world, objects are rarely perfect and are often very complex, which makes these environments especially difficult to generalize, and therefore, train on. In the next section, we finish the chapter with our typical exercises.

Exercises

As we progressed through this book, the exercises have morphed from learning exercises to almost research efforts, and that is the case in this chapter. Therefore, the exercises in this chapter are meant for the hardcore RL enthusiast and may not be for everyone:

1. Tune the hyperparameters for one of the sample visual environments in the ML-Agents toolkit.
2. Modify the visual observation standard encoder found in the ML-Agents toolkit to include additional layers or different kernel filter settings.
3. Train an agent with `nature_cnn` or `resnet` visual encoder networks and compare their performance with earlier examples using the base visual encoder.
4. Modify the `resnet` visual encoder to accommodate many more layers or other variations of filter/kernel size.
5. Download, install, and play the Unity Obstacle Tower Challenge and see how far you can get in the game. As you play, think of yourself as an agent and reflect on what actions you are taking and how they reflect your current task trajectory.
6. Build your own implementation of an algorithm to test against the Unity OTC. Completing this challenge will be especially rewarding if you beat the results of the previous winner. This challenge is still somewhat open and anyone claiming to do higher than level 20 will probably make a big impact on DRL in the future.

7. Replace the PPO base example in the Habitat Baselines module with an implementation of Rainbow DQN. How does the performance compare?

8. Implement a different visual encoder for the Habitat Baselines framework. Perhaps use the previous examples of `nature_cnn` or `resnet`.

9. Compete in the Habitat Challenge. This is a challenge that requires an agent to complete a navigation task through a series of waypoints. It's certainly not as difficult as the OTC, but the visual environment is far more complex.

10. Habitat is intended more for sensor development instead of visual development. See if you are able to combine visual observation encoding with other sensor input as a type of combined visual and sensor observation input.

The exercises in this chapter are intended to be entirely optional; please choose to do these only if you have a reason to do so. They likely will require additional time as this is a very complex area to develop in.

Summary

In this chapter, we explored the concept of 3D worlds for not only games but the real world. The real world, and to a greater extent 3D worlds, are the next great frontier in DRL research. We looked at why 3D creates nuances for DRL that we haven't quite figured out how best to solve. Then, we looked at using 2D visual observation encoders but tuned for 3D spaces, with variations in the Nature CNN and ResNet or residual networks. After that, we looked at the Unity Obstacle Tower Challenge, which challenged developers to build an agent capable of solving the 3D multi-task environment.

From there, we looked at the winning entries use of Prierarchy; a form of HRL in order to manage multiple task spaces. We also looked at the code in detail to see how this reflected in the winners modified PPO implementation. Lastly, we finished the chapter by looking at Habitat; an advanced AI environment that uses RGBD and depth based color data, to render real-world environments in 3D.

We are almost done with our journey, and in the next and final chapter, we will look at how DRL is moving toward artificial general intelligence, or what we refer to as AGI.

14
From DRL to AGI

Our journey through this book has been an exploration of the evolution of reinforcement and **deep reinforcement learning** (**DRL**). We have looked at many methods that you can use to solve a variety of problems in a variety of environments, but in general, we have stuck to a single environment; however, the true goal of DRL is to be able to build an agent that can learn across many different environments, an agent that can generalize its knowledge across tasks, much like we animals do. That type of agent, the type that can generalize across multiple tasks without human intervention, is known as an artificial general intelligence, or AGI. This field is currently exploding in growth for a variety of reasons and will be our focus in this final chapter.

In this chapter, we will look at how DRL builds the AGI agent. We will first look at the concept of meta learning, or learning to learn. Then we will learn how meta learning can be applied to reinforcement learning, looking at an example of model-agnostic meta learning as applied to DRL. Moving past the meta, we move on to hindsight experience replay, a method of using trajectory hindsight in order to improve learning across tasks. Next, we will move on to **generative adversarial imitation learning** (**GAIL**) and see how this is implemented. We will finish the chapter with a new concept that is being applied to DRL known as imagination and reasoning.

Here is a brief summary of the topics we will cover in this chapter:

- Learning meta learning
- Introducing meta reinforcement learning
- Using hindsight experience replay
- Imagination and reasoning
- Understanding imagination-augmented agents

In this last chapter, we will cover a wide variety of complex examples quickly. Each section of this chapter could warrant an entire chapter or book on its own. If any of this material piques your interest, be sure to do further research online; some areas may or may not have developed since this material was written. In the next section, we will look at ML and MRL.

Learning meta learning

The word "meta" is defined as "referring to itself or its type or genre". When talking about meta learning, we are talking about understanding the learning process of learning—that is, instead of thinking about how an agent learns a task, we want to think about how an agent could learn to learn across tasks. It is both an interesting and yet abstract problem, so we first want to explore what meta learning is. In the next section, we will explore how machine learning can learn to learn.

Learning 2 learn

Any good learning model should be trained across a variety of tasks and then generalized to fit the best distribution of those tasks. While we have covered very little with respect to general machine learning, consider the simple image classification problem with a deep learning model. We would typically train such a model with one goal or task, perhaps to identify whether a dataset contains a cat or dog, but not both, and nothing else. With meta learning, the cat/dog dataset would be one training entry in a set of image classification tasks that could cover a broad range of tasks, from recognizing flowers to cars. The following example images demonstrate this concept further:

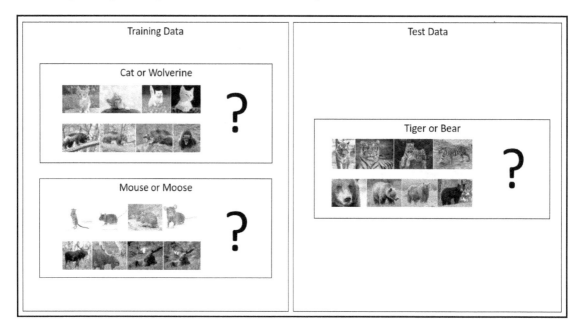

Example of meta learning applied to image classification (Image source Google)

The concept, then, involves training the model to classify the tasks of identifying a mouse or moose and cat or wolverine, and then, with meta learning, apply that to the task of identifying a tiger or bear. Essentially, we train the model in the same way that we test the model recursively—iteratively using collections of few-shot samples to expose to the network in learning sets or mini batches. You will have heard the term few-shot learning used in the context of meta learning to describe the small number of samples used for each task that are exposed to the model as a way of generalizing learning. The way that the model is updated through this process has been classified into the following three current schools of thought:

- **Metric based**: Solutions are so named because they depend on training a metric to gauge and monitor performance. This often requires the learner to learn the kernel that defines the distribution the network is trying to model rather than tune the network explicitly. What we find is that adversarial learning, using two somewhat opposing networks, can balance and refine this learning to learn the metric in a form of encoding or embedding. Some great examples of this type of approach are convolutional siamese networks for few-shot learning, matching networks, full-context embeddings, relational networks, and prototypical networks.
- **Model based**: Solutions define a group of methods that rely on some form of memory augmentation or context. Memory-augmented neural networks, or MANNs, are the primary implementation you will find using this solution. This concept is further based on a neural Turing machine (NTM), which describes a controller network that learns to read and write from memory-soft attention. An example of how this looks is taken from the following NTM architecture diagram:

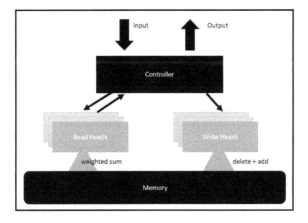

Example of a neural Turing machine

- The NTM architecture is used to power the MANN model for meta learning. Training a MANN requires some attention to the details of how the model memorizes and encodes the tasks. This model is often trained in such a way as to lengthen the amount of time that it takes for disparate training data to be reintroduced and remembered. Essentially, the agent is trained longer and longer for individual tasks, and then forced to recall memory of prelearned tasks later in further training. Interestingly enough, this is a method we humans will often use to focus on learning specific complex tasks. Then, we retest this knowledge later in order to reinforce this knowledge in memory. This same concept very much applies to MANN, and many believe that NTM or memory is a key ingredient to any meta learning pattern.

- **Optimization based**: Solutions are as much a combination of the two previous solutions as it is an antipattern. In optimization-based problems, we consider the root of the problem, and therefore the problem of optimizing our function, using not only gradient descent but also introducing gradient descent through context or time. Gradient descent through context or time is also known as **backpropagation through time** (**BPTT**), and is something we briefly touched on when we looked at recurrent networks. By introducing recurrent networks or **long short-term memory** (**LSTM**) layers into a network, we encourage the network to remember gradient context. Another way to think of this is that the network learns the history of the gradients it applied during training. The meta learner therefore gets trained using the process shown in the following diagram:

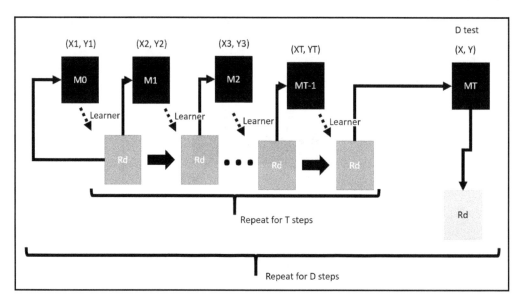

Training the meta learned with LSTM

The diagram was sourced from the paper *Optimization as a Model for Few-Shot Learning*, by Sachin Ravi and Hugo Larochelle, and it is a much-simplified version of the original. In the diagram, we can see how the meta learner is trained outside the regular model, often in an outside loop, where the inside loop is defined as the training process of the individual classification, regression, or other forms of learning-based task.

While there are three different forms of meta learning, we will pay particular attention to the optimization form, and in particular, a method that works by assuming an agnostic model, which we will explore in the next section.

Model-agnostic meta learning

Model-agnostic meta learning (**MAML**) is described as a general optimization method that will work with any machine learning method that uses gradient descent for optimization or learning. The intuition here is that we want to find a loss approximation that best matches the task we are currently undertaking. MAML does this by adding context through our model training tasks. That context is used to refine the model training parameters and thereby allow our model to better apply gradient loss for a specific task.

 This example uses the MNIST dataset, a set of 60,000 handwritten digits that is commonly used for base image classification tasks. While the dataset has been solved with high accuracy using a number of methods, it is often the base comparison for image classification tasks.

This will likely still sound abstract, so in the next exercise, we pull down a PyTorch ML framework called learn2learn and show how MAML can be used:

1. We will first create a new virtual environment and then download a package called learn2learn, a meta learning framework that provides a great implementation of MAML in PyTorch. Make sure that you create a new environment and install PyTorch and the Gym environment, as we previously did. You can install learn2learn with the following command:

   ```
   pip install learn2learn  # after installing new environment with
   torch

   pip install tqdm # used for displaying progress
   ```

2. In order to see how `learn2learn` is used in a basic task, we are going to review the basic MNIST training sample found in the repository, but we won't look at every section of the code example that has been provided in the source code `Chapter_14_learn.py`. Open the sample up and review the top section of the code, as shown in the following code:

```python
import learn2learn as l2l
class Net(nn.Module):
    def __init__(self, ways=3):
        super(Net, self).__init__()
        self.conv1 = nn.Conv2d(1, 20, 5, 1)
        self.conv2 = nn.Conv2d(20, 50, 5, 1)
        self.fc1 = nn.Linear(4 * 4 * 50, 500)
        self.fc2 = nn.Linear(500, ways)

    def forward(self, x):
        x = F.relu(self.conv1(x))
        x = F.max_pool2d(x, 2, 2)
        x = F.relu(self.conv2(x))
        x = F.max_pool2d(x, 2, 2)
        x = x.view(-1, 4 * 4 * 50)
        x = F.relu(self.fc1(x))
        x = self.fc2(x)
        return F.log_softmax(x, dim=1)
```

3. This top section of code shows the `learn2learn` import statement and the definition of the `Net` class. This is the network model we will be training. Note how the model is composed of two convolutional/pooling layers followed by a fully connected linear layer to an output layer. Note the use of `ways` as an input variable that defines the number of outputs from the last output layer.

4. Next, we will scroll down to the `main` function. This is where all the main setup and initialization occurs. This sample being more robust than most, it provides for input parameters that you can use instead of altering the hyperparameters in the code. The top of the `main` function is shown in the following code:

```python
def main(lr=0.005, maml_lr=0.01, iterations=1000, ways=5, shots=1,
tps=32, fas=5, device=torch.device("cpu"),
        download_location="/tmp/mnist"):
    transformations = transforms.Compose([
        transforms.ToTensor(),
        transforms.Normalize((0.1307,), (0.3081,)),
        lambda x: x.view(1, 1, 28, 28),
    ])

    mnist_train = l2l.data.MetaDataset(MNIST(download_location,
```

```
        train=True, download=True, transform=transformations))
        # mnist_test = MNIST(file_location, train=False, download=True,
    transform=transformations)

        train_gen = l2l.data.TaskGenerator(mnist_train, ways=ways,
    tasks=10000)
        # test_gen = l2l.data.TaskGenerator(mnist_test, ways=ways)

        model = Net(ways)
        model.to(device)
        meta_model = l2l.algorithms.MAML(model, lr=maml_lr)
        opt = optim.Adam(meta_model.parameters(), lr=lr)
        loss_func = nn.NLLLoss(reduction="sum")
```

5. Although we haven't gone through an image classification example before, hopefully the code will be relatively understandable and familiar to you. The main point to note is the construction of the `meta_model` using the `l2l.algorithms.MAML` model on the highlighted line of code. Note how the `meta_model` wraps the `model` network by using it as an input.

6. From here, we will scroll down to the familiar training loop we have seen so many times before. This time, however, there are some interesting differences. Look specifically at the code just inside the first iteration loop, as shown in the following code:

```
iteration_error = 0.0
iteration_acc = 0.0
for _ in range(tps):
    learner = meta_model.clone()
    train_task = train_gen.sample()
    valid_task = train_gen.sample(task=train_task.sampled_task)
```

Note how we are constructing a `learner` clone of the `meta_model` learner. The `learner` clone becomes our target learning network. The last two lines show the construction of a sampler for the training and validation tasks.

7. Next, let's see how `learner` is used to compute the loss again in an iterative manner using another loop, as shown in the following code:

```
for step in range(fas):
    train_error, _ = compute_loss(train_task, device, learner,
loss_func, batch=shots * ways)
    learner.adapt(train_error)
```

8. At this point, run the sample and observe the output to get a sense of how training is done.

Now that we understand some of the basic code setup, we are going to move on to explore how the sample trains and computes loss in the next section.

Training a meta learner

The `learn2learn` framework provides the MAML framework for building the learner model we can use to learn to learn; however, it is not automatic and does require a bit of setup and thought regarding how loss is computed for your particular set of tasks. We have already seen where we compute loss—now we will look closer at how loss is computed across tasks. Reopen `Chapter_14_learn.py` and go through the following exercise:

1. Scroll back down to the innermost training loop within the `main` function.
2. The inner loop here is called a **fast adaptive training loop**, since we are showing our network a few or mini batches or shots of data for training. Computing the loss of the network is done using the `compute_loss` function, as shown in the following code:

```python
def compute_loss(task, device, learner, loss_func, batch=5):
    loss = 0.0
    acc = 0.0
    dataloader = DataLoader(task, batch_size=batch, shuffle=False,
num_workers=0)
    for i, (x, y) in enumerate(dataloader):
        x, y = x.squeeze(dim=1).to(device), y.view(-1).to(device)
        output = learner(x)
        curr_loss = loss_func(output, y)
        acc += accuracy(output, y)
        loss += curr_loss / x.size(0)
    loss /= len(dataloader)
    return loss, acc
```

3. Note how the computation of loss is done iteratively over task training batches by iterating through the `dataloader` list. We then compute the average loss for all tasks by taking the total loss, `loss`, and dividing it by the number of dataloaders.

4. This average `loss` and accuracy, `acc`, are returned from the `compute_loss` function. From that learning instance, the learner is then adapted or updated using the following line of code:

```
train_error, _ = compute_loss(train_task, device, learner,
loss_func, batch=shots * ways)
learner.adapt(train_error)
```

5. After the fast adaptive looping and updating the learner through each loop, we can then validate the learner with the following code:

```
valid_error, valid_acc = compute_loss(valid_task, device, learner,
loss_func, batch=shots * ways)
iteration_error += valid_error
iteration_acc += valid_acc
```

6. The `valid_error` validation error and `valid_acc` accuracy are then accumulated on the total `iteration_error` error and `iteration_acc` accuracy values.

7. We finish by calculating the average iteration and accuracy errors, `iteration_error` or `iteration_acc` values, and then propagating that error back through the networks with the following code:

```
iteration_error /= tps
iteration_acc /= tps
tqdm_bar.set_description("Loss : {:.3f} Acc :
{:.3f}".format(iteration_error.item(), iteration_acc))

# Take the meta-learning step
opt.zero_grad()
iteration_error.backward()
opt.step()
```

8. The training for this example is quite quick, so run the example again and observe how quickly the algorithm can train across meta learning tasks.

Each meta learning step involves pushing the loss back through the network using BPTT, since the meta network is composed of recurrent layers. That detail is abstracted for us here, but hopefully you can appreciate how seamlessly we were able to introduce meta learning into training this regular image classification task. In the next section, we will look at how we can apply meta learning to reinforcement learning.

Introducing meta reinforcement learning

Now, that we understand the concept of meta learning, we can move on to meta reinforcement learning. Meta-RL—or RL^2 (RL Squared), as it has been called—is quickly evolving, but the additional complexity still makes this method currently inaccessible. While the concept is very similar to vanilla meta, it still introduces a number of subtle nuances for RL. Some of these can be difficult to understand, so hopefully the following diagram can help. It was taken from a paper titled *Reinforcement Learning, Fast and Slow* by *Botvinick, et al. 2019* (`https://www.cell.com/action/showPdf?pii=S1364-6613%2819%2930061-0`):

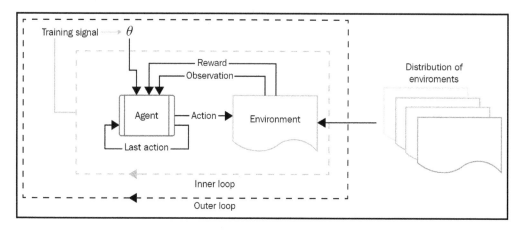

Meta reinforcement learning

In the diagram, you can see that familiar inner and outer loops that are characteristic of meta learning. This means that we also go from evaluating a policy π for any observed state to also now including the last action, last reward, and observed state in meta-RL. These differences are summarized as follows:

- Reinforcement learning = $\pi_\theta(s_t) \rightarrow$ distribution over A
- Meta reinforcement learning = $\pi_\theta(a_{t-1}, r_{t-1}, s_t) \rightarrow$ distribution over A

As we have seen with regular meta learning, there are a number of variations that are used and experimented on within meta-RL, but they all share the following three common elements:

- **Model memory**: We add memory to our model in the form of recurrent network layers or LSTM. Typically, the outer loop is composed of the memory component engaged by LSTM layers.

- **Distribution of MDPs**: The agent/algorithm needs to be trained across multiple different MDPs, which is typically done by exposing it to different or randomized environments.
- **Meta-learning algorithm**: The agent needs a meta learning algorithm for itself to learn to learn.

 The Unity Obstacle Tower Challenge was most likely developed to encourage developers to build a meta-RL agent, but as we have seen, the winning entry used a variation of hierarchical reinforcement learning. While HRL is designed to accomplish the same function as meta-RL, it lacks the automatic generation of memory.

In order to get a sense of the diversity of meta-RL algorithms, we will look at a list of what appear to be the most current methods used:

- **Optimizing weights**: This is essentially MAML or another variation called Reptile. MAML is currently one of the more popular variations used, and one we will explore later in detail.
- **Meta-learning hyperparameters**: There are a few hyperparameters that we use internally to balance learning within RL. These are the gamma and alpha values that we have tuned before, but imagine if they could be autotuned with meta-learning.
- **Meta-learning loss**: This considers that the loss function itself may need to be tuned, and uses a pattern to evolve it over iterations. This method uses evolutionary strategies that are outside the scope of this book.
- **Meta-learning exploration**: This uses meta learning to build more effective exploration strategies. This, in turn, reduces the amount of time exploring and increases effective training performance.
- **Episodic control**: This provides the agent with a method to keep important episodes in memory and forget others. This sounds a lot like prioritized experience replay, but the method of control here is within the calculation of loss and not from replay.
- **Evolutionary algorithms**: These are gradient-free, optimization-based solutions that use a form of genetic search to find solution methods. The collision of evolutionary algorithms and deep learning is an ongoing endeavor that many have tried and failed with. Both methods are very powerful and capable on their own, so it is perhaps only a matter of time before they get combined into a working model.

As you can see, there is plenty of variation in meta-RL methods, and we will look at how one method is implemented in detail in the next section.

MAML-RL

The learn2learn repository holds another great example of how to use their library for a few variations of this method. A good method for us to look at will be an implementation of Meta-SGD, which further extends MAML by adopting per-parameter learning rates using vanilla policy gradients, and is often referred to as MetaSGD-VPG. This concept was originally presented in the paper *Meta Reinforcement Learning with Task Embedding and Shared Policy*, which was itself presented at IJCAI-19.

 Make sure that you have completed all the installation steps from the last exercise before proceeding. If you have troubles running the sample, repeat the installation in a new virtual environment. Some issues may be related to the version of PyTorch you are using, so check that your version is compatible.

Open up Chapter_14_MetaSGD-VPG.py and go through the following steps:

1. You will need to install the cherry RL package first by entering the following command in your virtual environment window:

   pip install cherry-rl

2. We won't review the entire code listing, just the critical sections. First, let's look at the main function, which starts the initialization and hosts the training. The start of this function is shown in the following code:

```python
def main(
        experiment='dev',
        env_name='Particles2D-v1',
        adapt_lr=0.1,
        meta_lr=0.01,
        adapt_steps=1,
        num_iterations=200,
        meta_bsz=20,
        adapt_bsz=20,
        tau=1.00,
        gamma=0.99,
        num_workers=2,
        seed=42,
):
    random.seed(seed)
    np.random.seed(seed)
    th.manual_seed(seed)

    def make_env():
        return gym.make(env_name)
```

In the definition of the `main` function, we can see all the relevant hyperparameters as well as their selected defaults. Note that the two new groups of hyperparameters for the adaption and meta learning steps are prefixed with `adapt` and `meta`, respectively.

3. Next, we will look at the initialization of the environment, policy, meta learner, and optimizer using the following code:

```
env = l2l.gym.AsyncVectorEnv([make_env for _ in
range(num_workers)])
env.seed(seed)
env = ch.envs.Torch(env)
policy = DiagNormalPolicy(env.state_size, env.action_size)
meta_learner = l2l.algorithms.MetaSGD(policy, lr=meta_lr)
baseline = LinearValue(env.state_size, env.action_size)
opt = optim.Adam(policy.parameters(), lr=meta_lr)
all_rewards = []
```

4. Here, we can see the three training loops. First, the outer iteration loop controls the number of meta learning repetitions. Inside that loop, we have the task setup and configuration loop; remember that we want each learning session to require a different but related task. The third, innermost loop is where the adaption occurs, and we push the loss back through the model. The code for all three loops is shown here:

```
for iteration in range(num_iterations):
    iteration_loss = 0.0
    iteration_reward = 0.0
    for task_config in tqdm(env.sample_tasks(meta_bsz)):
        learner = meta_learner.clone()
        env.set_task(task_config)
        env.reset()
        task = ch.envs.Runner(env)

        # Fast Adapt
        for step in range(adapt_steps):
            train_episodes = task.run(learner, episodes=adapt_bsz)
            loss = maml_a2c_loss(train_episodes, learner, baseline,
gamma, tau)
            learner.adapt(loss)
```

5. After the fast adaptive looping takes place, we then jump back to the second loop and calculate the validation loss with the following code:

```
valid_episodes = task.run(learner, episodes=adapt_bsz)
loss = maml_a2c_loss(valid_episodes, learner, baseline, gamma, tau)
iteration_loss += loss
iteration_reward += valid_episodes.reward().sum().item() /
adapt_bsz
```

6. The validation loss is computed over the second loop for each different task. This loss is then accumulated into the iteration loss, `iteration_loss`, value. Leaving the second loop, we then print out some stats and calculate the adaption loss, `adaption_loss`, and push that as a gradient back through the network for training with the following code:

```
adaptation_loss = iteration_loss / meta_bsz
print('adaptation_loss', adaptation_loss.item())

opt.zero_grad()
adaptation_loss.backward()
opt.step()
```

7. Remember that the divisors in both loss equations (iteration and adaption) both use a similar value of 20, `meta_bsz = 20`, and `adapt_bsz = 20`. The base loss function is defined by the `maml_a2c_loss` and `compute_advantages` functions, as shown in the following code:

```
def compute_advantages(baseline, tau, gamma, rewards, dones,
states, next_states):
    # Update baseline
    returns = ch.td.discount(gamma, rewards, dones)
    baseline.fit(states, returns)
    values = baseline(states)
    next_values = baseline(next_states)
    bootstraps = values * (1.0 - dones) + next_values * dones
    next_value = th.zeros(1, device=values.device)
    return ch.pg.generalized_advantage(tau=tau,
                                       gamma=gamma,
                                       rewards=rewards,
                                       dones=dones,
                                       values=bootstraps,
                                       next_value=next_value)

def maml_a2c_loss(train_episodes, learner, baseline, gamma, tau):
    states = train_episodes.state()
    actions = train_episodes.action()
    rewards = train_episodes.reward()
```

```
dones = train_episodes.done()
next_states = train_episodes.next_state()
log_probs = learner.log_prob(states, actions)
advantages = compute_advantages(baseline, tau, gamma, rewards,
                                dones, states, next_states)
advantages = ch.normalize(advantages).detach()
return a2c.policy_loss(log_probs, advantages)
```

 Note how the cherry RL library saves us the implementation of some tricky code. Fortunately, we should already know what the cherry functions `ch.td.discount` and `ch.pg.generalized_advantage` are, as we encountered them in previous chapters, and so we won't need to review them here.

8. Run the example as you normally would and observe the output. An example of the generated output is shown in the following code:

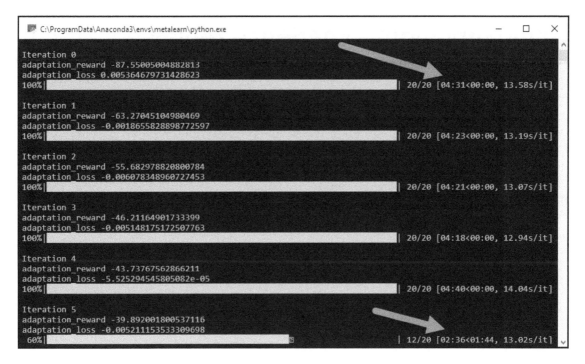

Example output from Chapter_14_MetaSQG-VPG.py

Note the amount of training time that the sample expects to take when running on a CPU when it first starts. While the prediction comes down significantly from five days to just over two in less than an hour, it still demonstrates the computational requirements for this type of training. Therefore, if you plan to do any serious work on meta-RL, you will likely want to use a very fast GPU for training. When testing on a very fast GPU, the preceding sample took 1,000 times less time to process. Yes, you read that right, 1,000 times less time. While you likely may not experience such a vast difference, any upgrade from a CPU to GPU will be significant.

There is a strong belief that is held by many of those in the RL community that meta-RL is the next big leap that we need to solve in order to get closer to AGI. Most of the development of this field is still guided by what is currently the state of the art, and how and when changes will dictate the future of RL. With this in mind, we are going to look at some other potential next-level steps, starting in the next section with HER.

Using hindsight experience replay

Hindsight experience replay was introduced by OpenAI as a method to deal with sparse rewards, but the algorithm has also been shown to successfully generalize across tasks due in part to the novel mechanism by which HER works. The analogy used to explain HER is a game of shuffleboard, the object of which is to slide a disc down a long table to reach a goal target. When first learning the game, we will often repeatedly fail, with the disc falling off the table or playing area. Except, it is presumed that we learn by expecting to fail and give ourselves a reward when we do so. Then, internally, we can work backward by reducing our failure reward and thereby increasing other non-failure rewards. In some ways, this method resembles Pierarchy (a form of HRL that we looked at earlier), but without the extensive pretraining parts.

 The next collection of samples in the following sections has again been sourced from `https://github.com/higgsfield`, and are the result of a young man named Dulat Yerzat from Almaty, Kazakhstan.

Open the samples for `Chapter_14_wo_HER.py` and `Chapter_14_HER.py`. These two samples are comparisons of simple DQN networks that are applied with and without HER. Go through the following steps:

1. Both examples are almost the same, aside from the implementation of HER, so the comparison will help us understand how the code works. Next, the environment has been simplified and custom built to perform that simple bit shifting of a random set of bits. The code to create the environment is as follows:

```
class Env(object):
    def __init__(self, num_bits):
        self.num_bits = num_bits
    def reset(self):
        self.done = False
        self.num_steps = 0
        self.state = np.random.randint(2, size=self.num_bits)
        self.target = np.random.randint(2, size=self.num_bits)
        return self.state, self.target
    def step(self, action):
        if self.done:
            raise RESET
        self.state[action] = 1 - self.state[action]
        if self.num_steps > self.num_bits + 1:
            self.done = True
        self.num_steps += 1
        if np.sum(self.state == self.target) == self.num_bits:
            self.done = True
            return np.copy(self.state), 0, self.done, {}
        else:
            return np.copy(self.state), -1, self.done, {}
```

2. We never really went over how to build a custom environment, but as you can see, it can be quite simple. Next, we will look at the simple DQN model that we will use to train, as shown in the following code:

```
class Model(nn.Module):
    def __init__(self, num_inputs, num_outputs, hidden_size=256):
        super(Model, self).__init__()
        self.linear1 = nn.Linear(num_inputs, hidden_size)
        self.linear2 = nn.Linear(hidden_size, num_outputs)
    def forward(self, state, goal):
        x = torch.cat([state, goal], 1)
        x = F.relu(self.linear1(x))
        x = self.linear2(x)
        return x
```

3. That is about as simple a DQN model as you can get. Next, let's compare the two examples by viewing the code side by side, as shown in the following screenshot:

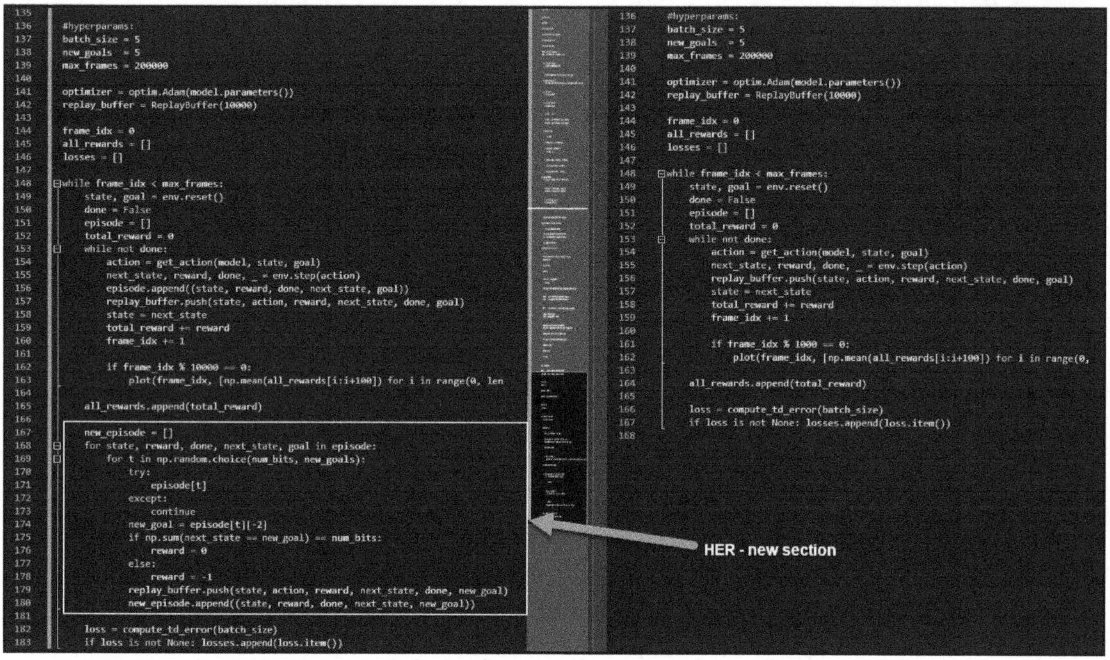

Comparison of code examples in VS

4. The new section of code is also shown here:

```python
new_episode = []
  for state, reward, done, next_state, goal in episode:
    for t in np.random.choice(num_bits, new_goals):
      try:
        episode[t]
      except:
        continue
      new_goal = episode[t][-2]
      if np.sum(next_state == new_goal) == num_bits:
        reward = 0
      else:
        reward = -1
      replay_buffer.push(state, action, reward, next_state, done,
new_goal)
      new_episode.append((state, reward, done, next_state,
new_goal))
```

5. What we see here is the addition of another loop not unlike meta-RL, but this time, instead of wrapping the inner loop, it sits as a sibling. The second loop is activated after an episode is completed from the first inner loop. It then loops through every event in the previous episode and adjusts the goals or targets based on the returned reward based on the new goal. This is essentially the hindsight part.

6. The remaining parts of this example resemble many of our previous examples, and should be quite familiar by now. One interesting part, though, is the get_action function, as shown in the following code:

```
def get_action(model, state, goal, epsilon=0.1):
    if random.random() < 0.1:
        return random.randrange(env.num_bits)
    state = torch.FloatTensor(state).unsqueeze(0).to(device)
    goal = torch.FloatTensor(goal).unsqueeze(0).to(device)
    q_value = model(state, goal)
    return q_value.max(1)[1].item()
```

Note here that we are using an epsilon value that is defaulted to .1 to denote the tendency for exploration. In fact, you might notice that this example uses no variable exploration.

7. Continuing with the differences, the next key difference is the compute_td_loss function, as shown in the following code:

```
def compute_td_error(batch_size):
    if batch_size > len(replay_buffer):
        return None

    state, action, reward, next_state, done, goal =
replay_buffer.sample(batch_size)

    state = torch.FloatTensor(state).to(device)
    reward = torch.FloatTensor(reward).unsqueeze(1).to(device)
    action = torch.LongTensor(action).unsqueeze(1).to(device)
    next_state = torch.FloatTensor(next_state).to(device)
    goal = torch.FloatTensor(goal).to(device)
    mask = torch.FloatTensor(1 -
np.float32(done)).unsqueeze(1).to(device)

    q_values = model(state, goal)
    q_value = q_values.gather(1, action)

    next_q_values = target_model(next_state, goal)
    target_action = next_q_values.max(1)[1].unsqueeze(1)
    next_q_value = target_model(next_state, goal).gather(1,
```

```
target_action)

expected_q_value = reward + 0.99 * next_q_value * mask

loss = (q_value - expected_q_value.detach()).pow(2).mean()

optimizer.zero_grad()
loss.backward()
optimizer.step()
return loss
```

8. Run the example without HER first and observe the results, then run the example with HER. The output for the example with HER is shown in the following excerpt:

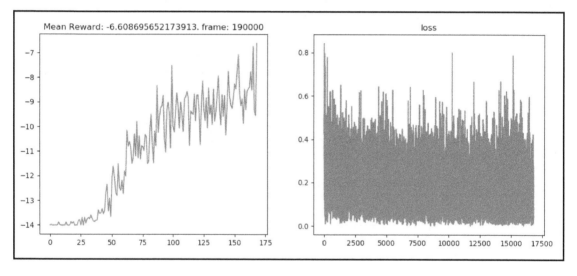

Example output from Chapter_14_HER.py

Compared to the example without HER, the preceding output is significantly better. You will have to run both examples yourself to see the exact difference. Note how the calculation of loss remains consistently variable and doesn't converge, while the mean reward increases. In the next section, we move to what is expected to be the next wave in RL—imagination and reasoning.

Imagination and reasoning in RL

Something that we can observe from our own experience of learning is how imagination can benefit the learning process. Pure imagination is the stuff of deep abstract thoughts and dreams, often closer to a hallucination than any way to solve a real problem. Except, this same imagination can be used to span gaps in our understanding of knowledge and allow us to reason out possible solutions. Say that we are trying to solve the problem of putting a puzzle together, and all we have are three remaining, mostly black pieces, as shown in the following image:

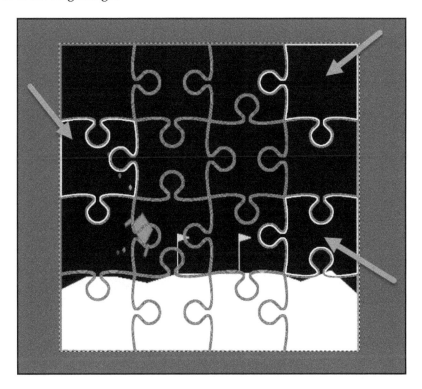

Imagining what the three missing puzzle pieces may look like

Given the simplicity of the preceding diagram, it is quite easy for us to imagine what those puzzle pieces may look like. We are able to fill in those gaps quite easily using our imagination from previous observations and reasoning. This use of imagination to fill in gaps is something we use all the time, and it is often said that the more imaginative you are, the more intelligent you are as well. Now it remains to be seen if this path to AI will indeed prove that theory, but it certainly looks like a possibility.

Imagination is not pulled from a vacuum, and likewise, in order to give our agents imagination, we have to essentially bootstrap their memory or previous learnings. We will do this in the next exercise in order for us to later generate the imagination from these learnings. Open sample `Chapter_14_Imagine_A2C.py` and go through the following steps:

1. The base agent we will use to generate the training bootstrap for our imagination will be a simple A2C Vanilla PG method. Let's first scroll down in the file and look at the `ActorCritic` class that defines our agent:

```
class ActorCritic(OnPolicy):
    def __init__(self, in_shape, num_actions):
        super(ActorCritic, self).__init__()
        self.in_shape = in_shape
        self.features = nn.Sequential(
            nn.Conv2d(in_shape[0], 16, kernel_size=3, stride=1),
            nn.ReLU(),
            nn.Conv2d(16, 16, kernel_size=3, stride=2),
            nn.ReLU(),
        )
        self.fc = nn.Sequential(
            nn.Linear(self.feature_size(), 256),
            nn.ReLU(),
        )
        self.critic = nn.Linear(256, 1)
        self.actor = nn.Linear(256, num_actions)
    def forward(self, x):
        x = self.features(x)
        x = x.view(x.size(0), -1)
        x = self.fc(x)
        logit = self.actor(x)
        value = self.critic(x)
        return logit, value
    def feature_size(self):
        return self.features(autograd.Variable(torch.zeros(1,
*self.in_shape))).view(1, -1).size(1)
```

2. What we can see is a simple PG agent that will be powered by an A2C synchronous actor-critic. Next, we come to another new class called `RolloutStorage`. Rollout storage is similar in concept to experience replay, but it also enables us to have an ongoing calculation of returns, as shown in the following code:

```
class RolloutStorage(object):
    def __init__(self, num_steps, num_envs, state_shape):
        self.num_steps = num_steps
```

```
        self.num_envs = num_envs
        self.states = torch.zeros(num_steps + 1, num_envs,
*state_shape)
        self.rewards = torch.zeros(num_steps, num_envs, 1)
        self.masks = torch.ones(num_steps + 1, num_envs, 1)
        self.actions = torch.zeros(num_steps, num_envs, 1).long()
        #self.use_cuda = False
    def cuda(self):
        #self.use_cuda = True
        self.states = self.states.cuda()
        self.rewards = self.rewards.cuda()
        self.masks = self.masks.cuda()
        self.actions = self.actions.cuda()
    def insert(self, step, state, action, reward, mask):
        self.states[step + 1].copy_(state)
        self.actions[step].copy_(action)
        self.rewards[step].copy_(reward)
        self.masks[step + 1].copy_(mask)
    def after_update(self):
        self.states[0].copy_(self.states[-1])
        self.masks[0].copy_(self.masks[-1])
    def compute_returns(self, next_value, gamma):
        returns = torch.zeros(self.num_steps + 1, self.num_envs, 1)
        #if self.use_cuda:
        # returns = returns.cuda()
        returns[-1] = next_value
        for step in reversed(range(self.num_steps)):
            returns[step] = returns[step + 1] * gamma *
self.masks[step + 1] + self.rewards[step]
        return returns[:-1]
```

3. If we scroll down to the `main` function, we can see that there are 16 synchronous environments that are being run with the following code:

```
def main():
    mode = "regular"
    num_envs = 16


    def make_env():
        def _thunk():
            env = MiniPacman(mode, 1000)
            return env


        return _thunk
```

```
envs = [make_env() for i in range(num_envs)]
envs = SubprocVecEnv(envs)

state_shape = envs.observation_space.shape
```

4. We will talk more about the `RolloutStorage` class later. For now, move down to the training section of code. It is the typical double-loop code, the outside loop controlling episodes and the inside loop controlling steps, as shown in the following code:

```
for i_update in range(num_frames):
        for step in range(num_steps):
                action = actor_critic.act(autograd.Variable(state))
```

The rest of the training code should be familiar, but it should be worth reviewing in detail on your own.

5. The next major difference we want to observe is at the end of the outer training loop. This last block of code is where the loss is calculated and pushed back through the network:

```
optimizer.zero_grad()
loss = value_loss * value_loss_coef + action_loss - entropy *
entropy_coef
loss.backward()
nn.utils.clip_grad_norm(actor_critic.parameters(), max_grad_norm)
optimizer.step()
```

6. Note the highlighted line in the preceding code block. This is unique in that we are clipping the gradient to a maximum value that is likely to avoid exploding gradients. The last section of code at the end renders out the playing area and shows the agent playing the game.

Exploding gradients are when a gradient value becomes so large that it causes the network to forget knowledge. The network weights start to be trained in wild fluctuations and any previous knowledge will often be lost.

7. Run the code as you normally would and observe the output.

Running the preceding code will also create a saved-state dictionary of memories that we will use to populate the imagination later. You must run this last exercise to completion if you want to continue working with later exercises. In the next section, we will explore how these latent traces can be used to generate an agent's imagination.

Generating imagination

In the current version of this algorithm, we first need to bootstrap the memories that we populate in the agent with a previous run by an agent, or perhaps a human. This is really no different than imitation learning or behavioral cloning, except we are using an on-policy agent that we will later use as an off-policy base for our imagination. Before we combine imagination into our agent, we can see how the predicted next state will look compared to what the agent's actual state will be. Let's see how this works by opening up the next example `Chapter_14_Imagination.py` and go through the following steps:

1. This example works by loading the previous saved-state dictionary we generated in the last exercise. Make sure that this data is generated and saved with a prefix of `actor_critic_` files in the same folder before continuing.

2. The purpose of this code is to extract the saved-state observation dictionary we recorded earlier. We then want to extract the observation and use it to imagine what the next state will look like. Then we can compare how well the imagined and next state resemble each other. This amount of resemblance will in turn be used to train an imagination loss later. We can see how the previous model is loaded by looking at the following line of code:

```
actor_critic.load_state_dict(torch.load("actor_critic_" + mode))
```

3. The preceding line of code reloads our previously trained model. Now we want to use the imagination to (for instance) reasonably fill in the areas where the agent may not have explored. Scrolling down, we can see the training loop that will learn the imagination part of the agent:

```
for frame_idx, states, actions, rewards, next_states, dones in
play_games(envs, num_updates):
    states = torch.FloatTensor(states)
    actions = torch.LongTensor(actions)
    batch_size = states.size(0)
    onehot_actions = torch.zeros(batch_size, num_actions,
*state_shape[1:])
    onehot_actions[range(batch_size), actions] = 1
    inputs = autograd.Variable(torch.cat([states, onehot_actions],
1))
```

4. This loop loops through the previously played games and encodes the actions using one-hot encoding. Scrolling down, we can see how the `imagined_state` state and the `imagined_reward` reward are learned:

```
imagined_state, imagined_reward = env_model(inputs)

target_state = pix_to_target(next_states)
target_state = autograd.Variable(torch.LongTensor(target_state))
target_reward = rewards_to_target(mode, rewards)
target_reward = autograd.Variable(torch.LongTensor(target_reward))

optimizer.zero_grad()
image_loss = criterion(imagined_state, target_state)
reward_loss = criterion(imagined_reward, target_reward)
loss = image_loss + reward_coef * reward_loss
loss.backward()
optimizer.step()
losses.append(loss.item())
all_rewards.append(np.mean(rewards))
```

This is the section of code that learns to correctly imagine the target state and reward from playing through the previously observed observations. Of course, the more observations, the better the imagination, but at some point, too many observations will eliminate all of the imagination entirely. Balancing this new trade-off will require a bit of trial and error on your own.

5. Scrolling down to the bottom of the file, you can see where an example of the imagination and target states are outputted with the following code:

```
while not done:
    steps += 1
    actions = get_action(state)
    onehot_actions = torch.zeros(batch_size, num_actions,
*state_shape[1:])
    onehot_actions[range(batch_size), actions] = 1
    state = torch.FloatTensor(state).unsqueeze(0)
    inputs = autograd.Variable(torch.cat([state, onehot_actions],
1))
    imagined_state, imagined_reward = env_model(inputs)
    imagined_state = F.softmax(imagined_state)
    iss.append(imagined_state)
    next_state, reward, done, _ = env.step(actions[0])
    ss.append(state)
    state = next_state
    imagined_image = target_to_pix(imagined_state.view(batch_size,
-1, len(pixels))[0].max(1)[1].data.cpu().numpy())
    imagined_image = imagined_image.reshape(15, 19, 3)
```

```
    state_image = torch.FloatTensor(next_state).permute(1, 2,
0).cpu().numpy()
    plt.figure(figsize=(10,3))
    plt.subplot(131)
    plt.title("Imagined")
    plt.imshow(imagined_image)
    plt.subplot(132)
    plt.title("Actual")
    plt.imshow(state_image)
    plt.show()
    time.sleep(0.3)
    if steps > 30:
        break
```

6. The following example screenshot shows the best the original author was able to get by training the agent for a considerable amount of time:

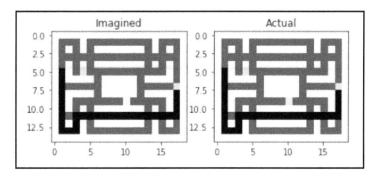

Example comparison of imagined versus actual

7. Run the example and your output: depending on your previous amount of training, it may not look as good. Again, the quality of the imagination will be based on the previous experiences and amount of training to refine the imagination itself.

8. One last thing to note is how the imagined image is getting extracted. This is done using an inverted CNN in the `BasicBlock` class that converts the encoding back to an image of the correct resolution. The code for the `BasicBlock` class is shown here:

```
class BasicBlock(nn.Module):
    def __init__(self, in_shape, n1, n2, n3):
        super(BasicBlock, self).__init__()
        self.in_shape = in_shape
        self.n1 = n1
        self.n2 = n2
```

```
                   self.n3 = n3
                   self.maxpool = nn.MaxPool2d(kernel_size=in_shape[1:])
                   self.conv1 = nn.Sequential(
                       nn.Conv2d(in_shape[0] * 2, n1, kernel_size=1, stride=2,
        padding=6),
                       nn.ReLU(),
                       nn.Conv2d(n1, n1, kernel_size=10, stride=1, padding=(5,
        6)),
                       nn.ReLU(),
                   )
                   self.conv2 = nn.Sequential(
                       nn.Conv2d(in_shape[0] * 2, n2, kernel_size=1),
                       nn.ReLU(),
                       nn.Conv2d(n2, n2, kernel_size=3, stride=1, padding=1),
                       nn.ReLU(),
                   )
                   self.conv3 = nn.Sequential(
                       nn.Conv2d(n1 + n2, n3, kernel_size=1),
                       nn.ReLU()
                   )
               def forward(self, inputs):
                   x = self.pool_and_inject(inputs)
                   x = torch.cat([self.conv1(x), self.conv2(x)], 1)
                   x = self.conv3(x)
                   x = torch.cat([x, inputs], 1)
                   return x
               def pool_and_inject(self, x):
                   pooled = self.maxpool(x)
                   tiled = pooled.expand((x.size(0),) + self.in_shape)
                   out = torch.cat([tiled, x], 1)
                   return out
```

As we can see, training the imagination process itself is not that difficult. The real difficulty is putting this all together in a running agent, and we will see how this is done in the next section when we learn about I2A.

Understanding imagination-augmented agents

The concept of **imagination-augmented agents** (**I2A**) was released in a paper titled *Imagination-Augmented Agents for Deep Reinforcement Learning* in February 2018 by T. Weber, et al. We have already talked about why imagination is important for learning and learning to learn. Imagination allows us to fill in the gaps in our learning and make leaps in our knowledge, if you will.

Giving agents an imagination allows us to combine model-based and model-free learning. Most of the agent algorithms we have used in this book have been model-free, meaning that we have no representative model of the environment. Early on, we did cover model-based RL with MC and DP, but most of our efforts have been fixed on model-free agents. The benefit of having a model of the environment is that the agent can then plan. Without a model, our agent just becomes reactionary through trial and error attempts. Adding imagination allows us to combine some aspects of using a model of the environment while being model free. Essentially, we hope to achieve the best of both worlds using imagination.

We have already explored the core role of imagination in the I2A architecture. This was the part we looked at in the last section that generated the imagined features and reward, essentially the model part. The following diagram illustrates the I2A architecture, the imagination core part, and the rollout encoder:

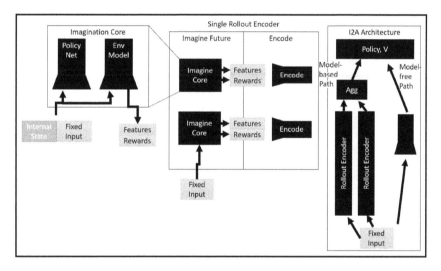

Summary of the I2A architecture

The I2A architecture demonstrates the complexity of the systems that we can start to build on top of DRL in the hopes of adding additional learning advantages, such as imagination. In order to really understand this architecture, we should look at a code example. Open up `Chapter_14_I2A.py` and go through the following steps:

1. We have already covered the first part of the architecture, so at this stage, we can start with the policy itself. Look at the I2A policy class:

```
class I2A(OnPolicy):
    def __init__(self, in_shape, num_actions, num_rewards,
```

```
                hidden_size, imagination, full_rollout=True):
            super(I2A, self).__init__()
            self.in_shape = in_shape
            self.num_actions = num_actions
            self.num_rewards = num_rewards
            self.imagination = imagination
            self.features = nn.Sequential(
                nn.Conv2d(in_shape[0], 16, kernel_size=3, stride=1),
                nn.ReLU(),
                nn.Conv2d(16, 16, kernel_size=3, stride=2),
                nn.ReLU(),
            )
            self.encoder = RolloutEncoder(in_shape, num_rewards,
    hidden_size)
            if full_rollout:
                self.fc = nn.Sequential(
                    nn.Linear(self.feature_size() + num_actions *
    hidden_size, 256),
                    nn.ReLU(),
                )
            else:
                self.fc = nn.Sequential(
                    nn.Linear(self.feature_size() + hidden_size, 256),
                    nn.ReLU(),
                )
            self.critic = nn.Linear(256, 1)
            self.actor = nn.Linear(256, num_actions)
        def forward(self, state):
            batch_size = state.size(0)
            imagined_state, imagined_reward =
    self.imagination(state.data)
            hidden = self.encoder(autograd.Variable(imagined_state),
    autograd.Variable(imagined_reward))
            hidden = hidden.view(batch_size, -1)
            state = self.features(state)
            state = state.view(state.size(0), -1)
            x = torch.cat([state, hidden], 1)
            x = self.fc(x)
            logit = self.actor(x)
            value = self.critic(x)
            return logit, value
        def feature_size(self):
            return self.features(autograd.Variable(torch.zeros(1,
    *self.in_shape))).view(1, -1).size(1)
```

2. For the most part, this is a fairly simple PG policy, except with the addition of imagination elements. Note how, in the `forward` function, the forward pass refers to the imagination needed to extract the `imagined_state` and `imagined_reward` values.

3. Next, we scroll down a little bit more and come to the `ImaginationCore` class. The class encapsulates the functionality we have seen before, but all wrapped in a single class, as shown in the following code:

```
class ImaginationCore(object):
    def __init__(self, num_rolouts, in_shape, num_actions,
num_rewards, env_model, distil_policy, full_rollout=True):
        self.num_rolouts = num_rolouts
        self.in_shape = in_shape
        self.num_actions = num_actions
        self.num_rewards = num_rewards
        self.env_model = env_model
        self.distil_policy = distil_policy
        self.full_rollout = full_rollout
    def __call__(self, state):
        state = state.cpu()
        batch_size = state.size(0)

        rollout_states = []
        rollout_rewards = []

        if self.full_rollout:
            state = state.unsqueeze(0).repeat(self.num_actions, 1,
1, 1, 1).view(-1, *self.in_shape)
            action = torch.LongTensor([[i] for i in
range(self.num_actions)]*batch_size)
            action = action.view(-1)
            rollout_batch_size = batch_size * self.num_actions
        else:
            action =
self.distil_policy.act(autograd.Variable(state, volatile=True))
            action = action.data.cpu()
            rollout_batch_size = batch_size

        for step in range(self.num_rolouts):
            onehot_action = torch.zeros(rollout_batch_size,
self.num_actions, *self.in_shape[1:])
            onehot_action[range(rollout_batch_size), action] = 1
            inputs = torch.cat([state, onehot_action], 1)

            imagined_state, imagined_reward =
self.env_model(autograd.Variable(inputs, volatile=True))
```

```
            imagined_state =
F.softmax(imagined_state).max(1)[1].data.cpu()
            imagined_reward =
F.softmax(imagined_reward).max(1)[1].data.cpu()

            imagined_state = target_to_pix(imagined_state.numpy())
            imagined_state =
torch.FloatTensor(imagined_state).view(rollout_batch_size,
*self.in_shape)

            onehot_reward = torch.zeros(rollout_batch_size,
self.num_rewards)
            onehot_reward[range(rollout_batch_size),
imagined_reward] = 1

            rollout_states.append(imagined_state.unsqueeze(0))
            rollout_rewards.append(onehot_reward.unsqueeze(0))

            state = imagined_state
            action =
self.distil_policy.act(autograd.Variable(state, volatile=True))
            action = action.data.cpu()
        return torch.cat(rollout_states),
torch.cat(rollout_rewards)
```

4. Now that we have seen how these big pieces work, it is time to get to the `main` function. We will start by looking at the first dozen or so lines of code:

```
envs = [make_env() for i in range(num_envs)]
envs = SubprocVecEnv(envs)
state_shape = envs.observation_space.shape
num_actions = envs.action_space.n
num_rewards = len(task_rewards[mode])

full_rollout = True

env_model = EnvModel(envs.observation_space.shape, num_pixels,
num_rewards)
env_model.load_state_dict(torch.load("env_model_" + mode))
distil_policy = ActorCritic(envs.observation_space.shape,
envs.action_space.n)
distil_optimizer = optim.Adam(distil_policy.parameters())

imagination = ImaginationCore(1, state_shape, num_actions,
num_rewards, env_model, distil_policy, full_rollout=full_rollout)

actor_critic = I2A(state_shape, num_actions, num_rewards, 256,
imagination, full_rollout=full_rollout)
```

Note the flow of code. The code goes from instantiating an environment model
`env_model` and the `distil_policy` from an `ActorCritic` class. Then the code
sets up the optimizer and instantiates the `imagination` object of
the `ImaginationCore` type with inputs of `env_model` and `distil_policy`. The
last line creates the `actor_critic` I2A policy using the `imagination` object as
input.

5. Jump down to the training loop. Note that it looks fairly standard:

```
for i_update in tqdm(range(num_frames)):
    for step in range(num_steps):
        action = actor_critic.act(autograd.Variable(current_state))
        next_state, reward, done, _ =
envs.step(action.squeeze(1).cpu().data.numpy())
        reward = torch.FloatTensor(reward).unsqueeze(1)
        episode_rewards += reward
        masks = torch.FloatTensor(1-np.array(done)).unsqueeze(1)
        final_rewards *= masks
        final_rewards += (1-masks) * episode_rewards
        episode_rewards *= masks
```

6. After the inner episode loop is complete, we then jump down to the loss
calculation and update the code, as shown here:

```
_, next_value = actor_critic(autograd.Variable(rollout.states[-1],
volatile=True))
next_value = next_value.data

returns = rollout.compute_returns(next_value, gamma)
logit, action_log_probs, values, entropy =
actor_critic.evaluate_actions(
autograd.Variable(rollout.states[:-1]).view(-1, *state_shape),
        autograd.Variable(rollout.actions).view(-1, 1)
        )
distil_logit, _, _, _ = distil_policy.evaluate_actions(
        autograd.Variable(rollout.states[:-1]).view(-1,
*state_shape),
        autograd.Variable(rollout.actions).view(-1, 1)
        )
distil_loss = 0.01 * (F.softmax(logit).detach() *
F.log_softmax(distil_logit)).sum(1).mean()

values = values.view(num_steps, num_envs, 1)
action_log_probs = action_log_probs.view(num_steps, num_envs, 1)
advantages = autograd.Variable(returns) - values

value_loss = advantages.pow(2).mean()
```

```
action_loss = -(autograd.Variable(advantages.data) *
action_log_probs).mean()

optimizer.zero_grad()
loss = value_loss * value_loss_coef + action_loss - entropy *
entropy_coef
loss.backward()
nn.utils.clip_grad_norm(actor_critic.parameters(), max_grad_norm)
optimizer.step()
distil_optimizer.zero_grad()
distil_loss.backward()
optimizer.step()
```

7. One thing to pay attention to here is that we are using two loss gradients to push back the loss to the `distil` model, which adjusts the `distil` model parameters and the `actor_critic` model or policy and its parameters. Without getting too bogged down in details, the main concept here is that we train the `distil` model to learn the imagination and the other loss for general policy training.

8. Run the example again. Wait until it starts and then you may want to shut it down after a few rounds, because, this sample can take upwards of an hour per iteration on a slower CPU, possibly longer. The following is an example screenshot of the start of training:

Example of Chapter_14_I2A.py training

Now, if you want to run this exercise to completion, you should use a GPU at the very least. Ten thousand hours of CPU training would take a year, and is not something you will likely want to spend time on. If you do use a GPU, you will have to modify the sample to support a GPU, and this will require uncommenting sections and setting up PyTorch so that it can run with CUDA.

This completes this section and the content for this chapter, as well as the book. In the next section, we will look at the last set of exercises.

Exercises

The following is a mix of simple and very difficult exercises. Choose those exercises that you feel appropriate to your interests, abilities, and resources. Some of the exercises in the following list could require considerable resources, so pick those that are within your time/resource budget:

1. Tune the hyperparameters for sample `Chapter_14_learn.py`. This sample is a standard deep learning model, but the parameters should be familiar enough to figure out on your own.
2. Tune the hyperparameters for sample `Chapter_14_MetaSGD-VPG.py`, as you normally would.
3. Tune the hyperparameters for sample `Chapter_14_Imagination.py`. There are a few new hyperparameters in this sample that you should familiarize yourself with.
4. Tune the hyperparameters for the `Chapter_14_wo_HER.py` and `Chapter_14_HER.py` examples. It can be very beneficial for your understanding to train the sample with and without HER using the same techniques.
5. Tune the hyperparameters for the `Chapter_14_Imagine_A2C.py` example. What effect does this have on running the `Chapter_14_Imagination.py` example later?
6. Upgrade the HER example (`Chapter_14_HER.py`) to use a different PG or value/DQN method.
7. Upgrade the `Chapter_14_MetaSGD-VPG.py` example to use a more advanced PG or DQN method.
8. Adapt the `Chapter_14_MetaSGD-VPG.py` example to train on different environments that use continuous or possibly even discrete actions.

9. Train the `Chapter_14_I2A.py` sample to completion. You will need to configure the example to run with CUDA, as well as install PyTorch with CUDA.

10. Tune the hyperparameters for the `Chapter_14_I2A.py` sample. You may decide to do only partial training runs using just the CPU, which is acceptable. Therefore, you could train a couple of iterations at a time and still optimize those new hyperparameters.

Do the exercises of most interest to you and remember to have fun.

Summary

In this chapter, we looked beyond DRL and into the realm of AGI, or at least where we hope we are going with AGI. More importantly, though, we looked at what the next phase of DRL is, how we can tackle its current shortcomings, and where it could go next. We looked at meta learning and what it means to learn to learn. Then we covered the excellent `learn2learn` library and saw how it could be used on a simple deep learning problem and then a more advanced meta-RL problem with MAML. From there, we looked at another new approach to learning using hindsight with HER. From hindsight, we moved to imagination and reasoning and how this could be incorporated into an agent. Then we finished the chapter by looking at I2A—imagination-augmented agents—and how imagination can help fill in the gaps in our knowledge.

I just want to thank you for taking the time to work through this book with us. It has been an amazing journey covering almost the entire RL and DRL alphabet of concepts, terms, and acronyms. This book started with the basics of RL and went deep, very deep, into DRL. Provided you have the mathematical background, you can likely venture out on your own now, and build your own latest and greatest agent. RL, and in particular DRL, suffers from the myth that you require extensive computational resources to make valuable contributions. While for certain research this is certainly the case, there are a lot of other more rudimentary elements that still need a better understanding that can be improved upon. The field of DRL is still relatively new, and it is quite likely that we have missed things along the way. Therefore, whatever your resources, you likely still could make a valuable contribution to DRL in the coming years. If you do plan to pursue this dream, I wish you success and hope that this book contributes to your journey.

Other Books You May Enjoy

If you enjoyed this book, you may be interested in these other books by Packt:

Reinforcement Learning Algorithms with Python

Andrea Lonza

ISBN: 978-1-78913-111-6

- Develop an agent to play CartPole using the OpenAI Gym interface
- Discover the model-based reinforcement learning paradigm
- Solve the Frozen Lake problem with dynamic programming
- Explore Q-learning and SARSA with a view to playing a taxi game
- Apply Deep Q-Networks (DQNs) to Atari games using Gym
- Study policy gradient algorithms, including Actor-Critic and REINFORCE
- Understand and apply PPO and TRPO in continuous locomotion environments
- Get to grips with evolution strategies for solving the lunar lander problem

Hands-On Deep Learning for Games
Micheal Lanham

ISBN: 978-1-78899-407-1

- Learn the foundations of neural networks and deep learning.
- Use advanced neural network architectures in applications to create music, textures, self driving cars and chatbots.
- Understand the basics of reinforcement and DRL and how to apply it to solve a variety of problems.
- Working with Unity ML-Agents toolkit and how to install, setup and run the kit.
- Understand core concepts of DRL and the differences between discrete and continuous action environments.
- Use several advanced forms of learning in various scenarios from developing agents to testing games.

Leave a review - let other readers know what you think

Please share your thoughts on this book with others by leaving a review on the site that you bought it from. If you purchased the book from Amazon, please leave us an honest review on this book's Amazon page. This is vital so that other potential readers can see and use your unbiased opinion to make purchasing decisions, we can understand what our customers think about our products, and our authors can see your feedback on the title that they have worked with Packt to create. It will only take a few minutes of your time, but is valuable to other potential customers, our authors, and Packt. Thank you!

Index

Lightning Source UK Ltd.
Milton Keynes UK
UKHW031834081220
374847UK00005B/162

9 781839 214936